THE LAST YORKISTS

THE LAST YORKISTS

EDMUND AND RICHARD DE LA POLE

RICHARD ANDERTON

For Mary

The author would like to offer special thanks to Dr Anthony Gross for his permission to use the portrait of Richard de la Pole which features in the colour plate section of this book.

First published 2025

Amberley Publishing
The Hill, Stroud
Gloucestershire, GL5 4EP

www.amberley-books.com

ISBN 978 1 3981 2169 0 (hardback)
ISBN 978 1 3981 2170 6 (ebook)

British Library Cataloguing in Publication Data.
A catalogue record for this book is available from the British Library.

1 2 3 4 5 6 7 8 9 10

Typesetting by SJmagic DESIGN SERVICES, India.
Printed in the UK.

Appointed GPSR EU Representative: Easy Access System Europe Oü, 16879218
Address: Mustamäe tee 50, 10621, Tallinn, Estonia
Contact Details: gpsr.requests@easproject.com, +358 40 500 3575

CONTENTS

William de la Pole m. Katherine
c. 1290–1366 d. 1382

Five others

Michael de la Pole, 1st Earl of Suffolk m. Catherine of Wingfield
c. 1338–1389 1340–1386

Michael, 2nd Earl of Suffolk 1361–1415

Thomas 1363–1415

William b. 1365

Richard 1367–1402

John 1369–1415

Anne b. 1373

Elizabeth b. 1377

Margaret b. 1386

Michael, 3rd Earl of Suffolk 1394–1415

William, 1st Duke of Suffolk 1396–1450 m. Alice Chaucer 1404–1475

Alexander d. 1429

John d. 1429

Thomas 1397–1433

Katharine d. 1473

Isabelle d. 1466

Elizabeth

Katharine d. 1410

Elizabeth d. 1422

Margaret Beaufort m. John, 2nd Duke of Suffolk 1442–1492 m. Elizabeth of York 1444–1502

John, 1st Earl of Lincoln 1464–1487

Edward 1466–1485

Elizabeth 1468–1489

Edmund, 3rd Duke of Suffolk 1471–1513

Humphrey 1417–1513

Anne 1476–1495

Catherine 1477–1513

William 1478–1539

Richard, 4th Duke of Suffolk 1480–1525

Introduction

THE ORIGINS OF THE DE LA POLES

At the end of the Middle Ages, an obscure family from Humberside, called de la Pole, came within touching distance of England's throne – but they were not part of England's ruling elite. Like many newly wealthy families, the earls and dukes of Suffolk added a French-sounding prefix to their name in an attempt to convince their social superiors that they were descended from Norman knights, but the de la Poles enter history as humble Yorkshire wool merchants from the lost town of Ravenser Odd, which once graced the mouth of the Humber.

The first de la Pole of note was William, who rose to be Chief Baron of the Exchequer and principal moneylender to Edward III. He was born around 1290, and though his origins are obscure it is likely that his father was also called William. The older William, who was knighted in 1296,[1] made a lot of money exporting fine Yorkshire fleeces to the weavers of Flanders and his sons transformed the small fortune they inherited into a very large one by lending huge sums of money to the Crown.

In 1325, the younger William and his brothers loaned £2,800 to Edward II for his war in Gascony and spent £306 of their own money improving the defences of Hull.[2] After Edward's gruesome murder, William funded the bid for power made by the late king's widow, Queen Isabella, and her lover, Roger Mortimer. He also provided a loan of £4,000 to renew the war against the Scots.

The fall of Mortimer and Isabella did nothing to disrupt William's financial career and when Edward III revived his claim to the French throne, thereby igniting the Hundred Years War, he lent the Crown so much money the king was unable to repay him in full. Perhaps inspired by the fate of the Knights Templar in France, Edward had his benefactor arrested on trumped-up charges of wool smuggling and William had to cancel all the king's debts in exchange for a pardon.[3]

Despite William's fall from royal favour, his son Michael (d. 1389) continued the de la Poles' unswerving loyalty to the Crown. Michael fought bravely for Edward III during the Hundred Years War and became a favourite of Richard II, the king's grandson and eventual successor. Michael also moved the de la Pole power base to East Anglia and increased his fortune by marrying the wealthy Suffolk heiress Catherine Wingfield. In 1385, Michael de la Pole was created 1st earl of Suffolk but his association with the weak and feckless Richard II almost led to his destruction. Barely a year after his ennoblement, Michael was impeached on charges of embezzlement and treason, whereupon he fled to France and never saw England again.

Though Michael de la Pole was stripped of his lands and titles *in absentia*, his son and heir, also called Michael (d. 1415), was allowed to succeed him as 2nd earl of Suffolk in 1398. By maintaining a relatively low profile during Henry IV's successful usurpation of his nephew's throne, the second earl managed to keep his coronet and in 1408 he was appointed Henry IV's chief ambassador at the Council of Pisa, which tried to end the Western Schism that had split the Catholic Church between the Rome and Avignon papacies.[4]

In 1415, though he was nearly fifty years old, the 2nd earl of Suffolk joined Henry V in France when the bellicose young king renewed the Hundred Years War. The ageing earl was accompanied by two of his sons, another Michael (d. 1415) and another William (d. 1450). The latter was badly wounded at the siege of Harfleur but worse was to follow. Before Henry V could lead his men into the breach, Michael senior died of dysentery and Michael junior had the misfortune to be one of the few Englishmen killed at the battle of Agincourt. Poor Michael had been the third earl for just seven weeks, but his brother William survived his wounds and became the 4th earl of Suffolk.

Following Henry V's sudden death in 1422, William remained in France and commanded the English garrison defending Orléans from Joan of Arc. The story of the Maid's relief of Orléans has been told too often to be repeated here; suffice to say that, although the English army managed to retreat to the nearby town of Jargeau, William was ultimately forced to surrender. To compound his disgrace, rumours began to circulate that William had been too busy ravishing an ex-nun to organise the English defences.[5]

Despite this ignominious episode, William was able to resume his position at Henry VI's court after he was ransomed, and in July 1448 he was created 1st duke of Suffolk. However, William's jealous enemies never forgave him for the loss of their possessions in France and they conspired to have 'Jackanapes'[6] deposed.

In a desperate attempt to revive his ailing fortunes, William arranged for his eight-year-old son John (d. 1492) to marry the king's equally young cousin Margaret Beaufort (d. 1509),[7] but this could not save him. The best Henry could do for his favourite was to order his banishment, sparing him the headman's axe, and on 1 May 1450 the exiled duke of Suffolk left Ipswich for Calais. Yet his enemies were not to be denied. William's ship was intercepted as it entered the Channel, and his headless corpse later washed up on a beach beneath Dover's White Cliffs.[8]

The faction that planned William's murder was led by Richard, duke of York, and these nascent Yorkists also succeeded in having John's marriage to Margaret annulled on the grounds of the bride and groom's extreme youth. However, they could not prevent the 2nd duke of Suffolk from inheriting his late father's title and estates. It is one of those ironies of history that John de la Pole, the son of a leading Lancastrian at the court of Henry VI, was destined to father the last Yorkist claimants to the throne, while his ex-wife would be the mother of their most implacable enemy: Henry Tudor.

BOOK ONE

Edmonde Poole Erle of Southfolke, sonne to Ihon duke of Southfolke, and lady Elizabeth sister to kyng Edward the IV, beyng stoute and bolde of courage, and of wyt rashe and hedy, was endited of homicide & murther, for sleyng of a meane person in his rage and fury.

Edward Hall, *Hall's Chronicle; Containing the History of England* (1548)

1

NO SLIGHT DISTINCTION

The hour was late one night in 1498 when the four drunken noblemen and their sleepy attendants left the tavern in London's Cheapside. Tired as they were, their good humour continued as Edmund, de la Pole, 6th earl of Suffolk, Lord William Courtenay, heir to the earldom of Devon, William Brandon and Thomas Neville tottered along Seething Lane, but as they passed the Church of All Hallows-by-the-Tower the laughing stopped. Standing in their way was a gang of ruffians.

Whatever words were exchanged between the two parties are lost to us now, but Edmund certainly felt his honour had been brought into question – and he was not one to shy away from a confrontation. The furious fight that followed may have been nothing more than an ugly street brawl, but when it was over three of the footpads were lying face down in the mud.

The sight of the corpses likely brought the surviving brawlers to their senses, and they soon scattered, but even in the fifteenth century the arm of the law was long. A few days after the battle of Seething Lane, Sir Reynold Bray arrived at Edmund's lodgings in Thames Street to formally arraign the earl of Suffolk for the murder of a man named Thomas Crue.[1]

Though the subsequent investigation was a farce, and no witnesses came forward to give evidence, Edmund was almost certainly guilty. Contemporary historians describe him as being, rash, headstrong and proud,[2] and the killing of commoners by nobles was no great crime in medieval Europe.

Since the beginning of Henry's reign at least two members of the noble jousting set[3] had been acquitted of murder in similar circumstances, but Crue had been a plaintiff in a case that was about to be heard by the Privy Council and England's first Tudor king was determined to show his subjects that no one was above the law. Edmund was therefore offered a full pardon, as he expected, but only if he admitted his guilt in open court.[4]

Given the choice between humiliation or beheading, Edmund reluctantly chose the former. Yet in the months following the Thomas Crue affair, he began to realise that being forced to plead for his life had been part of a carefully orchestrated campaign to destroy his credibility as a claimant to the throne.

To be fair to Henry, his deep distrust of the de la Poles was not without foundation. Edmund's father, John, 2nd duke of Suffolk, was married to Richard III's sister Elizabeth of York, and in the months before the climactic battle of Bosworth in August 1485, England's last Yorkist king had begun the process of making the most senior of his nephews his successor. The eldest of John de la Pole's eleven children was also called John, and to distinguish him from his father he is generally known by his courtesy title, earl of Lincoln.

Following the death of his own son Edward of Middleham, Richard III had appointed Lincoln as his Lieutenant in Ireland and President of the Council of the North. These important positions were usually given to the king's heir, and Richard had also betrothed Anne de la Pole, his seven-year-old niece, to the twelve-year-old duke of Rothesay, son and heir of the Scottish King James III,[5] but the Yorkist defeat at Bosworth had changed everything.

At first, Lincoln had accepted the Tudor victory and had sworn the required oaths of loyalty at the coronation of the victorious Henry, but the proud earl had too much Yorkist blood in his veins to stomach a descendant of Lancastrians on the throne for long. Just two years after Henry seized the throne, Lincoln threw in his lot with the ill-starred pretender Lambert Simnel, who had been groomed by a priest named Robert Simon to impersonate the imprisoned earl of Warwick.

Despite being only ten years old and barred from the succession by an Act of Parliament, the real Warwick had been sent to the Tower immediately after Bosworth because Henry feared that this nephew of Edward IV had a better claim to the throne than his own. Now, Warwick/Simnel's supporters claimed that the boy had escaped from his Tudor prison and was ready to reclaim his Yorkist birthright.

In truth, Lincoln was probably using Simnel as a 'stalking horse' to disguise his own bid for the throne. The fact that he convinced his aunt Margaret, dowager duchess of Burgundy, to finance the plot gives weight to this theory. In any case, their dream of restoring the House of York had ended in the slaughter of Stoke Field. To this day the shallow ditch on the outskirts of Newark, where Lincoln and his army of German mercenaries met their grisly end, is known as the Bloody Gutter. The Yorkist defeat would have a serious consequences for the entire de la Pole family.

The rebel earl's treachery was punished by the forfeiture of his lands and titles, which was the usual fate of those who took up arms against the king, but Henry went much further. Even though the ageing duke of Suffolk had been too old, and his brothers too young, to play any part in the Simnel rebellion, the king seized all the estates that Lincoln *would* have inherited from his father in addition to the lands he had acquired during his lifetime.[6] At a stroke, Henry had successfully disinherited the duke's seven surviving children, thereby depriving them of the means to mount another rebellion.

Most of Lincoln's siblings were more interested in winning crowns in heaven than on earth. After the collapse of her marriage plans, Anne de la Pole had joined the nuns of Syon Abbey, and she eventually became their prioress. Her brother Edward was appointed Archdeacon of Richmond and Craven in 1484, but he died the following year. Another brother, Humphrey, took a degree in law at Cambridge,[7] but spent most of his life as an obscure parish priest.[8]

No doubt Edmund would also have taken Holy Orders had it not been for the catastrophe of Bosworth. Five years before the fateful battle, he had been sent to Oxford to study theology at the whim of his other uncle, Edward IV. By sending his nephew to Oxford, Edward hoped to restore the university's flagging reputation.

The boy's tutor could barely contain his glee at being given a prince to educate. 'Our community if it had a thousand tongues, could not recount how much it is indebted to you ... that you have sent the Lord Edmund Pole, your nephew, to your University, to its no slight distinction,' he wrote in a letter dated 28 March 1482.[9] He goes on to describe Edmund as 'a penetrating, eloquent and brilliant genius', which is impressive considering the boy was only eleven years old. The learned don's effusive reports stand in stark contrast to the barely literate letters that Edmund wrote as an adult, but, in fairness, it has to be said that he never completed his education.

Had Edward IV survived the unknown illness that killed him, Edmund might have followed his brothers and sister into the cloister. But the disappearance of the Princes in the Tower, the accession of Richard III and the sudden death of new king's son meant the de la Pole brothers all took a step closer to the throne.

In theory, the brothers' cousin Warwick had a better claim to the throne than any of the de la Poles. However, his father, the duke of Clarence, had rebelled against Edward IV. After Clarence's execution, his son was barred from the succession by an Act of Parliament and so the de la Poles became the clear favourites to continue the Yorkist line. Edmund was one of the seventeen Knights of the Bath created on the eve of Richard III's coronation, where his father had carried the king's sceptre,[10] but then came the battles of Bosworth and Stoke Field.

Despite the calamity of Lincoln's rebellion, for a while it seemed as if Henry was prepared to forgive the de la Poles and the family might recover all it had lost. In 1487, barely five months after Lincoln's death, the young Edmund accompanied his father to another coronation – that of his cousin Elizabeth of York, wife and queen of the new king Henry VII. Thereafter Edmund became a noted member of the Tudor court. In 1488 he spent the festivals of Easter, Whitsun and All Hallows with the royal family at Windsor, and the following year he celebrated Christmas at Henry's palaces of Sheen and Westminster.[11]

No doubt the ageing duke and duchess of Suffolk watched their eldest surviving son's progress at court with a growing sense of hope. If the new king continued to favour Edmund, they might be able to persuade Henry to reverse the Act of Attainder that had ruined them. However, to reach the next rung on the ladder of royal favour, Edmund would have to distinguish himself in battle.

The first opportunity for Edmund to win his spurs came in June 1489 when Henry decided to invade France. Ostensibly, Henry was trying to open a second front in the Franco-Breton War and repay Brittany's duke, Francis II, who had sheltered the Tudor pretender for fourteen years, but the details of this complex conflict need not concern us here. All that needs be said is that a large contingent of Henry's expeditionary force was commanded by Henry Lovell, Lord Morley, who had married Edmund's older sister Elizabeth.[12]

To disguise their true purpose, it was announced that these troops were to strengthen the garrison at Calais. In fact, Morley's mission was to reinforce Lord Daubeney's attack on the French besieging the Flemish town of Dixmude.[13] Thanks to the efforts of Sir James Tyrell, who had saved a local man from being lynched and recruited him as a guide, the Englishmen were able to find a way though the French siege lines and catch their enemy by surprise. The unsuspecting French were slaughtered in their trenches, but at the very moment of his triumph Lord Morley was shot and killed.[14]

In truth, Morley's death was avoidable – he had refused to dismount or discard the elaborate coat that marked him as an officer. Regardless, the vengeful English were so incensed by their captain's death that they killed all their prisoners in cold blood. Elizabeth de la Pole was heartbroken, and for many years she refused to celebrate Christmas. She also spurned every offer to remarry, remaining single until her death around 1520.[15]

Although Edmund is not mentioned in the contemporary sources as being at the siege of Dixmude, it is highly likely that the young heir to the Suffolk dukedom was one of the squires under Morley's command.[16] We know that he and Morley often attended court together,[17] and the Suffolk-born Tyrell was a de la Pole family friend. We also know for certain that Edmund was in the English army that took the field against the French three years later.

On this occasion, Henry's *casus belli* was French support for another Yorkist pretender, Perkin Warbeck. Like Simnel five years before, Warbeck was a fraud who had been groomed by unscrupulous Yorkists to impersonate an heir to the throne.

This time the claimed identity was that of Richard, duke of York, the younger of the missing sons of Edward IV. Once again the conspirators had managed to convince Margaret of Burgundy to bankroll their attempt to put a 'White Rose' on the throne, but the plotters' attempt to raise an army in Ireland against the Tudors had come to nothing and Warbeck had been forced to seek sanctuary in France.[18]

Naturally, the French king, Charles VIII, was quite willing to back anyone who could cause trouble in England, so Henry responded by attacking Boulogne. For this campaign, the king took command of his army in person. One of the 12,000 Englishmen who marched out of Calais on 19 October 1492 was Edmund de la Pole,[19] though he had little choice in the matter because he was now duke of Suffolk.

The old duke had died in May 1491 and Edmund, as his successor, had to fulfil his father's feudal obligations to fight for his sovereign, even though the rich manors to which he should have succeeded had been seized by the king following his late brother's attainder. Edmund was one of the poorest peers in England, but he still lived in a world in which land and wealth could be won – or regained– by the sword.

Unfortunately for Edmund, Henry quickly decided against storming Boulogne's heavily defended walls and instead set up camp outside. Protracted sieges rarely provided an opportunity for noteworthy heroics. In fact, the only English casualty during the entire campaign was Sir John Savage, who had the misfortune to be ambushed while reconnoitring the enemy fortifications.[20] A lack of action notwithstanding, the siege of Boulogne served Henry's purpose admirably; the French king signed the Treaty of Étaples at the beginning of November 1492.

Under the terms of this humiliating treaty, Charles banished Warbeck from France and rewarded Henry with 745,000 ducats in war reparations and a personal pension of 25,000 ducats a year. The colossal former sum was equal to an entire year's revenue for the English Crown, but Henry's nobles grumbled that their feudal obligation to raise, pay and equip the men of the royal army had reduced them to penury.

Thankfully for the already impoverished Edmund, he had not been required to bring a large retinue to Boulogne. Nevertheless, the new duke of Suffolk was already living beyond his means and an entry in the king's accounts for March 1492 noted that Henry had paid Edmund 13*s* 4*d* to hire minstrels.[21] Employing musicians suggests that Edmund was desperately trying to keep up appearances, but Henry was not deceived for a moment. It was not long before he insisted on downgrading the Suffolk title from duke to earl.

The king's reasoning – that Edmund no longer had sufficient income to justify the lofty rank he had inherited from his father – was sound, but he could not resist turning the screw. In order to receive enough of the forfeited Suffolk inheritance to qualify even as an earl, Edmund had to pay an indemnity of £5,000 in yearly instalments of £200 during his mother's life, rising to £400 after her death.[22] Worse was to follow.

It had long been Henry's policy to try and convince any sceptical nobles that the Tudors were the true heirs to the illustrious House of York. To this end, he had married Edward IV's daughter Elizabeth of York, disinherited Edward IV's de la Pole nephews and waged war against the French, who had backed Warbeck's claim to be Edward IV's son Richard, duke of York. However, the pretender had now fled to the court of Edward IV's sister Margaret of Burgundy, and this threatened to wreck all his carefully laid plans. Henry VII therefore planned a new propaganda campaign whereby his younger son, the future Henry VIII, would be created duke of York.

By conferring a title that had been held by the younger of the missing Yorkist princes on his own son, Henry would outflank Warbeck. Moreover, by giving Edmund a prominent role at both the investiture ceremony and the lavish tournament that had been planned to celebrate the little prince's elevation, he would demonstrate to the world that the de la Poles had been surpassed in the Yorkist succession.

Accordingly, Edmund led the procession of the Three Estates, which customarily opened the ceremony of investiture, and bore his sword pointed down to symbolise his surrender.[23] A week later, Edmund captained the 'challengers', who would battle the 'answerers' chosen to defend the young prince's honour; it was no accident that all the members of his team had blood ties to the House of York or connections to East Anglia.

First of the four men chosen to fight alongside Edmund was Henry Bourchier, 2nd earl of Essex, nephew of Edward IV's queen, Elizabeth Woodville. Another, George Neville, 5th Baron Bergavenny, was a cousin of Richard III's queen, Anne Neville. Sir John Peche was next; his father had been a favourite of Edward IV. Finally, Sir Robert Curson was a wealthy Suffolk *parvenu* whose brand-new Ipswich mansion covered more than 2 acres.[24] Curson, Essex and Bergavenny would all feature in Edmund's future, and we will hear more of them later.

To drive home Henry's message, the 'answerers' facing down Edmund's company were prominent Lancastrians or ex-Yorkists who had deserted the white rose and adopted the red. Their captain was George Talbot, 4th earl of Shrewsbury, who had fought Edmund's brother during the Simnel crisis. Sir Edward Darrell[25] and Sir Edward Burrough had also distinguished themselves at Stoke Field, while the 6-foot-8-inch Sir John Cheney, who had served as Edward IV's master of horse, had joined the exiled Henry Tudor in Brittany after falling from Yorkist favour. Other 'answerers' included Sir Thomas Brandon, whose brother had been killed at Bosworth defending Henry's standard, and the Breton nobleman Sir William de la Riviere, who had been appointed Henry's master of henchmen.

The great tournament took place over three separate days at the beginning of November 1494 and there was plenty of feasting and dancing at the end of each day's contest. Besides celebrating his triumph over the House of York, Henry hoped these sumptuous festivities would mark the dawn of a new Golden Age. He ordered wooden grandstands to be constructed in the grounds outside Westminster Hall to hold the thousands of spectators who had paid handsomely to watch the contest.

Among the illustrious names on the guest list were Edmund's mother and her daughters.[26] The attendance of the last Yorkist kings' sister and nieces would be a very public demonstration of their acceptance of Henry's rule, and if the de la Pole ladies were present it is reasonable to assume that the dowager duchess of Suffolk's youngest sons, William and Richard, were with them.

At the time of the Westminster tournament, the boys would have been in their early teens[27] and it is easy to imagine them idolising their glamorous big brother. Indeed, Edmund must have looked like Lancelot reborn as he entered the tiltyard clad in a glittering suit of gilded armour – but his show of splendour was a sham.

Due to his state-imposed poverty, Edmund had been forced to take out an eye-watering loan to equip himself for the event, but at least he had spent the money well. Besides his enormously expensive armour, which contemporary chroniclers described as a masterpiece of the goldsmiths' art, golden bells had been braided into the mane of his mighty warhorse and silver bells had been stitched into its bridle, which, cheekily, had been trimmed with ducal ermine.[28]

At the beginning of the tournament, Edmund and his team entertained the crowd with feats of horsemanship but at the sound of a trumpet they retreated to the far end of the field to allow the 'answerers' to enter. Once these preliminaries were over, Edmund opened the contest by running six bruising courses against Sir Edward Burrough. Later that same day, he ran another six courses against the battered Sir Edward and twelve against Sir William de la Riviere.[29]

The second day of competition was even more spectacular than the first with the combatants entering the field under large, portable pavilions that identified them to the cheering crowds. These elaborate canopies were embroidered with each knight's heraldic emblems and Edmund's was especially splendid. It was made of ruinously expensive red silk, embroidered with his motto – 'For to accomplish' – and his crest of a golden lion with a forked tail and a spangled coronet.[30]

Another departure from the opening day's contest could be observed in Edmund's clothing. On the first day he had worn the Tudor colours of white and apple-green, but on the second he was clad in the old blue and mulberry of York. No doubt this change of costume was intended to symbolise the Tudor absorption of their Yorkist rivals, but it did not affect Edmund's martial prowess. During his third bout with the battered Sir Edward Burrough, an epic battle that lasted twenty-three strokes, he broke his sword and earned the day's prize of a golden ring set with a large diamond.[31]

The third day of the tournament required the combatants to fight for the honour of a lady. The chosen maidens, all dressed in gowns of pure white silk with sleeves of crimson velvet, entered the field riding snow-white palfreys. Edmund received the favour of his cousin Lady Elizabeth Stafford, Countess of Sussex,[32] and it hardly needs to be said that this pairing was loaded with hidden meaning.

Lady Elizabeth's mother was Catherine Woodville, sister of Edward IV's queen, while her father, the 2nd duke of Buckingham, had been executed by Richard III for abandoning the Yorkist cause and leading a rebellion. The widowed Catherine Woodville had later married Jasper Tudor, Henry's uncle, and the career trajectory of her brother Edward, 3rd duke of Buckingham closely resembled that of Edmund de la Pole. Though Buckingham had kept his dukedom, his loyalty to his Tudor kin was always suspect because of his Yorkist blood.

It is impossible to know how much Edmund was aware of these subliminal messages, but he certainly wasted no time in striking the first blow for his lady. In the first pass, he and the luckless Sir Edward Burrough broke their lances into splinters but Edmund scored the winning blow by hitting his opponent's helmet. When it came to the swordplay, Edmund gave the unfortunate Burrough a thrashing so brutal that he may have sustained brain damage.[33]

Sometime after the Westminster tournament, poor Sir Edward was barred from taking his seat in Parliament on the grounds he had become 'distracted of memory'.[34] Though there was a long history of madness in Sir Edward's family, the effects of being repeatedly beaten about the head cannot have improved his mental health. He was, at least, awarded the day's prize of another diamond ring.[35]

Considering, that the earl of Suffolk was the clear victor in all his bouts with Sir Edward, the presentation of such a valuable ring to the loser was surely a snub. Even so, the success of the Westminster tournament marked an apparent upturn in Edmund's fortunes. Less than a year later, Henry paid Edmund the honour of staying with him at Ewelme,[36] the de la Poles' principal residence in Oxfordshire. Yet even this outward display of royal favour disguised another calculated insult.

2

DEPARTED OUT OF THIS REALM

For its day, the magnificent house at Ewelme was one of the most modern in the Chilterns, boasting among its many innovations iron beams that supported the roof of its great hall. The Elizabethan antiquarian John Leland was particularly fulsome in his praise when he visited the manor sometime around 1540, describing the lodgings as 'exceeding fair and lightsome'.[1]

Whether Henry VII was similarly impressed is not recorded but, perhaps in a fit of pique, he signed the Act of Parliament ratifying Suffolk's demotion from duke to earl shortly after his visit.[2] Besides downgrading Edmund's title, Henry also decided to keep several de la Pole manors that had important feudal honours attached.

One of the estates that was to remain with the king 'in perpetuity' was the manor of Kettlebaston in Suffolk, whose lord had the right to carry a gold sceptre at the coronation of a king or one of ivory at that of a queen.[3] In 1487, the sixteen-year-old Edmund had watched his father exercise this right at the enthronement of his cousin Elizabeth of York,[4] so he must have understood that by this act the de la Poles' connection to royalty was being symbolically severed.

On the other hand, the same Act of Parliament that robbed Edmund of Kettlebaston returned to him his chief residence in the city of London, which was located in the parish of St Laurence Pountney, and designated him as one of the lords responsible for hearing petitions from Gascony and other overseas territories.[5] Although the reduction of England's French possessions to a few square miles around Calais meant this post had lost much of its original importance, Edmund's appointment did suggest that he was at least on probation. The turn of the year brought more royal favour when Edmund was made a Knight of the Garter.

Shortly before Christmas 1495, the king's beloved uncle Jasper Tudor, duke of Bedford, had died, and it was his place in the Order of the Garter that Edmund now occupied.[6] This was especially significant because the de la Poles had played a small, but important, role in the rise of the family that would eventually destroy them.

After the death of Catherine de Valois, widow of Henry V and mother of Henry VI, her sons Jasper and Edmund, a product of her later marriage to Owen Tudor, had been placed in the care of the nuns at Barking Abbey, whose abbess was Katherine de la Pole. Katherine was the sister of William de la Pole, who was the king's chief advisor at the time, and through him she was able to persuade Henry VI to take an interest in his half-brothers.[7]

Thanks to Katherine, Jasper Tudor was married to Catherine Woodville while his brother Edmund was married to Margaret Beaufort, whose brief marriage to John de la Pole had been annulled on the grounds of the bride and groom's extreme youth. Henry VII was a child of the Beaufort–Tudor union.

Considering Henry's longstanding antipathy to the de la Poles, replacing his Tudor uncle in the Order of the Garter with a possible rival for the throne seems like an extremely foolish idea. However, elevating Edmund to England's highest order of chivalry was consistent with his policy of trying to make peace with prominent Yorkists. Edmund may also have helped his own cause by settling down and marrying Margaret Scrope, one of Lord Richard Scrope's nine daughters, who soon gave birth to a baby girl named Anne.[8] Becoming a father appeared to suit the earl of Suffolk, and he was not among those arrested for supporting Perkin Warbeck when he began causing trouble once more.

After being expelled from France by the terms of the Treaty of Étaples, Warbeck had found a warm welcome in the Low Countries, where Margaret of Burgundy had officially recognised him as her long-lost nephew. Even more importantly, Burgundy's feudal overlords, Archduke Philip and his father Holy Roman Emperor Maximilian, had been so incensed by Henry's failure to seek their approval before signing the Treaty of Étaples that they too endorsed Warbeck's claim to England's throne.

Financed by Margaret, and with the tacit support of Philip and Maximilian, Warbeck attempted to land a small army near Deal in Kent but was driven off by the locals.[9] Undeterred, the pretender sailed to Ireland where he found a much warmer welcome from Maurice FitzGerald, 9th earl of Desmond. The FitzGeralds were locked into their own private war with the pro-Tudor earls of Ormond, and the chance to strike at their enemy's patron was too good to miss. Desmond and Warbeck laid siege to Waterford, but the new cannons in the city's Reginald Tower sank several of the pretender's ships and the rebels were forced to withdraw.

Following these failures, the irrepressible Warbeck fled to Scotland where he persuaded the Scottish king, James IV, to back his cause; not that his host needed much persuading. No true Scot would decline an opportunity to make mischief south of the border, and James duly announced that Warbeck was the younger of the missing princes, whom he intended to see crowned King Richard IV as soon as possible. To seal this renewal of an earlier Scots–Yorkist alliance, Warbeck married Lady Katherine Gordon, daughter of the earl of Huntly.[10]

As soon as these nuptials were over, James mustered an army to invade England and the Scottish host marched out of Edinburgh on 14 September 1496. At their head was a specially made Yorkist banner of red, white and blue taffeta embroidered with threads of gold and silver,[11] but the Scots were more interested in plunder than restoring the House of York.

The ferocity of his allies so terrified Warbeck that he deserted his own army as soon as they crossed the River Tweed into England. He tried to salvage some dignity by claiming he could not be party to an invasion that would cause his subjects to suffer, and while these sentiments may be laudable it is more likely he feared that the Scots would be furious when they realised that he had grossly exaggerated his support in England. Warbeck was certainly right to be worried, and when the extent of his deception was discovered James angrily declared he would have nothing more to do with a man 'who did everything by guile'.[12] Yet the saga was far from over. Indeed, Warbeck's continued intrigues would have a profound effect on the lives of both Edmund and Richard de la Pole.

In the aftermath of Warbeck's failed invasion, Henry raised taxes on Cornish tin in order to fund an army that would punish the Scots for supporting the pretender. Paying for a war that had little to do with Cornwall was deeply unpopular in the Stannaries, and those who resented Henry's attempts to fleece them soon raised the flag of revolt. These rebels were led by an ambitious Bodmin blacksmith named Michael An Gof[13] and a silver-tongued lawyer named Thomas Flamank, who assured the Cornishmen that presenting a peaceful petition to Henry would resolve all their grievances without any repercussions.[14]

For the most part, the march of the 16,000 Cornishmen to London was indeed bloodless. A detested tax collector was lynched at Taunton, however, and when the rebels reached Blackheath, near Greenwich, Henry began to panic. The Cornish camp was just over a mile from his favourite quarters, the Palace of Placentia, and he was so unnerved by this proximity that he tore up the rules of war.

Shortly after the Cornishmen's arrival, Henry announced that he would observe the Sabbath and not give battle until the following Monday – this was a lie, and he launched his attack on the Saturday.[15] Having been lulled into a false sense of security, the Cornishmen did not notice as their camp was slowly surrounded. When Henry sounded the charge, they were caught completely by surprise.

Though Lord Daubeney, Henry's field commander, managed to get himself captured, the rebels did not kill him in case it damaged their cause. They need not have been so cautious. Henry was not in a forgiving mood, and more than 2,000 Cornishmen were hacked to death by the royal forces. Those who survived quickly surrendered, and their leaders An Gof and Flamank suffered the usual fate of rebels on 27 June 1497.[16]

This massacre, dubbed the battle of Blackheath (and also known as the battle of Deptford Bridge), was a notable victory for Henry VII and it is a measure of his relief that almost seventy of his men were immediately rewarded for their valour with knighthood or promotion to knight banneret. Among them were Thomas Lovell, Charles Somerset, Sir Reynold Bray, Richard Guildford,

Thomas Green, Sir James Tyrell's brother Thomas, and Edmund's brother William.[17]

The surviving sources make no mention of Edmund's other brother, Richard, which suggests that he was not yet old enough to wield a sword and therefore must have been the youngest of the de la Poles, not William as is stated in some sources. Ironically, Edmund also saw little of the fighting because he was part of the 'great company of archers and horsemen'[18] ordered to cut off the rebel retreat and the Cornishmen surrendered before he could don his spurs. However, as Edmund's life began to unravel, a scurrilous rumour began to circulate about his conduct earlier in the campaign.

According to the gossips, Edmund had been caught in bed with Lord Bergavenny, one of his jousting cronies, when he should have been defending a vital bridge over the River Thames at Wallingford.[19] Whatever the truth of this slander – and there will be more to say on this later – the battle of Blackheath did not put an end to Henry VII's Cornish troubles.

Though Scotland's king had supposedly washed his hands of the pretender, the serious unrest in the West Country presented James with a unique opportunity. If Warbeck formed an alliance with the Cornish rebels and succeeded in overthrowing Henry, Scotland would have a friendly king on England's throne; equally, if the pretender failed, James would be rid of an ally who had become an embarrassment. To this end, James gave Warbeck a ship, the aptly named *Cuckoo*, and sent him to Ireland to raise another army while he laid to siege to the Northumberland castle of Norham, which guarded an important ford over the Tweed.

By now the pretender had little support even in the former Yorkist stronghold of Ireland. Undeterred, he nonetheless continued to Cornwall and landed a ragtag force of 300 English exiles and Flemish mercenaries at Whitesand Bay, 2 miles north of Land's End. Warbeck was welcomed by the survivors of Blackheath, who were eager to avenge the slaughter of their countrymen, but this would prove the peak of his success.

Having raised his standard at Bodmin,[20] Warbeck marched on Exeter but while he managed to recruit several thousand disaffected Cornishmen along the way, most of the West Country failed to rise up against the Tudors. When Exeter was reached on 17 September, the earl of Devon, who commanded Exeter's garrison, refused to surrender. Several attempts to storm the city's walls were then repulsed.

The bloodied and increasingly desperate Cornishmen withdrew to Taunton, which had no walls, but the defenders of the town's castle refused to open the gates. Without a secure base the Second Cornish Rebellion was doomed, and the final nail in its coffin was the news that Lord Daubeney was approaching at the head of a large army. How the beleaguered Cornish must have rued their decision to spare Daubeney after his capture at Blackheath.

Warbeck was the first to lose his nerve. Just as he had done during his earlier invasion of Northumberland, the pretender deserted his men and galloped away to the Channel coast. Whether by accident or design, he found refuge with the monks of Beaulieu Abbey, in the heart of Hampshire's New Forest, but Daubeney's men soon discovered his whereabouts. Realising he had run out of options, Warbeck surrendered and threw himself on the king's mercy.[21]

Warbeck was paraded through the streets of London before being sent to the Tower.[22] Despite the trouble he had caused, his life was spared; his capture meant Henry now had three Yorkist pretenders at his mercy. After being pardoned on the grounds of his youth, Lambert Simnel had been put to work as a spit-turner in the royal kitchens; Edward, earl of Warwick, meanwhile, was now joined in his captivity by Warbeck.

It may be recalled that the unfortunate Warwick had a claim to the throne through his father, the attainted duke of Clarence, who was brother to Edward IV and Richard III and uncle to Edmund de la Pole. Though Warwick had been barred from the succession by an Act of Parliament, he still had a stronger claim to the throne than the Tudors, so Henry had kept the boy a prisoner in the Tower ever since his victory at Bosworth.

With Warbeck and Warwick safely under lock and key, the only potential Yorkist claimants still at large were Edmund, William and Richard de la Pole, and the collapse of the pretender's latest rebellion meant Henry had a free hand to deal with them. It can hardly be a coincidence, then, that the arrest of Warbeck marked a sudden cooling in the earl of Suffolk's relations with England's first Tudor king.

After the relatively good years of 1496 and 1497, the downward spiral was renewed early in 1498 when Edmund was summoned to a civil court to answer a suit relating to his late father's estates. The cause of this dispute has been lost in the mists of time but, whatever it was, Edmund refused to settle the matter[23] and this was only the beginning of his legal troubles. Soon after Warbeck joined Warwick in the Tower, Edmund was charged with the murder of Thomas Crue during the brawl in Seething Lane.

The timing of Edmund's court appearance suggests that the whole affair had been carefully orchestrated by Henry, and that Crue had been paid to either murder Edmund and make it look like a common robbery or goad the hot-headed young earl into committing an offence for which he could be arrested. In either case, if Henry was trying to bring the de la Poles to heel, he failed.

Being arrested for murder was the final straw for Edmund. After being demoted from duke to earl, bankrupted by having to take part in royal tournaments and humiliated in both the civil and criminal courts, he decided that he could no longer live under Henry's tyranny. His last public engagement was in April 1499, when he attended a chapter of the Order of the Garter at Windsor, after which he retired to what was left of his estates and awaited an opportunity to flee abroad. That chance presented itself at the end of June when Henry took a short holiday at Godshill, on the Isle of Wight.[24]

As soon as Henry left London, Edmund slipped across the Channel.[25] His absence was quickly discovered, and the news that his bird had flown sent Henry into a panic. Writs were sent to the royal sheriffs in East Anglia, Kent and the Cinque Ports instructing them to round up suspected Yorkists. One of those charged with hunting down Edmund's supporters was Sir John Paston, whose family had been embroiled in a long-running feud with the de la Poles. The dispute concerned the validity of an oral will made by Sir John Fastolf, a kinsman of the Pastons as well as the model for Shakespeare's Falstaff, and his descendant needed no encouragement to arrest a de la Pole.

On 20 August 1499, the king commanded his officials to stop all Englishmen travelling abroad. Also on that day, Paston received a letter from the earl of Oxford ordering him to compile a list of those who may have fled with Edmund and to keep watch for any

Yorkist exiles trying to sneak across the Channel. Paston was also to arrest anyone who had helped the fugitive earl reach the coast and force them to sign a financial bond guaranteeing their good behaviour.[26]

What Henry feared most was that Edmund would follow in his late brother's footsteps and make straight for his aunt's court in Mechelen in Flanders. Once safe there, he would persuade Margaret of Burgundy to revive the Yorkist cause, with himself in the role of pretender. But Henry had not only misjudged Edmund, he had misjudged Margaret as well. The ageing Yorkist matriarch had grown weary of squandering her wealth on doomed rebellions,[27] and Edmund must have been aware of this because he did not to go to Flanders as everyone expected. Instead, he sailed for Calais and made his way to the castle of Guînes, whose captain was Sir James Tyrell.

It has been Sir James's utter misfortune to have been damned in the eyes of history as the murderer of the so-called Princes in the Tower, and his part in this most notorious act will be examined later. For now, suffice to say that the Tyrells were an ancient Suffolk family and Sir James had remained a steadfast member of the White Rose party even after his father had been beheaded for plotting to assassinate Edward IV.

Tyrell's bravery during the 1482 Yorkist invasion of Scotland had earned him both a knighthood and an invitation to Richard III's coronation, but he was in France on official business when his patron was killed at Bosworth.[28] Although the victorious Henry VII had seized some of the absent Tyrell's richer lands, he had later compensated him with estates in Wales and made him captain of Guînes, one of the two castles that guarded the southern approaches to Calais.[29] Though a grizzled ex-Yorkist was hardly the obvious choice for this strategically vital fortress, Sir James had never given Henry any reason to doubt his loyalty – that is, until Edmund knocked on his door.

As Tyrell had been a loyal servant of the Tudors since Bosworth, Edmund's decision to seek refuge in Guînes may seem strange. However, the two men would have known each other well; along with their Suffolk connections, Sir James had served in the Dixmude and Boulogne campaigns, in which Edmund likely took part, while his younger brother Thomas had been made a knight banneret at Blackheath.[30] Sir James was, therefore, an ideal choice of sanctuary, and a crucial lifeline for Edmund as Henry's bloodhounds picked up his trail.

The men ordered to bring Edmund home were Master Richard Hatton, who was Clerk of the Parliaments, and Sir Richard Guildford, one of those disaffected Yorkists who had suffered under Richard III but prospered after the Tudor victory; Guildford was also among those knighted after Blackheath. Henry considered his envoys' mission so important he paid them the considerable sum of £50 6*s* 8*d* to cover their expenses.[31]

At this point, Henry was still labouring under the delusion that Edmund had sought refuge with his aunt in Flanders, so he ordered Guildford to go to Brussels and remind Philip, archduke of Burgundy, of the treaty he had signed three years earlier. This treaty, dubbed the *Intercursus Magnus*, had lifted the trade embargo Henry had imposed on Burgundian goods as punishment for Margaret's support of Perkin Warbeck, and under its terms both monarchs had agreed not to support each other's rebels.

Yet Henry did not want it widely known that a new pretender was on the loose, so he ordered Guildford and Hatton to seek out Edmund *before* they approached the archduke. Once they had tracked Edmund to his lair, they were to read out a personal letter from the king in which he offered the wayward earl a free pardon if he returned to England of his own accord. If he refused this olive branch, Henry's envoys were to remind him that the rulers of France, Scotland, Spain, Portugal and the Holy Roman Empire were all bound by treaties similar to the *Intercursus Magnus*, so they too were required to banish English rebels. Guildford was also instructed to warn Edmund that taking service with foreign princes in wars against their Tudor allies would be considered proof of his treachery and forever place him beyond the king's power to forgive.[32]

Should this softly-softly approach succeed, Guildford and Hatton were to abandon their mission to Brussels and accompany Edmund back to England. But why was Henry so fearful? Edmund had served Henry loyally in both peace and war, and the only serious stain on his character was the possibly trumped-up charge of killing Thomas Crue. Even allowing for Margaret of Burgundy's reluctance to back another rebellion, the fact that Edmund had turned to Sir James Tyrell rather than his bellicose aunt offers more proof that treason was the last thing on his mind.

Instead of raising his flag of revolt, it seems far more likely that Edmund had left England in a simple fit of pique and was hoping to wait for the scandal of the murder trial to blow over. Unfortunately for the much-wronged earl of Suffolk, so entrenched was the king's fear of a Yorkist uprising that nothing could convince him of Edmund's loyalty.

Henry still had good reason to be wary. Six months before Edmund's disappearance, the king's spymasters had arrested Ralph Wilford, a twenty-year-old student at Cambridge who believed he was the son of the long-imprisoned earl of Warwick. Wilford's real father was a shoemaker in London's Bishopsgate, but he was encouraged in his delusions by an Augustinian friar called Patrick. Having failed to raise a rebellion in the boy's native Suffolk, the scheming priest and his misguided protégé had travelled to Kent and tried again, but this time Patrick insisted that Wilford was the actual earl of Warwick, rather than his son.[33]

It was a good idea for Patrick to make this tweak considering Wilford was only four years younger than his supposed father, but it hardly mattered. The two fraudsters had not been as discreet as they had imagined, and they soon attracted the attention of the authorities. The witless Wilford was sent to the gallows on Shrove Tuesday 1499, but the treacherous priest claimed 'benefit of clergy' and was merely imprisoned for life.[34]

Despite the preposterousness of the latest pretender's claim, the effect on Henry had been profound. The king appeared to age twenty years in a few weeks, and he began to show an increasing interest in the health-restoring powers of astrology and alchemy, even though he had outlawed such practices at the start of his reign.[35]

The king's accounts for 1499 reveal that a man from Perpignan had been paid £2 for demonstrating a youth-giving 'quintessence', while a physician named Wulf had received two instalments of £8 6*s* 8*d* for some undisclosed remedies. An astrologer called William Parron had been paid £1 to cast the king's horoscope and an unnamed alchemist had been given the huge sum of £33 6*s* 8*d* to a set up a laboratory in in the Tower of London, where he planned to turn base metal into gold,[36] but by far the worst of these charlatans was a priest who claimed have the gift of prophecy. This self-styled seer told Henry that he was in great danger, prophesying that England would never know peace so long as there were two warring parties in his kingdom, but it did not take an astrologer to realise that the Tudor struggle with the Yorkists was far from over.[37]

Though Edmund was not directly implicated in the Wilford plot, the fact that its chief architect came from Suffolk cannot have escaped Henry's attention, and his spies uncovered a much more serious Yorkist conspiracy whilst Wilford's body was still rotting on its gibbet.

The authors of this new intrigue, Robert Cleymond and Thomas Astwode, planned to assassinate Henry, seize the Tower, fire its magazine and use the ensuing confusion to free Perkin Warbeck and the real earl of Warwick, but their plot was quickly betrayed. It is thought that Warbeck himself might have turned informer in the hope of avoiding the gallows, but it is equally likely that Cleymond had owned up after being threatened with the rack; it is telling that he was not named in the indictment that condemned the others.

Whoever talked, the true victim was the wretched Warwick.[38] The last in the direct male line of Plantagenets had become so befuddled by his long years of captivity that he clutched at his first chance of rescue with all the desperation of a drowning man. A dagger and book of codes smuggled into his cell served to raise his hopes, but he supposedly could no longer 'discern a goose from a capon',[39] let alone sniff out the trap that had been carefully set for him. For three desperate weeks, Warwick believed that his hour of salvation was at hand; in fact, Henry was deliberately letting the plot play out because he wanted to catch bigger fish than Cleymond and Astwode. No doubt the king was secretly hoping that the earl of Suffolk would be implicated, but how much Edmund knew about the plot remains a matter of conjecture.[40]

Regardless of his complicity in the Wilford, Warbeck and Warwick affairs, Edmund would have been acutely aware of the corrosive atmosphere of suspicion created by these conspiracies, so it is hardly surprising that he had decided to leave England until matters improved. However, Guînes was still English territory and Henry's reach was long.

Perhaps on the advice of Tyrell, who may have feared for his own head if he spent too long in the company of a convicted murderer, Edmund decided to seek refuge outside the Calais Pale and so, on a moonless night at the beginning of September 1499, he slipped out of Guînes. A few days later Edmund was spotted in St Omer, which was at this time on the Flanders side of the Franco–Flemish border, and from here he wrote to Burgundy's archduke asking for his protection.[41]

Unfortunately for Edmund, moving to Flanders was a serious mistake because it confirmed to Henry what he had suspected all along. Moreover, the envoys Henry had sent to remind Burgundy's archduke of his legal duty not to harbour English rebels had already arrived in Brussels and Archduke Philip had assured them that he had every intention of honouring the *Intercursus Magnus*. For once, Philip was as good as his word and he ordered St Omer's captain, Denis de Morbecque, to inform Edmund that he was not welcome in Burgundy.[42]

Realising that he had been outflanked, Edmund meekly took ship for England sometime in the early autumn of 1499 and Henry kept his promise to be lenient. The earl's conviction for murder was conveniently forgotten and Edmund's only punishment was a fine of £1,000 for having left the country without royal permission. Relatively speaking, Sir James Tyrell was treated much more harshly, being forced to pay a huge bond of £300 to ensure his future good behaviour and losing one of his lucrative royal demesnes.[43]

Yet those who suffered most in the aftermath of Edmund's flight to Guînes were the two Yorkists in the Tower.

3

THE GOODLIEST PLUMES

The half-baked scheme to free Warbeck and Warwick from the Tower gave Henry the excuse he needed to send them both to the scaffold, along with their chief supporters. Warbeck, Astwode and John Awater, a former mayor of Cork who had backed the impostor from the beginning, were hanged at Tyburn on 23 November 1499. Five days later, the confused earl of Warwick was beheaded on Tower Hill.

Even though Warwick posed no threat to Henry, the poor befuddled earl had to die because Ferdinand of Aragon would not let his daughter Catherine of Aragon marry Henry's eldest son, Arthur, until the Tudors were secure on the throne.[1] The last of the Plantagenets in the male line therefore went to the scaffold at the insistence of the Spanish king, but one stubborn problem remained: what was to be done with Edmund?

If Henry was going to convince Ferdinand that he was in full control of his realm, he would have to keep the earl of Suffolk on very a tight leash. As a result, he continued with his shameless persecution of the de la Pole family and their retainers. To begin with, two of Edmund's servants, Thomas Wyndham and John Wiseman, were fined for failing to appear before the King's Council while their master was hiding in St Omer. Then, as soon as Edmund set foot on English soil, he found himself back in court, not once or twice but three times.

The earl's first reappearance in the dock occurred in the autumn of 1499, when he was ordered to surrender several manors to raise the

£1,000 he had been fined for being absent without the king's leave. Six months later, in May 1500, Edmund lost a civil case concerning another valuable manor in Norfolk, but by far the most serious charge he had to answer on his return to England was that of kidnapping.[2]

Edmund was accused of seizing a man named William Renet, who lived in the Suffolk village of Rishangles, and keeping him in custody against his will. According to the Queen's Bench Plea Roll for the Trinity Term of 1499, Edmund had appointed William Fisher and John Jenour as his advocates, and these lawyers claimed that their client's actions were fully justified because Renet owed him money. Perhaps inevitably, the verdict went against Edmund and he was ordered to pay his victim £100 in damages.[3]

This whole sorry incident fits Henry's policy of using the courts to control his delinquent nobles, but the king was not really interested in these minor transgressions. What Henry really wanted was an excuse to put the earl of Suffolk on trial for high treason, and this campaign of harassment was designed to force Edmund into a corner from which rebellion was the only way out.

If Edmund took the bait, Henry could send his rival to the scaffold with a clear conscience; there is little doubt that the luckless earl of Warwick had been lured into just such a trap. Yet, despite being humiliated by the king and hounded by the courts, the earl of Suffolk showed no signs of putting his head into the king's carefully prepared noose.

When this strategy failed to produce the desired results, Henry ordered Edmund's wife, Margaret, to be placed under surveillance but no evidence of Edmund's treason was forthcoming. By the spring of 1500, Henry was forced to admit that the eldest of Richard III's surviving nephews was not cut from the same rebellious cloth as his older brother. He reluctantly allowed Edmund to resume his place in the front rank of England's nobility.

The earl of Suffolk's rehabilitation began on 5 May 1500 when he was included in the royal entourage accompanying the king to Canterbury. Here Henry and the Spanish ambassador would ratify the treaty that would marry Arthur, Prince of Wales, to Catherine of Aragon and Edmund's name appears at the top of the list of dignitaries who witnessed this momentous event.[4]

What Tudor loyalists such as Lord Daubeney and Sir Richard Guildford, who had helped negotiate the treaty, thought of this is not recorded but Henry had good reasons for permitting the earl of Suffolk to make such a prominent return to public life. Rather than demonstrating any newfound trust in Edmund, Henry was showing the crowned heads of Christendom that the titular head of the House of York had wholeheartedly accepted Tudor rule.

Ferdinand of Aragon was not the only target of this fiction. Besides reassuring the Spanish king, Henry wanted to convince the archduke of Burgundy that there was no future in supporting English rebels. This was particularly important because Philip was married to Catherine of Aragon's older sister Joanna of Castile, who would succeed to Spain's twin thrones on the death of her parents, Ferdinand of Aragon and Isabella of Castile. In addition to Castile and Aragon, Joanna would also inherit all Spanish possessions overseas, such as the Mediterranean islands under Aragonese rule and the nascent Castilian empire in the New World.

Though the infant son of the king of Portugal, Miguel de la Paz, had a better claim to the Spanish thrones than Joanna,[5] the sickly little boy was not expected to live beyond his second birthday, and Archduke Philip fully intended to supplant his wife once the boy was dead. Already, the ambitious Philip was alarming the Spanish nobility by spreading rumours that Joanna was unfit to rule because she was mentally unstable.

It had not escaped the notice of Europe's other monarchs that the archduke of Burgundy was heir to the Habsburgs' sprawling empire in central Europe. Even though the imperial throne was theoretically elective, it was more than likely that Philip would succeed his father as Holy Roman Emperor and the Habsburgs also ruled vast domains in Germany, Austria and Italy in their own right. Should all these lands be gathered into the Habsburg fold, Philip would rule a Hispano-Italo-Germanic superpower that stretched from Portugal to Poland.

Ever mindful of his own tenuous grip on power, Henry decided it was time to build stronger bridges with Philip, so he invited the archduke to a diplomatic summit which was to be held in Calais for his guest's convenience. As an added bonus, crossing the Channel would allow the Tudor court to escape an outbreak of the dreaded sweating sickness that held London in its deadly grip.[6]

The first members of Henry's party arrived in Calais on 8 May 1500, and among the minor courtiers who formed the vanguard of the royal entourage was Edmund's younger brother William. The earl of Suffolk himself landed on 13 May and the rest of the Tudor court, including Richard de la Pole, the youngest of Edmund's brothers, disembarked on 4 June.[7]

Five days later, the king and queen of England left Calais accompanied by a glittering array of England's leading nobles. One Calais burgess, Richard Turpyn, noted that three men stood out from the rest. The first noble to catch Turpyn's attention was the duke of Buckingham, the second was the earl of Northumberland and the third was the earl of Suffolk, who was dressed from head to foot in cloth of gold as well as a hat decorated with gold chains and 'the goodliest plumes of white ostrich feathers that ever I saw'.[8]

The Calais chronicler also tells us that the conference was to be held in the small church of Our Lady and St Peter, which lay a few miles outside of the city on the road to St Omer. This was because Philip was reluctant to enter walled towns after his father had been kidnapped by Flemish rebels during a visit to Bruges,[9] and Turpyn adds that the previously unassuming St Peter's had been transformed into a sumptuous palace for the occasion.

Besides carpets strewn with roses, lavender and other sweet-smelling flowers, the church's altar and choir had been decorated with red banners emblazoned with the three gold lions of England, and blue banners decorated with French fleurs-de-lis. This combination was intended to highlight Henry's claim to the crown of France.

The two private chambers where the summit's business would be conducted were decorated with ruinously expensive wall hangings similarly loaded with symbolism.[10] The tapestry in the larger chamber told the story of Esther, a Jewish princess who had married a Persian king in order to save her exiled people from being massacred, and it was here that Henry and Philip discussed their plans for two dynastic marriages. The first would join the king of England's four-year-old daughter, Mary Tudor, to the archduke's young son Charles (the future Emperor Charles V). The second would betroth Henry's second son, Henry, duke of York, to Philip's daughter Eleanor of Austria.[11]

The tapestry adorning the smaller chamber depicted the Fall of Troy, the Homeric scenes acting as a reminder to Philip that

England's kings could trace their lineage back to a Trojan prince whereas the Habsburgs' Swiss ancestors were mere counts. It hardly needs to be said that the story of the Trojans' arrival in the Devon port of Totnes is a myth, but Tudor chroniclers such as Hall accepted these legends as historical fact.[12]

Whether Philip took the hint is not recorded, but Turpyn informs us that the feast prepared for the delegates was legendary in its own way. The archduke was treated to a banquet that included a whole roast ox, hot and cold venison pasties, a surfeit of strawberries and cream and seven cartloads of cherries. Indeed, there was so much food and drink that it could not all be consumed in one day, so Henry ordered the leftovers to be distributed among the local peasantry.[13]

Among those who had been present at this sumptuous feast were the three de la Pole brothers,[14] and Henry's reasons for inviting them became clear the next day. Besides arranging the marriages of his youngest children and boosting Anglo-Flemish trade, Henry was desperate to invite the archduke to the spectacular tournament he was planning as a celebration of the imminent marriage of his eldest son, Arthur, and Philip's sister-in-law, Catherine of Aragon.

As before, Henry wanted to use this tournament to demonstrate to everyone who mattered that the de la Poles were now loyal Tudors. It is therefore no surprise that Edmund's name would top the list of challengers. Tellingly, the official call to arms was made at the end of the Calais summit and required Edmund, as the captain of the challengers, to swear a public oath of loyalty to Henry in front the archduke of Burgundy, most of England's nobility, the entire corps of foreign ambassadors to the English court, and his own brothers.

It appears that Edmund took this oath willingly, and a copy of the official call to arms was presented to Philip as well as the kings of Spain, France and Scotland.[15] Such wide circulation further underlines Henry's desire to maximise the event's propaganda value. Forcing Edmund to take part would also drain his purse faster than a dozen court cases, and depriving him of the means to look like a prince would make it harder for him to claim he was a true Yorkist king-in-waiting. However, Henry had once again underestimated Edmund.

Even as the Tudor heralds were carrying the earl of Suffolk's challenge to all the royal courts of Christendom, a plot was being hatched to breathe new life into the de la Poles' claim to the throne. In brief, the new plot involved the Holy Roman Emperor financing another Yorkist invasion of England. While he was at the Calais summit, the conspirators informed Edmund of their plans and assured him that Emperor Maximilian had already agreed to champion their cause.

The man who brought this momentous news to Edmund was Sir Robert Curson, his former jousting partner, who had only recently returned from the imperial court. Curson's true loyalties have always been open to question. He might have been telling the truth, but equally he could have been a double agent working for Henry.

Curson's past does not make it easier to tease out his intentions. It is a matter of record that he had strong connections to the de la Poles, being born in Suffolk and having been a member of Edmund's team of 'challengers' at the 1494 Westminster tournament. However, he also owed everything he had to Henry.

Born of humble stock,[16] Curson was among those who had been knighted to celebrate the betrothal of the infant Prince Arthur to the equally young Catherine of Aragon.[17] Why he was singled out for such an honour is not clear, but afterwards Curson became a popular member of the Tudor court. He regularly played tennis with the king, and though he was unwise to win so many of their games he quickly climbed the ladder of royal patronage.

In 1491, Curson and another Suffolk gentleman, Sir James Tyrell, had welcomed the French ambassadors to the peace talks that had ended the siege of Boulogne. He also served Henry as Sheriff of Norfolk and Suffolk before being appointed captain of Hammes, sister fortress to the castle of Guînes, but tongues began wagging when Curson sought permission to resign his prestigious post. In his letter to the king, Curson asked that his request be granted so he could join a crusade against the Turks being proposed by Holy Roman Emperor Maximilian.

Curiously, Curson had only recently taken up his position at Hammes and the only way he could raise the eye-watering 800 marks required to purchase such a lucrative commission was through a shameless act of robbery. In March 1498 he had married

Anne Southill, the wealthy widow of the late Sir George Hopton. Shortly afterwards, he and a group of his kinsmen had seized the manor of Westleton, which had been bequeathed to Anne's son by her first husband.[18] There is evidence that the episode caused the king to question Curson's conduct; his friends were required to pay further sureties to guarantee his good behaviour before he was allowed to take up the captaincy of Hammes.

Of course, if Curson was part of a secret Tudor plot to discredit the earl of Suffolk, all this would have been mere window dressing designed to convince Edmund that relations between the king and his new captain were strained. Whatever the truth of the matter, Curson had managed to secure his appointment by the spring of 1499. Significantly, though, while on his way to Hammes he stopped at Guînes, where Edmund was then hiding.

The gathering of Sir Robert Curson, Edmund de la Pole and Sir James Tyrell under one roof certainly looked like a Yorkist council of war, but some think this meeting was the beginning of Curson's work as a double agent on behalf of the Tudor regime. We do not know what was discussed, and the three men soon went their separate ways. Edmund returned to England to resume his place at court, Tyrell stayed in Guînes and Curson took up his post in Hammes, where he remained until his request to go on crusade was granted.[19]

If Curson was a secret Yorkist and the king was unaware of it, Henry could be forgiven for granting his request. After all, delivering a respected knight into Maximilian's service was a boon to Anglo-Imperial relations, which had become strained over Henry's repeated refusal to send troops or money to support a war on the Danube. If this was Henry's intention, his scheme backfired because Edmund now accepted Curson's proposal to make an anti-Tudor pact with the Emperor.

Some historians[20] have insisted that Curson fled Hammes because the executions of Warbeck and Warwick caused him to fear for his own life. In this scenario, joining Maximilian's crusade was simply a ruse to get him away from Henry's clutches before he could be implicated in any plots, but we will return to this debate in a later chapter. For the time being, we will assume that Curson was a passionate Yorkist and his offer to broker an alliance with Maximilian was genuine.

Though Curson served in the imperial army for less than a year, Maximilian was sufficiently impressed to make him a baron of the Empire. This ennoblement prompted Curson to change his personal standard from the Tudoresque dragon's head on a green-and-white background to a more imperial-looking charge of red and yellow stripes strewn with the severed heads of wolves. The new imperial baron also adopted a crest featuring a turbaned Turkish archer dressed in a red tunic, and changed his motto from 'Nothing restrains me' to 'Speak as you will',[21] which is exactly what he proceeded to do.

As soon as Curson had the Emperor's ear, he announced that honest Englishmen could no longer stomach the oppressive rule of the Tudors and that Edmund de la Pole was ready to take up the cudgels against the Welsh despot. Incredibly, Curson's pleas for imperial support found an appreciative audience and Maximilian declared that 'if he might have one of king Edward's blood, he would help him recover the crown of England, or else he would spend as much money as his whole lands were in value for a whole year'.[22]

The contemporary account of Curson's apparent treachery is contained in a curious document entitled *A Statement Concerning Edmund de la Pole*, which was written sometime in 1501. Although the author is anonymous, it was likely penned by Sir Thomas Killingworth, Edmund's unerringly faithful steward;[23] what is certain, however, is Curson's impeccable timing.

Henry's determination to secure a Spanish match for his son had convinced the Emperor that the marriage was nothing more than a concerted attempt by Henry and Ferdinand to block Maximilian's scheme to unite Spain and the Habsburg empire under the rule of his son Philip, archduke of Burgundy.[24] Making Edmund king of England was one way to put an end to Henry's plans.

Moreover, Maximilian had his own longstanding ties to the House of York. Besides being the sister of Edward IV, Margaret, duchess of Burgundy had been the stepmother of Maximilian's first wife, Mary. After her death in a riding accident, the Yorkist matriarch had ruled the Low Countries as regent for Philip, her step-grandson, until 1494 when he had come of age. In return, the Emperor had supported Margaret's scheming with John de la Pole and Perkin Warbeck.

Backing the first two attempts to revive the White Rose had led to the trade war that had severely damaged the Burgundian economy. Philip took his archducal oath to defend his subjects' interests seriously,[25] and so he had quickly abandoned his father's anti-Tudor policy and agreed to both the *Intercursus Magnus* and the Calais summit, producing a significant warming in Anglo-Burgundian relations. If Maximilian wanted to keep Henry on the back foot, he could not rely on Philip to stoke the fires of Anglo-Habsburg hostility. Fortunately for him, Edmund's humiliation at Calais meant he was more than ready to accept Curson's proposal.

Like the Emperor, Edmund had good reason to fear the new world order that would be ushered in by the Prince of Wales's marriage to a Spanish princess. Not only would Henry's proposed wedding tournament bankrupt him, but any child of Arthur and Catherine would push the de la Poles further into the dynastic wilderness. Worse still, Henry would be able to draw on Spain's vast military power once the marriage had taken place, and this would doom to failure any Yorkist attempt to seize the throne by force.

The thought of leading his once illustrious family into historical oblivion would have been intolerable for a proud man like Edmund, and he began to share his late brother's belief that the only hope of Yorkist salvation lay with the Emperor.[26] Ironically, the royal wedding that was supposed to bind Edmund to the House of Tudor offered him the perfect opportunity to slip unnoticed out of England. This time, he intended to do much more than lie low in Guînes and St Omer.

Edmund now believed he could revive the Yorkist–Habsburg alliance that had financed his brother's rebellion, but before he set sail for Flanders he needed to re-establish his ties to England's other senior Yorkists. Not even the Emperor could bring about a White Rose restoration without their support, so Edmund held two secret meetings with his potential allies.

Top of the guest list were Thomas Grey, 1st Marquess of Dorset, Henry Bourchier, 2nd earl of Essex, and Lord Edward Courtenay, 1st earl of Devon, whose son was one of the young bucks who had been drinking with Edmund on the night Thomas Crue was murdered. All three of these prominent nobles were connected in some way to Elizabeth Woodville, late wife of Edward IV.[27] Dorset was Elizabeth's son by her first marriage to John Grey, Essex was her nephew and Courtenay was her son-in-law by virtue of his marriage to Catherine of York, Edward IV's ninth child by his Woodville wife.[28] Such proximity to the toxic Woodvilles had been dangerous even before Bosworth, and each of Edmund's guests had spent the last twenty years walking a political tightrope.

In the 1480s, after being forced into exile by Richard III, Dorset had sought refuge with the future Henry VII in Brittany. Although England's only marquis had sat firmly on the fence during the Bosworth campaign, Henry had allowed him to keep his head and his titles. Similarly, although Essex had been in Edmund's team of Yorkist challengers during the 1494 tournament, he had fought for Henry at Boulogne and Blackheath. Courtenay, meanwhile, had backed the Woodville-Beaufort conspiracy against Richard III and had held Exeter for Henry VII against Warbeck.[29]

If all three of these noblemen had made their peace with the Tudors, we are left to wonder why Edmund approached them in the first place. Perhaps he hoped to exploit the fact that Elizabeth Woodville and her sister Anne were sisters-in-law to his mother, but if he hoped that blood was thicker than water he was soon disappointed. The reactions of Dorset, Essex and Courtenay to Curson's proposal were, at best, lukewarm.[30] However, Edmund's second clandestine rendezvous, with Courtenay's father, was more encouraging.

To begin with, the earl of Devon broke with protocol by meeting Edmund at the outer gate of his house in Warwick Lane, which inferred that he was acknowledging Edmund as his king. Devon then compounded his guilt by inviting Edmund to raise his flag of rebellion in an area of the West Country under his control. Unbeknown to him, one of Devon's servants was an informer.

It is possible that Edmund knew he was being watched, as the informant's account of the meeting tells us that Devon's offer was met with a cryptic reply:

> He answered no more but this, I see well there is many pretty castings of eyes made to any countenance that was showed me ... let them judge by outward countenance what they will.[31]

Perhaps Edmund was advising the earl of Devon to be careful of how he acted in public. All that can be said for certain is that the earl was well aware of the Yorkist *coup d'état* that was being plotted, yet he did not betray Edmund's plan to seek aid from Maximilian. In any event, Edmund had received all the assurance he needed. He left England for the second time at the end of August 1501, and this time he was not alone.

4

MY MOST DEAR AND WELL-BELOVED COUSIN

It was dawn on a late summer's day in 1501 when a small rowing boat, carrying three hooded figures, approached one of the merchant vessels anchored in the Harwich Roads.[1] In answer to a whispered cry from the boatman, a rope ladder was dropped over the ship's side and the smaller boat's passengers scrambled aboard. After a purse of gold had been dropped into the captain's outstretched hand, the mysterious men were allowed to disappear into the ship's cavernous hold, where they would be hidden from watchful eyes.

An hour later, the tide began to turn so the stubby, round-hulled cog hauled up its anchor and unfurled a square sail to catch the freshening wind. By the time the sun was high in the sky, the merchant vessel was well on its way to Flanders. As soon as the secretive cargo heard the sea breaking against the ship's bow, they felt it was safe to venture on deck. Moments later, Edmund de la Pole, his brother Richard and their steward, Sir Thomas Killingworth, emerged blinking into the summer sunlight.

After spending several hours in the foetid stench of the ship's hold, the fresh sea air must have been very welcome. But it was the red-and-white pennant of the Hanseatic League streaming from the ship's masthead that announced to the fugitives that they were free. No one, not even King Henry, dared interfere with ships belonging to this powerful confederation of German ports. Even so, the brothers' elation at having successfully outwitted their enemies must have been tempered by fear for those they had left behind.

Fleeing King Henry's realm meant Edmund had abandoned his mother, sisters, wife and daughter to the king's mercy, and medieval monarchs were quite capable of venting their fury on the innocent relatives of those who had displeased them. Edmund had also left behind his brother William, whose striking good looks had caught the attention of a wealthy widow. The lady in question was Katherine Stourton, who had been left 50,000 crowns by her second husband, the Derbyshire magnate Lord Henry Grey of Codnor. Katherine was also William's sister-in-law through her brother, the 5th Baron Stourton, who had married the de la Poles' sister, who was also called Catherine.[2]

Although William was almost thirty years the widowed Katherine's junior, she was determined to make him her third husband and their affair became the talk of the Tudor court. A Venetian living in England at the time remarked that Katherine 'played her cards well' and that William 'patiently wasted the flower of his youth' in the hope of inheriting his wife's fortune.[3] Yet we should not think too harshly of William, for there may have been more to his gold-digging than the gossips imagined.

The late Lord Grey had controlled vast areas of the strongly Yorkist Nottinghamshire and Derbyshire, so William's marriage to his wealthy widow could have been intended to provide Edmund with a substantial war chest, as well as powerful allies in the Midlands. On the other hand, William may have decided that life with a wealthy widow was infinitely preferrable to an uncertain future as a penniless exile. All we can say for certain is that William remained in England while Edmund fled abroad with his steward and their youngest brother, Richard.

Sadly, we know nothing about Richard's motives for following his brother into exile. On the other hand, we have more information concerning Killingworth's thinking. Towards the end of his career, Edmund's steward tried to bolster Maximilian's support for the Yorkist cause by writing a polemic in which he carefully listed the reasons why his master must be king. In this so-called *Memorial* Killingworth claimed that he had left everything he loved behind so as not to be unnecessarily burdened and because it was his duty.[4]

This sense of duty would be sorely tested in the years to come, but at the time of their escape Killingworth, Richard and Edmund must have been elated when they landed in Flanders. They had outwitted one of the most efficient security services in Europe, and to reap the harvest Sir Robert Curson had sown all Edmund had to do was present himself at the imperial court. However, finding Maximilian was no easy task.

In common with most medieval monarchs, the Emperor spent most of his reign journeying around his sprawling domains dispensing justice, collecting taxes and renewing the feudal oaths which were the only ties binding together his disparate territories. The late summer of 1501 found Maximilian inspecting the imperial treasury at Innsbruck,[5] so Edmund was forced to make a long and difficult journey to the Alps.

Considering the appalling state of medieval roads, the little party of Yorkists would probably have travelled by boat along the Rhine, Main and Danube, which may explain why they ended up in St Johann, 130 miles to the east of Innsbruck. Though Edmund had overshot his mark by some distance, it was from here that he wrote to Maximilian to explain the indignities he had suffered at the hands of his Tudor enemy.[6]

Although the Emperor's reply took several weeks to arrive it was worth the wait. In his letter addressed to 'my most dear and well-beloved cousin', dated 9 September 1501, Maximilian declared that he fully understood why Edmund had been forced into exile and he promised to receive the Yorkists warmly.[7] Yet, when the Yorkists arrived in Innsbruck, they were told that the Emperor had decided to go hunting and was staying in the village of Telfs, 30 miles to the west. With a shrug, Edmund and his companions repacked their bags and set off up the Inn Valley. Before they reached Telfs, however, Edmund was told that Maximilian had not been satisfied with his lodgings in that village so he had moved to Pettnau.[8]

Cursing the inconstancy of monarchs, Edmund moved to Pettnau only to be informed that the Emperor had transferred the imperial court to Imst. Maximilian may have come to the Inn Valley for the hunting, but it was the Yorkists who were being led on a wild goose chase.

The Emperor's final destination was, most likely, the castle of Berneck, which he had purchased after his previous hunting lodge in the area, at Tratzberg, had burned to the ground. Typically, Maximilian had acquired Berneck for nothing because its previous owners, two brothers called Veit-Jakob and Simon Tänzl, were managers of the imperial silver mines. Maximilian had simply reminded the Tänzls that they owed their lucrative positions to him and, shortly afterwards, they had made their employer a gift of their fairy-tale castle. In return, Maximilian gave them the smoke-blackened shell of Tratzberg.[9]

If the duke of Suffolk – as Edmund was now styling himself – heard this story, it should have set alarm bells ringing as to the value of imperial promises. For the time being, at least, Maximilian was as good as his word. His Imperial Majesty greeted Edmund warmly, called him kinsman and listened carefully as his guest listed the Tudor crimes against the Yorkists. Having recounted his catalogue of woes, Edmund insisted that the Emperor had a duty to act because Henry had planned to murder both himself and his brother Richard, but at the end of his carefully worded speech there was an uneasy silence.[10]

For some minutes, Maximillian rubbed the long chin for which the Habsburgs were famous. When he did speak, he did not repeat the ringing endorsement of the Yorkist cause he had given Curson. Instead, the Emperor suggested that his guests should take lodgings in the nearby village while he decided what to do.[11] After a journey of 500 miles through bandit-infested forests, Maximilian's somewhat curt dismissal must have come as a complete shock to Edmund – and worse was to follow.

A few days after his audience, Edmund was visited by the imperial chancellor, Dr Newdek, who told him that urgent business with the French ambassador had forced Maximilian to leave Imst unexpectedly. Worse still, he said that nothing could be done to help the Yorkists as the Emperor's hands were tied by the *Intercursus Magnus*. While Edmund struggled to comprehend what he was being told, Newdek explained that even though the treaty had been signed by Maximilian's son, Archduke Philip, its terms also applied to the Emperor because he too had made his peace with Henry.[12]

This was the last thing Edmund had expected to hear, but the chancellor did offer a small crumb of comfort. The *Intercursus Magnus* notwithstanding, Newdek claimed that the Emperor still had Edmund's best interests at heart and was, therefore, prepared to grant the Yorkists permission to stay in the Habsburg-controlled territory of their choosing.[13]

Newdek's visit was only the first of many surprises Maximilian had in store for his guests. The following day, while Edmund was wondering where in the vast Holy Roman Empire he should go, the duchy of Burgundy's treasurer, Jehan Bontemps, arrived at the Yorkists' inn with news of another astonishing *volte face* by the Emperor.

After apologising for what Newdek had said, Bontemps declared that Maximilian had every intention of helping the Yorkists but required some time to decide exactly what action to take. If Edmund could be patient, he would have a decision to his liking within eight days. Unsurprisingly, the treasurer's estimate was optimistic. Instead of a week, the exiles were left kicking their heels in Imst for almost two months, and Maximilian's replies to Edmund's letters asking him to explain the delay were worryingly evasive.

'Although we had determined and it was our desire to inform you of our news; nevertheless, owing to the great and urgent affairs which have come upon us since our departure for Imst, we have not been well able to do so,' Maximilian wrote on 6 November 1501.[14]

When Bontemps eventually returned to Imst, he did bring good news. In spite of all that had gone before, he presented Edmund with Maximilian's plan to raise an army of between 3,000 and 5,000 German mercenaries who would fight for the Yorkists for anywhere from one to three months as necessary. These mercenaries would be commanded by Walter Yngar, son of Count Heinrich von Ardek, and Edmund would have to repay the cost of their recruitment on his accession. The debt could be settled either immediately in cash or by supplying Englishmen to fight for the Emperor as and when they were required.[15]

Though this army may seem small by modern standards, Edmund would have known that his rival had conquered England with a similar number of French mercenaries in a campaign that lasted just over two weeks.[16] Nor was he unduly worried by the third condition Maximilian attached to his offer, which required him to move to Aachen for the planning phase.[17] As one of the

Holy Roman Empire's free cities, Aachen enjoyed almost complete independence and was conveniently located near an area renowned for supplying the famed *landsknechts*.

The Emperor had created these utterly ruthless 'servants of the country' in the 1480s in order to defend his territories from a growing number of revolts as well as French attempts to seize the Burgundian lands bequeathed to Maximilian's first wife, Mary. He had modelled their weapons and tactics on the successful Swiss armies of the High Middle Ages and recouped the cost of his own wars by hiring these professional soldiers to the highest bidder. His only stipulation was that no *landsknecht* should ever fight for France.[18]

The promise of being given several thousand of these highly efficient killers was more than enough to restore Edmund's faith in his imperial patron, so he eagerly accepted Maximilian's offer and sent Killingworth to the imperial court to act as his envoy.[19] In the meantime, Edmund, Richard and Curson set off for Aachen as they had been instructed. They left the Tyrol in high spirits; despite some anxious moments, Edmund had secured the full backing of the Emperor.

However, his enemy had not been idle either. As with Edmund's first flight to the Continent, Henry was so desperate to have his rebel earl returned to England that he sent two of his biggest diplomatic heavyweights to bring him home.[20] On this occasion, those ordered to close the Yorkist bolthole were Henry's cousin and vice-chamberlain Charles Somerset[21] and master of the rolls William Warham.[22]

In spite of Dr Newdek's insistence that Maximilian was already bound by *the Intercursus Magnus*, Somerset and Warham were authorised to make a large contribution to any forthcoming crusade if Maximilian handed over the Yorkists. This was a complete reversal of Henry's earlier policy of staying out of any war in the east, and it represented a considerable loss of face, but the detailed instructions he gave to his ambassadors were woefully lacking in the necessary tact.

At their first audience with Maximilian, Somerset and Warham loftily declared that the king of England now endorsed the Emperor's claim to be the 'principal maintainer, defender and relief of Christ's Church'.[23] So far so good, but they went on to say that any discussions regarding a new crusade could not begin until a dispute over a previous Anglo-Imperial agreement, supposedly brokered by Burgundy's admiral Lord Bevers, had been resolved.

This Flemish nobleman had negotiated the *Intercursus Magnus* on behalf of Burgundy's archduke back in 1496, but he had told Maximilian that England's king was so grateful he would happily contribute 50,000 crowns to fight the Turks. The parsimonious Henry had later insisted that Bevers had no authority to make such a statement and refused to pay up.[24] Now, in order to secure Edmund's extradition, Henry ordered his envoys to offer the Emperor an outright gift of £10,000, or a loan of no more than 20,000 angel-nobles,[25] provided Maximilian signed a treaty ending imperial support for the Yorkists.

Again, so far so good, but Henry went too far when he insisted that any agreement to expel the de la Poles from the Empire had to be signed by Maximilian in his own hand and the relevant edicts had to be read out in every corner of the Empire. The last straw was Henry's demand that his envoys be given irrefutable proof of the Yorkists' departure.[26]

The Emperor was not a man who appreciated being given orders by the *parvenu* ruler of a fog-bound island on the edge of the civilised world, but he was also far too shrewd to merely refuse Henry's requests. Rather, he passed the draft treaty to an imperial committee and told them to examine its proposals in more detail. Without doubt, Maximilian ordered his commissioners to take their time while he pondered a way to turn the situation to his advantage; if the delay annoyed Henry, so much the better. All Somerset and Warham could do was write to their master and insist that the hiatus was not their fault.[27]

Meanwhile, back in Aachen, Edmund was becoming increasingly aware of what Somerset and Warham were up to. He confided his fears in several letters he sent to the Emperor early in 1502, and though Maximilian told Edmund to be patient and all would be well[28] such assurances were no longer enough. Edmund demanded that he be given an official position so that he could deal with Henry's spies and assassins, whom he believed were hiding around every corner. Dismayed, Maximilian replied that Edmund should not develop ideas above his station, warning that making a nuisance of himself would only harm his cause.[29]

Unbeknown to Edmund, who continued to complain, his Tudor nemeses were equally exasperated. By now the imperial commissioners had delayed meeting Warham and Somerset for several weeks, and when they did present their findings, Henry's envoys were confronted with a tangled knot of legalistic gobbledegook.

To begin with, the commissioners claimed that Henry's demand for the Yorkists to be expelled from *every* part of the Holy Roman Empire was completely unworkable. This, they explained, was because the imperial constitution combined territories that were part of Maximilian's personal patrimony with a kaleidoscope of semi-independent states whose rulers could not be bound by a treaty made without their consent.[30] In other words, while Maximilian was happy to banish the Yorkists from the territories under his direct control, the exiles could easily take up residence in another part of the Empire unless separate treaties had been made with all of its princes, dukes, burghers and bishops.

The imperial commissioners had a point, but they went on to undermine their own argument by suggesting that this situation might be remedied if the king of England pardoned Edmund and restored him to all his lost lands and titles.[31] If Henry was amenable to this, the commissioners promised that the Emperor would use his influence to persuade Edmund to abandon his claim to the throne. Such extortion came at a price, however. As payment for ending the Yorkist threat to Henry's fledgling dynasty, the 50,000 crowns originally promised by Lord Bevers would have to be paid in full.[32]

The offer to broker a deal that would end the Wars of the Roses plunged Henry's envoys into confusion. There was nothing in their detailed instructions that provided for Edmund being pardoned, so Somerset and Warham wrote to Henry asking for guidance.[33]

By this time, the Emperor's annual procession through the Alps had reached Bruneck, in northern Italy, and Sir Thomas Killingworth was among the legion of scribes, servants and foreign envoys accompanying the imperial court. Whether the Yorkist envoy ever met his Tudor counterparts during his time in the Tyrol is not recorded but he certainly shared their frustration with the glacial pace of imperial bureaucracy. In particular, Killingworth was worried that nothing had been done to recruit the promised army of *landsknecht* mercenaries. When Count Heinrich von Ardek finally appeared at court to inform the Emperor of his progress, he brought bad tidings.

According to Ardek, the promise of an easy campaign with cartloads of booty had failed to impress potential recruits. The count therefore told Maximilian that if the most venal mercenaries in Christendom could not be persuaded to fight for the White Rose, then the Emperor was under no obligation to honour any agreement he had made with the Yorkists.[34] Fortunately for Edmund, Maximilian had set his heart on restoring the House of York – at least that is what he told Killingworth.

As quickly as the Yorkists' hopes were dashed by Ardek, Maximilian raised them up again by declaring that he was still determined to help the wronged duke of Suffolk depose the wicked Tudors. Even more encouraging was the Emperor's declaration that he had decided to take personal charge of the operation, and he informed Killingworth that he had sent his chaplain, a man named Bastiam, to hire a fleet of transport ships from the king of Denmark. He also assured Killingworth that a 30,000-guilder war fund would be delivered to Edmund by St George's Day.[35]

Scarcely able to believe this turnaround in Yorkist fortunes, Killingworth hurried back to Aachen to await the White Rose's hour of deliverance, but when he reached Ulm he received a letter from Edmund instructing him to go back to Bruneck and make sure the Emperor kept his word. Edmund was no longer prepared to accept Maximilian's promises at face value, and for once he had read the situation correctly. When the saddle-sore steward caught up with the imperial court, he found that Bastiam had fallen ill and had not left for Copenhagen after all.

Even more worrisome was the news that Bastiam's replacement, a bishop, was reluctant to undertake the long and difficult journey to Denmark.[36] Instead of setting off immediately after his appointment, the bishop had begged a week's grace to put his affairs in order. Yet he spent so long attending to his diocesan business that it was almost Easter before he was ready to leave. At this point, the bishop claimed he could not go to Denmark because his cardinal needed help gathering pardon money from the local flock.[37]

A third ambassador, Ufford, was nominated but the feast of England's patron saint came and went without any sign of the promised invasion fleet or the 30,000 guilders Maximilian had sworn would be in Edmund's hands by this date.[38] To Edmund and Killingworth it must have seemed as if nothing Maximilian said could be trusted, but the Emperor did have a valid reason for suddenly postponing the Danish plan.

In the early spring of 1502, a border dispute between the imperial duchies of Cleves and Guelders suddenly escalated into open war, which meant the men and money that should have put Edmund on England's throne had to be diverted to the Low Countries. This long-running revolt will be discussed later, but the upshot is that Maximilian continued his negotiations with Somerset and Warham while simultaneously telling Killingworth and Edmund that the Yorkist invasion would go ahead as soon as the Guelders rebels had been crushed.

On the other side of the Channel, Henry, watching these developments with interest, shrewdly realised that Maximilian was trying to keep the Yorkist–Tudor pot boiling for his own nefarious ends. To counter this, he decided to enlist God himself in his struggle to have the de la Pole brothers returned to England. Thanks to the eternal struggle for Italy, Pope Alexander VI was extremely keen to add England to his Holy League, which had been founded in 1495 to preserve papal independence, so when Henry asked His Holiness to excommunicate the rebel earl of Suffolk and his supporters, he readily agreed.

The ceremony placing Edmund and five others, including Sir Robert Curson, outside the protection of the Church was performed on the second Sunday of Lent[39] at St Paul's Cross, the open-air pulpit in the churchyard of London's famous cathedral. It was here that all royal decrees were made public, and the large crowd gathered that day looked on in awe as the priest solemnly shut the Holy Bible, tolled a funereal bell and dashed a burning candle to the floor.

However, Londoners were not the only audience for Henry's chilling propaganda. By having Edmund pronounced 'openly accursed with book, bell and candle',[40] Henry had rendered irrelevant Maximilian's claim that he lacked jurisdiction over many parts of his empire. Anathematised by no less a person than Christ's Vicar on Earth, Edmund could not be offered sanctuary in any Christian territory; any ruler who disregarded this fact risked eternal damnation.

After trumping Maximilian's ace with this masterstroke, Henry now turned his attention to rooting out the last vestiges of Yorkism in England.

5

I THOUGHT AT THIS HOUR TO HAVE BEEN VERY NEAR ENGLAND

The ruthless efficiency with which suspected Yorkists were rounded up during the spring of 1502 was a distinct feature of the darker side of Henry's reign, but most of the fish caught in the Tudor net were pretty small. Typical of these low-level Yorkists, most of whom were gutted like herring on the scaffolds of southern England, was William Baskerville, porter of Beaulieu Abbey.[1]

It was no accident that Henry's attack dogs began their latest reign of terror at this isolated monastery. Five years earlier, the last significant Yorkist rebellion had ended here when Perkin Warbeck had been cornered and forced to surrender. Even more significantly, Beaulieu had been the refuge of several prominent Yorkists in the past including Anne Beauchamp, wife of Warwick 'the Kingmaker' and mother-in-law of Richard III. Anne had fled to Beaulieu in 1471, after her husband's defeat and death at the battle of Barnet, and had spent fifteen years under the abbot's protection before she was pardoned by Henry.

The importance of Beaulieu as a place of sanctuary dated back to its foundation, by King John and Pope Innocent III, as an 'exempt abbey'. This elevated status meant Beaulieu was under the direct jurisdiction of the Pope, rather than a local bishop, and such independence gave its abbot the power to grant asylum to anyone needing to hide from their political enemies, the king's constables or their creditors.[2]

At this time, there were at least ten such 'sanctuary men' living at Beaulieu and they were kept under close surveillance by the controller of customs at Southampton, John Dawtrey. Should these men set foot on unconsecrated soil they would be arrested by Dawtrey's constables, but Baskerville must not have known he was under suspicion because he was clapped in irons the moment he left the abbey's precincts. The unlucky porter was almost certainly tortured, and as the rack slowly dislocated his limbs he screamed three names: Hugh Holmes, John Langton and Richard Badcock. The latter was a sailor, and Baskerville also confessed that a ship full of Cornish tin had already reached Flanders.[3]

Apart from the loss of the tolls that such a valuable cargo attracted, the porter's testimony must have given Henry several sleepless nights because it pointed to a resurgence of Yorkism in the West Country. The trouble caused by Warbeck and the Cornish tin miners, not to mention the fact that three of the region's most prominent nobles had dined with Edmund shortly before his second flight to the Continent, had not been forgotten.

Of course, a man in extreme pain will admit to anything and there is no independent evidence to prove the mangled porter's claim that Edmund's revolt was being funded by smuggled Cornish tin. Nevertheless, Baskerville's confession was enough to make Henry regret his policy of trying to rehabilitate his former enemies by placing them in positions of trust. The man who topped the list of ex-Yorkists now under suspicion was Sir James Tyrell, captain of Guînes.

As previously noted, Tyrell had been a loyal member of the Tudor establishment ever since Bosworth and though he had harboured Edmund during his first flight from England, he had probably been given little choice in the matter. Tellingly, there is nothing to suggest that Edmund had contacted Sir James either before or after his second escape; even so, the Tyrell family's connections to the de la Poles were enough to damn him in the eyes of the king.

The task of relieving Tyrell of his command was given to Sir Sampson Norton, who had his own Yorkist skeletons to bury. Norton had fought for Edward IV during the Wars of the Roses, but Henry had appointed him controller of customs for Southampton until he was succeeded by Dawtrey. Sometime before 1500, Norton had been given the key post of serjeant-porter of Calais, which required him to oversee the city's general security and also to ensure that goods landed were delivered to their proper destinations.

Never a man to do things by halves, Norton marched the entire Calais garrison to Guînes, but when he arrived at the castle he found its drawbridge raised. What followed was a scene of almost Pythonesque farce as the two grizzled ex-Yorkists resorted to hurling insults at each other before settling down to a siege. This was not the swift and decisive action that Henry had wanted,[4] and he duly sent his crafty chancellor of the exchequer, Sir Thomas Lovell, to Guînes with orders to use more effective means of persuasion.

Along with Sir Richard Empson and Sir Edmund Dudley, Lovell was the man who applied Henry's fiscal thumbscrews to anyone suspected of disloyalty to the Crown. By forcing those suspected of straying from the Tudor fold to sign extortionate financial bonds ensuring their future good behaviour, Henry kept his nobles in line while filling his depleted treasury. Lovell was particularly good at squeezing the last pennies out of his victims, so winkling Tyrell out of Guînes would be child's play for a man of his dark talents.

Ironically, we know what happened next thanks to a letter sent by Edmund to Killingworth. In this letter, which is dated 12 May 1502, Edmund told his steward that Tyrell was promised immunity from prosecution by Lovell provided he went to the king and took an oath of loyalty.[5] Sir James agreed to this but he still suspected a trap so he took the wise precaution of instructing Thomas, his son, Robert Wellesbourne, his servant, and Sir John Wyndham, stepfather of Edmund's wife, to remain in the fortress.[6]

After the short ride from Guînes to Calais, Tyrell was bundled aboard a fast ship for England, and no doubt he pondered what he would say to Henry as he watched the French coast slip beyond the horizon. Lost in thought, Sir James suspected nothing until Lovell barked an order and two burly sailors grabbed the ex-captain of Guînes by the arms. There was a brief struggle and before Tyrell knew what was happening, he found himself being dangled over the ship's side by his heels.

'Tell your son to surrender the castle of Guînes or I will teach you to swim!' Lovell is supposed to have cried.[7] The mere threat of a watery grave was enough to break the old man. Tyrell agreed to send a secret signal that would persuade his son, together with Wellesbourne and Wyndham, to surrender. Within a matter of days, Tyrell and the others were locked up in the Tower along with two of their underlings, a yeoman named Matthew Jones and a pursuivant (attendant) called Curson (not to be confused with the erstwhile imperial crusader).[8]

No doubt Tyrell bitterly regretted his moment of weakness, which had brought such ruin to those closest to him, but at least his son was released after a mere two years in the Tower. Eventually, Thomas Tyrell was reinstated to his ancestral estates in Suffolk and he seems to have died peacefully in his bed sometime around 1520;[9] his father and the others would not be so lucky. Ever the master of propaganda, Henry was determined to use Sir James Tyrell to blacken the de la Pole name for all time, and the linchpin of his plan was to force Tyrell into admitting that he had arranged the murders of the young Yorkist king Edward V and his brother Richard, duke of York.

As the missing Princes in the Tower were Edmund's cousins, having a man with strong connections to the de la Poles confess to their killing would utterly discredit Edmund's claim to the throne. However, Henry did not concoct this scheme out of nothing. The finger of suspicion had always pointed at one of Tyrell's stable hands, a man called Dighton, who was not properly interrogated until after his master's arrest. According to the Elizabethan chronicler Richard Grafton, Tyrell and Dighton were interrogated together and it was during this questioning that they admitted smothering the innocent sons of Edward IV.[10]

Strangely, Dighton not only kept his head but was quickly released and lived out his days in Calais, where he eventually died 'in great misery'.[11] This suggests that Dighton had bought his life by incriminating Tyrell, and even more damning is Polydore Vergil's *Anglica Historia*. In this much earlier chronicle, Vergil states unequivocally that Tyrell's motives for murdering the boys was to propel Edmund de la Pole closer to the throne:

> On that occasion James could, without danger to his own life, have spared the boys, rescued them from death and carried them to safety ... but he would not do this in order

> that he might afterwards try, against all human and divine injunctions, to help Earl Edmund, son of Edward's sister.[12]

Whether or not this is true, and regardless of who actually committed the crime, the inclusion of this statement in what was intended to be the official history of Henry's reign shows his determination to use Tyrell to discredit Edmund. Furthermore, it is Vergil's version of events that was much embellished by the saintly Sir Thomas More, whose *History of King Richard III* had the most influence on later writers.[13] Discussing the veracity of these works lies outside the remit of this book. What is important to our story is that Tyrell's confession had far-reaching consequences for Edmund and his kin.

The first to be swept away by the ensuing maelstrom was William de la Pole, who was happily spending his wife's money and blissfully unaware of the cruel trick that fate was about to play on him. On 25 January 1502, William attended the ceremony that betrothed Henry's oldest daughter, Margaret, to the king of Scotland.[14] He was never seen again outside the Tower of London. There was no trial; William's Yorkist blood was enough reason for his arrest, and he has the dubious honour of being the Tower's longest-serving prisoner. He died sometime in 1539, having been incarcerated for almost four decades.

For the first few years of his long captivity, William shared his imprisonment with his sister Catherine who, like her brother, had married into the Stourton family. Considering the Stourtons' own connections to the House of York it is curious that only she was sent to the Tower, but Fate is no respecter of guilt or innocence. Catherine died, possibly while still a prisoner, sometime before 1512.[15]

The fate of Catherine notwithstanding, several prominent de la Pole and Stourton women were left at large. These included Edmund's mother, the dowager duchess of Suffolk, his widowed sister Lady Elizabeth Morley and his wealthy sister-in-law Lady Katherine Stourton. Though these ladies were allowed to live out their lives quietly, their male kinsmen were at the top of Henry's hit list. Lord William Courtenay, heir to the earldom of Devon, who had married a de la Pole niece, joined William in the Tower though he had done nothing more than dine with Edmund shortly before his escape.[16]

Even Tudor apologists such as Edward Hall admit that the two Williams were entirely innocent of any treason,[17] yet their suffering was mild compared to those lower down the Yorkist food chain. Within weeks of Tyrell's arrest, Henry's spymasters had a list of individuals that included the captain of the ship that had taken Edmund to Flanders,[18] a London barber called James Holand[19] and the captain of Portchester Castle, Sir Charles Rippon.[20]

It mattered not that Rippon had fought on the king's side at Blackheath or that the evidence against him was no more than the babbling of men broken on the rack. Rippon was from East Anglia and he had been under suspicion ever since his kinsman Robert had joined Warbeck's rebellion. Though Sir Charles had been arrested and acquitted during the 1494 trawl for Yorkist sympathisers,[21] there was no escape this time. The captain of Portchester was beheaded in Winchester marketplace on the eve of Palm Sunday 1502.[22]

Besides profaning the start of Holy Week, Henry's insatiable thirst for Yorkist blood was extended to those whose crimes did not quite amount to treason. On the last day of April 1502, two youths were sent to the pillory for 'defaming of the king's council' and, after being pelted with sharp stones and filth for several hours, had their ears sliced off.[23] Three days later, Sir James Tyrell, Sir John Wyndham and the unnamed captain of Edmund's ship were tried at the Guildhall and, predictably, sentenced to death.

The ship's captain, being a commoner, was dragged to Tyburn on a hurdle where he was half-strangled, castrated and disembowelled before being beheaded. Thanks to their rank, the two noblemen were spared such butchery but they still died by the headsman's axe on 6 May 1502.[24]

The day after Tyrell and Wyndham's executions, two simultaneous trials were held, one at the Guildhall in the City of London and the other at Whitehall in the City of Westminster. At the first hearing, Sir John Wyndham's son and the London barber were arraigned on charges of treason. At the second, it was Tyrell's son, the yeoman Jones and the pursuivant Curson who were charged with abetting the others in their plot to overthrow the king. Interestingly, the chief witness against them was Sir James Tyrell's servant Robert Wellesbourne.[25]

No doubt Wellesbourne had agreed to turn informer after being shown the instruments of torture, and his evidence doomed Jones and Curson. The luckless duo were sentenced to be hanged, drawn and quartered at Guînes so that their lingering agonies would serve as a warning to the rest of the garrison.[26] Over in Aachen, Edmund learned of these executions from a man called Peter Harter, who was Sir Charles Rippon's servant,[27] and his gruesome tidings supposedly caused the earl of Suffolk 'great agony and fear'.[28] Yet in the depths of his despair, Edmund heard the news that Arthur, Prince of Wales, was dead.

To Edmund, the death of Henry's heir was a clear sign that God had at last turned his back on the bloodstained House of Tudor; he therefore wrote to the Emperor and urged him to make the most of this heaven-sent opportunity because 'the longer I reside out of England the stronger will be King Henry'. He also accused England's first Tudor king of resorting to every kind of bribery and corrupt practice in his effort to destroy the de la Poles.[29]

This letter to Maximilian is dated 12 May 1502, which is the same day Edmund wrote to Killingworth to inform him of Tyrell's dreadful fate. The latest round of executions had clearly rattled Edmund, and though he assured Maximilian of his undying loyalty in his first letter, in the second he instructed his steward to use whatever deception was necessary to keep the Emperor in the Yorkist camp. 'I fully perceive that the king of the Romans treats all things with me with a certain pretence; therefore I want you to use the same pretence with him,' he wrote.[30] He also informed Killingworth that he believed Maximilian was dragging his feet in the hope that the Yorkists' dwindling funds would force him to make peace with Henry.

The earl of Suffolk's secretary was unusually busy on 12 May because Edmund dictated a third letter that day, this one to the Burgundian treasurer Jehan Bontemps. In this missive, Edmund voiced his annoyance at his treatment and he urged Bontemps to press his case with Maximilian before Henry could recover from the loss of Arthur. 'Going upon the letter of credence you showed me at Imst ... I thought at this hour to have been very near England for the purpose of recovering my right,' Edmund grumbled,[31] but the tide that he hoped to take at the flood had already turned.

While Henry mourned the loss of a son, his envoys to the imperial court, Charles Somerset and William Warham, continued with their efforts to negotiate a treaty that would expel every Yorkist from the Holy Roman Empire. In spite of all that he had said before, their efforts bore fruit when Maximilian suddenly agreed to accept the £10,000 Henry had offered for his crusade in return for signing a treaty banishing Edmund.

The reason for Maximilian's unexpected decision to abandon the Yorkists can be summed up in one word: money. The revolt in Guelders had put an enormous strain on imperial finances and £10,000 would keep an army in the field for several months. Having weighed everything in the balance, the Emperor decided to throw the earl of Suffolk to the Tudor wolves. Sir Thomas Killingworth therefore arrived at the imperial court with his master's letters, little knowing that he was heading for a diplomatic minefield.

It was now early summer, and Maximilian had moved the imperial court to Augsburg, where the banking houses of Fugger and Welser were headquartered. The financial hub of his empire, Maximilian came here whenever he needed money but he also heard petitions from his subjects and foreign envoys in the great hall of Augsburg's *Kaiserpfalz*.

This enormous room was so big that several hundred courtiers, scribes and diplomats could gather under its vast, vaulted ceiling, yet it was surprisingly austere. The only decorations were the portraits of past emperors hanging in niches on the wall behind a gilded chair placed on a low dais. This chair served Maximilian as a throne and here, seated beneath a silken canopy, he held court. No doubt Killingworth's knees must have trembled a little every time he was ushered into the imperial presence, and on this occasion it did not help matters that the Emperor had been in a bad mood for many months.

When Killingworth arrived in Augsburg on 20 June 1502, he found that the forty-three-year-old Emperor was still suffering from the effects of a riding accident the previous year. However, the real cause of his malaise was the breakdown of his marriage to his third wife, the Milanese heiress Bianca Maria Sforza, whom he had wed in 1494. Much to the impecunious Emperor's annoyance, his young Italian bride had turned out to be a frivolous spendthrift who had shocked the Germans at the imperial court by sitting on the floor to play with her stepchildren.

After six years of purse-draining marriage, Maximilian's patience had become exhausted. Banishing his wife to the Tyrol had changed nothing, and she had continued to incur enormous debts. To these woes was added the extra expense of fighting the war in Guelders, so, with his finances and marriage in disarray, it is little wonder that Killingworth was told that there was no money for the White Rose. Yet Maximilian also gave Killingworth his personal assurance that the invasion of England would go ahead as soon as the Guelders rebels had been crushed.[32]

Once again the Emperor was sending mixed messages, and when the imperial party moved from Augsburg to nearby Ulm, Jehan Bontemps dropped another bombshell. According to the treasurer, the Emperor was now of the opinion that it would be best if Edmund made peace with his Tudor enemies, but as he had no wish to shirk his responsibilities he magnanimously offered to broker an agreement that would restore Edmund to all he had lost and allow him to return to England.

At first, Killingworth could not believe his ears. This was a complete reversal of the promise he had received only a few days earlier. The miserable steward had to inform his master of this latest disappointment, but Edmund no intention of giving up the fight.[33] Fearing that Killingworth's lowly rank might not be helping matters, he sent Sir Robert Curson to the imperial court, but the result was the same.

Though Curson and Killingworth were welcomed with the usual promises, as soon as their audience with the Emperor was over they were ushered into a side-chamber where Bontemps, the Spanish ambassador and one of Maximilian's favourites, Adolf of Nassau-Wiesbaden-Idstein, were waiting. Before Curson or Killingworth could ask what on earth was going on, they were told that if Edmund could not, or would not, come to terms with Henry he should try his luck with the French.[34]

This revelation prompted Curson to splutter that it would be impossible for Edmund to abandon his cause at such short notice, and that if the Emperor withdrew his support the Yorkist exiles would be destitute.[35]

In reply Bontemps suggested that Edmund should lodge with the ageing duchess of Burgundy during the proposed negotiations. As a further incentive, he promised that the Emperor would pay the Yorkists' most pressing debts as well as any expenses incurred during the talks. To further set Edmund's mind at rest, Bontemps told Killingworth and Curson that Maximilian had already spoken to the king of England and had received Henry's personal guarantee that the persecution of the de la Poles, their relatives and all their supporters would end the moment Edmund renounced his claim to the throne.[36]

In Maximilian's mind this was a very generous offer, and he probably believed himself to be one of the blessed peacemakers to whom Christ had promised the Kingdom of Heaven, but he had already decided that Edmund would be banished to Spain if he refused the offer of talks. This would explain the presence of the Spanish ambassador at such an extraordinary meeting,[37] and a report from one of the king of Aragon's envoys at the imperial court explained that Maximilian's offer to mediate had been prompted by the warming of relations between the rulers of England, Burgundy and Spain. However, the unnamed author of this report had completely underestimated Maximilian's capacity for contradicting himself.

Shortly after Bontemps dropped this bombshell, Maximilian granted Killingworth the rare honour of a private audience, probably at a castle near modern Donauwörth. During this clandestine meeting Maximilian assured Edmund's steward that he would never agree to anything that would result in Edmund's death and that if Henry refused to act with honour Edmund would be freed from all his obligations to England's king. He claimed that he would carry on supporting the Yorkists but, given the current diplomatic climate, any aid would have to be given in secret.[38]

This statement notwithstanding, Maximilian remained adamant that a peace conference was the only way Edmund could secure a future for himself, his family and his fellow Yorkist exiles. He also told Killingworth that Henry's emissaries were already on their way to Antwerp to finalise the details. As an added inducement, he said that he had sent a man named Casius to Aachen with a passport for Edmund plus 1,000 guilders to cover his immediate expenses.

Unfortunately for all concerned, the imperial courier never arrived.[39] Why Casius disappeared is not recorded, but once again Maximilian had failed to provide the Yorkists with what he had promised. It is hardly surprising that Edmund's frustration now turned to anger. Before Killingworth could return to Aachen, he sent another herald to Maximilian with an all-too-familiar letter of complaint. Typically, Edmund's new courier had trouble finding the imperial court, which had moved from Donauwörth to Antwerp via Dusseldorf.

Eventually the courier succeeded in delivering Edmund's demand that Maximilian either honour the agreements he had made in Imst or he would seek an alliance elsewhere, but this was exactly what Maximilian had already suggested. Nevertheless, the Emperor baulked at calling the Yorkist's bluff and, yet again, Killingworth was told that if Edmund could only be patient for another six days he would receive 'such answer as he should be pleased'.[40]

What Edmund thought about this is not recorded, but Maximilian was already beginning to regret his readiness to wash his hands of the de la Poles. Despite his desperate attempts to keep Henry in the Habsburg camp, French influence over England's king was growing just as the imperial position in Milan was deteriorating.

6

BURN THAT BOOK AND A VENGEANCE TAKE THE FIRST WRITER

The struggle for Milan, Naples and Sicily, which endured throughout the first half of the sixteenth century, was chiefly a four-cornered fight between Spain, France, the Holy Roman Empire and the Pope. However, in order to pursue their respective claims each side created a complex and continually shifting network of alliances that drew in other nations with no direct interest in the Italian conflict. Among these subsidiary combatants were the Republic of Venice, the Swiss Confederacy, the Kingdom of Scotland and the Kingdom of England.

To relate the often bewildering sequence of events that fuelled each phase of the Italian Wars would require a book of its own but, in brief, the situation was this.

On becoming king of France in 1498, Louis XII had revived his ancestral claims to Milan and Naples. He was in control of both cities by the spring of 1502, but Milan had been an imperial fief and its deposed duke, Ludovico Sforza, was related to Maximilian's spendthrift wife. Naturally Ludovico approached the Emperor for help to regain his ducal coronet, but, with his treasury empty and Guelders in revolt, Maximilian could do nothing without an ally.

The ideal candidates were the kings of Spain and England; if Ferdinand invaded southern France from northern Spain and Henry attacked from Calais, Louis' forces would be divided and this would allow Maximilian to reconquer Milan for

Ludovico. But herein lay the cause of his dilemma over the de la Poles.

While Ferdinand of Aragon's own ambitions in Italy could easily be exploited to provoke a war with Louis, Henry was determined to stay of out of any foreign entanglements. Henry had even made peace with the French a condition of the £10,000 bribe that Somerset and Warham had offered in the autumn 1501.[1] If Maximilian wanted to reverse Henry's position, the only lever he had was the White Rose of York.

On the one hand, Maximilian could force Henry into an anti-French alliance in return for abandoning Edmund. On the other, he could replace Henry with a grateful Yorkist king who would happily be his ally. While he made up his mind, Maximilian continued to play both sides against each other by making empty promises to support Edmund in secret at the same time as signing Henry's treaty expelling Yorkists from the Empire.

The treaty casting Edmund adrift was signed on 28 July 1502. As soon as the ink was dry, Henry paid the £10,000 he had offered to save the Empire from the Turks. Though this was a huge sum, it was much less than the £50,000 Maximilian had demanded, so the Emperor made no move to return Edmund to England.[2]

A veteran schemer like Maximilian must have known that his decision to allow the Yorkists to remain in Aachen would sour Anglo-Imperial relations, but his policy of using English rebels to keep Henry distracted seemed to work. It could hardly have escaped Henry's notice that the rulers of Milan, Naples and Florence had been recently deposed by their dynastic rivals, and he soon had hard evidence that he would never be safe on his throne unless Maximilian handed over the last Yorkists.

The source of this information was Robert Wellesbourne, the servant of Sir James Tyrell who had bought his life by informing on his master. The chief evidence that Wellesbourne became a full-time Tudor spy is the fact that he received a pardon shortly after his master's execution and he had adopted the alias Hodgkinson, perhaps in order to insinuate himself into Edmund's inner circle.[3] Also incriminating is the entry in the king's accounts for this period, which stated that Wellesbourne was paid a half-yearly retainer of 60*s* 10*d* for some unspecified service, and Killingworth wrote in his *Statement Concerning Edmund de la*

Pole that Wellesbourne had stolen several important letters while masquerading as a Yorkist refugee.[4]

Though Killingworth had seen through this disguise and recovered the missing letters, the damage had been done; Henry had learned that Edmund was plotting to recruit three towns on the River Ijssel to his cause, and because these inland ports were technically under Maximilian's jurisdiction, this was clear evidence that the Emperor was continuing to back a Yorkist rebellion in secret. To be sure, Edmund's approaches the burghers of Zwolle, Kampen and Deventer coincided with Maximilian's failure to hire Danish ships, but, while these ports would have been ideal points of embarkation for an invasion force, it has to be said that all three towns were members of the powerful Hanseatic League.

Though nominally under the control of the Holy Roman Empire, membership of the League that dominated trade in the North Sea and the Baltic throughout the Middle Ages gave these towns a large measure of independence. It is therefore possible that Edmund began negotiations without telling the Emperor, although Edmund's parlous finances meant he would not have an army to embark without Maximilian's backing. Whatever the truth of the matter, the veteran rebel Sir George Neville was put in charge of the talks.

Neville, not to be confused with George Neville, 5th Baron Bergavenny, was a recent addition to Edmund's inner circle, but he had been a thorn in the Tudor side for decades. Born in Cumberland sometime during the late 1440s, he must have been conceived out of wedlock because he is called 'The Bastard' in several official documents. Neville had served in the Calais garrison during the reign of Henry VI, and though he had fought for the Lancastrians at Tewkesbury, he had been granted a pardon by the victorious Edward IV.[5] Following Edward's death Neville had become one of Richard III's most trusted bodyguards.

After playing a key role in supressing the duke of Buckingham's rebellion in 1483, Sir George Neville had been rewarded with several key appointments, such as constable of Corfe Castle, but also with permission to marry Mary FitzLewis, widow of the Yorkist Anthony Woodville, 2nd Earl Rivers. However, his wife's sister-in-law had married Jasper Tudor and he may have followed her into the Tudor camp at the time of Bosworth or shortly after. Neville fought *for* Henry *against* Edmund's oldest brother, John de la Pole, earl of Lincoln at Stoke Field, and he received a knighthood in return.

Still not content to settle in his allegiances, Neville later joined Perkin Warbeck. In 1495 he was condemned to death for having taken part in the pretender's abortive invasion of Kent but he escaped,[6] and after the rebels' expulsion from Ireland he had accompanied Warbeck to Edinburgh on his mission to enlist the support of James IV, king of Scotland. As a consequence, Neville was declared a traitor in England once more.

A full pardon was first offered to Neville immediately before Edmund's second flight to the Continent,[7] which suggests that Henry knew what was being planned and he was trying to deprive the fugitive earl of the rebel's experience. Henry repeated his offer soon after Edmund's disappearance, and this may have been a failed attempt to recruit Neville as a Tudor spy, but once again the king's mercy was refused. Furious at being rebuffed in this way, Henry ordered his envoys at the imperial court to demand the arrest and execution of the ungrateful rebel if he had not yet been banished from Maastricht, where he was supposed to be hiding.[8]

Interestingly, Neville was not the only Warbeck supporter to snub the king. Also refusing Henry's forgiveness were John Parrelebene, about whom very little is known, and Sir Walter Blasset, a Franciscan friar who became Edmund's chaplain.[9] They too would serve Edmund as couriers and envoys, but it was Neville who undertook Edmund's diplomatic mission to Zwolle, Deventer and Kampen.

'And let this matter be handled as secretly as you can and keep it secretly to you twain as my trust is in you,' Edmund wrote to his ally, unaware that his letters were being intercepted by Wellesbourne.[10] The immediate effect of his betrayal was to persuade Henry to ramp up his repression of Yorkists in England.

In October 1502, the ceremony excommunicating Edmund and five other senior Yorkists was repeated.[11] A few weeks later, on Boxing Day 1502, Edmund and Richard de la Pole, Sir Robert Curson and five others were officially declared outlaws at the Suffolk County Court sitting in Ipswich.[12] Further down the social scale, a special commission headed by the earl of Oxford continued to persecute de la Pole retainers. Among those forced to enter into financial recognisances to ensure their loyalty were a knight named Sir William Waldegrave, twenty-four gentlemen, fifteen squires and dozens of former de la Pole tenants in Suffolk and Oxfordshire.[13]

The turn of the year brought no respite for the beleaguered Yorkists. The ceremony excommunicating Edmund, Curson and 'all that then aided against the king'[14] was performed for a third time on the first Sunday of Lent 1503, and Henry continued with his show trials. In July 1503, Oliver St John, a distant relation of the king's mother,[15] was executed at Tyburn along with the bailiff of Thurrock and two sailors.[16] Interestingly, Robert Wellesbourne was also arrested during this purge but he was now using the name Simpson. As before, the turncoat was soon pardoned, which suggests that he had infiltrated and betrayed a Yorkist cell operated by St John before he was unmasked by Killingworth.

Such repressive measures are all too familiar to students of modern dictatorships, but Henry had good reason to fear for his throne and in late 1503 two new plots were uncovered. Both dastardly schemes were centred on Calais, and Henry was well aware that the Yorkist earl of Warwick, 'the Kingmaker', had used the English enclave as a base for his anti-Lancastrian activities during his time as governor there.

Half a century later, the city was still a hotbed of Yorkist intrigue. The first threat came from Lady Lucy Browne, wife of Anthony Browne, the captain of Calais Castle. Lady Lucy was a distant cousin of the de la Poles and she had vowed to betray the city to Edmund. The second, more serious plot involved the city's governor at the time, Giles Daubeney, who was planning to place himself on the throne.

It may be recalled that Daubeney had led the Tudor armies that had crushed the Cornish and Warbeck rebellions of 1497; it is no coincidence that the man who brought both of the Calais plots to Henry's attention was John Flamank, brother of the Bodmin lawyer who had led the Cornish to defeat at the battle of Blackheath. As John had taken no part in the revolt he was spared Thomas Flamank's grisly fate, but he may have volunteered to spy on Calais' ruling class in order to prove his loyalty further. Whatever his motives, John was in a perfect position to observe the comings-and-goings of the city's elite because he was the son-in-law of Calais' deputy governor, Sir Richard Nanfan, who was also a Cornishman.

Before being sent to Calais, Nanfan had been part of the diplomatic mission that negotiated the betrothal of Arthur, Prince of Wales, to Catherine of Aragon. By 1492 he was a pillar of the enclave's establishment. Interestingly, Nanfan's chaplain at this time was an ambitious young cleric named Thomas Wolsey, and the future cardinal's biographer, George Cavendish, noted that Calais' deputy governor occupied 'a great room' in the town.[17]

Having such an important father-in-law may have helped insulate John Flamank from his older brother's treason, and for his part Nanfan had no compunction about employing his daughter's husband, though in what capacity is unknown. Furthermore, besides marrying Nanfan's daughter, Joyce, John Flamank became a close friend of his wife's illegitimate half-brother William, and this closeness to the Nanfan family meant he was invited to attend a secret meeting to discuss the crisis caused by the death of Arthur Tudor and the sudden decline in the king's own health.

Besides William Nanfan and John Flamank, the deputy governor had invited Sir Sampson Norton, who had failed to winkle Sir James Tyrell out of Guînes, and Sir Hugh Conway, who had helped smuggle to Henry the gold that had financed the Bosworth campaign. Conway's reward had been a series of increasingly important positions in the Tudor king's household, and by this time he was Lord Treasurer of Ireland.[18]

The clandestine conference was held in Nanfan's official residence at the end of September 1503. He and his guests had to be extremely careful;[19] in the aftermath of Arthur's death, Henry's illness and Edmund's escape, any talk of the succession would be considered treasonable. Nanfan therefore insisted that everyone take an oath of loyalty to the king.

'Ye shall be both sworn upon a book that ye shall never utter nothing that is now here spoken, without it be to the king's grace,' he said darkly, and Flamank did just that – he reported everything that was said to the king.

According to the resulting document, *Flamank's Information*, Conway opened the discussion by stressing that he too had only the king's best interests at heart and it was for this reason that he could no longer keep silent. He then revealed the astonishing news that Sir Giles Daubeney, who was Henry's lord chamberlain as well as governor of Calais, was planning to usurp the throne after the king's death. However, Conway went on to insist that Daubeney had no intention of rebelling while the king lived and only wanted to save England from the chaos that would inevitably follow if a regent had to be appointed for Henry's surviving heir.[20]

A regency was a distinct possibility because Prince Henry was still only twelve years old, and Conway's further claim that King Henry was 'a weak man and sickly, not likely to be long-lived' was not without foundation. As no one at the meeting wanted a return to the turbulent regencies that had followed the untimely deaths of Henry V and Edward IV, their talk now turned to those who had a better claim to the throne than Daubeney – and Conway had another unpleasant surprise:

> It happened at the same time I found myself to be among many great personages ... some of them spoke of my lord of Buckingham, saying that he was a noble man and would be a royal ruler. Others there were that spoke likewise of the traitor Edmond De la Pole, but none of them spoke of my lord prince [Henry].[21]

Again, everyone present would have known that Buckingham's father had tried and failed to depose Richard III, but what chilled Nanfan and Norton to the bone was Conway's insistence that people were considering Edmund as a future king.

The part Norton played in Tyrell's arrest has already been discussed, but it had been Nanfan who had warned the king that Edmund had taken refuge with Sir James during his 1499 flight from England. Unfortunately for Nanfan, Henry did not believe him.

This was not the first time Nanfan had been accused of slandering important courtiers out of pure malice. Six years earlier he had accused Sir Robert Clifford of being a Warbeck supporter, which was true, but Henry had also ignored this warning and the memory of being humiliated in this way still rankled. 'Never words went colder to my heart than they did,' Nanfan told his guests, and Conway said that he too had suffered from the king's reluctance to believe any charge made by one member of the Tudor court about another.[22]

In Conway's case, he had accused Thomas Lovell, the chancellor of the exchequer, of being up to no good, but it had been he who had been dragged before Henry to explain himself. No action had been taken against Lovell and the whole matter had been forgotten, but Conway and Nanfan's cautionary tales prompted Norton to remark that the king should trust his true knights better. No doubt Norton remembered how Lovell's false promises of safe conduct had persuaded Tyrell to surrender, and he now feared the terrible revenge Edmund would exact on those who had sent his friends from Guînes to the scaffold if he became king.

However, Conway insisted that Daubeney was the greater threat because he had been carefully placing men loyal to himself in the king's entourage. 'Look how strong he is in the king's court ... for the more party of his guard be of those that were my Lord Chamberlain's servants before,' he said. But he was not done, for next came his most startling revelation:

> And for troth I know well that he [Henry] cannot long continue for it is written of him that he shall no longer reign than King Edward, which was but twenty-two years and a little more ... and I shall shew you my book [of prophecies] that shall declare [to] you the same plainly to be as I have said and spoken.[23]

Those present were appalled. Though Henry's own fondness for prophecy was well known, it was treason for commoners to try and divine the time of a king's death and the shocked Norton told Conway to destroy the offending grimoire at once.

'Burn that book and a vengeance take the first writer!' he cried.[24]

Ignoring him, Conway turned his attention to Lady Lucy's plot. Warming to his subject, Conway declared that the constable of Calais' wife had spoken openly of surrendering the town to Edmund and that every Tudor loyalist would be murdered if the town fell to the Yorkists:

> [If] the king were once departed, she being in the castle here and Edmond de la Pole her cousin [be] at his liberty, she would help him in his causes with all her power and to let

> him come into this town by the postern of the castle to the destruction of us all.[25]

Though Lady Lucy's husband, Sir Anthony Browne, was a stalwart Lancastrian, having succeeded the late William Brandon as Henry VII's official standard bearer, he had married a known Yorkist as part of Henry attempts to reconcile the warring factions. Unfortunately, Browne's wife had never forgotten that she and Edmund were descended from the Yorkist matriarch, Cecily Neville, so a plot involving Lady Lucy had to be taken seriously – especially as Conway was adamant she had the support of several key members of the Tudor government.

According to Conway, those backing Edmund included Sir Richard Guildford, comptroller of Henry's household, Sir Edward Poynings, lord warden of the Cinque Ports, and Sir Thomas Bourchier, constable of Windsor Castle.[26] Yet Conway's accusations were extremely far-fetched because all these men had been mixed up in the duke of Buckingham's ill-fated rebellion against Edmund's uncle Richard III.

The consequences of Buckingham's short-lived rebellion, which collapsed in November 1483, shaped Yorkist and Tudor politics for decades, but the relevant information for us is that Sir Edward Poynings had plotted with his stepfather, Sir George Browne, brother of Lady Lucy's husband Sir Anthony Browne, to raise the men of Kent in support of Buckingham's bid to depose Richard III. Though Buckingham and Browne had been captured and executed, more than 500 of their supporters had fled to Brittany and transferred their loyalties to Henry Tudor – among them Sir Edward Poynings, Sir Giles Daubeney, the marquess of Dorset and the earl of Devon.

It would be extremely unlikely for all these men, who had been with Henry since before Bosworth, to turn their coats a third time. Furthermore, Daubney had his own plan for a *coup d'état*, Edmund's attempts to recruit Dorset and Devon had failed, and Poynings had no love for the earl of Suffolk because his mother was a Paston. The famous family of letter writers had a longstanding feud with the de la Poles, and Poyning's deep antipathy towards Yorkists had been much in evidence during his rule in Ireland. After serving Henry faithfully on the battlefields of Bosworth,

Stoke Field, Dixmude and Boulogne, Poynings had been appointed lord deputy of Ireland, with Sir Hugh Conway as his treasurer, and his orders were to purge the island of Yorkist rebels. Between 1494 and 1496, Poynings had ruthlessly crushed Irish Yorkism; indeed, he had personally led the army that had defeated Perkin Warbeck's attempt to land at Waterford.

Edmund was therefore unlikely to welcome Poynings into the ranks of his supporters, and the same might also be said about Sir Richard Guildford. Not only had Guildford taken part in Buckingham's plot to oust Edmund's uncle, but it had been he who had led the mission to extradite the fugitive earl of Suffolk from St Omer after he had fled the charge of murdering Thomas Crue.

The above notwithstanding, Conway remained utterly convinced that Lady Lucy's treason was well advanced and he was equally insistent that the Calais garrison was 'ready to follow her mind ... and do us the most mischief they can do'.[27] Yet, when pressed, Conway could only name someone called 'Raynold of the Chamber, a constable of the retinue', and two lowly spearmen, Richard Woodhouse and John Clinton, as being complicit in the scheme to seize Calais for Edmund. Nevertheless, Nanfan proudly declared that he would rather die than surrender the town and he urged his colleagues to waste no time in rounding up anyone whose loyalty was even slightly suspect.[28]

At this point, there is an abrupt halt in Flamank's account of Nanfan's secret talks and he claims that he could not, or would not, recollect any more of what was said. However, in a postscript to his report, Flamank delivered another body-blow to Henry by declaring that Sir Nicholas Vaux, the man who had replaced Sir James Tyrell as captain of Guînes, could no longer be trusted.

After the Tyrell affair, Henry had wanted someone with impeccable Lancastrian-Tudor credentials in command of the vital stronghold of Guînes, and Vaux certainly fit the bill. His mother, Katherine, had been lady-in-waiting to Henry VI's wife, Margaret of Anjou, and she had shared many of the queen's privations during her exile. Katherine de Vaux's devotion had been rewarded by Henry VII, who showered the family with honours, and Sir Nicholas had repaid his patron by slaughtering Lambert Simnel's German mercenaries at Stoke Field and Thomas Flamank's Cornish rebels at Blackheath.

In spite of his unimpeachable Lancastrian pedigree, Flamank insisted that Sir Nicholas had not given the king his unequivocal backing when he had been questioned by Sir Hugh Conway about the alleged Daubeney plot. Instead, Vaux had hinted that he would stay in his castle 'however the world turned',[29] and it did not help Vaux's case that his brother-in-law was Sir Richard Guildford. Besides being named by Conway as part of the Lucy plot, Guildford had recently fallen from the king's favour due to some financial irregularities that had occurred while he held several royal posts.

Reading between the lines of *Flamank's Information*, it appears that Conway was simply trying to find out which faction had the best chance of success. With everyone sitting on the fence, however, he decided to insert his own spy into the king's household so he could find out exactly what was going on. Unfortunately, the man he tried to recruit for this task was none other than John Flamank.

At a separate clandestine meeting, Conway told Flamank that such an enterprising young man as himself could easily obtain a position of trust with Henry and he offered him £10 a year to spy on the king, but only if Nanfan and Norton would commit to paying him as well.[30] Annoyingly, Flamank ends his report without telling us if the others agreed to pay up; nevertheless his findings gave Henry plenty to think about.

Ironically, Flamank was guilty of being motivated by malice and ambition whereas Conway, Nanfan and Norton were not. For a start, Flamank could avenge his brother by ruining Daubeney; added to this, by the time his report reached the king Flamank had also fallen out with his father-in-law. That said, everything Flamank had reported was largely true, and the seed he had planted did bear fruit – eventually.

Three years after receiving *Flamank's Information*, in 1506, Henry moved against all those he had named. Daubeney was fined £2,100 for embezzlement, and though Sir Anthony Browne had died, his wife, Lady Lucy, was punished for failing to ensure her late-husband's retainers had taken the proper oath of loyalty to the Tudors. Guildford had also died, but Sir Nicholas Vaux was still alive and he was made the subject of a huge financial indenture. As for Conway, Norton and Nanfan, they were all dismissed from their posts.[31] In 1507, Flamank was reinstated and given a position in the Calais garrison. Likewise, Conway and Norton were also rehabilitated, while Nanfan had wisely chosen to retire.

However, these punishments and reconciliations were in the future. Henry's *first* response to Flamank's accusations was to recruit a new spy. His name was Sir John Wiltshire.

7

PROVIDED THEY MAKE DECLARATION OF ALL THEY KNOW

The year before Nanfan's secret meeting, in 1502, Sir John Wiltshire had been appointed comptroller of Calais and tasked with overseeing the city's public finances. Wiltshire certainly had a good head for business, having made his fortune as a merchant despite humble origins. His financial nous had earned him a position at court, a knighthood and a castle at Stone, on the southern shore of the Thames estuary.[1]

Wiltshire's commission as comptroller of Calais required him to keep a second set accounts for the king's eyes only, not to be shown to Sir Richard Nanfan, the city's treasurer, under any circumstances.[2] This suggests that Henry was already suspicious of the Calais elite even before the controversial meeting recorded by Flamank, and the comptroller's covert activities did not stop at clandestine bookkeeping. As Henry's chief financial officer on the Continent, it was Wiltshire's responsibility to arrange the payment of the £10,000 Henry had promised Maximilian in return for the treaty expelling Yorkists from the Empire.[3]

It is typical of the micro-managing Henry that he specified how this treaty's provisions were to be enforced in minute detail. Firstly, the citizens of every area where the de la Poles and their supporters were resident had to be notified by public proclamation that all English rebels were now outside imperial protection and anyone aiding them would be punished most severely. Secondly, these proclamations had to be read out in French, German and Latin, using the exact form of words stipulated by the treaty, and the imperial heralds had to be accompanied by their English counterpart, the Norroy King of Arms.

Finally, Wiltshire was instructed to list all the Yorkists living in exile, together with their hiding places. Obviously this was a momentous task but, to help him complete it, Wiltshire was authorised to recruit more spies.[4] The commission touched specifically on Edmund:

> Also, he shall find means, to the best of his power, to engage some of the servants of Edmund de la Pole always to give him intelligence, promising them, on the king's part, his pardon ... Also, if there are any other of the gentlemen and servants of the said Edmund De la Pole who desire to have their pardon and absolution, the king is content to pardon them their lives, provided they make declaration of all that they know.[5]

This in itself was something of a tall order, but Wiltshire was helped by authorisation to make use of the highly effective network of spies created by Sir Charles Somerset.[6] The man who had persuaded Maximilian to sign the treaty banishing the Yorkists had been rewarded by being made Henry's permanent envoy to the imperial court, and one of his agents recorded his activities in an autobiographical paper entitled *Depositions Touching Edmund de la Pole.*

As this spy's identity was later redacted, to use a modern term, we shall call him Agent X. He begins his *Depositions* by telling us he was recruited to penetrate a secret organisation that spirited suspected Yorkists out of the country. To this end, Agent X was sent undercover into the Tower of London in an attempt to gain the confidence of a Yorkist prisoner named William Hussey. Though Hussey's father and brother were loyal Tudors, William had been mixed up in Edmund's jousting set and he had been imprisoned for non-payment of the sureties levied on him during the recent purge of suspected Yorkists.[7]

Once inside the Tower, Agent X managed to trick the unsuspecting Hussey into revealing the identities of the guests at Edmund's infamous farewell dinner parties. He also managed to convince Hussey that he knew an astrologer who could be extremely useful to the rebels. Suitably impressed, Hussey revealed the codes and recognition signals used by the Yorkists, after which his cellmate 'escaped' and made his way to Aachen.[8]

Having used what he had learned from Hussey to convince everyone that he was a genuine defector, Agent X was introduced to Edmund, whereupon he played his astrologer card. No doubt he hoped to learn the time and date of any Yorkist invasion through this subterfuge but Edmund, fearing a trap, had refused to reveal his date of birth. Without this information, an accurate horoscope could not be cast so Agent X was forced to spend the next few months trying to win Edmund's trust by running errands and passing on snippets of gossip.

'As I could get no counsel of the astronomers, because they had not his nativity, like as I promised, I kept me from his [Edmund's] company, and by reports of such news as I heard, got the most favour I could of him,' the spy admits in his *Depositions*.[9]

One such menial task involved the collection of an expensive crossbow that Edmund had ordered from Antwerp. As the Yorkists were running dangerously short of cash this may seem like an extravagance, but hunting was an important facet of nobility and the White Rose had to keep up appearances. Besides, the 12 florins needed to buy the crossbow had been provided by a well-wisher named John Chamberlain.

As well as much-needed money, Chamberlain had important information regarding a man who was offering Wiltshire's pardons to Edmund's servants provided they became informers. Chamberlain told Agent X that John Brit, someone named Hourts, Hourts' servant and an unnamed ship's captain had already turned their coats, but Agent X knew this because he too had been approached.

In his *Depositions*, Agent X names the Tudor mole as William Cowper and confirms that Sir John Wiltshire was controlling the operation. However, instead of telling Cowper that he too was working for Henry, he reported his fellow spy's activities to another of Edmund's servants, one Gilkin. Presumably, Agent X could not report the matter in person because he was still *persona non grata* with Edmund, but Gilkin's messenger 'lay sick' so it was he who informed the White Rose of the treachery in his household after all.

'So that Edmund, weening (believing) that all this advertisements had come from me, gave me great thanks,' wrote the spy proudly,[10] but his accusation that two more servants, Edward Awnsham and a man called Derick, were secretly working for the Tudors was less well received. 'And Edmund wrote again to Gilkin and me and bade us speak no more of Edward or Derick, for he knew all that matter.'[11]

The Derick referred to here is probably a Flemish gentleman called Derek van Riet who, with his brother Jan, had been recruited by Edmund to act as a courier and interpreter. As both the van Riet brothers are regularly referred to in letters written by Edmund after this date, Derek must have refused Cowper's offer; Edward Awnsham, on the other hand, is never heard of again.

Whether Awnsham escaped to England or ended up in a shallow grave somewhere in the Ardennes is not recorded, but Agent X continued to spy on Edmund and his *Depositions* go on to state that he had tried, and failed, to persuade Sir Robert Curson to reveal what he knew about Edmund's sources of income, his foreign allies, his supporters in England and any locations earmarked for an invasion. Curson would say nothing; as we shall see, he had his own reasons to keep his cards close to his chest.[12]

In any case, sacrificing Cowper and Awnsham did persuade Edmund to change his mind about consulting Agent X's astrologers. Now he had proved his loyalty, Edmund asked the spy to discover the most propitious time to take a trip and a horoscope was duly cast. The reply soon arrived:

> For any poverty or neediness make none hasty passage without ye be assured to pass strongly or else to find them before you in England that ye be assured of shall aid and strength you sufficiently against all that shall make resistance; and cast not away yourself for hastiness and without favour of astats [i.e. England's noblemen]. Trust not the commons, for in them without their heads never was [and] never shall be steadfastness.[13]

While this insight was typically vague, the soothsayers' advice struck a chord with Edmund because the purpose of the journey in question was to receive the Emperor's personal assurance that he would continue to fund the Yorkists in secret. Moreover, it seems as if Edmund followed the astrologers' advice because, on his return, he told Agent X that his mission had been extremely successful.

'And I did speak with him ... and he sayeth he had been with the king of Romans and the king gave him answers to such as he came for ... for his cousin of Suffolk aid should not be diminished nor his journey by one hour for that bond,' Agent X wrote.[14]

This offer of covert funding is confirmed by Sir Thomas Killingworth's *Statement Concerning Edmund de la Pole*, and while Henry would not have been aware of such collaboration at this time, he had every reason to believe Maximilian was still backing a Yorkist restoration because the plots against him continued.

In the summer of 1503, two new conspiracies were betrayed by a former woodcutter named Alexander Symson. This man had suddenly appeared at Sir Richard Guildford's country seat of Rolvenden, in the Weald of Kent, and told him that his neighbour, Sir Walter Roberts, was a closet Yorkist who had employed him to act as a courier and messenger for Yorkists on the Continent. This was particularly unsettling for Guildford because he owed his life to Roberts.

In the year of troubles that had followed the death of Edward IV, Guildford and his father had been drawn into the duke of Buckingham's plot to depose Richard III. The Guildfords had been recruited by Sir Reynold Bray, who had once been Margaret Beaufort's steward, and he may have been using his then master, the duke of Buckingham, as a 'false flag' for her son, Henry Tudor. Whatever the Guildfords believed, they recruited Sir Walter Roberts, who may have thought that he was fighting to free Edward V from the clutches of his wicked uncle. Indeed, there were many who thought the young prince and his brother were still alive, but Roberts may have been nothing more than a man with an eye for the main chance.

Roberts was descended from an eleventh-century Scot with the surname Rockhurst who had settled in Kent during the reign of Henry I. When Walter inherited the Manor of Glassenbury, he anglicized his name to Roberts in the hope of advancing his family; he may have joined Buckingham's rebellion for the same reason.[15] Unfortunately for Roberts, he had backed the wrong horse.

Once it became clear that both Princes in the Tower were dead most of the rebels had transferred their allegiance to the exiled Henry Tudor, but a violent storm had prevented them from uniting their disparate forces. Buckingham's Welshmen had been trapped behind the River Severn, which had become a raging torrent, while Guildford's forces were similarly marooned in Kent, and Henry could not cross the Channel with his French mercenaries.[16]

Once the Buckingham revolt had collapsed, the fugitive Guildfords had joined Henry in Brittany. But they could not have escaped without Robert's help, and when his 'misprision' was discovered he was attainted. Roberts' beloved Glassenbury was seized by the crown, and he was forced to seek sanctuary in a monastery, but his loyalty was not forgotten. After Bosworth, Sir Richard Guildford had made sure that Roberts' estates were restored and he was given the right to enclose his lands 'in consideration of good and gratuitous services rendered at great cost and heavy expense'.[17]

All this meant Guildford found it hard to believe that Roberts was now supporting Edmund, and he may have warned his friend that this woodcutter-turned-spy was trying to betray him. Consequently, it was Symson who was forced into hiding. This begs the question: why did Guildford fail to investigate the woodcutter's allegations? Even allowing for the debt of honour he owed Roberts, Guildford's behaviour is highly suspicious. It should not be forgotten that these events coincide with those described in *Flamank's Information.*

As mentioned earlier, Flamank had accused Guildford of plotting with Sir Giles Daubeney to seize the throne, and his brother-in-law, Sir Nicholas Vaux, was another of those alleged conspirators. Guildford must have known he was in trouble because he failed to attend that year's feast of St George, which he had not missed for some time; he may have been considering joining Edmund simply to save his own skin. If this was the case, it made perfect sense for him to join forces with his old friend and use the unwitting Symson to find out the strength of the Yorkist position.

On the other hand, Guildford and Roberts could have been working for Henry and Symson's employment on trips to Europe part of another 'false flag' plan to infiltrate a spy into Edmund's household. In other words, perhaps Symson believed he was working for the Yorkists when in fact the information he was supposed to obtain was destined for the Tudors. This scenario would certainly explain why Roberts was later promoted. Instead of ending his days at the end of a rope, Roberts was appointed commissioner of the peace for Kent and commissioner of delivery for Maidstone Gaol, and died in his bed at the age of eighty.[18]

By contrast, his erstwhile accuser soon fell back into bad company. Symson was dragged before the dreaded court of Star Chamber on 6 August 1503, charged with a different treasonable offence. However, the proceedings began with the luckless woodcutter repeating his allegations against Roberts.

> Alexander Symson of Cranbrook in the County of Kent, sawyer by his craft, sayeth that he hath belonged to Walter Robardes [Roberts] of Cranbrook, since a year before King Edward's decease. And he sayeth that soon upon Easter last past, the said Walter Robardes being in a strip of a meadow lying in the back side of Cranbrook aforesaid ... called this Alexander to him.[19]

Having met his hired hand in a secluded corner of his estate in the beautiful Kent countryside, Roberts asked him if he could be trusted. Symson replied that they had known each other too long to dignify such a question with an answer, and after this gruff exchange Symson heard nothing more for a month. Their next meeting took place while Symson was clearing a pond, and on this occasion Roberts offered him a job as a Yorkist courier and spy.

In addition to carrying Roberts' messages of support to Edmund, Symson agreed to travel to Aachen via the de la Pole heartlands in order to ascertain levels of anti-Tudor feeling. He set off shortly after Whitsuntide. He was paid 2 nobles in gold and 20 groats in silver for expenses, but he found no evidence that the people of Oxfordshire and Suffolk were yearning for a Yorkist restoration – at least that is what he told his interrogators.[20]

Nevertheless, the underground pipeline used by Agent X was still a reality, and on reaching the Continent Symson was given a warm welcome by a shoemaker who operated a de la Pole safehouse in Aachen. However, Edmund was now extremely wary of strangers claiming to be loyal Yorkists so he ordered Sir George Neville and Walter Blasset to interrogate the new arrival. Neville quickly concluded that Symson was indeed a Tudor spy and warned him to leave Aachen by eight o'clock the next morning or he would have his ears cut off. The terrified Symson did not need to be told twice, smuggling himself home aboard a herring boat.[21]

Following his return, Symson discussed the matter with his wife and it may have been she who persuaded him to report his employer's treason to Sir Richard Guildford. As a former sheriff of Kent, Guildford was certainly the obvious choice, but if the hapless Symson had known about Guildford's connection to Roberts they may have thought otherwise.[22] Yet there is more to the Symson affair than his abortive trip to Aachen, and to explore that we must now turn to the principal reason for his arrest in August 1503, which was a plot to kidnap a boy called James Ormond.

For this part of the story we have to rely on the evidence of Thomas Broke, a prosecution witness who made his living as a boatman in Erith on the south bank of the Thames estuary, where Symson had ended up after being sent packing by Sir Richard Guildford. Having failed to find honest work, he soon found himself leading a gang of Yorkist kidnappers. Symson had tried to recruit Broke, but the boatman had reported the conspiracy to Erith's constable.

In order to save himself from the gallows, Symson had turned King's Evidence. Besides betraying Roberts, he also revealed a scheme to snatch James Ormond. Though the precise identity of his intended victim is unclear, the fact that Symson described the boy as 'a great inheritor and next to the crown' suggests he was the son of Sir Piers Butler, who was the heir to one of Ireland's most important titles.

The Butler earls of Ormond boasted strong Lancastrian-Tudor connections and a longstanding feud with the Yorkist FitzGerald earls of Desmond. However, back in the 1460s, there had been several claimants to the Ormond inheritance. One claimant had tried to outmanoeuvre his rivals by allying himself to Edward IV, and though this plan had been wrecked by the Tudor victory at Bosworth, the claimant's son, Piers, had regained his place in the Ormond succession by the simple means of killing his rival. As Henry needed allies in Ireland, Piers was pardoned and in return resumed his family's pro-Lancastrian stance.

All this mattered to Edmund because the earls of Ormond not only controlled much of southern Ireland but were the lords of seventy-two manors in south-east England, a swath of land that could provide a useful bridgehead for an invasion. It hardly needs to be repeated that Kent had been at the forefront of Buckingham's rebellion, or that Ireland had played a key role in John de la Pole's plans to put Lambert Simnel on the throne.

If the boatman Broke was to be believed, Symson was following the same path trodden by his near-namesake Robert Simon, the Yorkist priest who had groomed the ten-year-old Simnel to impersonate the late earl of Warwick. Yet is highly likely that Simnel had been a mere stalking-horse for John de la Pole. and now, said Broke, Symson was planning to use the equally young James Ormond to secure Ireland for Edmund. That said, we should bear in mind that the boatman had been drunk when Symson explained his plans.

'The said Thomas sayeth that on St James's Day at night last past, he was at John Wilson's house in Erith, drinking. And as he sat there, comes in Alexander Symson and asked whether he were the good man of the house or not. And the said Thomas said he was and then the said Alex asked him whether he might trust him or not,' reads the transcript of Broke's testimony.[23]

After a little more verbal sparring, Broke insisted that Symson get to the point, whereupon the veteran plotter whispered that he was planning to kidnap a boy whose guardian was the 'master of Christ Church'. Though Broke does not mention the man's name, he has to be Thomas Goldston, prior of Christ Church Monastery in Canterbury, who had accompanied Lord Thomas Butler to France after the latter had been appointed Henry's ambassador to the French king. As most noblemen sent their sons to be educated by prominent clergymen it is highly probable that Goldston had been entrusted with James's education, but as no action was taken against him we can assume he was not a member of Symson's gang.[24]

The plot, when Symson finally got around to revealing it, was breathtakingly naïve. After snatching the boy from his Canterbury schoolroom, the heavily armed kidnappers would use a small boat to travel down the River Stour and join a larger ship waiting for them at the mouth of the Wantsum Channel. Although long since silted up, this waterway once separated the Isle of Thanet from the rest of Kent and Symson planned to hide in the isle's labyrinth of marshes if his plan went wrong.[25]

As his getaway would be by boat, Symson had need of a boatman so he offered Broke an annual pension of 40 marks if he agreed to take Ormond to 'any country of France or Zealand'. On hearing this, the boatman took one look at Symson's ragged clothes and asked how he could afford such an enormous sum, whereupon Symson admitted he had only 20 pence in his pocket and something worth 20 shillings back at his house. This did not impress Broke, who went straight to the constable.

Within days, Symson found himself in the Tower. Worse still, the boatman was not the only witness against him. James Ormond was also interviewed, and the boy's evidence was just as damning. He readily admitted he had been approached by Symson, who had offered 'to make him a great lord if he would be counselled by him', but the plot had been discovered before it could go any further.[26]

Ormond true complicity in this conspiracy is not known, but he too was spared the gallows owing to his youth and political importance. In any event he had no need of Symson to become a great lord because his father Piers succeeded his kinsman Thomas as the 8th earl of Ormond in 1515 and he in turn became the 9th earl in the fullness of time.

Curiously, there is no record of Symson's execution or his ultimate fate, which suggests he had indeed saved himself by turning King's Evidence. But how deeply was Edmund involved in these plots?

While there is no doubt that Symson was initially recruited by Roberts, perhaps under false pretences, it is equally likely that the woodcutter was acting on his own initiative when he came up with his plan to kidnap James Ormond. Whether this was a genuine, if overambitious, attempt to secure Ireland for Edmund or simple criminal extortion is not known, but the disastrous interview with Neville and Blasset suggests Edmund trusted neither Symson nor Roberts. Consequently, he would have wanted nothing to do with their schemes to raise Kent or kidnap James Ormond.

All that can be said for certain is that the exploits of Alexander Symson, Agent X, William Cowper and the rest of the spies in Aachen were making life intolerable for Edmund. Moreover, the Emperor's fickle prevaricating meant the Yorkist treasury was being emptied faster than it was being filled. As a result, despite the warnings of Agent X's astrologers, Edmund was forced to make increasingly desperate decisions.

8

WE AND KING HENRY OF ENGLAND, OF THE RED ROSE, HAVE MADE A CONTRACT

The ratification of the treaty expelling English rebels from the Holy Roman Empire was a body blow to the White Rose, and worse was to follow. Despite what Maximilian had said to Edmund and Killingworth in private, he had no intention of keeping his promise to continue funding the Yorkists in secret; at least, that is what he told Jerome Lay, his personal envoy to the rebellious duchy of Guelders.

Early in 1503, while Conway, Nanfan, Flamank, Daubeney, Guildford, Roberts and Symson were anxiously contemplating their own precarious futures, Maximilian wrote to Lay, who enjoyed the curious title of master of the hunt at Guelders, and instructed him to contact the authorities in Aachen with news of his change of policy towards the Yorkists:

> We and King Henry of England, of the Red Rose, have made a contract with one another which, amongst other things, contains that we are not in any way furthermore to encourage the same duke of Suffolk against the above-mentioned king of England.[1]

In Maximilian's defence, it ought to be said that his hands were tied, albeit loosely. The treaty with Henry did nothing to change the Empire's constitution, whereby Aachen and the other Free Cities lay outside imperial authority. This legal obstacle effectively prevented Maximilian from fulfilling his obligations to banish Edmund, so, to escape the impasse, he ordered Lay to tell three shameless lies. Firstly, the master of the hunt was instructed to inform the burghers of Aachen that Edmund had asked to leave their city of his own free will. Secondly, he was to tell them that the Emperor was prepared to settle Edmund's debts with an *ex gratia* payment of 3,000 Rhenish florins. Thirdly, Lay was to stress that Maximilian had never promised to help the Yorkists in the first place.[2]

Typically, the Emperor's charity disguised an ingenious piece of double-dealing. Maximilian knew that the burghers of Aachen were heartily sick of the Yorkists and were only allowing them stay in the hope their numerous outstanding bills would be paid. Therefore, by settling the Yorkists' debts, Maximilian could ensure that the Aachen authorities would do his dirty work for him. His letter to Lay explained that the required funds would be taken from the taxes collected by his son, Philip, archduke of Burgundy.[3]

What the Burgundians thought about their hard-earned cash being used to subsidise a foreign rebel is not recorded, but Maximilian did not abandon Edmund entirely, and he continued to believe that a negotiated settlement would prevent his kinsman's head from adorning a spike above London Bridge. To this end, he prepared a diplomatic ambush that would force Henry to pardon Edmund and restore him to his rank of duke.

The ace up Maximilian's sleeve was a minor clause in the banishment treaty that honoured each monarch by investing them with each other's highest order of chivalry. This was a common way of signifying a rapprochement between two nations, in this case through Henry accepting the imperial Order of the Golden Fleece while Maximilian agreed to be invested with English Order of the Garter. However, Maximilian had already received the Garter in 1489, and he thought this could save Edmund from the scaffold.

Put simply, the oath taken by Garter knights required them to support their fellow members in adversity. By inference, then, they could not put one another in jeopardy.[4] Because Edmund was also a Garter knight, Maximilian could not uphold his oath to protect him and at the same time comply with Henry's treaty requiring all English exiles to be declared outlaws. The only solution, Maximilian reasoned, was for Henry to pardon Edmund and return everything that had been taken from him since his brother John's death. The restored duke of Suffolk could then return home and the honour of everyone concerned would remain intact.[5]

The Emperor tabled this proposal during the conference convened to make arrangements for the investiture ceremony at the end of January 1503 in Antwerp's Abbey of St Michael. The chief imperial negotiators were Matthew Lang, provost of Augsburg Cathedral, Doctor Haydon, the imperial chamberlain, and the bishop of Laufenburg. On the other side of the table were Sir Thomas Brandon, brother of Henry's standard bearer at Bosworth, and Nicholas West, who was Henry's chaplain and a future bishop of Ely.[6]

Though Maximilian was absent during the initial phases of the conference, which discussed such weighty matters as whether or not the Garter oath could be taken on the Sabbath and where, exactly, in the abbey's church the ceremony should take place, he made it very clear he was unhappy with the terms of the treaty banishing Edmund once he did arrive.[7] As mentioned earlier, Maximilian's chief objection was the paradox created by having been inducted into the order already, but Brandon and West had their counterargument ready:

> Whereupon we showed that because his proxy came not to be en-stalled for him, and to present his helmet, &c. by the time limited by the said statutes, therefore as well [as] the receiving of the said order, [and] the giving of the oath, were void and of none effect, likewise as if they had never be done.[8]

In other words, the first investiture was not valid because the ceremony had not been performed within the time stipulated by the order's rules. With Maximilian's objection neatly neutered, Brandon and West asked the Emperor, plainly, if he intended to fulfil the terms of the treaty expelling Edmund. At this, Maximilian countered by asking if Henry's envoys had authority to negotiate Edmund's pardon:

> And immediately thereupon the said provost Lang asked of us whether we had any authority or not to commune [of] any

> matter concerning Edmund de la Poel [*sic*], whom he called the duke of Suffolk; for the king [of the Romans] intended to purchase his pardon and grace of your highness.[9]

Again, Brandon and West had their answer ready. Their response was to list all of Edmund's 'many-fold offences' to show why Henry could not contemplate giving pardons to any of the exiled Yorkists. Unfortunately, their attempt to seize the moral high ground was treated with utter disdain by the imperials and a whispered discussion between Maximilian and his courtiers produced 'a great laughing at the first word that the king spoke'.[10]

In their report to Henry, Brandon and West admitted they had no idea what the joke was, but it was they who had last laugh. Unbeknown to the Emperor, Brandon's men had intercepted a Yorkist courier, Robinet Ruffyn, who carried an incriminating letter. Addressed to Edmund's steward, Thomas Killingworth, it contained Maximilian's offer to continue supporting the Yorkists in secret, 'all contrary to the amity concluded and confirmed' with Henry.[11]

With ill-disguised glee, the Tudor envoys confronted Maximilian with this evidence of his double dealing. The Emperor had been caught in a web of his own lies, and though he excused himself by saying he had acted as he did because he thought Henry had no intention of keeping to the treaty, he promised 'never hereafter to give any manner of relief to the said rebels and to observe every point of the said amity'.[12]

A few days later Brandon and West were back at the negotiating table in the full expectation that the humiliated Maximilian would agree to their every demand, yet he continued to insist that he would not accept the Order of the Garter until Edmund had been pardoned. Furthermore, the Tudor envoys were astonished to hear that Maximilian had had sent his own ambassadors to England to discuss Edmund's pardon directly with Henry and he would not order any banishments until the matter had been settled to his satisfaction.[13]

The only concession Maximilian was prepared to make was to give Edmund fair warning that he would be required to leave Aachen in the near future and that all his creditors should submit their final invoices in anticipation of his imminent departure. On hearing this, Brandon and West must have thought they were at last making progress, but Maximilian suddenly 'discovered' another anomaly created by the banishment treaty.

The Emperor now claimed that he had promised the burghers of Aachen he would act as guarantor for the Yorkists' debts partly because he had ordered Edmund to move to the city in the first place and partly as a favour to the dying Margaret of Burgundy. Herein lay the problem: imperial honour would not allow Maximilian to order Edmund's departure from Aachen as required by the treaty until his bills were paid, but the Emperor was prohibited from settling those accounts by the same treaty.[14]

This was too much for the befuddled Brandon and West, who wrote to Henry saying that the Emperor would not budge on the matter of Edmund's pardon and that, though they had done their best to comply with their instructions, there was no power on earth that could untangle the Gordian knot of Maximilian's double dealing.[15] To be fair to Brandon and West, their hands were tied after Maximilian sent a second set of imperial ambassadors to Windsor to negotiate the matter of Edmund's pardon directly with Henry.

While all this was going on, where was the impoverished earl of Suffolk? The answer is that he was still spending money he did not have and searching for backers to fill the growing void in his finances. For all Maximilian's promises to settle Edmund's debts, he had seriously underestimated the amount owed by the Yorkist court-in-exile. The money that Lay had been ordered to deliver was quickly spent, and in July 1503 Maximilian had to instruct Martin Aichorn, the imperial chamberlain at Innsbruck, to send another 2,000 florins.[16]

The enormity of Edmund's debts is hardly surprising; after all, he had been forced to live far beyond his means in order to maintain the fiction that he was a king unjustly deprived of his throne. In an undated letter sent to Sir Thomas Killingworth around this time, Edmund complained that he was in desperate need of new clothes but any shirts purchased from a certain Monsieur Delenne had to be the best quality and his new bonnet had to be of 'rosy hue'. Edmund also asked Killingworth to buy him 'three quarters of satin for my doublet' and a new handkerchief.[17]

Besides looking like a prince, Edmund had to employ a sizeable retinue of courtiers, couriers and servants, several of whom we have already met. In addition to his steward, Sir Thomas Killingworth, his second-in-command, Sir George Neville, and his chaplain, Sir Walter Blasset, Edmund's inner circle included the Flemish merchant Claus Derrek and several Burgundians including John Griffon, who is also known as the Bastard of Oyskerk.[18] In truth, Oyskerk was not a passionate Yorkist but an imperial gentleman who had replaced Bontemps as Maximilian's principal liaison officer at Edmund's court-in-exile.

Further down the social scale, there were a number of ordinary folk in Edmund's employ. Among these minor functionaries were several Englishmen, such as John Parreleben, John Growet and John Griffith,[19] as well as a few natives of Flanders. The latter included Hans Wittershaw and the van Riet brothers, Jan and Derek, the latter of whom Cowper had tried to recruit as a double agent.[20] Edmund's letters also refer to a number of individuals who are identified by a single name such as Gilkin, Holland, Allen, Eustace, William and Peter.[21]

Maintaining even a relatively small entourage was enormously expensive, and with the river of imperial gold dwindling to a trickle it was Killingworth who had to keep the fiscal plates spinning. Another of Edmund's letters written at this time shows that the much-put-upon steward travelled to Arnhem, Utrecht, Wageningen and a number of other towns in the Low Countries in pursuit of loans and donations. Yet another missive orders the steward to seek out 'the ambassador with a clubbed foot' and enlist his help.

After reading these letters, we are left wondering why Edmund did not approach his aunt Margaret of Burgundy for money, but the truth is that she seems to have had little time for him. Perhaps she felt betrayed once she realised that Simnel was not her long-lost nephew, as the oldest of the de la Pole brothers had claimed. Whatever the reason, the ageing Yorkist matriarch never offered the earl of Suffolk the same levels of support she gave the earl of Lincoln.

So desperate was Edmund that he sought to refill his much-depleted coffers through Margaret's imminent demise, beseeching Killingworth, 'Do your best to recover more of that money of my lady my aunt's and also make as great labour as you can to my Lord Fiennes who is my lady's debtor for the 300 florins.'[22] But then, at the very nadir of his fortunes, salvation appeared in the form of a rich Pomeranian called Paul Zachtlevent.

Though he had been born in the coastal lowlands to the east of Denmark, Zachtlevent had settled in Amsterdam and made a great deal of money in the Baltic trade. Like many wealthy businessmen he held several public offices, including being schout of Amsterdam, which was similar to an English sheriff, and in the 1490s he had been part of a consortium of Baltic merchants who had financed the Warbeck plot. The pretender's capture meant his patrons had been left severely out of pocket, so when Edmund fled England, Zachtlevent had written to Henry and threatened to back the new White Rose unless the debt was settled.[23]

Unsurprisingly, Henry had refused to pay. Early in 1503, Zachtlevent therefore told Killingworth that he was prepared to aid Edmund with all his 'body and goods', provided Warbeck's loans were repaid when the White Rose recovered his throne. To convince Killingworth that the pretender's debts to him were genuine, Zachtlevent showed the steward 'certain writings under the sign and seal of the duke of York'.[24]

No doubt Killingworth thought this offer was manna from heaven, and he wasted no time in telling his master the good news, but Edmund knew he had to tread warily. One word uttered to the wrong person could lead to an agonising death, and he warned Killingworth that two of the couriers used by Zachtlevent, one called William and the other called Holland, were suspected informers. Nevertheless, Edmund was so desperate for funds he constantly asked Killingworth for updates on his progress with Zachtlevent, even though the support of a Pomeranian merchant could only take the Yorkist cause so far.[25]

What Edmund really needed was the backing of a powerful royal ally who could not be bribed or browbeaten by the king of England. The king of Hungary, Vladislaus II, was just such a monarch. Vladislaus not only loathed both Henry VII and Maximilian but had recently married the de la Poles' cousin Anne of Foix-Candale. Indeed, Maximilian had used Anne's marriage to taunt Henry's frustrated envoys during the Garter oath conference, and they had included this in the report they had sent to Henry at the end of February 1503:

> [The king of the Romans had heard that] the king of Hungary was to wed a lady out of France. How be it, [Maximilian] said, that he understood she was an Englishwoman, called the lord Kendal's daughter, whose lands he supposed to lie in England.[26]

Brandon and West's curt reply was that Anne was not English but her French ancestors had been subjects of the English Crown during the Hundred Years War.

The new queen of Hungary's late father was Gaston de Foix, whose ancestral lands lay on the French side of the Pyrenees, while her mother was the infanta Catherine, youngest daughter of the Navarrese Queen Eleanor. Anne had been brought up at the French royal court in Blois, and was thoroughly French, but her grandfather was the Gascon knight John de Foix, Vicomte de Castillon. John had been created earl of Kendal and a Knight of the Garter as a reward for his loyalty to the English Crown during the Hundred Years War.[27]

The most notable of John's exploits was his heroic defence of Bordeaux in 1446, and his connection to the de la Poles also begins at this time with his marriage to Margaret Kerdeston. Margaret's mother was Elizabeth de la Pole, sister of William, 1st duke of Suffolk,[28] but John had nailed his colours to the wrong mast. William had been impeached for losing everything that Henry V had won at Agincourt, and the thirty-first item of his indictment accused him of arranging the earl of Kendal's marriage 'for the singular enriching of his niece'.[29]

After William's impeachment, Henry VI had banished his disgraced favourite in an attempt to save his life. As we have discussed, 'Jackanapes' had been murdered on his way into exile, beginning the de la Poles' long decline. However, William's death had been equally calamitous for John de Foix.

The last battle of the Hundred Years War had been fought at Castillon, where John was vicomte, on 17 July 1453, and after this decisive French victory he had been in imprisoned in a French fortress for seven years. When he was finally released, John had fled to his English estates to avoid paying the huge ransom his captors had demanded, but England was now embroiled in the Wars of the Roses and once again he chose the wrong side. Captured by the Yorkists at the battle of Northampton, the Lancastrian earl of Kendal was placed in the custody of Richard Neville, earl of Warwick, but he was able to return to Castillon after the death of his nemesis, Charles VII, king of France.

Over the years, French tongues corrupted 'Kendal' to 'Candale', so John's descendants were dubbed Foix-Candale.[30] Thanks to the tangled web of royal marriages, his granddaughter Anne was also related to Maximilian's son Philip, archduke of Burgundy, as well as the heir to the French throne, Louis d'Angoulême, and Aragon's King Ferdinand. This impeccable pedigree meant she was groomed from birth to marry a king who could strengthen the French position against the growing power of the Habsburgs. Meanwhile, Hungary's strategic position on Austria's eastern flank made Vladislaus the prime candidate for her hand.

Annoyingly for French ambitions, Vladislaus was already married to Beatrice, a daughter of the infamous Ferrante, king of Naples, so Louis XII, Pope Alexander VI and Ferdinand of Aragon conspired with Vladislaus to have this marriage annulled. To add insult to injury, poor Beatrice had to pay the legal costs of her own annulment. Once his ex-wife was back in Naples, the forty-six-year-old Vladislaus was free to marry the eighteen-year-old Anne. His new bride was crowned queen of Hungary and Bohemia on the same day as her wedding.

Unquestionably, Anne's marriage made her an extremely attractive ally for Edmund, especially as her husband had his own reasons for disliking both the Habsburgs and the Tudors. For most of the 1480s, Vladislaus had fought Emperor Frederick III and his son and heir, Maximilian, who claimed the crowns of Bohemia and Hungary for themselves. Though the Habsburgs had lost, this long war had left the once-mighty kingdom of Hungary in no condition to repel a new threat from the Ottoman Turks.

In the spring of 1500, rumours began to circulate that a huge Turkish army was preparing to attack Austria and Hungary, so Maximilian and Vladislaus put aside their differences and formed an alliance. This was the crusade that Sir Robert Curson had resigned his captaincy of Hammes to join, but the king of England had refused to answer Vladislaus' call to arms. The miserly Henry had baulked at the cost of paying for Englishmen to fight so far from home, and his decision was vindicated when a rebellion in the

Ottomans' eastern provinces put an end to the Sultan's ambitions in the west – at least for the time being.[31]

Nevertheless, Vladislaus never forgot Henry's lack of cooperation and relations between the two kings had been strained ever since. This animosity made Hungary a very useful ally for Edmund, but he was reluctant to move to Buda, the Hungarian capital. As his Tudor rival had pointed out, the sheer distance of Vladislaus' realm from the Channel made planning any military operation involving England extremely difficult, so it was decided that Edmund should remain in Aachen while his brother led a Yorkist embassy to Vladislaus.

Now aged twenty-three, Edmund's youngest brother Richard was the ideal ambassador for this mission. By all accounts he was athletic and good looking, and though we do not know the level of his formal education his surviving letters suggest that he was far more literate than his brother. Richard had also proved his worth as a diplomat by conducting successful negotiations with another potential Yorkist ally, George the Bearded, duke of Saxony.

Interestingly, George's father, Albert, duke of Saxony, who was Maximilian's brother-in-law, had been the imperial lieutenant in Low Countries during the 1490s and in this capacity he had been heavily involved in the Warbeck conspiracy.[32] Edmund's dealings with George will be examined shortly, but first we must return to Richard's meeting with the Saxon duke's representative, William of Waldburg. These talks took place in March 1504, and following their success Richard set off for Buda,[33] but nothing more was heard from him until one of his servants suddenly reappeared in Aachen.

The valet was named Eustace and he told Edmund that he and two other servants, Allen and Derek,[34] had been summarily dismissed by Richard, who had now disappeared. The only light Eustace could shed on the matter was that Richard had been made very welcome by Queen Anne but soon afterwards had left Buda for an unknown destination. Adding to the mystery was Eustace's claim that Queen Anne had agreed to send secret letters, on Richard's behalf, to Philip, archduke of Burgundy and titular king of Castile.[35]

Incidentally, Maximilian's son claimed this title through his marriage to Joanna, daughter of the Spanish monarchs Ferdinand of Aragon and Isabella of Castile, but he was not content to be a mere consort. Though Joanna's parents were still alive, Philip was already plotting to supplant his wife as ruler of a united Spain. Furthermore, by welding Joanna's territories in Spain, southern Italy and the New World to the Habsburg lands he was due to inherit in northern Italy, the Low Countries and central Europe, Philip would create an unconquerable superpower. It therefore made perfect sense for Richard to cultivate Philip as an ally, especially as Maximillian had now turned his back on the Yorkists.

Unfortunately, such logic did not impress the increasingly nervous Edmund, especially as Richard had not seen fit to tell his brother about his attempt to use their Franco-Hungarian cousin to open a diplomatic backchannel to the next generation of Habsburgs. To Edmund, such furtive behaviour could only mean that the youngest of the de la Pole brothers was trying to set up a rival Yorkist court in Brussels, Philip's capital, and the fear that Richard had abandoned him made Edmund incandescent with rage.

'I see my lord Richard is not content, wherefore I would deal no further with him ... and methinks he will away as far as I can see,' he fumed in a letter to Killingworth,[36] though he was at pains to make clear that he harboured no ill will towards Richard's servants. 'And give fair words to Derrek as you can, to see if you can get him [to return] hither ... and also give Allen 2 florins and let him go to Acere or to Gelderland till the time comes that we be agreed with Master Pole [Paul Zachtlevent].'[37] He also instructed Killingworth to ask Oyskerk if he would go to Hungary to find out what was going on.

Though no information about Oyskerk's trip has survived, he must have succeeded in his mission because Richard reappeared in Aachen as suddenly as he had vanished. Moreover, future correspondence between the two brothers contains no hint of animosity. Either they had patched up their differences or Edmund had misread the situation completely.

Yet there *was* a traitor at the heart of the Yorkist inner circle, and his identity was about to be revealed.

9

AND AFTER ALL THINGS WERE KNOWN

On 25 January 1504, Henry VII recalled Parliament for the first time in seven years to tackle the threat of a Yorkist invasion. Accordingly, the first bill passed was an Act of Attainder that outlawed seventeen named Yorkists and 'divers other ill-disposed persons, falsely and traitorously imagining and conspiring the death and destruction of the King, our Sovereign Lord, and the subversion of this his realm'.[1]

Among those attainted were Edmund and his brothers William and Richard de la Pole, Thomas Killingworth, Sir George Neville, William Courtenay, James Tyrell, John and Thomas Wyndham, Charles Rippon, William Baskerville and the sanctuary men of Beaulieu Abbey.

It did not matter that many of those deprived of their rights and property were already cold in their unmarked graves or rotting away in the king's dungeons; their estates were seized, their surviving relatives impoverished and their descendants disinherited. Equally repressive was the catch-all clause retrospectively attainting anyone convicted of conspiring with the de la Poles since Edmund's first flight in 1499.[2] By wreaking vengeance on the dead as well as the living, Henry hoped to terrorise secret Yorkists into surrender – and his strategy appeared to score its biggest success when Sir Robert Curson was at last brought in from the cold.

'And after all things were known, opened, pacified and suppressed, he willingly returned and was received into high favour with the king, his master and sovereign lord,' wrote Edward Hall in his chronicle.[3]

Exactly when Curson abandoned the Yorkist cause is not known, but he arrived in England sometime before Easter 1504; his name not only appears in the Pardon Roll published on 5 May that year, but he is also described therein as a member of the royal household.[4] Less than a year later, on 10 April 1505, Curson's pardon was extended to cover all the offences he may have committed while in Edmund's service and he was also allowed to rent the Suffolk estates that had been seized from Sir Thomas Killingworth.[5]

All this points to Curson being Henry's man all along, his rapid return to royal favour the reward for his many years spent working undercover for the Tudors. Certainly that is what Edward Hall believed, and in his near-contemporary chronicle he congratulated Henry on using Curson's excommunication to deceive the Yorkists:

> Howbeit, the king like a wily fox, knowing the faithful intent of this Sir Robert, and intending to put him out of all jealousy and suspicion with the lady Margaret [of Burgundy], and Edmond de la Pole, caused the said earl and the said Sir Robert and five persons more to be accursed at Paul's Cross, the first Sunday of November in the seventeenth year of his reign, as enemies and rebels to him and his realm.[6]

Admittedly, Hall must have muddled his dates because other sources[7] state Edmund's first excommunication took place on the Second Sunday in Lent 1502, and earlier chronicler Polydore Vergil is a little more circumspect on the subject of Curson's treachery. In his *Anglica Historia*, which was written while Hall was still at school, Vergil says that although many people thought Curson was a double agent because he owed everything he had to Henry, 'he betook himself to the rebels enticed only by a foolish hope' and his return to England was a desperate attempt to save himself.[8]

After the passage of five centuries, we may never know for certain why Curson left Aachen but it is highly suspicious that his departure coincided with a complete reversal of Henry's policy towards the powerful Hanseatic League. Throughout his reign, Henry had tried to boost English commerce by limiting the League's activities in England. However, when he found out that Edmund was planning to use three Hansa ports on the River Ijssel – Deventer, Kampen and Zwolle – to transport an army funded by Paul Zachtlevent across the North Sea he repealed all the restrictions that he had placed on the League's trade in return for their promise not to aid the White Rose.[9]

This large slice of humble pie formed the basis of the second Act passed by Henry's parliament of 1504, and it worked. Edmund's scheme to use the Ijssel ports for his invasion never got off the ground, and there is the distinct possibly that his plans had been betrayed by Curson. Of course, the collapse of the Ijssel scheme does not prove whether Curson was a Tudor agent from the start or an opportunist who used what he knew to buy his way home once he realised the Yorkist cause was hopeless.

In any case, the Hanseatic League did not control every outlet to the North Sea. Frustratingly for Henry, the wild, windswept coast between Holland and Denmark, known as East Frisia, offered an alternative point of embarkation for Edmund's German mercenaries and this remote shoreline was under the control of the George the Bearded, duke of Saxony – at least in theory.

Before 1468, these lands had been a patchwork of fiercely independent chiefdoms but the avaricious dukes of Burgundy, and the equally covetous Holy Roman Emperors, had wanted this highly strategic area for themselves. Though the Habsburg Emperors had emerged the victors in this struggle, and appointed the uber-loyal dukes of Saxony as their viceroys, the Frisians had taken up arms against the foreign invaders and George was still fighting these rebels when Edmund appealed to him for help.

It is entirely possible that Maximilian instigated this alliance in order to use George as the conduit for the secret support he had promised; in return, Edmund would send an English army to help crush the Frisians once he was king. But someone leaked the details of this plan to Henry, and once again the prime suspect has to be Curson.

As with the Ijssel ports scheme, Henry moved quickly to block any Yorkist–Saxon pact and he contacted George the Bearded with an offer of his own *before* Richard de la Pole met William of Waldburg. If, said the Tudor envoy, George could lure the White Rose into his clutches and send him back to England in chains, Henry would provide the military support he needed for his war against the Frisians. These terms were entirely acceptable to George, and William of Waldburg baited the trap at his initial meeting with Richard.

Little knowing that he was being duped, Edmund had eagerly accepted the offer of a Saxon alliance brokered by Richard, and he agreed to meet George in person to sign the proposed treaty, but his departure was not without its own difficulties. As soon as Aachen's moneylenders, landlords and tradesmen heard that the White Rose was preparing to quit the city, albeit to seek new funds, they demanded that Richard stay behind as collateral for the brothers' debts.[10]

With his creditors mollified, at least for the moment, Edmund slipped out of Aachen, but his troubles were only beginning. His new patron was busy besieging the Frisian stronghold of Groningen, and travelling to this city meant crossing the war-torn duchy of Guelders, which was also in a state of revolt against its Habsburg overlords. Edmund therefore wrote to Guelders' duke, Charles of Egmond, asking him for safe-conduct.

Like the war in Frisia, the Guelders rebellion was a result of Habsburg attempts to add what had once been an autonomous dukedom to their rapidly expanding domains, but the seeds of this uprising had been sown thirty years earlier by Charles the Bold, duke of Burgundy.

Back in 1471, Charles of Egmond's grandfather Arnold had mortgaged his duchy to Charles the Bold in order to fund a war against his own son. When this loan could not be repaid, the duke of Burgundy had seized Guelders as payment but he had been killed, in 1477, at the battle of Nancy. As the late Charles the Bold had no male heir, both the king of France and the Habsburg Emperor claimed the Burgundian lands were theirs by right.

In the Middle Ages, such matters could only be settled by war. Five years of bloody fighting was only ended by the Peace of Arras, through which the Burgundian heartlands to the west of the Rhine were given to France while the Habsburgs retained control of the Low Countries, including the mortgaged duchy of Guelders.

This settlement did not impress the Guelderians, who declared their independence from the Holy Roman Empire and installed the bankrupt Arnold's grandson Charles of Egmond as their duke. With French help, this Charles kept his imperial foes at bay until

1502 when Maximilian decided to assert Habsburg authority in Guelders once and for all. A border dispute between Guelders and neighbouring Utrecht gave the Emperor the excuse he needed, and he promptly ordered his son Philip, archduke of Burgundy to raise an army.

For two years the *landsknecht* mercenaries employed by both sides had murdered, raped and looted their way across Gelderland, but the defeat of Louis XII in his war to drive the Aragonese out of Naples meant French could no longer support the Guelders rebels. By the spring of 1504, Charles of Egmond was in desperate need of a new ally – and it is at this point that Edmund's request for safe-conduct arrived.

Having read Edmund's letter, Charles had exactly the same idea as Henry and George the Bearded: if the White Rose could be lured into Gelderland, he could be captured and sold to the king of England in return for the resources he needed to continue his war. With a certain amount of moustache-twirling glee, Charles signed Edmund's passport and the unsuspecting earl of Suffolk crossed into Gelderland sometime in the early summer of 1504.

It had been arranged that Edmund would dine with the duke of Guelders at Hattem, on the Guelders–Frisian border, which was particularly ironic because the town's castle controlled access to the Ijssel ports that had been closed to the Yorkists by Henry's agreement with the Hanseatic League. The massive walls that gave Hattem's castle its nickname of *Dikke Tinne*, meaning 'thick battlements', were surrounded by a broad moat, and Edmund crossed the long wooden causeway that led to its entrance little knowing he was heading to his doom.

No doubt the treacherous duke of Guelders was extremely apologetic when he suddenly announced that he could not allow his English guest to leave. Before Edmund could protest, he found himself locked inside one of Hattem's impregnable towers.

In addition to its moat and 20-foot-thick ramparts, the castle of Hattem was supposedly protected by a ghostly hound, so Charles was supremely confident that his hostage would be well guarded. He was equally sure that Henry would pay whatever he asked to have Edmund sent back to England, but he was wrong. Henry was outraged by Charles's greed, telling the Aragonese ambassador to England, Rodrigo de Puebla, that he could not think of paying such a large ransom because 'it would be very derogatory to his royal authority'.[11]

The audience with de Puebla took place in late October 1504, and during these proceedings Henry also confided that, while he believed the king of France 'had a hand in the business',[12] he blamed Maximilian for having driven Edmund into the arms of French-backed rebels. Considering that Henry had done his utmost to have Edmund banished from the Holy Roman Empire his criticism is somewhat ironic, but he did have a point.

In a letter the captive Edmund sent to Sir Thomas Killingworth early in 1505, he insisted that he had only undertaken his perilous journey through Gelderland at the specific command of 'the king of the Romans', meaning Maximilian, but he ordered his steward to go to Brussels and ask the king of Castile, meaning Philip, for help.[13] Although this suggests that Edmund's relationship with Maximilian had broken down completely, it was Philip who was conducting the war against Guelders and it was he who had the military muscle to take Hattem by force if necessary.

Unhappily for Edmund, Maximilian's son had even less interest in restoring the House of York than his father; however, he was keen to prevent Henry from paying a ransom large enough to allow the Guelders rebels to continue their war. Long before Killingworth arrived in Brussels to plead his master's case, Philip had written to Henry and reminded him of the *Intercursus Magnus*, which obliged him not aid rebels against imperial authority.

'The king of England, in accordance with the alliance between Flanders and England, must assist [me], instead of lending money to the duke of Guelders, [and] I write to the king of England like a father writes to his son because a father will never do harm to his son,' writes Philip in a letter dated 29 October 1504,[14] and his delight at turning the tables on his English counterpart is clearly evident.

What Henry thought about being hoist by his own petard is not recorded, but Philip was in a conciliatory mood. He goes on to write that he will not grant an audience to Edmund's steward or his brother Richard, because he did not like to negotiate with rebels. This news must have reassured Henry that he had nothing to fear from Edmund so long as he was shut up in Hattem, but he could never forgive the Habsburgs for having allowed the White Rose to slip through their fingers in the first place.

Furthermore, Henry could not risk the Yorkist hydra growing another head by allowing Edmund's brother to remain at large in Aachen. He therefore summoned de Puebla and told him that the king of England would consider it a personal favour if the king and queen of Spain would put pressure on the king of the Romans to have Richard de la Pole arrested and sent back to England so his execution could serve as an example to others.[15]

Meanwhile, back in Hattem, news of Philip's refusal to see any Yorkist envoys reached Edmund and his response was to order his steward to approach Robert II de la Marck, the duke of Bouillon and seigneur of Sedan and Fleuranges.[16] Known as 'the Younger' to distinguish him from his father, Robert I, this powerful border lord controlled large estates in what is now southern Belgium and eastern France, and the de la Poles and the de la Marcks may have been distantly related – letters written by Richard de la Pole to de Bouillon's brother, Erhard de la Mark, bishop of Liège, are signed 'yours in consanguinity'.[17] What mattered most, though, was the duke's ties to both the French and Burgundian courts.

As Bouillon was technically imperial territory, Edmund may have hoped that the duke would use his influence with the Habsburgs to restore their faith in the Yorkist cause, but the de la Marcks had often sided with the kings of France in their frequent disputes with the Empire. It is a measure of Robert II's Francophilia that he sent his son and heir, Robert III, to be educated at the French court. Edmund's appeal to the pro-French duke of Bouillon therefore indicates that he was trying to contact the king of France in the hope Louis would persuade his client, the duke of Guelders, to release his English prisoner.

As we shall see, Louis had his own reasons for wanting to involve himself in the rapidly escalating row surrounding Edmund's kidnapping, the ramifications of which had now reached as far Scotland.

By another of those curious twists of medieval matrimony, the Scottish king, James IV, was related to both the king of England (by virtue of his marriage to Henry VII's eldest daughter, Margaret) and the duke of Guelders (through his grandmother Mary). Mary of Guelders was a daughter of the same Arnold of

Egmond who had mortgaged his ancestral lands to the duke of Burgundy, and she had played her own small part in the Wars of the Roses.

After the assassination of her husband, James II, Mary had acted as regent for her son, James III (father of the aforementioned James IV), and in this capacity she had sheltered the Lancastrian Queen Margaret of Anjou, who had fled over the Border following her defeat at the battle of Hexham. Fast-forward forty years, and once Henry VII had refused to pay the exorbitant ransom for Edmund, the duke of Guelders had decided to make use of his kinship with Mary's grandson to save his struggling rebellion.

In a letter to James IV dated 3 May 1505, the duke of Guelders asked the Scottish king to persuade Henry, his father-in-law, to agree to his demands, which he insisted were not unreasonable. He also claimed that Edmund had come to Guelders of his own free will in the hope of being granted asylum after his expulsion from the Holy Roman Empire by Henry's treaties with the Habsburgs and he only allowed Edmund into Guelders because he believed he could broker a peace between the errant earl of Suffolk and the king of England.[18]

This is the same argument that Maximilian had used to justify his granting asylum to Edmund, but Charles goes on to insist that Edmund had betrayed his host's trust by recruiting 6,000 men to overthrow England's king and hiding them in Guelders. He then insists that the ransom he had demanded was simply to cover the cost of disbanding this secret army, which had left him deeply out of pocket.[19]

Even by the standards of his day, the duke of Guelders was stretching a point. Edmund's letters to his supporters make it quite clear that he had only asked for safe-conduct across Charles's territories in order to meet George the Bearded. Certainly James saw through his blatant lies, and the long letter he wrote in reply is vehemently critical of his cousin:

> It is quite absurd for you to pretend, nor does it appear probable to us, that a needy man whom you supply with food keeps a thousand armed men in his pay. One of two things, I think you are attempting, either that the king of England

> through vain fear shall conciliate de la Pole, or that he shall expect to see him restored by your arms ... I wish, therefore, you had refrained from empty threats, and talking of his boasted power...
>
> Pray excuse me, illustrious cousin, if I deal not gently with you now. You treat kindly a rebel of England, an exile from the greater part of Christendom, to the disgust of your friends, and to the complication even of your own affairs, at a time when you ought to be conciliating princes rather than exasperating them. Is this what has come of our supplications? Is our bond of consanguinity at an end? Have your promises come to this?[20]

This relentless tirade continues over several paragraphs, and James ends by telling Charles that must rid himself of 'that perfidious man' if he wishes to recover his Scottish cousin's trust.[21] For one ruler to speak to another in such a manner was truly shocking, and it was of little comfort for Charles to know that his prisoner was having similar difficulties rallying his allies to his cause.

'Chase well the lords for money,' Edmund commanded Killingworth,[22] referring to the lords Chevers, Vele, Fiennes and Oyskerk, who were supposed to be his backers at the Burgundian and imperial courts. Edmund's many letters went unanswered, and it was not just his political situation that was becoming desperate. Although he had been treated well during his time at Hattem, his clothes were soon reduced to rags and the long-suffering Killingworth was ordered to do what he could to replenish his master's wardrobe.

'I have neither doublet, nor crest nor hose and I must buy fur for my gown ... and if you have money send me a red bonnet, with aiguillettes, like that I wore when you were here but let it be good ... for none of my friends will help me with a penny,' Edmund wrote,[23] further instructing Killingworth to pawn a valuable ring to raise the necessary funds.[24] However, when the clothing arrived he complained that the hat he had been sent lacked the aiguillettes (silk cords with ornate metal sheaths) that he had specifically requested.[25]

In another letter to his steward, Edmund remarked somewhat sniffly that Maximilian had promised to send a more suitable bonnet but this was 'a great deal too little'.[26] To be fair to Edmund, his complaint was somewhat justified. Replacement decorations for a hat were a poor substitute for the all-conquering army Maximilian had promised.

On a more serious note, Edmund admonished Killingworth for incurring unnecessary expense by sending John Parrelebene to Sir George Neville, which was against his explicit orders,[27] and for failing to keep him properly informed:

> I have nothing but you have it, and you put me to all the cost ... and yet you send not me my gear, that I thoke [took] you money to buy it. And all that I marvel not so much as of you, and of John Griffon, that you send not me word.[28]

Considering everything Killingworth had done for the Yorkist cause, this ingratitude must have been deeply hurtful. Nevertheless, the faithful steward continued to run around the Low Countries delivering Edmund's begging letters to potential supporters. On 1 July 1505, Killingworth received a passport allowing him to travel 'beyond the Zuider Zee'[29] and shortly afterwards he informed Edmund that he was travelling east to renew Warbeck's old alliance with Zachtlevent's friends in the Baltic.[30] No doubt Edmund was much cheered by this, but the rest of the news in Killingworth's letter was decidedly mixed.

On the debit side, Killingworth had been told by Zachtlevent that a shipload of supplies sent by Yorkists in England to help their exiled compatriots had been intercepted by Philip's coastal patrols. On the credit side, Killingworth had been given the schout's personal promise to send '4 ells of the best satin', along with 14 yards of velvet for a gown, with a proper sarcenet lining, and enough cloth for two pairs of hose.[31] This was the most concrete offer of help Edmund had received in many months, but Killingworth also warned his master that there were limits to Zachtlevent's generosity.

At some time during Edmund's preparations for his journey to meet the duke of Saxony, Sir George Neville and some of his servants had been sent on ahead to rent lodgings. Unfortunately,

Edmund's kidnap had left them stranded in Zwolle, across the river from Hattem, with no money, and for some unknown reason Zachtlevent not only refused to help but told Edmund 'he should not speak to him of such things'.[32] The impecunious Yorkists were duly thrown out of Zwolle, whereupon Neville had fled to The Hague. The entire affair must have given Edmund grave cause for concern.

The fact that Zachtlevent refused to pay a paltry tavern bill when he claimed he was able to finance an entire army suggested that the schout was stringing the Yorkists along merely to recover what he was owed by Warbeck. Yet this question was soon rendered moot by the sudden collapse of the Guelders rebellion.

10

TO KEEP THE BIT IN THE MOUTH OF THE KING OF ENGLAND

At the beginning of July 1505, eight hundred mercenaries fought their way into the besieged rebel stronghold of Arnhem. Their arrival was greeted with great rejoicing by the city's defenders, but the besieging imperials believed this was absolute proof that Henry was helping the Guelders rebels in defiance of the *Intercursus Magnus*. Philip therefore sent an envoy named Hermarich across the Channel with an angry demand that Henry cease giving his enemies this 'constant and considerable pecuniary assistance'.[1]

It has to be said that no other contemporary source indicates that Arnhem's reinforcements were either English or paid in English gold, but if Henry *was* supporting Guelders then Edmund would have been just as worried as Philip. Any such alliance meant it would only be a matter of time before he was sent back to England in return for Henry's aid. Even as the imprisoned earl of Suffolk and the megalomaniac king of Castile were pondering their very different situations, however, Lady Fortune was shuffling the deck and re-dealing the cards.

The last chapter in the epic story of Edmund de la Pole began when one of Philip's captains, named von Lichtenstein, led his foraging party into the vicinity of Hattem. As his force consisted entirely of horsemen, Lichtenstein had no intention of storming the town; nevertheless, the burghers of Hattem offered him their immediate surrender.[2]

To be fair to the craven city fathers, they had no way of knowing that Lichtenstein's force was not strong enough to capture Hattem. All they knew was that most of the town's garrison was away foraging for food so there was nobody left to man the walls. Such matters did not concern Lichtenstein, who happily accepted the keys to Hattem, but it was only the town that surrendered. The few men-at-arms who had been left behind to guard Edmund were made of sterner stuff than the townsfolk and they slammed shut the gates of their castle.[3]

Fearing reprisals, someone in Hattem revealed to Lichtenstein that an important English prisoner was being held inside *Dikke Tinne* and the captain was astute enough to realise the value of what he was being told. He immediately sent a message to Philip, informing him that the most valuable hostage in Christendom was ready to fall into his lap like a ripe plum, and within a matter of days Hattem's castle was under imperial siege. As soon as the understrength garrison saw that they now faced the full might of Philip's army, they too opened their gates.

High in his tower, Edmund's heart must have jumped for joy as he watched Philip's horsemen clattering across *Dikke Tinne*'s causeway to accept his gaolers' surrender; this was surely the answer to all the letters he had written. But his hopes of being released were quickly dashed. Instead of being treated as a rescued hero, Edmund was kept behind the locked door of his chamber, and the guard outside was doubled.

The problem for Edmund was that Anglo-Burgundian relations had failed to improve despite the treaties Henry had signed with Philip. According to Venetian ambassador Vincenzo Quirini, Flemish goods still could not be exported to England, and vice versa, so the trade fairs in cities such as Antwerp 'do not yield one-third of their usual profit'.[4] Moreover, Henry had recently impounded several Flemish galleys loaded with fine linen, so Philip could have wanted to use Edmund to secure the release of these ships,[5] but it is more likely he intended to use possession of the White Rose to further his scheme to steal Castile from his wife.

It had not escaped Philip's attention that the betrothal of Catherine of Aragon to the future Henry VIII had created a powerful Anglo-Spanish axis. With Henry firmly in the Aragonese camp, Ferdinand would be better placed to block Philip's planned coup in Castile, and he was also aware that his father-in-law had his own scheme to disinherit his eldest daughter.

Though Queen Isabella, who had died in 1504, was barely cold in the ground her widowed husband was already planning to marry Germaine de Foix, the young niece of Louis XII, king of France. Any son born to Ferdinand and Germaine would not only supplant Philip's wife in the Aragonese line of succession, which barred females from inheriting the crown, he would also weaken Joanna's hold on the Castilian throne.

This was because the Castilian nobles were beginning to believe the rumours being spread by both Philip and Ferdinand that Joanna was unfit to rule by virtue of her insanity. Any male heir born to Ferdinand and Germaine would, therefore, offer the Castilians an attractive alternative to Joanna 'the Mad', and once she had been removed from the throne her father planned to reign over a united Spain as regent for any son he might produce with his new wife. Likewise, Philip was plotting to use his wife's increasingly irrational behaviour to smooth his own path to power in Spain, but he planned to rule as king in his own right.

In this race to scrape the bottom of treachery's barrel, the backing of England's king would be crucial. Ferdinand should have had his nose in front, thanks to the betrothal of his youngest daughter, Catherine of Aragon, to Henry's second son. Yet the unseemly row that had followed the death of Catherine's first Tudor husband, Arthur, had soured Anglo-Aragonese relations.

In theory, the widowed Catherine should have been returned to Spain along with her dowry of 200,000 ducats, but half of this sum had still not been paid at the time of Arthur's death. Ferdinand wanted the return of both his daughter and the money that *had* been paid, but Henry had no intention of parting with 100,000 ducats. To settle the matter Catherine was duly betrothed to Henry's second son but Ferdinand refused to pay the rest of the dowry. Poor Catherine was kept a virtual prisoner in London while the row rumbled on, but as soon as Edmund fell into Philp's hands the scheming Ferdinand saw a chance to mend his fences with Henry while confounding the schemes of his surviving son-in-law.

On 22 June 1505, Ferdinand wrote to his ambassador in London telling him that Aragon would happily go to war 'against any prince, without exception'[6] who refused to deliver Edmund and Richard de la Pole to the king of England. Reading between these lines, Ferdinand wanted to use Edmund to widen the divide already separating Henry and Philip.

Back in Hattem, the White Rose knew nothing about his increasing importance on the international stage. The beleaguered earl of Suffolk the continued to write to his dwindling band of supporters, and one of these plaintive letters was addressed to Zachtlevent. The Neville affair notwithstanding, Edmund begged the schout to hasten to Hattem in the belief his imperial rank would carry enough weight to secure his release. Zachtlevent did nothing. In desperation, Edmund wrote again, claiming that Ferdinand had arranged for both his release and asylum in Spain but that Zachtlevent's money was needed to pay his immediate expenses.

> I beseech your lordship most urgently for the reason for which I have especially given you letters ... that by the providence of God and the support and protection of the most fearing Catholic king, we are to be delivered from this camp, and if I may say more truly, from this prison, and to thereafter to tarry a few days in a city near to Hattem, where it will be necessary to provide for us as soon as possible...[7]

But Edmund had failed to appreciate that any dealings with Ferdinand were fraught with danger. The mistake he made was to think that Don Juan Manuel de Villena y de la Vega, the Spanish diplomat at Philip's court with whom he was in contact, was loyal to Ferdinand of Aragon. Vega was actually a die-hard supporter of Castilian independence from Aragon, so his allegiance was to Joanna. It was he who had convinced Philip that he would have the backing of the Castilian nobility in any struggle with Ferdinand, little knowing that this would persuade Joanna's husband to pursue his own ambition to rule in Madrid instead of his wife. So, while Ferdinand had decided it was in his interest to send the de la Poles to Henry, Vega was working equally hard to keep them in the Low Countries for Philip.[8]

'The duke of Suffolk, called White Rose, is now in the power of the king of Castile, intelligence which greatly delights this country;

and his Majesty hopes by means of this individual to keep the bit in the mouth of the king of England,' the Venetian ambassador observed wryly.[9]

Unfortunately for Edmund, Richard and the Castilian party, Aragonese spies at Philip's court reported that Don Manuel had befriended the de la Poles and often dined with them. Ferdinand therefore wrote to de Puebla, his loyal ambassador in England, warning him that his counterpart in Brussels was a traitor to the kings of Spain and England for doing everything in in his power to prevent the brothers from being sent to Henry.[10]

As Edmund had little talent for this type of intrigue, he had no idea that he was at the centre of Philip and Ferdinand's tug-of-war. Zachtlevent, on the other hand, had realised what was going on, which is why he ignored Edmund's plea to come to Hattem. All the while, the youngest of the de la Poles was still under siege from his creditors in Aachen and he wrote of his plight in a short, desperate letter to his brother.

'Sir, I beseech your grace send me some[thing] what to help me with all,' Richard wrote,[11] and though no money was forthcoming Edmund did write a fawning letter to the burghers of Aachen in a desperate attempt to convince them that he had not fled to Guelders to avoid settling the brothers' debts. Having done his best to scotch these slanderous rumours, Edmund declared that he would be able to repay every florin he owed once Philip had been made fully aware of the situation.[12] He also wrote to Richard to assure him that the sun would soon shine again on the House of York:

> My dearest and most beloved brother. I commend myself to you with all the affection of my mind, certifying as to your loyalty to our cause, that I and the castle of Hattem have already been delivered into the hands of his majesty, the king of Castile. And I believe it is not unknown to you, my dearest brother, that it was on the safe conduct of Guelders' duke I proposed to cross [his] country to [meet] the Saxon duke and the count de Guidon, for certain promises had been made between us, especially for securing the debts of our creditors; for which singular reason I stood a long time in these perils; and although it was disbelieved by many, yet the truth of the matter is known to all...

> And as soon as it pleases God that I have that power (which I trust to be in a short time), I will restore you and I to liberty, and satisfy the debts of the creditors. To which matter I shall apply myself thoroughly with all my might.[13]

Such a statement indicates that Edmund was still labouring under the delusion that the archduke of Burgundy continued to have his best interests at heart. Unfortunately for Edmund, he had reckoned without Philp's inexhaustible capacity for overplaying his hand.

Once Philip had control of Edmund he had effectively won the war in Guelders because the rebels had lost their only means of securing foreign support. Without outside help, Charles had to admit defeat, and he duly agreed to swear a public oath of allegiance to Philip at Arnhem. As it would take several weeks for the protagonists to make their way to Gelderland's capital, the date for this lavish ceremony was set for 29 July 1505. In the meantime, Philip had to decide what was to be done with Edmund.[14]

On the one hand, keeping hold of the White Rose would give Philip the advantage in any future dealings with Henry; on the other, Edmund's continuing presence anywhere in Burgundian or imperial territory would violate the treaties that prohibited the Habsburgs from harbouring English rebels. Fearful that any breach of these agreements would persuade Henry to resume his support for the Guelders rebellion, but not wishing to lose the hold he had over the king of England, Philip decided to send Edmund back to Charles.

'The earl of Suffolk has been returned to the duke of Guelders, because, in accordance with the agreements between the kings of England and Castile, the latter could not keep the earl,' wrote an astonished Vincenzo Quirini on 7 August 1505.[15] He may not have seen it, but there was method in Philip's apparent madness.

The most pressing concern for Philip was to establish his rule in Castile before Ferdinand's marriage schemes came to fruition, but this could only be done if he and Joanna travelled to Spain and received the required oaths of loyalty from the Castilian cortes in person. Philip had not dared leave the Low Countries while Charles's rebellion was drenching Gelderland in blood, but now he had triumphed over the rebels he felt sure that the defeated duke of Guelders would meekly return Edmund whenever he was asked to do so.[16]

Unfortunately for Philip, Charles had merely being playing for time and in the few short weeks following the capture of Hattem he managed to rekindle his alliance with the French. King Louis XII was not a man to ignore his enemy's blunders, and he promised the duke of Guelders that he would either help him negotiate an advantageous peace or give him the men and money he needed to continue his rebellion. As ever, the price of this renewed French support was Edmund de la Pole.

According to Quirini, Louis' motive for 'obtaining possession of the earl of Suffolk' was to force Henry to cancel the annual pension of 50,000 crowns which had been imposed on the kings of France by the Treaty of Étaples, which had ended the English siege of Boulogne as well as French support for Perkin Warbeck.[17] In the thirteen years Henry's protection racket had been in operation, the French treasury had paid him the modern equivalent of £100 million, so it is hardly surprising that Louis wanted to end these ruinous payments, but he also needed Edmund to improve France's position in the international marriage market.

All the time that Edmund had been pacing the walls of Hattem's castle, the widowed king of England had been wooing the French princess Margaret d'Angoulême, sister of Francis d'Angoulême, heir to the French throne. Louis had welcomed Henry's suit because he was regretting allowing his niece Germaine de Foix to marry Ferdinand of Aragon. The childless Louis had realised that any son born to Germaine and Ferdinand would have a claim to the French throne, as well as those of Castile and Aragon, but it was too late; blocking the marriage at the eleventh hour would mean war with Spain.[18]

All Louis could do was try and limit the damage by arranging a dynastic marriage of his own, and for once the kings of England and France were in complete agreement. Early in 1505 the English ambassador to the French court, Sir Charles Somerset, recently ennobled as Lord Herbert, delivered a fifteen-page document setting out Henry's conditions for the marriage and the surrender of Edmund was at the top of this list. Louis replied that if Henry gave his solemn oath that the rebel earl would not be executed, he would force the duke of Guelders to hand him over.[19]

Though this was the same condition that Maximilian had used to frustrate England's king during their negotiations, Henry agreed. However, Louis could not resist tweaking his old enemy's nose. Knowing Henry's reputation for being careful with money, he insisted that Henry had to compensate the duke of Guelders 'for the costs and expenses for the keeping of the said de la Pole'.[20]

For his part, Charles was happy to sell Edmund to Louis in return for military aid. The first stage of this transfer was to send the luckless earl of Suffolk to Wageningen, 40 miles to the south of Hattem. No doubt Charles felt he could no longer rely on Hattem's pusillanimous citizens, whereas the heavily fortified river port of Wageningen, situated on the north bank of the Lower Rhine, had always been a steadfast supporter of Guelders' dukes. Before the bewildered Edmund could appreciate what was happening, he and his meagre possessions had been moved to a tavern in the centre of this town, and from here he could watch the new rebel army being assembled.

'The duke of Guelders has taken fifty thousand men more into the town of Waggone [*sic*] than there was,' he wrote in a letter to someone he called Don Peter.[21] Although we do not know who this man was, his Spanish title suggests he was part of de la Vega's entourage.

Elsewhere in this letter, Edmund apologised for not being able to come to Brussels in person to plead his case and explains that, although he had promised to return to Wageningen as soon as he had been granted an audience with Philip, he had been placed under house arrest by a local magistrate. Edmund also warned Don Peter that the duke of Guelders was about to restart his rebellion and that this would spell disaster for himself.

'And this meant not well for me, for if the K[ing of Castile] ... and the duke agree I care not, but if he agree not, I am as a man lost,' he wrote.[22]

In the light of this realisation, it is hardly surprising that Edmund decided to escape.

Some 15 miles south-west of Wageningen, on the banks of the River Waal, was the inland port of Tiel. If Edmund could reach it, he might be able to find a ship to take him to the Baltic, where his connections to Zachtlevent would ensure he would be given asylum. Indeed, Wageningen's magistrate may have suspected this is what Edmund intended when he refused to let his prisoner visit Brussels. If so, he should have had the White Rose watched more carefully because Edmund was able slip out of the town with surprising ease.

Though he had not a penny in his purse, or a sword on his hip, the fresh air of freedom must have tasted sweet to Edmund as he hurried down the dusty road towards Tiel. In his elation he perhaps gave a cheery wave to the company of foot soldiers marching towards him, but this was his first, and last, mistake. The presence of a stranger who spoke very little Dutch in a war zone was enough to alert the troops' captain, and when Edmund failed to give the right password he was marched straight back to Wageningen's magistrate.[23]

Unsurprisingly, Edmund found himself guarded more closely as a result of his failed bid for freedom, and a herald sent to the magistrate by the duke of Guelders to find out what had happened recommended that his English prisoner should be kept in a dungeon on trumped-up charges of drunkenness to make sure he stayed put. Fortunately for Edmund this advice was not taken, but he was confined to his inn and his English servants were removed.[24]

The worst of this situation was that Edmund was no longer able to communicate with Sir Thomas Killingworth directly and he was forced to rely on Burgundian go-betweens such as the Bastard of Oyskerk. Indeed, on 4 August 1505, Oyskerk wrote Killingworth to inform of these developments:

> I recommend myself to you, letting you know that my lord our master is brought into the town of Wagenynghe [*sic*] into the hands of the duke of Guelders, by command of the king [of Castile]. And my lord the master, commands you to keep a good manner, and not to speak too much, to all his people and servants; and you shall tell them so, for my lord our master wishes it, and is quite satisfied to be where he is; I am going to sound his whole case with the king … keep, nevertheless, a good countenance, for everything is for good by the grace of God.[25]

This cheerful optimism notwithstanding, Oyskerk also asked Killingworth how things stood with Zachtlevent and assured the steward that the schout would be granted safe passage to Wageningen to conduct any future negotiations. Once again Zachtlevent failed to accept the invitation, which was the last straw for Edmund. Having decided it was up to him to seize the initiative, he wrote to the duke of Guelders with an offer to ransom himself and, astonishingly, his proposal was accepted:

> The present writing testifies that I, lord Charles duke of Gelderland, etc., have negotiated, agreed, and promised Griffon Bastard D'Oysekerke, servant of lord Edmund, duke of Suffolk of England, that the aforesaid lord duke of Suffolk shall pay or cause to be paid to the aforesaid lord Charles de Guelders two thousand [florins] for the expenses of the same duke of Suffolk and his servants in the land of Guelders in the following form; that is to say, five hundred pieces of gold to be given within eight days immediately following the present. And within three weeks of the said eight days immediately following another five hundred in gold... the same lord Charles duke of Guelders hereby firmly undertakes and promises that immediately upon this the aforesaid lord Edmund, duke of Suffolk, shall have his full liberty, and depart from his hands and lands at the pleasure and will of the same lord Edmund without further delay.[26]

It is hard to believe that Charles intended to release Edmund and completely betray his agreement with Louis on the payment of a mere 2,000 florins, but the diplomatic situation was highly fluid. Perhaps Charles had suddenly realised he was in danger of losing control of Edmund to Philip for a second time.

While the duke of Guelders was trying to restart his rebellion with French help, Henry's plan to marry Marguerite of Angoulême collapsed. The political abyss between France and England was simply too wide to be bridged by a wedding, but Henry now feared that Louis would keep hold of Edmund if he was surrendered by Charles. There was no telling what trouble Louis would cause if the White Rose ended up in Paris, so Henry wrote to Philip and demanded that the king of Castile clear up the mess his blunder had caused.

At first Philip refused, following the same line of reasoning as his father: he could not surrender the rebel earl of Suffolk even if he wanted to because Henry's treaty had forced Edmund to be returned to the duke of Guelders. This argument cut no mustard with Henry, who insisted that because Philip claimed *he* was the lawful duke of Guelders, and Edmund was still in Gelderland, the responsibility for sending the White Rose back to England remained his.

The wretched Philip could hardly disagree, because to do so would undermine his entire *casus belli* for the Guelders' war. He therefore wrote to Charles and demanded that Edmund was returned to his custody immediately. Now it was the duke of Guelders' turn to be forced into a corner, and because the promised French aid had yet to materialise he had little choice but to obey. That said, Quirini tells us that Philip's offer of a truce and a substantial pension was enough to persuade Charles to hand over the unfortunate Edmund.[27]

At the end of October 1505, a troop of Burgundian horsemen arrived in Wageningen to take the earl of Suffolk in charge. However, he was not taken to Calais and put on a boat for England. Instead, the White Rose found himself locked up in the Burgundian castle of Namur, a fortress ten times stronger than any of his prisons in Gelderland.[28]

11

HERE AT THE KING'S COMMAND

The castle of Namur occupies a rocky promontory overlooking the confluence of two rivers, the Meuse and Sambre. This strategic headland had been fortified ever since the days of the Romans, and though the castle that existed in the early sixteenth century was smaller than those besieged by John of Austria in 1577, Louis XIV in 1692, William of Orange in 1695, French Revolutionaries in 1792 and Kaiser Wilhelm II in 1914, it was still a formidable fortress.

The only way to reach the hilltop citadel was by a narrow road winding its way up from the water's edge between two high walls. The entrance to this road was through a grim barbican, the first of three heavily fortified gateways that guarded the approach to the castle's square keep. To ensure that God added his divine protection to Namur's defences, the second-largest building behind the castle's massive curtain wall was an enormous chapel, the lofty spire of which towered above the ramparts.

Though his gaoler and gaol had changed, Edmund continued to receive some of the privileges due to royal prisoners. He was given comfortable apartments and permitted to roam freely behind the walls of the castle, but the windows of his chamber were barred and, as at Hattem, he was not allowed his own servants. Moreover, the six Burgundians appointed to attend him were ordered to report everything the prisoner did or said to the castle's governor.[1]

In spite of all this, Edmund continued to believe that the Habsburgs were his allies and he carried on writing to Killingworth, Oyskerk and the rest of his diminishing entourage in the hope that the king of Castile could be persuaded to support a Yorkist restoration. The first of these letters is dated 17 November 1505, and in it, besides making the usual exhortations for everyone to work for his release, he informed Oyskerk that he had used the last of his financial reserves to send his brother some much-needed cash.

'And touching my brother and king Henry I hope that I have put the matter in such security that my brother shall do as I would have him in everything, and that he will not neglect to do so for any danger or poverty in the world. And for the management of this thing I have helped my brother with my money,' he wrote.[2] Unfortunately for Richard, this meagre pittance was nowhere near enough to keep the wolves from his door.

On 24 November 1505, Richard wrote to Edmund and told him that Aachen's city council had tried to force Philip, rather than Maximilian, to settle the Yorkists' debts but that the king of Castile had refused pay up.[3] Worse still, the first Richard knew about this was when he was accosted in the street by his landlord, Martin, to whom he owed several months' rent. The irate innkeeper, who owned a seedy tavern known as The Pot, was flanked by several hired goons. Needless to say, the meeting did not go well for Richard.

'I gave them the best answer I could to satisfy them,' he wrote. 'At last they said to me: your brother is the falsest man that ever was of his promise, and we will do to him as he ought to be served. We will accuse him in this town and all the other towns belonging to the Empire, that all the world may know that he is a false perjured man; and we will have our money from you. And if you will not find a remedy for us, we will find one for ourselves; and therefore, make your answer to us in all haste.'[4] Richard goes on to tell his brother that Henry had persuaded Aachen's city council to put a price on his head.

> Sire, as far as I can perceive they have some encouragement to do this ... for I am apprised by two persons who are my good friends, that king Henry has desired the burgesses of

> Aix [Aachen] to deliver me 3 leagues out of the town of Aix [Aachen], and he will pay them. And so, I am advised no longer to go into the street, for if I am killed in the street, king Henry will pay them their money.
>
> I think in very truth, it was done to the end that I might be the more willing to do king Henry's pleasure, which is to abandon you, and do as he shall command me; which would be to your dishonour and mine all our lives long. Nevertheless, sire, if you will do towards me as I have deserved, and as a brother ought to do to his brother who is here in hostage for you, and I see that you do the best to ransom me according to your promise, you will find me your loyal brother, come what may.[5]

After rumours of his untrustworthiness blighted Richard's Hungarian mission the previous year, he may have felt it necessary to over-emphasise his loyalty now his brother was also a hostage. If so, his assurances did nothing to put Edmund at ease. Three days after hearing about the disturbing events in Aachen, Edmund wrote to Oyskerk and Killingworth and besides ordering them to tell the king of Castile about the shameless things being done in his name he berated his servants for persuading him that Philip was a faithful ally.

'[You] brought me word from the king [of Castile] that I should put no doubt in him. He was my good lord, and would do for me many things, but I cannot perceive it. I lie here, to my pain and shame, and also spend what I can get of my friends, and I have nothing but fair words,' he wailed,[6] but, in spite of all he had said in this and his previous letters, Edmund still believed the Habsburgs would rescue him from oblivion, if only they were told the truth.

'Wherefore me thinketh, if the king were advertised of me and my brother how we stand, and all by reason that I am here at the king's command, I put no doubt his grace will have some regard what danger my brother is in,' he wrote in a letter dated 27 November 1505.[7]

Whether Edmund was referring to Philip, as king of Castile, or Maximilian, as king of the Romans, is not entirely clear but in either case it is hard not to feel sorry for him. He may have been arrogant, vain, conceited, short-tempered and a trifle slow-witted, but Edmund's faults were no worse than those of most noblemen in his or any other age. True, he had killed a man in a drunken brawl, but he lived in violent times and he had rarely been the author of his own misfortune. It was his Yorkist blood, rather than any desire to rebel, which had made Edmund de la Pole a target for the new Tudor king, and it had been Henry's constant persecution that had caused him to flee abroad in the first place.

Similarly, it had been Henry's double agent, Sir Robert Curson, and his promises of imperial support for a Yorkist rebellion, that had persuaded Edmund to leave England for the second time, and it had been the false promises of Maximilian, Philip and the dukes of Guelders and Saxony that had led the White Rose to disaster. Sadly, none this was of much help to Edmund's impoverished supporters, and one of those whose belief in the White Rose was beginning to waver was Sir George Neville.

As Edmund's year of troubles drew to a close, Neville wrote to Killingworth from his refuge in The Hague asking if the steward believed the brothers were prepared to fight on; if they were not, he was 'very loth to tarry here without company'.[8] This letter is dated 31 December 1505, just ten days after Quirini had told the Venetian Signory that Henry had no idea his relentless campaign of threats and bribes was having its desired effect.

According to the omniscient Venetian, Henry still regarded Edmund as 'a great thorn in his eyes' and feared that 'the people of England love and long for him'.[9] Being locked up in a Burgundian castle had greatly reduced Edmund's power to topple the Tudors, but Henry knew full well that his formidable brother, Richard de la Pole, was quite capable of leading a rebellion. Indeed, the chroniclers of the time believed that Edmund's brother was the more capable leader.

In the words of Edward Hall, who was no admirer of Yorkists, Richard was 'an expert and politic man, so craftily conveyed, and so wisely ordered himself in this stormy tempest, that he was not so trapped either with net or snare'.[10] His forerunner Polydore Vergil was of the same opinion, describing Richard as 'a man of experience, who sailed the same sea so carefully that he encountered no terrible storm',[11] but neither Henry, Edmund nor Richard could guess how events in Spain would affect their respective futures.

While Edmund had been lambasting his supporters for not keeping him properly informed, the rogue Castilian diplomat Don Manuel de la Vega had been busy persuading Philip that now was time to do something about Ferdinand's attempt to deprive Joanna of her birthright. Although the late Queen Isabella had stated in her will that her husband should act as regent in the event of Joanna's absence or incapacity, Ferdinand's high-handed manner had alienated a sizeable section of the Castilian nobility and the head of the anti-Aragon party had moved quickly to make the most of this situation.

On the advice of de la Vega, Philip had written to Ferdinand and advised him 'to take himself back to Aragon' because Castile belonged to Joanna. Such arrogance was hardly likely to endear Philip to his father-in-law and Ferdinand had politely informed his daughter's husband that he was too young and inexperienced to rule Spaniards, who had to be governed differently from Belgians.[12]

Undeterred by this thinly veiled insult, Philip planned to travel to Spain under the pretext of persuading Aragon's king to join another anti-French Holy League being assembled by the newly elected Pope Julius II. Once he was safely in Madrid, Philip would rally the Castilian nobility and block Ferdinand's grand design to unite Spain under his rule as regent for the son he hoped to sire with his French bride.[13]

That said, Philip had no intention of relying on de la Vega's promises alone and he planned to overawe the Castilians with a display of Habsburg power. Accordingly, Philip recruited 2,000 battle-hardened *landsknechts* to act as his personal bodyguard and ordered his entire court, together with their wives and servants, to accompany him and Joanna on their historic voyage. Also taking ship for Spain were a number of foreign dignitaries including Vincenzo Quirini and Charles of Egmond, duke of Guelders.

After the Hattem fiasco, Philip had no intention of leaving Charles behind to restart his rebellion. He ordered the recalcitrant duke to join the Burgundian armada gathering at Middleburg, on what was then the island of Zeeland. Initially Charles had agreed, but as the day of departure drew near he sent word that he was too ill to travel.[14]

According to Quirini, who had already arrived at Middleburg, the real reason for Charles's refusal was his continued annoyance at the loss of the White Rose and the non-payment of the pension he had been promised by Philip.[15] Interestingly, he also mentions that he had discussed the king of England's proposed marriage to Marguerite of Angoulême with 'a discreet and prudent person of the court' who had insisted that Henry's true motive for the union was to 'get out of the hands of the king of Castile the duke of Suffolk, called White Rose'.

Even though Henry's wooing of Margaret had come to nothing and Charles had been forced to surrender Edmund, Quirini was convinced that Louis was still pulling the duke of Guelders' strings. As evidence for this, Quirini cites the French king's interference in the election of a new prince-bishop of Liège, which he argues gave Charles the means to ignore Philip's summons to Middleburg.[16]

The previous prince-bishop of Liège, John de Hornes, had died late in 1505, but instead of electing Philip's preferred candidate the canons had chosen Erhard de la Marck, brother of the anti-Habsburg, pro-French duke of Bouillon. Never one to miss a chance, the duke of Guelders asked Erhard for asylum, which was granted, and as soon as he was safe in Liège he began plotting yet another revival of his rebellion. Though he could no longer use Edmund to buy the French king's support, Louis was still keen to make trouble for Philip, but his adversary no longer cared about a sideshow like Guelders.[17]

As far as Philip was concerned, the only prize worth the fight was Castile and he knew his enemies in Liège and Paris could not make an alliance with England while Edmund was safely locked up in Namur. Moreover, time was of the essence because Germaine de Foix had married Ferdinand by proxy and she was now en route to Aragon. Although Philip could no longer prevent the wedding, he could still seize Castile before any child of the union was born – but Fate did not share his sense of urgency.

A lack of favourable winds kept the Burgundian ships at their moorings for more than a week, and when the capricious North Sea breezes finally changed direction, which they did on 10 January 1506, Philip's jubilance was almost palpable. While his fleet's crews raised the ships' anchors and unfurled the red and white banners of Burgundy, the court musicians played joyful music and the decks of every vessel became crowded with lords and ladies desperate to catch a last glimpse of home.[18] Philip may have been mightily relieved to be underway at last, but his courtiers knew that the voyage ahead, though relatively short, would be difficult.

To reach any of the ports on Castile's northern coast, Philip's ships would have to steer a course between the Scylla of France and the Charybdis of England. With a freshening north-east wind behind them, their initial progress was rapid. After just forty-eight hours at sea, the Burgundian fleet had reached the Isle of White. But here the weather changed for the worse.

Shortly before midnight on the second day of the voyage, the stars disappeared behind a thick bank of cloud and a furious storm descended on the forty vessels of the Burgundian armada. The sail-shredding winds and mountainous seas became so ferocious even experienced sailors began to fear for their lives, and when night fell it was so dark that a third of Philip's ships became separated from the rest. Daybreak brought no respite from the merciless gale, and the horizon was lost behind a curtain of icy, needle-like rain.[19]

Somehow the Burgundians fought their way into the Bay of Biscay, but now the winds veered around to the west and began blowing their ships back up the English Channel. Unable to make headway, the fleet's sailing masters had no choice but to turn their vessels around and run before the storm. Hour after hour, the exhausted sailors struggled to keep their battered vessels afloat and even Philip's enormous flagship, which had been built to ply the new ocean routes to India, began to founder.[20]

Realising the royal ship was carrying too much canvas, the captain ordered the mainsail to be lowered but it was too late. A particularly vicious gust tore the sail from the mast and sent it crashing to the deck. This was bad enough, but part of the sail fell into the sea and the weight of the waterlogged canvas caused the ship to list alarmingly. Within seconds, water began pouring through the starboard gunports, which were now underwater, and the frantic crew began throwing overboard guns, ammunition and anything else they could find to return the ship to an even keel. Despite their efforts, the flooding continued until a courageous sailor plunged into the freezing, churning waves to cut the sail free.[21]

It took three attempts to release the ship from the sail's grasping tentacles, and when the vessel finally righted itself the sudden movement dislodged several lanterns from their hooks. The hot oil from the shattered lamps spilled over the ship's tarred timbers and, despite the incessant rain, three separate fires broke out. Having narrowly escaped death by drowning, the crew now faced being burned alive. So desperate was the situation that even Philip had to help fight the flames.[22]

Dressed only in his doublet, the self-styled king of Castile manfully threw buckets of water over the conflagration until he was washed through an open hatch by a huge wave crashing over the ship's bow. The fall knocked Philip unconscious, and many of those aboard believed he had been killed. The thought of losing their monarch plunged the Burgundian nobles into despair, but, thanks to Joanna's careful nursing, Philip recovered his wits and scolded his terrified courtiers for their timidity, as recorded by Quirini:

> The King declared that he did not regret his own death, which was the will of God but deeply lamented first of all that he should cause the death of so many brave men whom he had brought with him, as he firmly believed that if his own ship, which was the biggest, and manned by so many pilots and skilful mariners, perished, there could be no salvation for the rest of the fleet. Secondly, he grieved to leave his children orphans at so tender an age; and thirdly, he deplored the ruin and confusion that might ensue in his territories.[23]

Whether Philip ever made such a grandiloquent speech is, perhaps, unlikely but Quirini had a point. The death of the Holy Roman Emperor's son would have altered the balance of European power in a way that could only end in war, but such concerns were a matter for the future. Though Philip and the heroic sailor had saved their ship from being dragged to the bottom or burned to the waterline, the entire Burgundian fleet was still in grave danger.

Three days of merciless winds and punishing seas had driven Philip's armada far to the north and ahead of them was the rocky coast of Cornwall. Fearing being driven onto the jagged teeth of the Lizard, Philip's captains decided to head for shelter as soon as the sun rose. At dawn, however, there was still no sign of land because the treacherous Cornish coast was hidden behind a blanket of fog.[24]

We can only imagine the dismay felt by the Burgundian courtiers as they faced this new terror, but the Flemish sailors were veterans of the English Channel and their superb seamanship guided those ships still afloat into the natural harbours at Falmouth, Plymouth and Dartmouth. Four of the armada's storm-tossed vessels found shelter in Devon's Tamar estuary and three limped into the mouth of the nearby River Dart, but most of the Burgundian fleet found sanctuary in the deep waters of Cornwall's River Fal. Among the latter was Quirini, yet he was far from grateful.

'I am at the extremity of the island, 250 miles from [South] ampton, in a wild spot where no human being ever comes, save the few boors who inhabit it,' he moaned,[25] but at least he was alive. Three of Philip's ships had sunk within sight of safety, and though most of the crews had been rescued, there was no sign of the vessel carrying their king.[26]

For three days, the survivors stranded in Falmouth tried to learn what had happened to the royal party but news travelled slowly in England's far west, even without the most fearsome gale in living memory transforming every road into a morass. Eventually, an exhausted, mud-spattered messenger arrived and told the anxious Burgundians that their prayers had been answered. Philip and Joanna's ship had found shelter in the lee of Portland Bill, a rocky headland on the Dorset coast, 150 miles to the east of Falmouth.

The Burgundian flagship had dropped anchor off Melcombe, a small fishing village which is now a suburb of Weymouth. While the locals were used to seeing strange fishing boats in their bay, the sudden appearance of one of the largest foreign warships afloat caused panic. Despite the ship's empty gunports and tattered rigging, the villagers believed they were under attack so they grabbed whatever weapons came to hand and hurried to drive off the invaders.[27]

From the deck of Philip's ship, the Flemish crew watched the farmers and fishermen gathering on the sand with growing concern. They knew only too well that castaways were easy victims for the wreckers and pirates who infested both sides of the Channel coast and the large crowd brandishing boathooks and pitchforks only increased their anxiety. Moreover, the trade war with Flanders was still simmering; even if they survived the murderous locals, they risked being interned and held for ransom by the Tudor authorities.

Fearing the worst, Philip's counsellors strongly advised him not to leave the safety of his ship until a truce had been negotiated, but the king of Castile was determined to go ashore and take his wife with him. Nothing his captains said could persuade the headstrong Habsburg to stay on board, and they watched in consternation as he and Joanna set off for *terra firma*.

After their brush with death, we can hardly blame the landlubbing king and queen of Castile for having had enough the sea, and as it happens luck was with them. Among those who had come to investigate were two local landowners, Sir Thomas Trenchard and Sir John Carew, and they not only realised to whom the ship belonged, they had brought with them enough armed retainers to prevent the foreigners from being lynched.

Having pacified the mob, Trenchard invited Philip and Joanna to stay with him while they recovered from their ordeal, but his offer was not made out of kindness. Both Trenchard and Carew knew that every effort had to be made to keep these supremely important castaways on English soil until Henry could be informed.

The king of England, they insisted, would never forgive them if they allowed their royal guests to leave without receiving a proper welcome. After all, the queen of Castile was sister to the dowager princess of Wales, and they felt sure that Henry would hurry down from Windsor the moment he knew that his illustrious relatives had arrived in his realm. At most, they added, Philip would have to wait no more than two or three days before he could continue his voyage.

Their guest was not fooled for a moment.[28] Even Philip knew that Henry could not possibly make the long journey to Dorset in so short a time, and when he glanced over his shoulder he noticed that the rowing boat that had conveyed the royal party to shore had mysteriously vanished. Slowly it dawned on Philip that he risked creating an international incident if he protested further, and he reluctantly accepted Trenchard's hospitality.

The journey to Wolfeton House, Sir Thomas Trenchard's fortified manor near Dorchester, was short – less than 10 miles – but the moment Philip passed through the squat, barrel-shaped towers of its gatehouse, which still stand today, he must have known that he was now in exactly the same predicament as Edmund de la Pole. While Philip pondered the irony of his situation, a swift rider galloped away to inform the king of England that Fate had presented him with the perfect opportunity to solve his Yorkist problem once and for all.

12

TILL HE MIGHT POSSESS HIS PREY

As soon as Henry learned about the shipwreck, he sent messengers to Carew and Trenchard urging them to keep hold of Philip and Joanna until arrangements could be made to bring them to him. A short while later, the earl of Arundel, accompanied by 300 torch-bearing noblemen, arrived at Wolfeton to escort the royal castaways to Windsor. However, while Philip was happy to make the trip, Joanna was left behind, probably at her husband's insistence.[1]

The king of Castile reached Henry's court on 31 January 1506, and for the last 5 miles of his journey he was accompanied by the prince of Wales and five hundred 'fine earls and diverse lords and knights'. Half a mile from Windsor, Philip was met by Henry himself and conveyed to his apartments in the castle with all due pomp and ceremony.[2]

The warmth and lavishness of Philip's welcome to Windsor contrasted sharply with Edmund's confinement, yet the contrast in the gilding of their cages could not disguise the fact that both men were prisoners. Yet despite Henry's eagerness to use Philip's misfortune to secure the return of the White Rose, he did not raise the matter for almost a week. Until then, the two monarchs hunted deer, watched horses baited and played tennis. During one match Philip gave the marquess of Dorset an advantage of 15, which may be the first recorded use of a handicap in the game.[3]

Eventually the questions of when and how Philip would be allowed to leave had to be addressed, but although the main item on Henry's agenda was Edmund de la Pole, he first insisted on revising the terms of *Intercursus Magnus*. According to Henry, the treaty had to be updated because the archduke of Burgundy was now the king of Castile and Philip was so desperate to reach Spain he was prepared to agree to anything. The hastily concluded agreement was therefore so favourable to the English it was dubbed the *Intercursus Malus*, or 'terrible treaty', by the Flemish merchants whose livelihoods had been ruined.[4]

Naturally, these trade talks were only the first round in Henry's bruising diplomatic prize-fight and before broaching the matter of Edmund he ramped up the pressure by investing his guest with the Order of the Garter. As with Maximilian, Henry hoped that taking the oath not to support the king of England's enemies would force Philip to surrender the White Rose, but this time, by holding the investiture ceremony *prior* to raising the matter of Edmund, he believed he had avoided the diplomatic minefield created when he made a similar offer to the Emperor. Unfortunately for Henry, Philip knew how to play the game just as well as his father.

At first all went well. Philip swore the Garter oath in Windsor Castle's Chapel of St George on 9 February 1506, and he signed the revised *Intercursus Malus* while still seated in his Garter stall,[5] but accounts differ regarding the subsequent discussion over Edmund.

The contemporary, though anonymous, *Narrative of the Reception of Philip, King of Castile*, insisted that Philip volunteered to surrender Edmund without being asked.[6] However, later chroniclers, such as Vergil, Hall and Bacon, maintained that Philip raised the same objections as Maximilian. In other words, he had no jurisdiction over Edmund and, even if he did, he could not send to his death a man under his protection because this would violate the Garter oath to protect a fellow knight.[7]

Considering everyone knew that Edmund was being held in Philip's castle of Namur, the first of these objections was ridiculous and the second was negated by Henry promising to take a public oath to forgive Edmund 'every injury and restore him to his confiscated property'. This guarantee was more than enough to satisfy Philip, and he agreed to send a messenger to Namur with a warrant for Edmund's extradition,[8] but the White Rose had realised that the game was lost at least two weeks *before* his captor had set sail for Castile.

On 26 December 1505, Sir Thomas Killingworth and another of Edmund's servants, John Griffiths, had met with Henry's representative John Chamberlain. This meeting was held in secret and without Philip's knowledge, and by its end Edmund had agreed to renounce his rights to the throne and return home voluntarily if everything he had lost was restored. A month later, on 24 January 1506, the earl of Suffolk issued a proclamation in which he announced he had decided to end his struggle to restore the House of York:

> Be it known to all princes, nobles and true Christian men by this present writing that we Edmund, duke of Suffolk of England, on the 26th day of December passed, had certain communications and words touching the troubles that are in the realm of England by reason that it standeth betwixt the king of England and me.[9]

The fact that Edmund was no longer in a position to decide his own fate, let alone that of England, was conveniently ignored.

Little knowing that he had been overtaken by events, Edmund issued another diplomatic *communiqué* four days later in which he set out the conditions by which he would end his campaign to overthrow the Tudors. This document is dated 28 January 1506, and it offers a unique insight into Edmund's state of mind at this time.

Somewhat understandably, the first condition insisted that Henry 'withdraw from the said duke his high displeasure and to put clearly out of his heart such grudge and malice as his grace hath against the said duke'.[10] Furthermore, in return for being restored to the rank and estates held by his grandfather and father, Edmund graciously declared he was willing to accept the king's pardon and promised to loyally serve Henry and his heirs.

The second and third conditions demanded the return of several lucrative estates that had been given to loyal Tudors specifically to reward them for hounding Yorkists. These included the castle of Orford in Suffolk, which had been given to Lord Willoughby for presiding over the purge of de la Pole retainers in East Anglia, and the manor of Filberdes, in Berkshire, which had been Sir Richard Guildford's reward for successfully persuading Edmund to return from his first exile in St Omer.[11]

The fourth condition is full of unintentional irony because it required Henry to pressurise Philip into ordering Edmund's release. Evidently, Edmund had no idea that his gaoler was himself a prisoner and the king of England was busy applying the diplomatic thumbscrews to achieve exactly what he was asking.

At the same time, Edmund is acutely aware of his own impotence and he implores Henry to show mercy to his wife, his daughter and his supporters, whether or not Philip granted him his liberty.[12] In particular, he asked that his wife, Margaret, be allowed to receive the revenues to which her husband would be entitled if he was pardoned yet remained Philip's prisoner, or to inherit the de la Pole estates should he die in Namur. Likewise, Edmund asked that his daughter, Anne, be allowed to inherit all the property seized from the de la Poles under their various Acts of Attainder if he died without siring a male heir.[13] Incidentally, Anne became a nun around this time but she entered the Order of Minoresses without Aldgate under the name of Elizabeth, perhaps to disguise the fact she was the child of an attainted rebel.[14]

The final condition made by Edmund was to insist that Henry pardon all those who had been punished for supporting the Yorkist cause and allow the heirs of those who had died in his service to inherit any property that had been seized by the Crown. Among those specifically named by Edmund as being worthy of a pardon were his brother William, who was entirely innocent, and Sir George Neville, who was entirely guilty, but Richard de la Pole's name is conspicuous by its absence.[15] Perhaps Edmund hoped his youngest brother would continue the struggle, or maybe Richard had simply refused to surrender.

Whatever Edmund and Richard's intentions, Killingworth and Griffith delivered the earl of Suffolk's terms to Chamberlain at the end of January 1506 but it was already too late. Philip was made a Knight of the Garter on the 9 February 1506 and that same day, in addition to the trade agreement dubbed the *Intercursus Malus*, he signed a second treaty that created a military alliance between England and Castile and formalised Philip's verbal agreement to hand over Edmund.[16]

The treaty's lengthy clauses prohibiting support for each other's rebels are nothing new, but what is surprising is that Philip signed the Anglo-Castilian alliance on behalf of his father, as well as himself, and he promised that the Emperor would ratify it within four months.[17] He had also exceeded his authority by making an alliance with Castile in Joanna's absence because, for all his pretentions, Philip was still only a king consort. In other words, any treaty he negotiated would have no legal force until it had been signed by Castile's queen regnant, Joanna, but she had been left in Dorset.[18]

Much to Philip's annoyance, Joanna had to be brought to Windsor with all speed, but he insisted that his wife used a side entrance to the castle when she arrived and he was even heard to mutter that he would rather not meet her at all. Joanna, on the other hand, was looking forward to seeing her sister, Catherine of Aragon, whom she had not met for several years, but neither Philip nor Henry wanted the sisters to discuss their poor treatment at the hands of their respective spouses and in-laws. Henry made sure that his daughter Mary Tudor and a gaggle of ladies-in-waiting were always present when Joanna and Catherine were together, and their reunion lasted just one afternoon.[19]

As soon as Joanna had ratified the Anglo-Castilian alliance, which she did on 12 February 1506, she was sent back to the West Country. Not so for Philip, however, as Henry insisted his captive accompanied him to Richmond to enjoy yet another week of lavish entertainment. Knowing only too well the Habsburgs' propensity for going back on their word, Henry was determined keep the king of Castile in England until Edmund had crossed the Channel; as Edward Hall put it, his goal was 'to protract the time till he might possess his prey'.[20]

While three of Philip's gentlemen journeyed to Flanders to fetch Edmund,[21] the king of Castile had to endure another round of jousts, feasts and solemn church services, but the most insidious of Henry's distractions was a tour of London. Travelling by river to Barking Abbey, Henry proudly showed Philip all the points of interest including Baynard's Castle, which had been the House of York's chief residence during the Wars of the Roses. In recent years, Henry had transformed this crumbling ruin into a luxurious palace for the singular purpose of hosting state visits[22] and this not-so-subtle metaphor was followed by a ceremonial cannonade as the royal barge passed the Tower of London.

Again, this honour was loaded with hidden meaning; for a start it reminded Philip that Henry had not forgotten his guest's fear of entering walled cities.[23] On a more sinister note, the gunfire served as a warning to Philip that he would join William de la Pole, who was still incarcerated behind the Tower's walls, if he failed to deliver Edmund. After this chastening experience, the king of Castile was finally taken to Barking Abbey where Edmund's great-aunt Katherine de la Pole had once been abbess. Her role in raising Henry's father and uncle, Edmund and Jasper Tudor, has already been described and it cannot be a coincidence that Philip's journey through London finished where the Tudor dynasty began.

By the end of his tour, Philip would have been left in no doubt that the Yorkist de la Poles were yesterday's men and England's future belonged to the Tudors, but at least the king of Castile's fate was in his own hands. Poor Edmund was still at the mercy of his Habsburg gaoler, yet Namur's prisoner had become almost bullish about his future once he had made his momentous decision to abandon his quest for the throne.

'But it goes well my father,' Edmund wrote in a letter to his kinsman Erhard de la Marck, and he goes on to recall a pleasant visit he had made to the newly elected bishop's brother, the duke of Bouillon, during which he had played tennis and drunk much ale.[24] The timing of this letter, which is dated 28 January 1506, is significant because it was written on the same day as Edmund's articles of surrender were published. Therefore Edmund's request that Erhard forward his baggage, and his promise to send 'better tidings' in the next fifteen days, suggests that he fully expected to be freed in the very near future. Sadly, Fate had other ideas.

In a despatch sent to the Venetian Signory on 17 March 1506, Quirini told his masters that when the three men Philip had sent to take Edmund to England arrived at Namur, the governor of the castle had refused to release his prisoner into their custody. Quirini also reported that the governor had been acting on the orders of the Great Council of Mechelen, which was the nearest thing Burgundy had to a parliament.[25]

The same informant told Quirini that the Great Council had become deeply concerned by Philip's extended stay in England

and his signing of the *Intercursus Malus*. The councillors were not only appalled at the unfavourable terms in the revised trade agreement, they feared Henry was planning to keep Philip in England permanently, in order to wring further concessions from him in the future. To counter this, they decided to prevent Edmund leaving Namur until the hated treaty had been torn up and Philip was safely on his way to Spain.[26]

Unfortunately for Mechelen's Great Council, Philip's eyes were firmly fixed on his wife's crown and the only thing preventing his departure for Spain was their refusal to release his English hostage. The irate Philip therefore sent the councillors a strongly worded rebuke and, in return, Henry allowed him to set off for Falmouth where his wife and fleet were waiting. As far as Philip was concerned all should have been well, but within hours of leaving Richmond he fell ill, requiring him to spend several days in the infirmary of Reading Abbey.[27]

Philip had doubtless feasted too hard and too long during his time as Henry's guest, but his illness was so sudden that there were many in Mechelen who suspected poison. Edmund's destiny might have been very different had the king of Castile died, but he soon recovered, and once he had resumed his journey, the Great Council of Mechelen handed the earl of Suffolk to the men who would take him to Calais.

The journey along the muddy roads of Flanders and Picardy proceeded without incident, and Edmund arrived in the English enclave on the eve of St Patrick's Day 1506, but the usual contrary winds delayed his departure for Dover for more than a week.[28] The uncooperative weather also prevented Philip from leaving Falmouth, and the Burgundian armada did not reach Spain until St George's Day 1506, but by that time Edmund was safely in England.

The task of escorting the Tudors' most dangerous enemy since Warbeck was given to Sir John Wiltshire, Sir Henry White and sixty fully-armed soldiers from the city's garrison.[29] Yet Edmund had every reason to be optimistic when he boarded a ship bound for the home he had not seen for five long years; after all, Henry had sworn on the Holy Bible and a stack of consecrated wafers that he would spare the earl of Suffolk's life and restore his lost rank and titles.[30] Nevertheless, the first glimpse of Dover's White Cliffs must have made him nervous.

Half a century earlier, a ship carrying Edmund's grandfather William de la Pole, 1st duke of Suffolk, into exile had been ambushed by his enemies within sight of these cliffs. The hated 'Jackanapes' had been captured, condemned to death by a sham trial and the sentence carried out in the ship's rowing boat. William's headless body had been found on the sands beneath the South Foreland, and Edmund's sense of foreboding must have increased when he saw Sir Thomas Lovell, the man who had trapped the Tyrells, waiting for him at Dover.[31]

After so many betrayals by so many princes, Edmund must have suspected that Henry would not keep his word, and his worst fears were confirmed when Lovell informed him that his destination was to be the Tower after all. At least the White Rose was not paraded through the streets of London like his predecessor, Warbeck, but throughout the journey Edmund's mind must have been filled with the thought of what had happened to Sir James Tyrrell.

Back in 1501, Lovell had tricked Tyrell into giving himself up and Henry's torturers had forced him to confess that he had arranged the murders of Edward IV's sons. Now Edmund was subjected to a similar interrogation, which was described by Vergil as 'exhaustive'.[32] Such a euphemism likely means that Edmund was also tortured into naming those who had offered him support during his years of exile. Certainly, Sir Thomas Green and the 5th Baron Bergavenny were 'hastily flung' into the Tower suspiciously soon after Edmund's return.[33]

It may be recalled that Green had been a close friend of Sir James Tyrell, and he had dined with Edmund shortly before his second escape. Though the charges against him were quickly dropped, Green died before he could be released.[34] The reasons for Bergavenny's arrest were equally spurious. True, he was descended from the Yorkist matriarch Cecily Neville and he had been one of Edmund's jousting partners in the 1494 tournament, but his loyalty had never been in doubt until Edmund pointed an accusing finger.

The incident that put Bergavenny in serious jeopardy had occurred at the start of the Cornish Rebellion, when Henry had been on his way north to punish the Scots for sheltering Perkin Warbeck. As London had been denuded of troops for the northern war, Henry had to buy sufficient time for the royal army to march south, so he ordered Edmund and Bergavenny to block a key bridge over the Thames at Wallingford.

Despite his East Anglian title, Edmund's principal seat was at Ewelme, which was very close to Wallingford, and Bergavenny owned vast estates in Kent and Sussex. Together, the two lords managed to raise a sizable force to defend Wallingford's bridge but the rebels never came.[35] When the Cornishmen discovered that the area was heavily defended, they decided cross the Thames at Staines, 30 miles to the south.

As soon as Henry learned of this, he had sent orders to Edmund and Bergavenny to move their men to Staines and deny its bridge to the rebels, but the courier hurriedly dispatched to Ewelme was in for a shock. Instead of sharpening their weapons or drilling their men, he was surprised to find the earl of Suffolk and the 5th Baron Bergavenny in bed together.[36]

Whatever the scurrilous gossips may have thought, the two cousins were probably doing no more than sharing a billet, and the real scandal was that Bergavenny had hidden under the bedsheets to avoid been recognised by the courier. At the time, nothing was said but the transcript of the proceedings against Bergavenny in 1506 resurrected this long-forgotten incident and a strange conversation between the baron and the earl is quoted *verbatim*.

'Why doth thou shrink and hide thyself so? Art thou afeared?' Edmund is reported to have said to Bergavenny once the bemused courier had left.

'Nay, but I would not that he saw me here, but if a man will do what he ought, what will you do now it is time?' Bergavenny is supposed to have replied.[37]

The inference is that Bergavenny was on the point of throwing in his lot with the Cornish rebels, perhaps with a view to putting himself on the throne, and he expected his cousin to support his *coup d'état*. However, instead of answering Bergavenny's question, Edmund had hidden his guest's shoes while he saddled his horse and galloped away to join the king.[38] At this, Bergavenny changed his mind, and he too fought for Henry when the rebels were defeated at Blackheath. But this begs the question: who revealed what was said at Ewelme?

As there were no outside witnesses to this conversation it must have been Edmund who told the story during his interrogation, yet Henry did not believe a word of it. According to Vergil, the king accused Edmund of deliberately lying in order to sow seeds of discord among the Tudor nobility,[39] which was the exactly same response that had caused Sir Richard Nanfan and Sir Hugh Conway such discomfort. Nonetheless, Bergavenny was fined £70,650 for keeping an illegal private army and banned from entering any county bordering London without the king's licence. Though this colossal sum was later reduced to a more realistic £5,000, Bergavenny had learned a very valuable lesson – others would not be so lucky.[40]

After the chastened Bergavenny was released, his place in the Tower was taken by another prominent scion of the House of York: Thomas Grey, 2nd marquess of Dorset. Grey, who had inherited the Dorset title in September 1501, was a grandson of Elizabeth Woodville and his father had dined with Edmund shortly before his escape, yet he should have quite been safe from persecution by virtue of his marriage to the king's cousin Eleanor St John.

It is a measure of the younger Dorset's standing with Henry that he had been granted the lucrative wardship of Wyverstone Forest, in the de la Poles' Suffolk heartlands, the year before Edmund's surrender, so the suddenness of his fall suggests that he had only been unmasked as a secret Yorkist after another 'exhaustive interrogation' of the White Rose. This time, Henry believed the allegations and Dorset joined the earl of Suffolk, William de la Pole and William Courtenay in the Tower.

Yet even now, England's first Tudor king could not sleep soundly. The imprisonment of Edmund, the two Williams and Dorset may have broken the back of the Yorkist cause, but the stem of the White Rose still bore its sharpest thorn. Its name was Richard de la Pole.

13

TO CAESAR'S GREATEST DISPLEASURE

The omission of Richard de la Pole from Edmund's articles of surrender indicates that the two brothers had decided to go their separate ways sometime before January 1506, but it is not known if their parting was amicable. Richard may have decided to keep the Yorkist torch burning against his brother's wishes, or he may have simply distrusted Henry. In either case, Edmund journeyed to Calais without his brother and Richard found his own path to safety.

After the disasters of the last few years the de la Poles had few allies left on the Continent, but one of those who had kept faith with them was Erhard de la Marck. Despite offering sanctuary to Edmund's nemesis, the duke of Guelders, the recently enthroned bishop of Liège was happy to do what he could for Richard, especially if it meant embarrassing the Habsburgs.[1]

Reading between the lines of Edmund's letters from Namur, it was Erhard who pacified the de la Poles' irate creditors so Richard could leave Aachen, but there was no question of him finding a permanent refuge in Liège. As Richard's recent confrontation with the landlord of The Pot had shown, Henry's tentacles had a long reach – and the perils of challenging a ruling monarch were graphically illustrated by the sudden death of Castile's putative king.

At first, Philip's attempt to usurp his wife had proceeded exactly as he had planned. Lengthy talks with Ferdinand had produced an agreement whereby Philip would rule Castile as king regnant in place of the supposedly mentally incapacitated Joanna, but his triumph was suspiciously short-lived. Less than two months after the two kings had signed the Treaty of Villafáfila, which disinherited Joanna, Philip was in his grave. So convenient was his death for Ferdinand that many suspected that the king of Aragon had ordered his son-in-law poisoned.

These rumours notwithstanding, the unexpected demise of the Emperor's son was terrible news for Edmund and Richard. Even though Philip had happily thrown the earl of Suffolk to the Tudor dragon the moment it suited him, the victorious Ferdinand was no friend of the Yorkists. Indeed, Don Manuel de la Vega, the only Spaniard who wanted to keep the de la Poles out of England, ended up in a dungeon on charges of treason.[2]

With no hope of finding a refuge in Spain, or the Empire, Richard had to look elsewhere for sanctuary yet he dared not approach the French king, who was the traditional protector of Englishmen fleeing their persecutors. This was because Louis had already tried to buy Edmund from the duke of Guelders and sell him to Henry in exchange for an advantageous alliance. Fortunately for Richard, the de la Poles' cousin Anne of Foix-Candale was proving to be a most effective queen of Hungary, and her husband had his own reasons to loathe both the Tudors and the Habsburgs.

As mentioned previously, the king of Hungary's antipathy towards his German cousins was rooted in the war he had been forced to fight with the previous Emperor, Frederick III, and his son and successor, Maximilian, in order to inherit his throne. Although the Habsburgs had suffered a crushing defeat, the imperial eagle continued to hover greedily over the middle reaches of the Danube,[3] and to compound Vladislaus' woes the Turkish Sultan, Bayezid II, was determined to add Hungary to the Ottoman Empire.

Again, we have already seen how Henry was content to let Sir Robert Curson go to Hungary but he was less keen to send an entire English army to the Danube on the grounds it would cost too much. Considering Vladislaus' old enemy Maximilian had happily joined his anti-Ottoman alliance, the king of England's refusal to fight the Turks had been taken as a calculated insult. Consequently, Henry's attempts to stop Yorkists finding a refuge in Hungary met with a frosty response.

Two years after the Ottoman scare, in 1502, Henry had sent Dr Thomas West to demand that Vladislaus sign a treaty requiring him to turn away any Yorkist refugees who may appear on his border.[4] Though the Ottoman threat had receded, it had not disappeared, so the king of Hungary repeated his request for English help to fight the Turks in return for expelling English rebels. Vladislaus had even sent his envoys to England with his offer of an alliance, but Henry had rudely told them they should have stayed at home and 'those who are unable to make war upon the Turk should make peace; so no assistance will be obtained'.[5]

The king of Hungary had responded to this outrageous snub by sending Dr West back to England with a similar diplomatic flea in his ear, and as a result of Henry's short-sightedness Richard de la Pole had found a warm welcome in Buda when he first visited Vladislaus' court in 1504.

As the situation had not improved in the intervening years, Richard had every reason to believe he would be safe with Vladislaus now that he had to leave Aachen permanently, but by this time both Maximilian and Philip had signed the treaties requiring imperial officers to arrest Yorkists on sight. Sadly, no account of Richard's perilous journey has survived but we know he managed to evade Henry's carefully constructed web and he reached Vladislaus' court in the autumn of 1506.[6]

We can only imagine the huge sense of relief Richard must have felt as he entered Buda's castle high above the Danube. In recent years, Italian craftsmen had built shady loggias, marble balustrades and walled gardens that had transformed this once grim gothic fortress into a glittering Renaissance palace. Yet the colossal bronze statue of Hercules that greeted visitors to Vladislaus' court was festooned in black crepe when Richard arrived, and he could scarcely believe his ears when he was told by a grieving courtier that Queen Anne was dead.

Although she was only twenty-two years old, the Hungarian queen had died giving birth to a son, the future Louis II, and she had been laid to rest just a few weeks before her English cousin's arrival. Such a cruel turn of events must have made Richard fear for his future.

He had no need to worry. As Anglo-Hungarian relations were still at an all-time low, Vladislaus had no hesitation in refusing

Henry's demand for Richard's extradition when it arrived. Indeed, the Tudor envoys, hastily dispatched from the English embassy in Venice, were not even allowed to disembark when their ship docked at a port in Hungarian-controlled Croatia. Moreover, to underline his annoyance with Henry, Vladislaus gave Richard permission to stay in Hungary for as long as he wished as well as a handsome pension on which to live.[7]

At this point, the story of the last Yorkists could have ended in Buda. With a wealthy and reliable patron, Richard could have lived out his days in comfort. But Philip's sudden death in far-off Castile had restored the Yorkists' political value, and the first person to take advantage of this was Sir Thomas Killingworth.

Even before Edmund left on his final journey to Calais, it was feared that the untrustworthy Henry would renege on his oath to pardon the de la Poles. It was therefore agreed that Killingworth would remain in Aachen in case he had to persuade Maximilian to rekindle the fight for a Yorkist restoration. This proved to be a wise precaution because it soon became clear that although Henry had no intention of executing Edmund, he would never allow him to go free. Enraged by Henry's duplicity, Killingworth hurried south to seek an audience with Maximilian, who was spending the summer touring his Alpine domains.

In the post-Philip world, Maximilian was prepared to listen to Killingworth and he assured him that the utmost would be done to force Henry to abide by his own treaties and oaths. Bolstered by this, Killingworth remained with the imperial court as it journeyed through the Tyrol and Bavaria, but as the weeks dragged on with no noticeable improvement in Edmund's situation he began to suspect that the Emperor was up to his old tricks of promising everything yet delivering nothing.[8]

When Maximilian stopped at Bolzano, in northern Italy, Killingworth was told that any action taken on Edmund's behalf would have to be done in secret. By the time the imperial juggernaut reached Constance, in southern Germany, Maximilian was always too busy to see him. The steward was forced to submit any new petitions through an intermediary, the lord chancellor of Sarentiner, which was exactly the same pattern of prevarication that he and Edmund had experienced in Imst six years earlier.[9]

Nevertheless, Killingworth had learned from one of the French king's chamberlains that Louis was still interested in finding a Yorkist stick with which to beat his English enemies. This man's name was Argenteyn and he also claimed that Queen Anne's death had made Richard so fearful for his future in Hungary that he was seriously considering Louis' proposals.[10]

As far as Killingworth was concerned, this was worrying news indeed. To begin with, there was a strong possibility that Louis' offer of asylum was a trap whereby Richard would be sent to England in exchange for an Anglo-French alliance. Alternatively, if Louis was truly backing a Yorkist invasion led by Richard, Henry would have Edmund executed in retaliation.[11]

With these thoughts preying on his mind, Killingworth begged the Emperor to let him to go to Hungary to persuade Richard to abandon his negotiations with the French and renew the brothers' previous pact with the Habsburgs, but once again the steward had been overtaken by events. To Killingworth's utter astonishment, he was politely informed that his proposed trip was unnecessary because Richard had already made contact with the imperial court and arrangements were being made for him to be transferred to a castle in Austria.

To compound his humiliation, Killingworth was told to go back to Aachen and wait there until negotiations with Richard had been concluded, but the steward desperately needed to do something to restore his battered reputation. He therefore decided to visit Richard in defiance of Maximilian's order, but by the time he set off for Hungary the Alpine passes were blocked by winter snow.[12]

To reach Buda, Killingworth had to take a circuitous route via Ulm and he arrived in this city early in February 1507. Here, quite by chance, the exhausted steward bumped into Derek van Riet, who had found a position with Richard after Edmund's surrender. Riet was delivering Richard's letters to Maximilian, but he and Killingworth discussed the de la Pole situation for the next two days. Eventually, they decided that the steward's plan to go to Hungary to help Richard resist the siren songs of the French was a good one.[13]

Once they had agreed to work together, the two men went their separate ways. Killingworth arrived in Buda on 1 March 1507, but a few weeks later he was back in Constance trying to explain why he had not gone to Aachen as instructed.[14] The hapless steward set out his reasons for disobeying the Emperor in three official petitions, dubbed memorials by nineteenth-century archivists, in which he always refers to himself in the third person.

Killingworth initially blamed van Riet for convincing him to press on to Buda, but he admits that he had been forced to return to Constance earlier than he had planned because his connections to Maximilian had made him a target for Hungary's anti-Habsburg faction. Nevertheless, Killingworth insisted that it was he who had persuaded the Hungarian foreign minister, Cardinal Tamás Bakócz, archbishop of Esztergom, and a royal advisor named Doctor Heydon to back the Emperor's plan to move Richard to Austria.[15]

Opposing the pro-imperial party was a powerful group of nobles who could not forget that Maximilian had led the Austrian army that had tried to conquer Hungary in the 1480s. As mentioned earlier, Vladislaus had won this war but in the minds of many at the Hungarian court the continuing threat from the Habsburgs meant France was their natural ally.

Even with Vladislaus' closest advisors in the pro-imperial camp, the pro-French party steadily gained ground with Richard and he began to believe the rumours they spread about his brother's steward. It seems that the mutual suspicion that had soured Richard and Killingworth's relations after the former's first trip to Hungary now returned, because the steward was suddenly declared *persona non grata* and sent back to Constance.[16]

'Your majesty knows well these Hungarians and Bohemians, there is no faith to be applied to them,' Killingworth moaned in his third memorial,[17] but ignoring the imperial order to go to Aachen had destroyed what little credibility he had with Maximilian. With no cards left to play, the steward's future looked extremely bleak. However, the sudden deterioration in the king of England's health presented a chance for Killingworth to save himself and his master.

The argument the steward used in an attempt to shame Maximilian into action went something like this: if Henry died, a new Tudor king would have Edmund executed in order to deprive any Yorkist rebellion of a figurehead, and this was more than likely because the prince of Wales had not taken an oath to spare

Edmund's life. Therefore, with Henry slipping away, Maximilian had to act quickly or the de la Poles' blood would be on his hands.

'And if anything bad should happen to my lord (which God forbid!), I well know that it would be to Caesar's greatest displeasure,' he wrote,[18] and he repeats his belief that Edmund and William de la Pole would be executed if Richard ended up plotting an invasion with Louis.

Though Killingworth had a point about growing French influence over Richard, Maximilian had no need of a servant who had fallen out of favour with his master and the steward's plaintive memorials were totally ignored. By now Killingworth was also running terminally short of cash, and his last desperate throw of the dice was to suggest that he could earn his keep by being reinstated as an imperial envoy. To this end, he reminded Maximilian of his long years of loyal service to the Houses of York and Habsburg:

> And the aforesaid Thomas begs Caesar that his majesty, remembers that the same Thomas left his parents, everything he owned and his homeland for the service of the aforesaid lords, and for that reason he has nothing to live on.[19]

The subtext here is that if a lowly steward can stand by his friends then an emperor could do the same, yet the silence from the imperial court remained deafening. Even letters to Oyskerk went unanswered, and Killingworth was forced to return to Aachen as Maximilian had originally ordered. Here, he wrote once more to the Emperor, only this time he abandoned the formal style of a memorial in the hope that a more personal note would produce a response.

> Most sacred Caesar, I humbly beseech your sacred majesty, if you would like to recall your most noble memory, that I have waited here these thirty weeks at your sacred majesty's command, will and pleasure... and I am in weakness and in the greatest need and misery.[20]

Still there came no reply. After one more begging letter, written to an imperial courtier called Dionysus,[21] we hear no more of the long-suffering Sir Thomas Killingworth.

We can only assume that the steward died in Aachen sometime in 1508, and while it hardly needs to be said that poverty, malnutrition and fatal illness are common bedfellows it is just as likely that Martin of The Pot's bully boys ambushed the unsuspecting Killingworth and caved in his skull for the price Henry had put on his head. All that can be said for certain is that the de la Poles had lost their most loyal supporter. However, although their steward now lay in a pauper's grave, their chief antagonist was also not long for this world.

By the spring of 1509, Henry knew he had only a few weeks to live so he did everything a dying king could to ensure the survival of his dynasty. Naturally, his most pressing concern was to neutralise any potential challenge to the Tudor heir from the few Yorkists left alive, and his principle targets were William Courtenay, heir to the earldom of Devon, and Thomas Grey, 2nd marquess of Dorset.

It may be recalled that although their Yorkist blood was thin, these hapless kinsmen of the Woodvilles had been sent to the Tower for being distantly related to Edmund, and Henry had not sworn a public oath to spare their lives. As soon as the consumptive king of England felt the cold hand of death upon his shoulder, he ordered both men to be taken to Calais, where they could be quietly put to death once he had breathed his last.[22]

The planned murders of Grey and Courtenay were cruel enough, but the contemporary French chronicler Martin du Bellay tells us that Henry compounded this sin by adding a codicil to his will instructing his son to have Edmund executed the moment he ascended the throne.[23] Admittedly, Bellay's account of events may have been coloured by his friendship with Richard de la Pole, whom he came to know well, but he was not the only French writer who was appalled by Henry's breach of his oath.

In the mid-sixteenth century, the Gascon essayist Michel de Montaigne published a monograph on ethics entitled *That the Intention Is Judge of Our Actions* in which he cites Henry's posthumous command for his son to do his dirty work as an example of how a man cannot use his own death, or a proxy, to release him from an obligation taken under oath. As a precedent for this principle, Montaigne quoted a story from Herodotus in which an Egyptian mason who had sworn never to tell anyone about a hidden door he had built into a pharaoh's treasure chamber was still guilty of breaking his oath even though he only revealed the secret to his son on his deathbed.[24] The parallels with Henry VII are clear, but it was not philosophy that persuaded Henry's son to ignore his father's wishes.

As tradition demanded, the dying Henry VII had tried to make his peace with God by issuing a general pardon for all criminal offences committed before 10 April 1509. He passed away ten days later, and two days after his accession the new king, Henry VIII, had granted 'a more ample pardon, for all things except debt, to everyone who will sue for it'.[25]

Indeed, despite Henry VIII's later willingness to use judicial murder throughout his long reign, either he or his advisors understood that the imprisoned Edmund and William de la Pole could be used as hostages to ensure that Richard did not raise a rebellion. This would explain why the imprisoned brothers were not only kept alive but specifically excluded from the amnesty that was customarily granted to all prisoners on the death of a monarch.

By issuing his declaration of clemency on St George's Day 1509, Henry VIII hoped to begin his reign on a note of patriotic optimism, but he was informed by his advisors that the wording he had used meant Edmund and the other Yorkist prisoners would have to be released should they ask for their freedom. To rectify this error, Henry promptly issued an addenda whereby eighty named individuals, including all three de la Pole brothers and Sir George Neville (the veteran rebel, not Bergavenny), were specifically excluded from the royal mercy.[26]

Also named in the exclusion were Thomas Grey and William Courtenay, who had not been beheaded after all. Warrants for their execution had failed to reach Calais before the old king had died, yet the new king not only commuted their death sentences but ignored his own list of exclusions from the general pardon and ordered their release. Scarcely able to believe their luck, the two men emerged blinking into the Calais sunshine, and though Courtenay died eighteen months later, he did live long enough to carry a sword at Henry VIII's coronation. Grey fared even better; having been restored to his Dorset title, he served the Tudors loyally until his death in 1530.

Those lower down the Yorkist ladder did not do so well, and typical of their fate is the sobering tale of John Parrelebene. Both he and Neville had supported Warbeck, but although they had been pardoned in 1501[27] they chose to follow Edmund into exile. We have already seen how Edmund had admonished Killingworth for allowing Parrelebene to join Neville, 'thereby incurring more expense',[28] and though we know nothing of this man's activities while he was in Aachen, we do know that he tried to take advantage of the general pardon and that Henry ordered that he must never be granted mercy under any circumstances.

'Parlaben [*sic*], one of the most errant traitors and railers against the king's father beyond the seas, has come over and been arrested. He is endeavouring to obtain the General Pardon, which the King expressly desires may not be passed or delivered,' states the official response to Parrelebene's application, which was issued on 21 October 1509.[29]

While Parrelebene's ultimate fate is unknown, his end was almost certainly unpleasant. Edmund and William, meanwhile, still in the Tower, continued to keep their heads. Indeed, their living conditions actually improved under the new king. There were no more 'exhaustive interrogations', with both men now housed in proper apartments and outfitted with clothing suitable to their standing.

By the new king's order of 23 July 1509, Sir Andrew Windsor, master of the King's Wardrobe, and Sir Richard Cholmeley, deputy lieutenant of the Tower, were instructed to provide the brothers with two gowns, one red trimmed with fox fur and one tawny trimmed with the costly black lambskin called bogue.[30] In addition to clothes made from these expensive imported fabrics, which cost 5 shillings a yard, Edmund and William were to be provided with two doublets apiece, one of black satin, the other of black velvet, three pairs of hose, three shirts, three pairs of sheets, a black bonnet, three pairs of shoes or slippers, three dozen silk points (laces) and a ribbon girdle.[31]

Buying fine apparel for the Tower's most important prisoners is further evidence that Henry VIII had no intention of executing Edmund and William. Furthermore, such leniency may have persuaded Richard that he and his surviving brothers would be pardoned if he too surrendered. Yet, he could not merely go home.

At the very least, Richard had to negotiate safe passage through Habsburg territory and receive cast-iron assurances from the new king of England that the Acts of Attainder passed in 1504 and the exclusions to the general pardon of 1509 would be repealed.

To have any chance of achieving this, Richard would have to enlist the help of the Emperor after all. He therefore set off for the imperial court, which was planning to spend Christmas at Freiburg in the Black Forest. He crossed the Alps in late autumn and reached his destination early in December, but while Maximilian was again prepared to listen to his Yorkist kinsman, he had no intention of doing anything himself. Instead, he asked his daughter Margaret to intercede with the new king of England on Richard's behalf.

Involving Margaret was logical because she had ruled the Low Countries as regent for her nephew, the future Emperor Charles V, ever since the death of her brother Philip. In this capacity, she had played an increasingly important role on the diplomatic stage and successive historians have remarked on how well Margaret and her father worked together. This was in sharp contrast to the constant battles Maximilian had waged with his son, but it is a measure of the de la Poles' decline in international importance that the Emperor's letter to his daughter mentions Richard only in passing.

The chief subject of Maximilian's letter, which is dated 22 December 1510, was a request for Henry to provide 2,000 English archers to serve as an escort during his forthcoming official visit to Rome. At long last, Pope Julius had agreed to formally crown Maximilian Holy Roman Emperor, and along with the English bowmen Margaret was instructed to ask Henry to send three pedigree hunting dogs, which were to be a wedding present for Ulrich, duke of Württemberg, who was engaged to Maximilian's niece.

Sandwiched between these requests was Maximilian's instruction for Margaret to ask the king of England 'to pardon to the young duke of Suffolk who is at our side, and to consent to him returning to his said kingdom'.[32]

Unfortunately for Richard, Maximilian could not reach Rome without entering French or Venetian territory, and the doge of Venice in particular had no intention of allowing such a large imperial force to cross his borders. As a result, the imperial coronation had to be postponed. Maximilian's archers remained in England, Ulrich never received his hounds, and 'the young duke of Suffolk' did not receive his pardon. But why not?

Accepting Richard's surrender would have given Henry VIII an opportunity to send the last of the de la Poles to the Tower, and when all three brothers were safely under lock and key, or dangling from a gallows, the Tudor dynasty would have been firmly fixed on England's throne. Yet Henry missed his chance to finally put an end to the War of the Roses and Richard continued to be a thorn in his side for many years to come.

Perhaps Margaret never forwarded her father's requests to Henry, or Richard may have simply recovered his mettle and decided to fight on. Whatever it was that scuppered his attempt to make peace with the Tudors, after Christmas 1510 the last Yorkist still at large vanishes from the historical record for almost two years.

BOOK TWO

I was informed by the bishop of Zamora of this country, the which was prisoner in France, that, as he heard said, that your said rebel was made a captain of the Almaynys that went into Navarre.

Letter from Sir John Stiles to Henry VIII,
Brewer (1920 ed.), *Letters & Papers of Henry VIII, Vol. 1 Part 1, 1509*, 3584, p. 694

14

AN EXALTED INDIVIDUAL

It is curious to think that Thomas Grey, 2nd marquess of Dorset, who had suffered a great deal for his tenuous connections to the House of York, would be instrumental in propelling Richard de la Pole back into the political limelight. It is even more strange to think that the two men would find themselves on opposite sides in a war for control of the kingdom of Navarre, but such are the tides of history, and the current that swept both men towards the Pyrenees was the latest eddy in the maelstrom known as the Italian Wars.

During the previous round of fighting, which had ended in 1504, Ferdinand, king of Aragon and Louis XII, king of France, had made common cause with Venice to drive Maximilian out of Milan and conquer the kingdom of Naples, which was ruled by a cadet branch of the Aragonese royal family. Though Louis and Ferdinand had easily defeated the Neapolitans and Milanese, they had quarrelled over the division of the spoils and a brief Franco-Spanish war had ensued. The end of this war had left Ferdinand in control of Naples and southern Italy, but Louis and his Venetian allies had kept their conquests in Milan and Lombardy.

The chief losers in the north were the Holy Roman Empire, which lost Milan and Genoa to the French, and the Papal States, which lost several key cities to Venice. As for the latter, the bellicose Pope Julius II was determined to recover what was his. He therefore encouraged Maximilian to attack Venice and, in return, offered to perform the coronation that would confirm Maximilian as Holy Roman Emperor. It may be recalled that Maximilian's previous attempt to receive the most prestigious diadem in western Christendom had been blocked by the Venetians, and he was eager to avenge that insult.

Meanwhile, a highly toxic atmosphere of mutual suspicion had so strained French relations with their Venetian allies that when Louis proposed a conference to discuss curbing Venetian power, his former enemies were happy to attend. The envoys from France, Aragon, the Empire, the Papal States and England met in the autumn of 1508 in the Flemish city of Cambrai where, besides clipping Venetian wings, they discussed such weighty matters as ending the revolt in Guelders and the disputed succession in Navarre.[1] It would be this struggle that would involve Richard de la Pole and the marquess of Dorset – but not yet.

While the delegates failed to settle the Guelders and Navarrese questions, the fate of Venice was sealed on 10 December 1508 when an anti-Venetian alliance, dubbed the League of Cambrai, was signed. The League's aims were simple: once Venice had been defeated, its possessions would be divided among the victorious members, namely Ferdinand, Louis, Pope Julius, Maximilian, the Swiss Confederacy and the pro-French Italian duchy of Ferrara. Curiously absent was the king of England.

Though Henry VII had been invited to join the League, and Sir John Wingfield had been sent to Cambrai to represent Tudor interests, England's king had been under the impression that the conference had been convened to discuss the proposed marriages of his youngest daughter, Mary, to the ageing Louis XII and his youngest son, Henry, Prince of Wales, to either Maximilian and Ferdinand's granddaughter Eleanor of Austria[2] or Ferdinand's widowed daughter Catherine of Aragon.

The realisation that the other envoys at Cambrai had come to plot the dismemberment of Venice came as a shock to Henry, who not only refused to join the League but sent a secret message to the Doge warning him he was about to be attacked.[3] His decision is hardly surprising. Besides Henry's customary reluctance to spend money on expensive foreign wars, he knew he was dying and he was too busy trying to ensure his son's succession to worry about a struggle in which England had no interest. Nevertheless, Henry's decision to remain neutral would have a huge impact on the surviving de la Poles.

Although Henry VII died in April 1509, his refusal to join League of Cambrai's war and subsequent victory over the Venetians, which was completed by the end of 1510, meant Richard became an irrelevance once more. No doubt it was this political redundancy that ended Habsburg interest in helping Richard negotiate his surrender, which is why he had to leave Freiburg empty handed. With nowhere else to go, Richard returned to Hungary; but while he was cooling his heels in Buda, the League of Cambrai fell apart.

The rapidity and scale of French victories over Venice caused a concerned Pope Julius to reconsider his position, and late in 1510 he defected from the League. The beleaguered doge was only too happy to accept the papal olive branch, and the anti-Venetian League of Cambrai was reconstituted as the anti-French Holy League, which Louis' hereditary enemies clamoured to join.

Besides the Doge and himself, the members of Julius' new League included Ferdinand, Maximilian and Henry VIII, all of whom hoped to seize large chunks of French territory for themselves. Ferdinand wished to annexe the pro-French Navarre, Maximilian wanted to recover Milan and Henry VIII had dreams of reconquering England's lost possessions in Normandy. From Louis' point of view, any revival of the Hundred Years War meant that replacing the pro-Spanish Tudor with a pro-French Yorkist became a top priority. As a result, when Richard re-enters our story he does so as a client of the French king.

As far as Richard was concerned, the death of Henry VII and the relatively comfortable imprisonment of his brothers may have given him the confidence to ignore the late Sir Thomas Killingworth's warnings about Tudor reprisals if he tried to continue the Yorkist struggle with French help. Yet it was the exploits of his distant French cousin Gaston de Foix that drew Richard inexorably towards the Pyrenees.

Before his stellar career was cut short by a Spanish arquebus ball at the siege of Ravenna, Gaston had earned the nickname 'the Thunderbolt of Italy' while fighting for Louis, but it was his close kinship to the Navarrese royal family that would have far-reaching consequences for the House of York.

As previously noted, the de la Poles were related to the House of Foix, and Richard had already used his ties to the late Anne of Foix-Candale, queen of Hungary, to secure asylum in Buda, but she was not the only female monarch to be descended from this ancient Gascon family. Gaston's sister Germaine was queen of Aragon by virtue of her recent marriage to Ferdinand, and their cousin Catherine de Foix was queen of Navarre.

This relationship gave Gaston and Germaine a tenuous claim to the Navarrese throne, and once the Thunderbolt of Italy had been laid to rest his rights to his cousin's crown passed to his sister. The existence of a senior heir, Henri d'Albret, did not prevent Ferdinand from using his wife's Navarrese blood as a pretext for annexing this fiercely independent mountain kingdom.

By now, Ferdinand had successfully sidelined his daughter Joanna and united Castile and Aragon under his personal rule, but he would not be king of all Spain until he had conquered Navarre. Naturally, Louis, had no intention of letting his niece's husband seize this key buffer state on France's south-western border, and the Franco-Aragonese struggle for Navarre would become a separate theatre in the ongoing Italian Wars.

The battles in this phase of the war, which lasted from 1512 to 1516, would be fought from Naples to Northumberland, as well as across the Pyrenees, but fighting on multiple fronts would stretch Spanish resources as well as French. What Ferdinand needed was an ally, and by this time his daughter Catherine had married the ambitious, warlike Henry VIII.

From the moment of his coronation, Henry VIII was determined to emulate Henry V in the hope that repeating his illustrious predecessor's triumphs at Harfleur and Agincourt would enhance his own right to rule England. This was grist to Ferdinand's mill and so, to further his own ambitions in Navarre, he convinced Henry that he ought to recover former English possessions in neighbouring Gascony as well as Normandy. In November 1511, Henry eagerly signed the Treaty of Westminster with Ferdinand whereby an English attempt to seize Gascony would be supported by a Spanish army that had marched through neutral Navarre. Their first target would be the vital port of Bayonne.

The man put in charge of the English expeditionary force was Thomas Grey, 2nd marquess of Dorset, but why he was chosen is something of a mystery. Perhaps Henry was trying to atone for his father's poor treatment of England's only marquis, or maybe his skill in the tiltyard had won the new king's favour. Whatever the reason, Dorset received his commission on 2 May 1512, but his army did not reach Spain until 3 June.

As ever, the capricious weather had refused to cooperate and storms in the Bay of Biscay pushed the English fleet too far south. The exasperated Dorset had to disembark his men at Pasajes,[4] on Spain's northern coast, and although this Castilian port was only 30 miles from Bayonne, his troubles were only beginning.[5] In his arrogance, Ferdinand had demanded free passage for his army through Navarre on the grounds that the Anglo-Spanish attack on France had been sanctioned by the Pope's Holy League. The Navarrese saw through this ruse, which would have allowed Spanish troops to occupy their kingdom.

At this time, Navarre was ruled by the co-monarchs Catherine – who was closely related to Louis XII – and her French husband, John d'Albret. Not only did they refuse permission for Ferdinand's troops to cross Navarre, but they even signed a mutual defence pact with their French kinsman.[6] Ferdinand's response was to persuade Pope Julius that the Navarrese were heretics who had to be brought back to Holy Mother Church by force; he was successful, and a papal bull granting the king of Aragon permission to invade Navarre 'for the extirpation of the accursed schism' was published on 21 July 1512.[7]

Within days of receiving papal authority, a Spanish army led by the duke of Alba crossed the border and began laying waste to the Navarrese countryside with a ruthlessness learned in the Moorish Wars.[8] Meanwhile, Dorset moved the English army from Pasajes to the Spanish border town of Fuenterrabía,[9] but the cavalry and supplies that had been promised by Ferdinand never materialised. Without these vital reinforcements Dorset could not launch his invasion, so he ordered his men to make camp on the banks of the River Bidasoa, which marked the boundary between France and Spain.

The arrival of the English in Fuenterrabía caused consternation in Bayonne, and this worsened when a strong force sent to block the English advance was met by a hail of arrows. As at Crecy, Poitiers and Agincourt, the French were forced to retreat with heavy losses but the pusillanimous Dorset failed to exploit his advantage. Instead of marching to Bayonne and occupying the practically undefended city, he ordered his men to return to camp and await the reinforcements promised by Ferdinand.[10]

It was at this point that Ferdinand dropped his pretence and argued that, because Dorset's tardiness had allowed Bayonne's garrison to be strengthened, the English had lost their opportunity to conquer Gascony. Therefore, Ferdinand insisted, Dorset's only option was to support the Spanish conquest of Navarre. The English captain-general was astute enough to realise he was being blackmailed and steadfastly refused to march on Navarre, on the grounds that he had been ordered to attack only Bayonne,[11] but his refusal only convinced an increasingly irate Ferdinand that he was being double-crossed by his English ally.

'Many Spaniards have their suspicions, or firmly believe, that some of the persons who served in the [English] army entertained a secret understanding with the French,' Ferdinand confided in a letter to his ambassador in England.[12] No doubt Ferdinand had remembered that Dorset's father had been close to Edmund de la Pole and that his son's arrival in Spain had coincided with Louis' promise of support for Richard.

'The current rumour is that the king of France has exalted a certain individual, son of the deceased sister of the king, who was killed by the late king of England, it being said that he purposes sending him to England, and helping him to the crown,' reads the entry in Venetian Marino Sanuto's diary for 8 June 1512.[13]

Fuelling Ferdinand's suspicions was a curious incident involving the visit of a Navarrese bishop to Dorset's camp. The bishop, who arrived during a storm, offered much-needed supplies and a large personal bribe to Dorset if he stayed out of Navarre. Beyond merely accepting this offer, Dorset declared he would never break his knight's oath by violating Navarrese neutrality and promised to pay for everything that was delivered.[14]

That said, Dorset's men were suffering dreadfully in the unseasonal foul weather because the tents, food and other supplies promised by the Spanish had failed to arrive. This concern for the welfare of his men is certainly to Dorset's credit, but rumours began to circulate that the English captain-general was deliberately sabotaging the Bayonne expedition in the belief that the 'Sun of York' was about to rise again. Whatever the truth of the matter, a now incandescent Ferdinand wrote to Henry insisting that Dorset's obstinacy was jeopardising the success of the entire campaign.

'The combined Spanish and English forces might have conquered as much of Guyenne [Gascony] as the rate of their marches would have permitted ... even Bayonne would have surrendered within three months, without being regularly besieged, if the combined Spanish and English armies had occupied all the country around,' he howled,[15] and Henry agreed with his father-in-law. Echoing Ferdinand's stinging rebuke, Henry wrote to Dorset telling him to attack Navarre at once, but the weeks of idleness had left the English troops in no condition to fight anybody except the local landlords and brothel keepers.

Once the July storms had given way to the dog days of August, Dorset's bored soldiery did what bored young men do best: they got drunk and started brawling in the streets. In the worst of these riots, an Englishman who had punched a Spaniard in the face was lynched, whereupon the German mercenaries in Dorset's army began an orgy of rape, pillage and murder under the pretext of avenging their English comrade.

It was only with the greatest of difficulty that Dorset managed to regain control of his men, and he was forced to hang seven of the Germans who had tried to escape to France with their booty.[16] To add to Dorset's woes, many of the English soldiers were suddenly struck down by a mysterious fever, which the chronicler Edward Hall believed was caused by eating too much foreign food:

> Their victual was much part garlic, and the Englishmen did eat of the garlic with all meats and drank hot wines in the hot weather and did eat all of the hot fruits that they could get which caused their blood to boil in their bellies, that there fell sick 3,000 of the flux and thereof died 800 men.[17]

This particular pestilence was so virulent even Dorset had to take to his bed, and when he recovered he announced that his army had been so decimated by the disease that he had no choice but to return home. When Ferdinand protested, Dorset insisted that it was the Spaniards' failure to provide the necessary supplies that had robbed them of the opportunity to conquer Gascony, further pointing out that the twenty-five-day limit for the campaign, set by the Treaty of Westminster, had passed weeks ago. As a final insult, Dorset demanded that Ferdinand honour the clause in the treaty requiring the Spanish to provide the ships he needed to take his army home.[18]

By now Ferdinand had realised that his allies were more of a hindrance than a help, so he happily sent a fleet to take the querulous, drunken English back to their misty, muddy island. Dorset's army left Spain at the end of October and by this time the conquest of Upper Navarre, on the Spanish side of the Pyrenees, was complete. Queen Catherine and King John had fled to the safety of Lower Navarre, on the French side of the mountains, at the first sight of Alba's army and the people of Pamplona, the Navarrese capital, had opened their city's gates to avoid a brutal sack.[19] The annexation of Upper Navarre had taken little more than two weeks, but the conquest of Lower Navarre would not be as easy.

Thanks to Dorset's departure, which had removed the threat to Bayonne, Louis was able to send 30,000 men to help the Navarrese fight the Spanish. While the nominal head of this enormous army was the eighteen-year-old heir to the French throne, Francis, comte d'Angoulême, actual command was wielded by three veterans of the Italian Wars, namely Jacques de la Palice, marquis of Chabannes, Charles, duke of Bourbon, and Louis d'Orléans, duke of Longueville. These exalted noblemen would shape Richard de la Pole's future in ways he had yet to imagine, and he met them all in Navarre.

Although the campaign season was drawing to a close, Louis ordered Palice, Bourbon and Longueville to retake Pamplona before winter snows closed the Pyrenean passes. To stiffen their largely feudal army, he sent them 10,000 German and Dutch *landsknechts*. Some 7,000 of these mercenaries were commanded by Robert III de la Marck, son of the duke of Bouillon, and the remaining 3,000 were led by Richard.

As mentioned earlier, Edmund de la Pole had been close enough to Bouillon's duke to play tennis with him in happier times and ask for his help when he was a prisoner. Likewise, Bouillon's brother Erhard de la Marck, bishop of Liege, had provided Edmund with money while he was held captive in Namur and helped Richard escape from Aachen. Shortly after Richard's arrival in Buda, he had written to Erhard and thanked him for the help he had given the de la Poles throughout their exile:

> Most dignified and most illustrious Prince, I commend myself to your dignity with all the affection of my heart for your kindness and giving thanks on account of that love, benevolence and favour which you have shown me and, by the grace of God, extended to my brother.[20]

Unsurprisingly, he soon made friends with his benefactor's nephew. To avoid confusion with his father, Robert II duke of Bouillion, Robert III de la Marck is generally referred to by his courtesy title of seigneur de la Fleuranges, and it is under this name that he wrote an autobiography entitled *Memoirs of the Marshal of Fleuranges, Called the Young Adventurer*. Thanks to Fleuranges, we know a good deal about Richard's involvement in the Navarrese War of 1512, but the 'Young Adventurer', as he liked to call himself, began his military career in Italy, fighting for France alongside Richard's cousin Gaston de Foix.

We have already seen how the de la Marcks' relations with their Habsburg overlords had become so strained that Fleuranges' father had thought it wise to send his eldest son to be educated at the French court. Consequently, the Young Adventurer had grown up with the heir to the French throne, the comte d'Angoulême, who was now in titular command of the French forces on the Guyenne–Navarre front. The two men had formed a lasting friendship as boys, and on reaching manhood Fleuranges had fought for his adopted country in Italy.[21]

While serving with the French garrison in Ferrara, Fleuranges had been entertained by the soon-to-be infamous Lucrezia Borgia and had been with Gaston de Foix as he cut a bloody swathe through the Spanish-Papal armies of Northern Italy.[22] After Gaston's death, Fleuranges had been sent back to the Ardennes to recruit *landsknechts* for the liberation of Navarre and he succeeded in enlisting 7,000 veterans of the Guelders rebellion to fight for the French in the Pyrenees. These men called themselves the Black Band because they blackened their breastplates with smoke to prevent them from rusting. Unfortunately for Fleuranges, their habitual drunkenness made marching his new army across France extremely difficult.[23]

In his *Mémoires*, Fleuranges commented that *landsknechts* preferred camping in places where strong wine was available because it 'was better than boiling water', but bypassing the laborious process of pasteurisation was not without its own problems. On at least one occasion, Fleuranges' drunken recruits refused to march another step until they had negotiated an increase in wages and their captain could only quell the mutiny by digging deeper into his war chest.[24]

It was typical of *landsknechts* to try and raise their pay by such extortion, and Richard would experience similar problems with his own mercenaries,[25] yet when they did choose to fight they were extremely effective. It is therefore hardly surprising that these men were chosen to spearhead the French counterattack in Navarre.

'The king added my *landsknechts* who numbered 7,000 to another company led by the duke of Suffolk, who we called White Rose,' wrote Fleuranges,[26] and it is interesting that he refers to Richard by the same *nom de guerre* used first by Warbeck and later by Edmund. Clearly Richard's adoption of this title indicates his determination to take up the Yorkist cudgel, but he would have to prove himself in Navarre before he could invade England.

The first objective given to Richard and Fleuranges' men was the recapture of Saint-Jean-Pied-de-Port, which guarded the principal road over the Pyrenees from France to Pamplona. The invading Spaniards had occupied this heavily fortified town during the initial phase of the war but their commander had been ordered to avoid a pitched battle so he sent out his skirmishers to delay the mercenaries' advance.[27]

Though the lightly armed Spaniards should have been no match for the heavily armed Germans, who brandished double-handed swords, 8-foot halberds and 18-foot pikes, Fleuranges tells us that many of his best men were lost in the bloody melee that followed. Nevertheless, the *landsknechts* gave as good as they got and soon as the main body of the French army arrived the Spaniards threw down their weapons and fled.[28]

Encouraged by the recapture of Saint-Jean-Pied-de-Port, the Navarrese king, Jean d'Albret, wanted to push on to Pamplona but the French insisted that it was too late in the season to cross the Pyrenees. This tense situation was not helped by Richard and Fleuranges' quarrelsome *landsknechts*, who started a riot in which 500 of their Gascon allies were killed. Though the Young Adventurer does not tell us the reason for this unrest, he does say that many more would have died had it not been decided to divide the French army in two.[29]

While Longueville took the greater part of the army to winter quarters in France, Palice marched 8,000 Frenchmen, 7,000 Gascons and Richard's 3,000 grumbling Guelderians through the Roncesvalles Pass into Upper Navarre. This flying column reached Pamplona on 24 October 1512, but the delay caused by the disagreements in the French high command, not to mention the rioting mercenaries, meant the element of surprise had been lost.[30]

15

I PRAY YOU GIVE ME THIS DAY SOMETHING

The king of Navarre's eagerness to recover his and his wife's throne was somewhat uncharacteristic given that Fleuranges described Jean d'Albret as being man so pious he preferred to hear two or three masses a day rather than prepare his country for war.[1] Moreover, his devout inertia had prompted his wife, Queen Catherine, to complain that 'had I been king, and you queen, we would be reigning in Navarre at this moment'.[2]

Though Catherine's acid remark is most likely apocryphal, it is ironic that by ignoring Jean d'Albret's plea for swift action the French commanders had given the duke of Alba time to repair Pamplona's dilapidated fortifications. Consequently, when Palice and his men reached the Navarrese capital they found that the city could only be taken by siege. Like countless armies throughout the ages, the French dug trenches and artillery pits in an effort to starve their enemies into submission but it was their own positions that came under repeated attack.

As part of the improved defences, Alba had built a fort for his skirmishers in the town of Puente la Reina, which lay 12 miles to the south-west of Pamplona. From this fort lightly armed Spanish horsemen, known as *jinetes*, could raid the French siege lines with impunity, and these attacks became so serious that Palice ordered the Chevalier Bayard, his favourite captain, to do something about them.

In the pantheon of French medieval heroes, the name of Bayard is ranked as high as Roland, Joan of Arc and Bertrand du Guesclin. Dubbed the 'Good Knight Without Fear or Reproach' by his servant and biographer Jacques de Mailles, Bayard had won his glittering reputation on the battlefields of Italy, where his chivalrous treatment of prisoners and civilians had won him many admirers on both sides. That said, Bayard was ferocious in battle and much feared by his enemies.

The Good Knight's particular talent was conducting daring operations behind enemy lines, so the capture of the Puente la Reina fort was meat and drink to him. He quickly put together a strong strike force, which included four cannon and two companies of Richard's *landsknechts* as well as the men under his own command.[3]

With more than a thousand troops at his disposal, Bayard's little army greatly outnumbered the Spanish garrison so, in keeping with his reputation for being the most chivalrous knight on any battlefield, he offered his enemies generous terms. When the Spaniards declined, Bayard ordered his cannon to open fire. It took less than an hour for the French heavy guns to demolish a section of the fort's walls, but when Bayard ordered Richard's *landsknechts* to storm the breach, they refused unless they were given double pay.[4]

Through the mercenaries claimed it was customary for danger money to be paid before any such assault, Bayard was not a man to submit to such blackmail and he attacked the breach with his own men, led by a captain with the splendidly Robin Hood-esque name of Little John de la Vergne. Whilst Bayard's cannon fired a diversionary barrage, Little John and his band of merry men scaled an undefended section of the fort's walls and the Spaniards did not realise they had been tricked until it was too late.[5]

Having captured the fort and installed a garrison of loyal Navarrese, Bayard prepared to march his men back to the main French camp. Before his trumpeters could sound the withdrawal, however, he was waylaid by two *landsknechts* and their interpreter. Despite taking no part in the attack, the shameless mercenaries repeated their demand for double pay. On hearing this, Bayard exploded with rage and pointed out that, because it had been his men who had captured the fort, the mercenaries were not entitled to a penny.

'Tell your rascally *landsknechts* that I would sooner give each of them a noose with which to hang himself! I shall indeed speak of it to the Lord La Palice or his Grace of Suffolk, their captain-general, but it will be in order to have them dishonourably discharged, for they are not worth a sou!' Bayard is said to have cried,[6] but it wasn't until he threatened to turn his own men loose on the mutineers that they agreed to waive their bonus.

According to Mailles' account of the event, the Good Knight returned to the French camp where he was congratulated on his victory by the king of Navarre, the lord de la Palice and all the other captains, including Richard, duke of Suffolk, but this was not the end of the matter.[7] There was at least one man who could not forget the damage done to his honour – and his pocket – by the debacle at Puente la Reina.

Later that same evening, Richard and Bayard were dining together when a drunken *landsknecht* burst into their tent. The sozzled mercenary threatened that unless he was paid his danger money Bayard would suffer the consequences. As the man had his razor-sharp *katzbalger* (cat-skinner) sword in his hand, there was little doubt as to his intentions, but the man's accent was so heavy all the Frenchmen burst out laughing. Bayard then called the mercenary's bluff by challenging him to a duel. Mailles recorded their subsequent exchange.

> 'Is it you who wants to kill Captain Bayard? Very well, I am here, defend yourself!' said the Good Knight, and the poor *landsknecht*, who had turned a beautiful colour, replied in his terrible French.
>
> 'It's not just me alone who wants to kill Captain Bayard, it is all the *landsknechts*.'
>
> 'Ha! Upon my soul!' said the Good Knight. 'Then I will be quiet, because I am not going to argue against 7,000 *landsknechts* all by myself. Let's have a drink and talk about this my friend, for the love of God!'
>
> All the company began to laugh loudly at such a wonderful proposal and they made the *landsknecht* sit at the table, face to face with the Good Knight, which made him abandon his assassination before he had begun. And so, before the *landsknecht* left there, he promised that as long as he lived, he

> would defend Captain Bayard against all who came between them, and he swore that Bayard was a good man, who had good wine. When the king of Navarre and the Lord de la Palice heard about the events of that evening, they laughed as loud as the others![8]

Incidents such as this are a graphic illustration of the difficulties faced by Richard and his fellow captains when trying to control battle-hardened veterans who fought only for money. Yet the exiled pretender to the English throne was more than equal to the task, and under his direct command his *landsknechts* acquitted themselves well in the final battle for Pamplona.

The problem facing every medieval commander was keeping a besieging army in the field once the surrounding countryside had been denuded of food and fodder. This was especially true during the winter months, and as soon as the weather began to worsen Palice decided to abandon the siege because of a lack of firewood.[9] However, Jean d'Albret managed to persuade his French allies to make one last attempt to recapture his wife's capital.

On 24 November, the French guns began to pound Pamplona walls with renewed vigour. After three days of ceaseless bombardment, a breach wide enough for an assault had been made. On the morning of 27 November, Palice ordered a full-scale attack and Fleuranges tells us that Richard was in the thick of the fighting.[10]

'They pressed the attack very firmly, where Monsieur de Suffort and the *landsknechts* did their duty well,' he wrote,[11] but he adds that many of the attackers never made it beyond the breach and those that did 'were pushed back very hard'.[12]

Once inside the city, the struggle for Pamplona degenerated into a bloody street fight where short swords and brass-knuckled fists were the weapons of choice. Both sides fired the city's wooden buildings to flush out their enemies, and through the smoke from the burning houses Richard's men would have seen their captain, clad in his azure-blue surcoat emblazoned with the three gold leopard heads of Suffolk's dukes, hacking his way through his foes. Yet it was all to no avail; inch by inch, yard by yard, the French attackers were driven out of the city.

The defeat proved to Palice that Pamplona could not be taken by force or siege. In spite of Navarrese objections, he decided to take his army back to France and so the French struck their camp on 30 November 1512.[13] A few days later, winter arrived in the war-torn Pyrenees; frost covered the ground, snow flurries filled the air and Mailles tells us that the retreating French were particularly vexed by a shortage of shoes.

'One sorry pair for a footboy cost a crown,' he says ruefully,[14] but he adds that the French troops' misery was largely of their own making. During their advance, Palice's men had burned so many barns full of crops in order to deny these supplies to the Spanish that there was nothing for them to eat on the way back. Consequently, many Frenchmen died of starvation long before they reached home.[15]

All the while, Palice's starving army was harassed by Spanish skirmishers and Navarrese collaborators. When the roads were turned into quagmires by the winter storms, he ordered his heavy siege guns to be abandoned. According to Mailles, these guns were spiked before they were left at the entrance to the narrow pass of Belate, but Sir John Stiles, the English ambassador to Spain, reported that they were captured intact.[16] In either case, the thirteen French cannon taken at Belate adorned the region's coat of arms until 1979 when they were removed 'as a gesture of friendship'.[17]

Whatever really happened in that lonely Pyrenean pass, the only French commander to emerge with his honour intact was Richard de la Pole. Mailles is full of praise for the Yorkist exile, with the following anecdote typical of his respect for Richard:

> That duke of Suffolk, surnamed the White Rose, captain-general of the *landsknechts*, was present at this retreat and once, when this noble personage had undergone as much fatigue as he was capable of sustaining, and had neither eaten nor drank the whole day, it being necessary to retreat from a skirmish, he went late to the Good Knight and spoke to him thus:
>
> 'Captain Bayard, my friend, I am dying of hunger, so I pray you, give me this day something to sup, because my people tell me there is nothing to be had in my billet!' The Good Knight, who was astonished by nothing, replied: 'Ay marry, my Lord, you shall be well entertained.'

> Then he called before him his steward and said to him: 'Monsieur Mylieu, go ahead and make supper quickly, and let us fare as well as if we were in Paris.' At these words the duke of Suffolk laughed for quarter of an hour because they had eaten nothing but bread made of millet for the last two days.[18]

Even when the footsore and starving survivors reached Bayonne, Mailles tells us that many of them died from overeating.[19] Fortunately, Richard was not among them but although he had survived the disastrous Navarrese campaign, the war that had begun in 1508 would continue for another four years.

The anti-French Holy League created by Pope Julius II in 1511 had left Louis XII dangerously isolated, but he could always rely on the king of Scotland to side with him in any fight that involved the English. Consequently, when Henry VIII and Ferdinand of Aragon declared war on France in the spring of 1512, Louis hastily rekindled the Auld Alliance with Scotland.[20]

Though the kings of England and Scotland had signed the Treaty of Perpetual Peace in 1502, and the Scottish monarch, James IV, had married Henry VII's daughter Margaret Tudor to ensure the two countries' 'friendship, league and confederation would last for all time coming', Henry VIII's determination to be a warrior king was enough to convince his brother-in-law that Scotland had to prepare for war. As a result, James and Louis signed their Treaty of Mutual Help within days of Dorset's expedition setting sail for Bayonne.[21]

The reconquest of Gascony was supposed to be the first step on a road that would lead Henry VIII to his coronation in Paris, but as soon as Scotland entered the fray he had to move quickly to secure his northern border. Henry could not forget that Perkin Warbeck had rallied the Scots to the Yorkist cause, and even though Edmund was safely in the Tower and Richard was in far off Navarre, he could not risk another invasion of Northumberland with most of the Tudor army in Guyenne.

No doubt Henry was kept informed of what was happening in Edinburgh by his sister. So, when it became clear that his three deadliest enemies had made common cause, he sent Dr Nicholas West,[22] his father's old chaplain, and Lord Dacre, warden of the

Western Marches, to warn James that he would derive no benefit from any alliance with Louis or Richard.

'The entertaining of our said rebel is as contrarious to the king of Scots' weal and possibility of succession as to ours; so that, everything well considered, our said brother of Scotland hath little cause thus to favour the French King and his against us as he doeth,' declared Henry in the letter that Dr West delivered to James,[23] but the king of Scotland had already told his brother-in-law that he did not support Louis' recognition of a Yorkist as England's king.

In a letter to Lord Dacre dated 18 July 1512, James had declared that French support for the White Rose was 'contrary to the possibility of our interests'.[24] He had also offered to send the bishop of Moray to Paris to negotiate both Richard's extradition and a treaty of 'universal peace'.[25] However, Henry realised that this olive branch was simply an attempt to disguise the recent renewal of the Auld Alliance.[26] In his reply to James's letter, dated 31 July 1512, Henry thanked the king of Scotland for his co-operation in the matter of Richard de la Pole but declined the offer to negotiate a universal peace on the grounds he could not make such a treaty without consulting the other members of the Holy League.[27]

After this exchange, war between England and Scotland was inevitable. Henry commissioned his master of the Wardrobe to make battle flags displaying the cross of St George, the red dragon of the Tudors and the royal arms, while the key border fortress of Norham was restocked with bows and arrows.[28] Unfortunately, Dorset's bungling of the Bayonne campaign had seriously damaged Henry's attempt to portray himself as a new King Arthur. Even as the hapless marquess was re-embarking his men, Ferdinand was writing to his son-in-law to express his disgust at his English ally's incompetence.

'In a combined action they will never assist the troops, or act in concert with a commander of another nation. More time is spent in concerting any measure with them than the whole execution of it requires,' he wrote. On a more conciliatory note, Ferdinand conceded that the English are 'strong, stout-hearted, stand firm in battle and never think of taking flight'. He also said that once Henry's men had learned to use modern tactics he would be more than happy to undertake another Anglo-Spanish operation.[29]

Having vented his spleen, Ferdinand proposed a new campaign whereby Henry would invade northern France from Calais whilst Spanish troops seized Guyenne on Henry's behalf. This strategy, Ferdinand argued, would avoid the friction that had blighted the first attack on Bayonne and, by splitting the French forces, both the conquest of Navarre and the recovery of all England's lost territories in France would be assured.[30]

Of course, Ferdinand's proposed campaigns in northern and southern France were inextricably linked to the wider struggle for Italy where the Holy League was on the point of total victory. Despite Gaston de Foix's Pyrrhic victory at Ravenna in April 1512, French-occupied Milan had been captured by Swiss mercenaries in the pay of Pope Julius in May and this was only the beginning of Louis' troubles. By the end of the year, the French had been driven back over the Alps, as well as the Pyrenees.

When Henry, Ferdinand, Maximilian, Julius and the other members of the Holy League checked their balance sheet for 1512, it showed only Dorset's expedition to Bayonne had failed to meet its objectives. A court of enquiry, hastily convened after Dorset's return, heard evidence from Lord Herbert and the marquess's own brother that their captain-general was to blame and a chastened Henry had no option but to accept Ferdinand's strategy for renewing the war.[31] A new Anglo-Spanish treaty was quickly signed and the ageing Pope Julius granted 'plenary indulgence' to any Englishman who fought the French for at least six months.[32]

All this was carefully noted in Scotland, and James wrote to the king of Denmark, who was his uncle, to solicit his help. In a letter dated 12 January 1513, James claimed that the English were about to attack Scotland because Henry could not conquer France until his northern border was secure.[33] James also tells his Danish uncle that the English were rearming and asked for a fleet to help defend Scotland's coast. Interestingly James does not mention that the French had already sent 200,000 gold crowns for the Scottish war chest and twenty pieces of artillery.[34]

The Franco-Scottish allies were certainly right to be fearful. In the spring of 1513, Maximilian agreed to support the English invasion of Picardy, provided Henry contributed 250,000 crowns to the imperial treasury and if the Emperor shared Ferdinand's fears about conducting a joint operation with the English he did not show it.[35] Under the treaty creating a new Anglo-Spanish-Imperial axis, which was ratified on 5 April 1513,[36] it was agreed that Ferdinand would attack Louis in Guyenne and Navarre while Henry and Maximilian invaded northern France from Calais and Flanders.

The next phase of the war would begin in June 1513, and this time Henry was determined not to entrust command of the English army to an underling such as Dorset. Instead, Henry would take personal charge of the campaign,[37] but his decision to follow in the footsteps of Henry V created its own problem: what was to be done with Edmund de la Pole?

Though Edmund had now been in the Tower for the best part of seven years, he was far from a forgotten man. Henry's spymasters knew that the de la Pole brothers were writing to each other,[38] and, to add to Henry's woes, a new tax to fund the forthcoming Scottish War had to be cancelled after the whole of northern England threatened to rebel. It was circumstances similar to these that had caused Cornwall's tin miners to march on London, and their rebellion had been exploited by James IV and Perkin Warbeck for their own ends.

As a child, Henry had witnessed at first hand the panic that had seized the Tudor court every time Warbeck popped up in France, Ireland or Scotland. Now he was king, Henry feared that his absence in France would provide his Yorkist enemies with an opportunity to snatch Edmund from the Tower and place him on the throne.[39] This is precisely the scenario that had sent Warbeck and the befuddled earl of Warwick to the scaffold, and the situation in Navarre had done nothing to ease Henry's concerns.

If Louis could send Richard de la Pole across the Pyrenees at the head of 3,000 *landsknechts* he could just as easily send him across the Channel with an army of comparable size, and this situation was also not without precedent. Though Henry had not been born when John de la Pole tried to put Lambert Simnel on the throne, the earl of Lincoln's landings in Ireland and northern England, at the head of an army of Irish and German mercenaries, was still fresh in the minds of many.

Incredibly, Simnel was still alive, and slowly working his way through the ranks of royal servants from spit-boy to falconer, so his presence must have been a constant reminder to Henry of the fragility of royal power. With the living Simnel and the ghost of Perkin Warbeck haunting the corridors of Windsor and Westminster, Henry felt he could not invade France *and* keep his crown unless Edmund de la Pole was in his grave.

It was all over with unseemly haste. On 4 May 1513, the earl of Suffolk was dragged from his chamber in the Tower and bundled towards the steps of a hastily built scaffold. As prayers were said for his soul, Edmund was forced to kneel before the bloodstained block. Seconds later, his head was struck from his body. He was forty-two years old.[40]

Whatever monster Henry VIII became in his later life, he was exceedingly pious as a young man and if he had any qualms about ordering Edmund's execution he could salve his conscience with the thought that he was carrying out his father's dying wish. Henry could also justify his actions by claiming his rival had been condemned to death by the Act of Attainder[41] that had been passed five years before he ascended the throne, but several contemporary observers cited Richard de la Pole's decision to ally himself with the kings of France and Scotland as the reason why his brother had to die.

'Nothing fresh was heard of the English, save that they had beheaded the earl of Suffolk, who was King Henry's prisoner, because his brother was there at the French court; it being said that he [Richard] was the rightful heir of that realm,' noted Roberto Acciajuolo, who was Florentine ambassador to the French court.[42] Acciajuolo's report is dated 20 May 1513 and his opinion is echoed by Peter Martyr d'Anghiera, an Italian tutor at the Spanish court:

> There was a certain duke of Suffolk named Emond de la Pulla [*sic*] of the great nobility in England, sprung of the fourth daughter of King Edward. He was shut up in the Tower; was much in debt; fled into Burgundy, returned, resumed his old habits, and fled a second time to the duke of the Siccambri, called of Guelders; came into the hands of Philip on the conquest of that duke; and was delivered by him to Henry VII, but on condition confirmed by oath that his life should be spared. Henry his successor, has ordered him to be put to death because he held correspondence with Richard De la

> Pole his brother, an exile in France, and commander of the French fleet [*sic*], for a rising in England.[43]

Interestingly, one man who did *not* go to the scaffold in the spring of 1513 was Edmund and Richard's brother William. Perhaps even Henry struggled to find a reason to execute a man whose only crime was to marry a wealthy widow. On the other hand, William could have been spared because there was no point in killing him now that Richard had become the only Yorkist able to realise the de la Poles' claim to the throne.

16

A MARVELLOUSLY PRETTY ARMY

Despite dying a traitor's death, Edmund's remains were not cast into an unmarked grave. Instead, the last of the de la Pole earls of Suffolk was laid to rest in the Abbey of the Minoresses of St Clare without Aldgate. Two years later, Edmund's wife, Margaret, and their daughter, Anne, who had entered the convent under the name of Elizabeth, fell victim to an outbreak of the plague and they too were buried in the House of the Poor Clares.[1]

With Edmund safely under six feet of earth, and his few remaining supporters in disarray, Henry VIII could safely cross the Channel. Moreover, recent developments in Italy made him supremely confident of victory.

On 6 June 1513, 12,000 Swiss mercenaries in the pay of Pope Julius and Massimiliano Sforza, the restored, pro-imperial duke of Milan, routed 20,000 French troops who had been trying to recapture all the Italian territory they had lost to the Holy League the previous year. This crucial battle was fought at Novara, 30 miles west of Milan, and the French defeat was so complete that Louis' demoralised troops had been forced to retreat over the Alps. With no French army to stop them, marauding bands of victorious Swiss were able to ravage Louis' kingdom as far north as Dijon, so the French were already on the back foot when Henry and Maximilian launched their invasion of Picardy.

As was customary, the army raised by Henry at the beginning of 1513 was divided into three 'battles' called the vanguard, middle-guard and rearguard. After appointing himself captain of the middle-guard, Henry chose George Talbot, 4th earl of Shrewsbury,[2] to lead the vanguard while the rearguard was given to Charles Somerset. This was the same Charles Somerset who, with Bishop Warham, had persuaded Maximilian to withdraw his support for the de la Poles in 1503, and he had been given the title Lord Herbert after becoming chamberlain to the royal household in 1508.

In 1464, following the death of his father, Henry Beaufort, the Lancastrian duke of Somerset, at the battle of Hexham, the young Lord Herbert had been exiled to Flanders so he was familiar with the ways of the imperial court and well liked by the Emperor. Herbert had also served in the Bayonne campaign; indeed, he was one of the captains who had alerted Henry to the marquess of Dorset's deficiencies. No doubt Henry appointed Herbert to address Ferdinand's criticism that Dorset was incapable of cooperating with other nationalities, but Henry seems to have ignored the rumours that the marquess had colluded with his de la Pole kinsmen to sabotage the attack on Bayonne.

Despite Dorset's failure, he was not sent back to the Tower, where he had spent nearly two years during the reign of Henry VII. Instead, the marquess was invited to join Henry's general staff[3] along with the earl of Essex, who had been a member of Edmund de la Pole's jousting set. As both Dorset and Essex were closely connected to the Yorkist Woodvilles,[4] as well as the de la Poles, Henry probably wanted them on his staff so he could keep an eye on them.

With his senior commanders in place, Henry began sending his men across the Channel but he had to do so in stages because Calais could not accommodate his entire army all at once. Consequently, the 8,000 men of Herbert's vanguard, together with the 6,000 men of Shrewsbury's rearguard, disembarked on 10 June 1513 and Henry planned to join them with the 11,000 men of the middle-guard two weeks later. In the meantime, Herbert and Shrewsbury were ordered to capture Thérouanne, a French town on the border with Flanders.

In one respect, the choice of Thérouanne as the expedition's first objective was strange because successive English armies had always besieged Boulogne as a precursor to any campaign in northern France. Capturing Boulogne neutralised any threat to Calais' rear but the attack on Thérouanne, which lay 30 miles to the south-east of the English enclave, had been agreed under the treaty Henry had signed with the Emperor.

If Maximilian shared Ferdinand's qualms about conducting a joint operation with the English, he could not afford to show it because he needed to protect imperial Flanders from a French invasion while he concentrated on securing his position in Italy. As Thérouanne controlled the western approaches to Maximilian's Flemish territories, the town had to be taken and he promised to send 8,000 battle-hardened imperial mercenaries to provide the untested English forces with some much-needed experience.[5]

For his part, Henry was so desperate to make amends for his failure in Gascony he readily agreed to Maximilian's plan and the strategic importance of Thérouanne was also apparent to the French. The town was protected by a broad moat, steep ramparts and strong walls bristling with the latest types of artillery. Indeed, the town was so heavily fortified the Anglo-Imperial army pitched their camp almost a mile from Thérouanne's battlements. Even so, French guns could shoot further than English longbows. 'And as certain captains were in council in the lord Herbert's tent, suddenly out of the town was shot a gun, the pellet whereof slew a noble captain called the Baron of Carew, sitting therein council, which sudden adventure dismayed much the assembly,' noted Edward Hall in his chronicle.[6]

It may have been an incredibly lucky shot, but the death of Carew convinced Herbert that Thérouanne was too strong to take by direct assault and the town would have to be starved into submission, yet he did not have enough men to enforce a complete blockade. All Herbert could do was order a wide ditch to be dug around the entire town and wait for the rest of the army to arrive, but Henry was still in England.

It was not until 30 June that the middle-guard, with Henry at its head, made the short crossing to Calais and John Taylor, clerk of the parliaments, left an eyewitness account of this momentous event. According to Taylor, the king looked resplendent in his suit of the latest German armour and a surcoat of cloth of gold decorated with the cross of St George. He also tells us that the king's army was welcomed to Calais 'with such firing of guns from the ships and from the towers, you would have thought the world was coming to an end',[7] but although Henry looked like a warrior king, he was in no hurry to go to war.

Rather than marching on Thérouanne with all speed, Henry wasted three weeks attending church, entertaining imperial envoys and practising archery with the men of his bodyguard. Naturally, Henry won every one of these contests but his insistence on demonstrating his prowess with a bow meant the opportunity to seize Thérouanne was lost.[8]

While Henry prayed, played and feasted in Calais, Louis put his defeat at Novara behind him and mustered a new army to oppose the Anglo-Imperial invaders. This hastily assembled force made camp at Blangy-sur-Ternoise, 16 miles to the south of Thérouanne, and among the feudal lords and mercenary captains who answered Louis' call to arms was Richard de la Pole with 6,000 *landsknechts*.[9]

The French tents at Blangy were pitched just 3 miles from the battlefield at Agincourt and two of Richard's ancestors had been among Henry V's band of brothers. His great-grandfather had died of fever during the siege of Harfleur, and his great-uncle Michael had been one of the few Englishmen killed on St Crispin's Day 1415. Incidentally, three more of Richard's great-uncles, Alexander, John and Thomas, would also die in France during the last phases of the Hundred Years War.

In an age still underpinned by magic and superstition Richard must have wondered if the ghosts of his forefathers approved of their descendant taking service with the hated French, but he knew that fighting for Louis XII gave him his best chance of toppling the Tudors. At Blangy, Richard was reunited with several veteran captains from the Navarre campaign, all of whom would be vital in maintaining support for a Yorkist restoration at the French court. These notables included Palice, Fleuranges and Bayard, but the most important person Richard met at Blangy was John Stewart, 2nd duke of Albany.[10]

Despite being born in France to a French mother, Albany was the heir presumptive to the throne of Scotland and he, like Richard, had been forced to live in exile by the rebellion of his relatives. In Albany's case, it was an attempt by his father, Alexander, to depose his unpopular older brother, James III, which had caused all the trouble, and this had been done with the help of Richard de la Pole's uncles Edward IV and Richard III.

Under the Treaty of Fotheringhay, signed 11 June 1482, Alexander had promised to rule Scotland as Edward IV's vassal in return for English help and it was the future Richard III who had led the 20,000 men of a Yorkist army over the border. Despite some initial success, which included the capture of Berwick-upon-Tweed, Alexander's bid for the throne had ended in abject failure and he had fled to France, where he had married Anne de la Tour d'Auvergne, an enormously wealthy French heiress. Their son, the aforementioned John, had been born in his mother's castle but soon afterwards Alexander had been killed in a jousting accident.

After his mother's remarriage to a French nobleman, Albany had remained in France and had grown up more French than Scottish. At the battle of Novara he had commanded 500 French men-at-arms, and during the next twelve years he would become a hugely important instrument of French foreign policy as well as a key supporter of the Yorkist cause. However, at this point in their careers, both Richard and Albany were just two of the captains trying to stop Henry VIII from capturing Thérouanne.

On paper, the French chances of driving the invaders back into the sea looked extremely good. By tarrying too long in Calais, Henry had committed the cardinal military sin of dividing his forces in enemy territory, but Louis failed to capitalise on his enemy's mistake. Instead of attacking each section of the weakened English army in turn, Louis instructed his captains to avoid a pitched battle at all costs. To be fair to the French king, he had good reason for his caution; because the greater prize was Milan, Louis did not want to squander his strength in a northern sideshow. He therefore told the Venetian ambassador, Marco Dandolo, that he would send his new army into Italy as soon as he had dealt with the king of England, who was at last on the march.[11]

On 21 July 1513, more than four weeks after the siege of Thérouanne had begun, Henry led his middle-guard out of Calais with all the pomp and ceremony he could muster but his enemies were not impressed. With ill-disguised sarcasm, Fleuranges described the English host as 'a marvellously pretty army', but he did admire the imperial mercenaries Maximilian had hired to Henry. 'The said king of England had with him 7,000 *landsknechts* who call themselves the Black Band. A handsome bunch and well-armed,' he wrote,[12] but this Black Band should not be confused with Richard's men, who used the same name. In the language of heraldry the colour black was associated with fortitude and constancy, which made it a popular livery for mercenaries of the period.

Fleuranges was equally impressed by the English cannon. 'And their camp was marvellously furnished with more artillery than in any war we have ever seen,' he noted,[13] and he was referring to the twelve huge siege guns which Henry had ordered from the imperial armourers in Mechelen. Each of these *curtals*, which tipped the scales at over 3 tons, was decorated with the image of an apostle but their weight meant they could only be dragged a few miles in a day.[14] The English advance was further hampered by Henry's determination to sleep in a prefabricated, two-roomed wooden cabin complete with iron chimneys. This ingenious structure could be taken apart and re-erected at will, but it required twelve carts to transport it from one battlefield to another.[15]

No less cumbersome was Henry's personal entourage of more than 2,000 servants, including 49 valets, 15 chamberlains, 10 minstrels, a lutenist, 115 churchmen and 276 cooks.[16] Clearly, Henry had no intention of suffering the same privations that the Chevalier Bayard and Richard de la Pole had endured during the Navarrese campaign, but while Henry was warming his toes in his comfortable, collapsible billet, his Yorkist rival was eagerly awaiting a chance to avenge his brother.

Unfortunately for Richard, the captains of the French army were determined to obey Louis' order to avoid a battle and they were content to merely shadow the invaders. Nothing was done to prevent the border village of Ardres from being burned to the ground by Henry's Black Band, who were so intent on plunder not even the churches were spared. To his credit, Henry was so outraged by this sacrilege he hanged three of the errant *landsknechts*, and losing one of his precious Twelve Apostles did not improve his humour.[17]

According to Fleuranges and Mailles' accounts of the campaign, a party of Louis' horsemen captured the cannon called the St John the Evangelist in a daring raid on the English column, though Hall insists that the great gun had been lost when it fell off its carriage and rolled into a pond.[18] Besides blaming the negligence of the English carters, Hall goes on to say that another cannon, an iron bombard called the Redde Gonne, became wedged in a narrow lane but Henry could not wait while these guns were retrieved because his patrols had reported the approach of the main French army.[19]

Such was Henry's eagerness to win a great victory that would equal Agincourt, he left his pioneers to extricate the stranded guns while he hastily deployed the rest of his troops at the edge of a wood near the modern village of Tournehem-sur-la-Hem. Nightfall prevented an attack by either side, but the following day English pickets reported that 11,000 French foot and 4,000 French horse were less than 2 miles away. Hall tells us that among the French battle flags was the azure-blue banner emblazoned with the three gold leopard heads that heralded the presence of Richard de la Pole.[20]

Once the French had been sighted, Henry ordered his trumpeters to sound the alarm and his infantry took up a good defensive position on the crest of a low ridge while his cavalry rode off to secure the English flanks. Soon afterwards, the French horse made a half-hearted charge towards the English lines but a few shots from Henry's field guns forced them to retire. This sudden retreat prompted Henry's 'northern men' to give chase, but despite inflicting large numbers of casualties they found themselves in danger of being surrounded by the French infantry, whose advance had been screened by a hill.[21]

The northerners' rash charge had left a company of spearmen, led by the earl of Essex, dangerously exposed but Sir Rhys ap Thomas, the man said to have cut down King Richard III at Bosworth, spotted the danger. Riding to the rescue with his knights and 200 mounted archers under Sir Thomas Guildford, Sir Rhys managed to extricate Essex from the French pincer movement, but the enemy's 'great battalion' was too large to attack. Sir Rhys therefore halted his men to await reinforcements but the French suddenly lost their nerve.

Had the French counterattacked Sir Rhys' men, whom they heavily outnumbered, they could have punched a massive hole in the disordered English lines, but the senior French commanders were mindful of Louis' order not to fight a pitched battle so they ordered a general withdrawal. At this point Sir Rhys could have inflicted serious damage on the retreating French but he did not press home his advantage because he too suspected a trap.

Though the English had been left in possession of the field, this non-battle of muddle and missed opportunities could hardly be called a victory. Indeed, those Englishmen who had taken little part in the fighting sarcastically referred to the engagement as Dry Wednesday because they had been kept at their posts for most of the day without food or water.[22] On the other side of the battlefield, the French were now convinced that there was wisdom in Louis' decision to refuse battle and they returned to using guerilla tactics to harass Henry's advance.

One of the French raiding parties ambushed the English engineers trying to recover the St John the Evangelist from its watery casemate. The unarmed carpenters were slaughtered to a man and the enormous cannon was carried off to Amiens in triumph, but the earl of Essex managed to prevent the Redde Gonne from suffering a similar fate.[23] Meanwhile, Henry continued his march to Thérouanne but torrential rain prevented the middle-guard from joining the rest of the English army until 3 August.

By the time Henry reached his destination, Shrewsbury and Herbert had been besieging the town for more than a month but their light guns had done nothing more serious than demolish a house where 'many dozen fair young women had sought shelter'.[24] Equally ineffective had been the ditch that the English sappers had dug in a vain attempt to prevent supplies reaching the defenders; the entire length of the ditch could not be properly guarded, so the French had little difficulty re-victualling the semi-beleaguered town. Henry's arrival, however, turned the tide in favour of the English.[25]

Now he had sufficient men, Henry could plug the gaps in the leaky English blockade but Louis was fully aware of the situation. He therefore he ordered his army at Blangy to make sure Thérouanne's defenders had enough food and ammunition to last until the winter weather made further campaigning impossible *before* the town was completely closed off.[26] The dutiful French captains were happy to oblige and they soon came up with a plan: while Richard de la Pole's *landsknechts* kept the English busy, French pioneers would fill in the ditch with bundles of sticks and this makeshift bridge would allow a squadron of light cavalry to gallop into the town with the much-needed supplies strapped to their saddles.[27]

The horsemen chosen for this task were the Albanian *stradiots*, with whom Richard had previously served in Navarre, and they were commanded by the redoubtable Imbaud de Fonterailles. These forerunners of nineteenth-century hussars were instantly recognisable by their long Balkan coats, tall beaver-fur hats, short spears and curved swords, and they excelled at conducting lightning raids behind enemy lines.[28]

The ensuing fight was brief but bloody. The 3,000 English footmen who tried to prevent Fonterailles' horsemen from entering the town were blown to pieces by the defenders' cannon and Richard's mercenaries prevented the besiegers from sending more men to destroy the improvised bridge.[29] The *stradiots* delivered their flitches of bacon and satchels of powder to the grateful defenders but Edward Hall tells us that Henry's remaining eleven apostles 'sore beat the town's walls'.[30]

With the English siege guns slowly reducing Thérouanne's defences to rubble, Louis suddenly realised that his situation was much worse than he feared. To compound his peril, the 10,000 *landsknechts* he had recruited to reinforce his army at Blangy had failed to arrive.[31] These mercenaries were led by none other than Charles of Egmond, duke of Guelders, whose fortunes had greatly improved in the seven years since the collapse of his first revolt.

As mentioned earlier, Charles's attempt to use the captive Edmund de la Pole to blackmail Henry VII into funding his rebellion may have failed but Philip of Habsburg's bungling had allowed the rebel duke to escape to Liège, from where he had been able to renew his alliance with Louis. With the French king's help, Charles had restarted his war of independence and during this second revolt he had been obliged to fight the English because Henry VIII had sent 1,500 archers to help his imperial ally crush the Guelders' rebels. These Englishmen, who were led by Sir Edward

Poynings, had acquitted themselves well but Maximilian had lost the war and Charles had recovered his duchy.

With Guelders free from Habsburg domination, at least for the time being, Charles had repaid Louis by recruiting 6,000 of his countrymen to fight for France in the Italian Wars. He had marched his men to Lombardy in person, but his intervention had failed to prevent the French defeat at Novara. Had Charles and his men reached Picardy Richard de la Pole would have found himself sharing a billet with his brother's betrayer, but their paths were not yet destined to cross.

In a rare moment of military foresight, Maximilian persuaded Henry to detach the imperial *landsknechts* serving with the English army and send them east to block the duke of Guelders' march. This tactic worked simply because the 10,000 German *landsknechts* in the pay of the French had refused to fight their countrymen in the pay of the Emperor. As a result of this bizarre stand-off, the Guelders reinforcements never arrived in Thérouanne and Richard was spared the embarrassment of having to fight alongside his brother's nemesis.[32]

On a similar note, the duke of Albany was being asked to fight on the same side as the man who stood between himself and the throne of Scotland, James IV, but the Franco-Scottish nobleman was no rebel. Despite the fact that there was no love lost between the various branches of the Stewart dynasty, Albany was totally loyal to his French king so he welcomed James IV's support in any war against the hated English.

The moment Henry's troops embarked for France, James had offered Louis a fleet of Scottish ships to blockade Calais and, in a letter to the French king dated 4 August 1513, he expressed surprise that his partner in the Auld Alliance had not already asked him to do this. James also promised to invade England by land with an army of 60,000 men no later than 16 September, and it hardly needs to be said that Louis was delighted with these proposals.[33]

By now Henry had joined his army besieging Thérouanne, so James had to send his herald to Picardy to deliver his declaration of war. The Scottish envoy arrived at the English king's portable cabin on 11 August 1513, but despite the warm summer weather his reception was decidedly frosty.

'The king of England being in his rich tent, the herald of the king of Scots was brought to him and recited his message that, having besieged Turwyn [*sic*] two months without being fought, and having by his invasion caused the king of France to recall his army from Milan, Henry should be content and return home without making further war,' wrote an anonymous chronicler of the time, but although Henry listened to the herald with 'sober countenance' he kept his hand on his sword throughout the interview.[34] He gave full vent to his fury in a letter which the herald took back to Scotland.

In this letter, the king of England accused his Scottish counterpart of being a faithless oath-breaker and a malicious schismatic for daring to attack a member of the Pope's Holy League. Furthermore, wrote the outraged Henry, to declare war on England while her king's back was turned was an act of infamy that would dishonour the name of Scotland forever.[35]

Considering that James must have lied in his previous letters assuring his brother-in-law that he earnestly desired peace between their kingdoms, Henry had a point. On the other hand, it should be not be forgotten that the king of Scotland's offer to secure Richard de la Pole's extradition from France had been snubbed. In other words, both monarchs had been playing each other false.[36]

This game of bluff and counter-bluff notwithstanding, James's declaration of war proved to Henry that the Scots and French had been planning to foment a new Yorkist rebellion all along, which was exactly the scenario that the execution of Edmund de la Pole had been designed to prevent, and Henry's spies soon confirmed that the Yorkist hydra had indeed grown a new head.

17

THE HUNGRY MAN OF PAMPLONA

The first inkling that James IV of Scotland, Louis XII of France and Richard de la Pole had formed an alliance to depose England's second Tudor king came in July 1513 when Henry received a report from Antwerp identifying a Normandy priest as the man who had been smuggling messages from the late Edmund de la Pole to his brother. The author of this report was Thomas Spinelli, a Florentine financier employed by Henry to represent Tudor interests in Antwerp from 1509 until his death in 1522.[1]

Although little is known about Spinelli's life prior to Henry VIII's coronation, we do know that he was related to a family of Italian bankers whose financial tentacles spread across Europe. Spinelli's uncle ran a prominent Burgundian banking house, with offices in Bruges and Antwerp, while one of his brothers had been chamberlain to the Pope. Another of his brothers may have been Lorenzo Spinelli, head of the Medici bank in Lyon, who presented a sword and a cap to Henry VIII in 1514.[2] Whatever Thomas Spinelli's origins, he was certainly well placed to provide Henry with details of Yorkist plots hatched in the Low Countries and his account of the Normandy priest's activities is typical of his reports.

According to Spinelli, this shady cleric, who had a 'brown visage and a left eyebrow higher than the other', was planning to sabotage the English attack on Picardy with the help of his cousin, a lawyer from Rouen, a French merchant with an English wife and a gunner in Henry's army. This gunner, who was already in the pay of the French, was called Denys le Charon and his task was to destroy the English powder mills at Guînes with Greek fire.[3]

Curiously, imperial spies had known about this plot for some time but had chosen not to pass on this vital information until Henry had agreed to attack Thérouanne. Now it suited the imperials, the unfortunate priest was arrested and interrogated in Spinelli's presence. Though Spinelli thought the man was 'a poor fellow, ill-arrayed, and with a sharp tongue', he insisted that he was quite capable of sowing 'suspicion and division'.[4]

Whatever the level of threat posed by the cockeyed priest and his motley crew of saboteurs, the existence of any Franco-Yorkist cell underlined the fact that Henry could not afford to ignore the continuing presence of Richard de la Pole at the French court. In other words, with a Scottish invasion of England now a certainty, Henry had to win in Picardy before he was forced to withdraw his army to deal with the Scots. Ironically, Louis was equally desperate to resolve the impasse at Thérouanne because the Swiss victors of Novara were now besieging Dijon.

Fortunately for Louis, the success of Richard and Fonterailles' mission to resupply Thérouanne had convinced him that the town could keep the Anglo-Imperial army pinned down while he destroyed the Swiss, provided the garrison could hold out. Consequently he ordered his army at Blangy to make one more delivery of supplies before marching south, but now that the English had strengthened their blockade the French tactics would have to be different.[5]

Instead of Richard's infantry making a diversionary attack to allow Fonterailles' lightly armed Albanians to dash into the town, Louis planned to have his heavily armoured mounted knights, known as *gendarmes*, punch a hole through the English lines and hurl their sacks of food and ammunition into the ditch at the base of the town's walls. Once darkness fell, these supplies could be easily retrieved by the defenders.[6]

On 16 August 1513, the dukes of Vendôme, Longueville and Alençon, the lords de la Palice and de la Piennes, who was the king's Viceroy in Picardy, and the Chevalier Bayard left Blangy at the head of 1,200 nobly born, steel-clad horsemen. Unfortunately for the French, the English archers were waiting. The ensuing

1. Church of St Mary and almshouses, Ewelme, Oxfordshire. The magnificent manor house built by the de la Poles is long gone but the medieval parish church and almshouses they endowed have survived to this day. (Poliphilo, CC 2.0)

2. The gatehouse of Wingfield Castle, Suffolk. The ancestral seat of the de la Poles was built by Michael de la Pole, 1st Earl of Suffolk, in 1384. (Public domain)

3. Warwick Lane, City of London. It was in a house on this busy London thoroughfare that Edmund de la Pole held his council of war before fleeing England for the second time. (All photographs author's collection unless otherwise stated)

4. Paul's Cross, churchyard of St Paul's Cathedral. This plaque marks the spot where the wooden pulpit known as Paul's Cross once stood. It was here that Edmund and Richard de la Pole were 'accursed with bell, book and candle' at the beginning of Lent, 1502.

5. The Pontor (Bridge Tower), Aachen, Germany. One of the two surviving medieval gateways into the city where Edmund and Richard spent much of their exile between 1501 and 1504.

6. The walls and moat of *Dikke Tinne*, Hattem, Netherlands. Edmund was imprisoned in this Gelderland fortress from the summer of 1504 to the autumn of 1505.

7. Adelaarshoek (Eagle's Corner), Hattem, Netherlands. This is the only part of *Dikke Tinne* from Edmund's time to survive to this day. The building now houses an excellent fine-dining restaurant.

8. Site of the Abbey of the Minoresses of St Clare without Aldgate, The Minories, City of London. After his execution in 1513, Edmund was buried here alongside his late wife and daughter. What remained of the abbey after Henry VIII's dissolution of the monasteries was destroyed by fire in 1797 and its site is now occupied by this futuristic office block.

9. Maximilian I, Holy Roman Emperor, painted by Joos van Cleve *circa* 1530. (Rijksmuseum, Amsterdam)

10. Maximilian's son, Philip, archduke of Burgundy and king of Castile, painted by an unknown artist, southern Netherlands, *c.* 1500. (Rijksmuseum, Amsterdam, currently loaned to Noordbrabants Museum, 's-Hertogenbosch)

11. Portrait of Erhard de la Marck, painted by Jan Cornelisz Vermeyen, *c.* 1528. Erhard was appointed bishop of Liège in 1506 and he may have been distantly related to the de la Poles. He used his position to provide Edmund with money during his imprisonment and he helped Richard escape to Hungary. (Rijksmuseum, Amsterdam)

12. Portrait of Richard de la Pole. This enigmatic sixteenth-century painting is reproduced by kind permission of Dr Anthony Gross, whose meticulous research has identified the sitter as Richard. Those interested in his findings should read his excellent essay 'The Last Yorkist Revealed? Richard de la Pole, Charles Duc de Bourbon and a contentious panel portrait of the 1520s' (part of *The Fifteenth Century, Volume XX: Essays Presented to Rowena E. Archer*, ed. Linda Clark) published by The Boydell Press and available online at: JSTOR, https://doi.org/10.2307/jj.12771047.

13. Porte des Allemands (the Germans' Gate), Metz. This is the heavily fortified south-eastern entrance to the city where Richard de la Pole spent much of his exile.

14. Palais de Justice, Rue Haute Pierre, Metz. This elegant eighteenth-century building, which now houses the city's law courts, stands on the site of Richard's magnificent palace of Haute Pierre.

Above: 15. La Maison des Têtes, rue en Fournirue, Metz. Richard's lover, Sebille, and her cuckolded husband, the goldsmith Nicolas, lived on this street, in a house similar to this rare survivor from the sixteenth century. The plaque on the door to the extreme left of the building reads 'SALON DES ORFÈVRES' (Goldsmiths' Hall).

Right: 16. Église Sainte-Barbe de Sainte-Barbe, Metz. In 1519, Richard accompanied the comte de Guise to this church, dedicated to the patron saint of artillerymen, to give thanks for surviving the twenty-two wounds he had received at the battle of Marignano. Coincidentally, this church had been renovated by Richard's former landlord, Claude Baudoiche, in 1513.

Above: 17. Place Saint-Louis, Metz. These medieval buildings once housed the city's bankers and moneylenders, hence the square's alternative name of Place du Change. No doubt Richard was a familiar sight in this square whenever he tried to raise funds for his invasions.

Left: 18. Francis I, king of France, painted *c.* 1532 by Joos van Cleve. (Philadelphia Museum of Art)

19. Pierre Terrail, seigneur de Bayard, better known as the Chevalier Bayard. Richard became firm friends with France's most famous renaissance knight during the Navarre and Picardy campaigns. (Musée Carnavalet, Histoire de Paris)

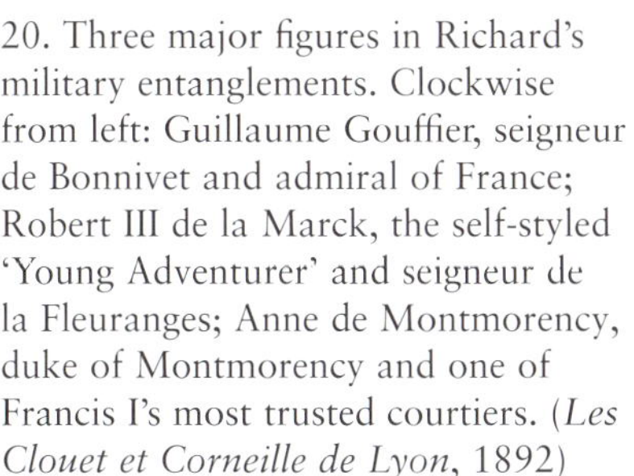

20. Three major figures in Richard's military entanglements. Clockwise from left: Guillaume Gouffier, seigneur de Bonnivet and admiral of France; Robert III de la Marck, the self-styled 'Young Adventurer' and seigneur de la Fleuranges; Anne de Montmorency, duke of Montmorency and one of Francis I's most trusted courtiers. (*Les Clouet et Corneille de Lyon*, 1892)

Left: 21. Charles V, Holy Roman Emperor, painted in 1548. Often attributed to Titian, this famous portrait is now thought to be by his student Lambert Sustris. (Alte Pinakothek, Munchen, CC-BY-SA 4.0)

Below: 22. *Landsknechts*, contemporary engraving by Daniel Hopfer, *c.* 1500–10, illustrating their characteristic flamboyance. (Rijksmuseum, Amsterdam)

Right: 23. John Stewart, 2nd Duke of Albany. A portrait of Scotland's reluctant regent drawn later in his life by an unknown artist. (*Exposition de portraits peints et dessinés du XIIIe au XVIIe siècle avril–juin 1907*)

Below: 24. Wark Castle, Northumberland. All that is left of the once mighty border fortress besieged by the duke of Albany's Franco-Scottish army in 1523. (Alljengi, CC 2.0)

Above: 25. Castel Mirabello, Pavia, Italy. During the siege of Pavia, the French baggage train was based in and around this hunting lodge, built by the Visconti dukes, at the centre of their vast deer park to the north of the city. In the battle, the baggage train was brutally sacked and hundreds of camp followers were massacred.

Below: 26. Porta Repentina, Pavia, Italy. The third camp occupied by the king of France, Francis I, and Richard de la Pole during the siege of Pavia was located near this ancient farmhouse, now called the Cascina Repentita. According to tradition, the French king was imprisoned here after his capture and he was given a reviving broth of stale bread and poached eggs which is still known as Zuppa Pavese (Pavian soup). *Inset*: a plaque on the farmhouse's wall reads: 'Francis 1st, King of France, opposed on these fields by the fate of arms, on 24 February 1525, fell prisoner to his rival Spain, proud of such a triumph.'

27. The battlefield of Pavia, Italy. The battle of Pavia was fought across the entire deer park, but Richard was killed at a spot somewhere to the west of the Mirabello hunting lodge, probably near the grey barn in the centre left of this picture.

28. The battle of Pavia, as depicted in a Flemish work painted *c.* 1525–30. The death of Richard de la Pole is depicted just to the right of the tower on the far left and the caption next to his supine figure reads, 'Duc de Svffoc dit Blance Rose' ('the duke of Suffolk, also called the White Rose'). (© Ashmolean Museum, Oxford)

29. The Basilica St Pietro in Ciel d'Oro, Pavia, Italy. After the battle, Richard's funeral was held in this twelfth-century church, which contains shrines to the fifth-century theologian St Augustine of Hippo, the sixth-century philosopher Boethius and the eighth-century Lombard king Liutprand.

30. The crypt of St Pietro in Ciel d'Oro, Pavia. Following his funeral, Richard's body was interred in San Pietro's crypt. Though his mausoleum was destroyed by Napoleon's troops, who turned the church into an arsenal, his remains still lie somewhere in these vaults.

battle became known as the Day of the Spurs after the speed of the *gendarmes*' retreat.

The English had learned of the French plan through the diligence of their spies and by interrogating prisoners, so it was easy to lay a trap. Firstly, Henry moved the bulk of his infantry south, to bar the road between Thérouanne and the French camp at Blangy. He then ordered his cavalry to search the countryside for any French formations trying to outflank the English foot soldiers' position.[7] Consequently, the French relief force found their way blocked by 10,000 English archers, supported by ten cannon, and the result was Henry's coveted repeat of Agincourt.

According to Bayard's loyal servant, who was present, the French were still under Louis' express orders to avoid a pitched battle so they began to retreat they moment they realised the English positions were impregnable. However, the first volley of English arrows turned what should have been a measured withdrawal into a rout and those French knights who survived the first fall of arrows became entangled with their advancing comrades. To compound French misery, the cleverly sited English guns could not miss this struggling mass of men.[8]

Typically, Bayard's biographer tried to put a positive spin on the debacle by claiming that his master's heroic defence of a key bridge allowed many of Louis' knights to escape. Nevertheless, numerous senior French commanders, including Longueville, Palice, Piennes and Bayard himself, were taken prisoner and sent back to England for ransom.[9] Of the French high command based at Blangy, only the duke d'Angoulême, heir to the French throne, the seigneur de la Fleuranges and Richard de la Pole escaped, and only then for the simple reason that this had been a cavalry engagement and they commanded the infantry.

Despite the defeat of the French horsemen, Richard and Fleuranges' foot soldiers managed to make an ordered withdrawal to Ancre on the River Somme but this skilful manoeuvre was not enough to save Thérouanne. Realising he could not relieve or resupply the town without cavalry, a distraught Louis gave its defenders permission to surrender.[10] A week after the Day of the Spurs, the captain of Thérouanne's garrison, Lord Pont-Remy, handed over his sword.

Three weeks later, Louis' Scottish allies suffered an even worse defeat in far-off Northumberland. On 9 September 1513, 25,000 Englishmen under the earl of Surrey cornered and crushed James IV's army of 40,000 Scots shortly after it crossed the River Tweed. The two sides met at Flodden, near the modern village of Branxton, and a few hours later the flower of Scottish chivalry was lying face-down in the rich earth of the Cheviots.[11] King James himself was among dozens of noble lords who were butchered by the English billmen, and Surrey's victory was the third of four military disasters suffered by the French in the summer of 1513.

Following hard on the heels of la Trémoille's defeat at Novara in June, the shameful rout of the French cavalry at Thérouanne in August and the slaughter of Scots at Flodden in September came the humiliating capitulation of Dijon, whose citizens had to pay the Swiss 20,000 crowns to raise their siege and go home.[12] These catastrophes left France without an army, without a nobility and without allies. Yet, despite this advantage, instead of marching on an undefended Paris, Henry was persuaded by the Emperor to besiege the Franco-Flemish town of Tournai.

Although this border stronghold surrendered on 23 September 1513,[13] it was of little use to Henry, so by the end of the year's campaigning season he was no nearer to making himself king of France than his Plantagenet predecessors. Yet there was one thing that Henry's Picardy campaign could still accomplish. The string of disastrous French defeats had forced Louis to open peace negotiations with the victorious Holy League. If Henry could make the surrender of Richard de la Pole a condition of ending hostilities, he would have taken a huge step towards eliminating the Yorkist threat forever.

It could hardly have escaped Henry's notice that his father had been able to make handing over Richard's brother Edmund the price of peace between England and the late king of Castile, but, in the words of one contemporary chronicler, Louis was 'a more rigid observer of the laws of hospitality than Dom Philippe'.[14] Consequently, when Louis received Henry's demand that Richard must be sent to England if he wanted the war to end, his reply was unequivocal: 'I would prefer to keep my faith and my word than surrender an ally to face certain death at the hands of an enemy.'[15]

Of course, Louis' motives for protecting Richard were not entirely altruistic. While Henry was still threatening to wage war in France, maintaining French support for the last Yorkist still at large was the best way to keep the pressure on his English enemy. Louis therefore instructed the captured duke of Longueville to secretly fan the flames of Henry's paranoia. This was not as difficult as it may sound because, being a nobleman, Longueville was allowed to move freely around his gilded Tudor cage.[16]

In the tennis courts and tiltyards of Windsor and Greenwich, Longueville quietly whispered to all who would listen that the king of France was ready to send Richard de la Pole into England at the head of 12,000 *landsknechts*. Longueville also delivered Louis' official warning to Henry that he had better prepare for war if the peace negotiations broke down, and a raid on the Sussex coast in the spring of 1514 demonstrated that the French were far from beaten.[17] Henry's response to the burning of 'the poor village of bright Helmston [*sic*]'[18] was to send Sir John Wallop to ravage the Normandy coast, and at this point Richard re-enters the story.

The sudden renewal of hostilities prompted Louis to send Richard and his mercenaries to the areas devastated by Wallop. Their orders were to protect the French coast from English raids, but Louis also promised to transport the White Rose and his men to England as soon Normandy was secure. Richard had been waiting for this moment for ten long years, but, unfortunately for the Normans, his men behaved worse than the English.

A popular story of the time told how a particularly riotous *landsknecht* was kicked out of Heaven for refusing to repent of his many sins and turned away from Hell because his behaviour frightened the Devil.[19] Indeed, Edward Hall tells us that the behaviour of Richard's men was 'so vile and shameful' that Louis was forced to send them to St Malo to await the French fleet that would to take them to England.[20]

The news that Richard was marching his men to Brittany may have come as a blessed relief to the people of Normandy, but the same could not be said for the king of England. St Malo was just a few days' sail from the perennially rebellious Cornwall and Ireland, and Tudor spies had learned that Louis, Richard and the duke of Albany were now plotting to seize control of Scotland as a precursor to their attack on England.[21]

After James IV's death at Flodden, he had been succeeded by his seventeen-month-old son and heir, James V, with the infant's mother, Margaret Tudor, acting as regent. Though being ruled by the king of England's sister was difficult for many Scots to bear, Margaret was largely accepted until she undermined her own position by marrying the deeply unpopular Archibald Douglas, 6th earl of Angus. Eager to be free of the hated Tudors and Douglases, a cabal of rebellious Scottish nobles offered the regency to Albany, and Louis encouraged his protégé to accept their offer in the hope of forcing Henry to negotiate. This tactic worked beautifully; facing a Yorkist invasion in the west and another Scottish attack in the north, Henry agreed to talk.

Of course, nobody told Richard. When he arrived in Brittany there were no ships waiting to take him to England, only excuses. Typically, Louis blamed the lack of transports on contrary winds, and the astonished Richard was told to be patient, but the king of France was playing a double game. While the White Rose waited obediently at St Malo and dreamed of avenging the deaths of his brothers, Louis was preparing to sacrifice a pawn for a queen.[22]

In a strange mirror of Henry VIII's future troubles, Louis' wife, Anne of Brittany, had died on 9 January 1514 without providing the king of France with a male heir. However, the sudden outbreak of peace with England provided him with an excellent opportunity to rectify this situation by marrying Henry's beautiful younger sister, Mary Tudor.

Though the eighteen-year-old Mary was already betrothed to Maximilian's grandson and heir, Charles, prince of Castile, Henry saw her marriage to Louis as a way of conquering France without further bloodshed. He therefore tore up his arrangement with the Emperor and a truce with Louis was proclaimed on 16 August 1514. As a gesture of his good faith, Henry dropped his demand for Richard to be sent back England but he did insist that Louis banish the White Rose from France.[23]

It is hard to underestimate the dismay Richard must have felt when heard the news that he, like his brother, had been betrayed by his supposed ally. Despite all the hardships he had endured in the service of the French king, Richard was back to being a stateless refugee but his position wasn't quite as bad as it had been in 1506. Back then, Richard had been forced to flee Aachen to escape his outraged creditors but now Louis gave Richard a handsome pension of 36,000 ecus, which was in addition to the annuity he was already receiving from the king of Hungary. Louis also arranged for Richard to be given political asylum in Metz.[24]

Today Metz is located in the French *département* of Moselle, but for most of the Middle Ages it was a Free City of the German Holy Roman Empire. This status gave Metz almost complete autonomy, and the Messines guarded their independence jealously. Over the centuries successive pro-French dukes of Lorraine had tried to conquer Metz, and the scars of a siege that had taken place in 1473 could still be seen in Richard's time. Despite these conflicts, the city's culture, traditions and language had become steadily more French and the drift towards Paris was exacerbated by Maximilian's frequent attempts to tax Metz to pay for his numerous wars.

Most recently, in 1512, the Messines had invoked their ancient right not to pay tribute to any prince or lord,[25] but while this steadfast refusal to accept foreign authority made Metz the ideal sanctuary for an exile, Louis' request presented the city fathers with a dilemma. Granting asylum to a Yorkist pretender might anger the Emperor, who was still an ally of the English king, and Henry's recent capture of Tournai had placed a hostile Anglo-Imperial army on the Messines' doorstep. On the other hand, refusing Louis' request could result in the French king attacking the city himself, or at the very least withholding any future aid.[26]

Caught between an imperial devil and the French deep blue sea, the Messines came up with an ingenious solution: they would grant Richard permission to remain in their city for a maximum of eight days, and this could be renewed on application as often as the city fathers saw fit.[27] This was hardly the secure refuge Louis had promised, but Richard accepted these conditions because his only other option, Hungary, was too far from the centres of power should he need to act quickly. This would prove to be a wise decision as the political tide was about to turn.

Having decided on his destination, Richard paid off all but sixty of his faithful *landsknechts* and arrived in his adopted city on Saturday 2 September 1514. As their custom required, the burghers of Metz presented Richard with the traditional gifts of two half-vats of wine, one of red and one of *clairet*, and twenty-five measures of oats for his horses.[28] Yet his welcome was not quite as warm as Richard had been led to expect, and there was an unseemly delay in finding him a suitable place to live.

At first, Richard was lodged in the Court of St Martin, which was a house belonging to the duke of Lorraine, but there was not enough room for his retinue and they had to be billeted in a nearby inn called The Angel.[29] Such an arrangement could not last for long and the man put in charge of finding more permanent accommodation for the Messines' guest was a successful haberdasher named Philippe de Vigneulles. Besides making a great deal of money in the cloth trade, Vigneulles' chief claim to fame is as the author of the *Gedenkbuch des Metzer Burgers*, which is our chief source of information about Richard's time in the city, and he came to know the English exile well. [30]

For three days, Vigneulles searched for a property that Richard could buy or rent but he could find nothing that was appropriate to the Yorkist's rank. Eventually the burghers of Metz pressurised their fellow alderman Claude Baudoiche, seigneur des Moulins, into leasing his house to the White Rose. The house in question was called Pastimes and it was hardly a coincidence that it was chosen because Baudoiche was a favourite of the French king and related to Richard's long-standing benefactors and kinsmen, the de la Marcks.[31]

Pastimes was a handsome waterfront property, located near the Abbey of St Vincent, and it had come into the possession of the Baudoiche family in 1494, when Claude's father, Pierre, married Bonne de la Marck. Previous notable guests had included the duchess of Lorraine, titular queen of Sicily, Yolande of Lorraine, landgravine of Hesse, and even Maximilian, who had stayed here in 1498 during one of his attempts to borrow money from the Messines.[32]

It was not only Pastimes that was very much to Richard's liking. Metz was one of the greatest cities in northern Europe, with strong walls, lofty towers and many fine churches. Chief among these was the imposing Gothic monolith of St Stephen's Cathedral, which still boasts the largest expanse of medieval stained glass in the world. Between these churches, wide boulevards intersected with attractive squares. Sixteenth-century Metz was clearly a very pleasant place to spend a lifetime in exile. Yet Richard had no intention of abandoning his quest for England's throne, especially as he was constantly being reminded of what he had lost.

Early in 1514, Richard learned that the dukedom of Suffolk, which had been created for his grandfather, had been given to Henry's new favourite, Charles Brandon, Viscount Lisle, who had distinguished himself at Thérouanne. Henry had hoped to marry Brandon to the Emperor's daughter Margaret of Austria, but to do so he needed to be of a higher rank than viscount. Brandon therefore became England's third duke on 4 March 1514, and he kept the title even though the planned marriage to Margaret never took place.

The elevation of Brandon notwithstanding, Richard continued to style himself duke of Suffolk for the rest of his life. However, his chances of exchanging a dukedom for a kingdom were dealt a serious blow by another diplomatic marriage which did take place. In October 1514, the fifty-two-year-old Louis XII married Henry VIII's eighteen-year-old sister Mary, but if England's king believed this union would drive a Tudor wedge between the White Rose and his French patron he was mistaken. In fact, the wedding marked a turning point in Richard's fortunes because less than three months after his wedding Louis was dead.

Upon their marriage a Parisian wit had remarked that 'the king of France hath been sent a white mare from England who would soon carry him gently to heaven or hell',[33] and this bawdy prophecy led many to believe that the French king had worn himself out trying to produce a male heir with his lusty young wife. If this was the case, he failed. The childless Mary was sent back to England, where she resumed her love affair with the aforementioned Brandon.

Once the late king had been laid to rest in the Basilica of St Denis, Louis was succeeded by his distant cousin and son-in-law Francis, duke d'Angoulême. This was the same Francis who had commanded French forces during the Bayonne and Thérouanne campaigns, and it was he and Richard who had extricated the French infantry from the disastrous Day of the Spurs. The new king of France was crowned at Reims on 25 January 1515 and he immediately declared his intention to renew the war to recover Milan.[34] This was the moment for which Richard had been waiting, and he wasted no time in returning to the French court.

The White Rose left Metz on 23 February 1515, taking with him only his page and his personal chef. According to Vigneulles, Richard had no desire to repeat the hardships of the retreat from Navarre so 'the hungry man of Pamplona did not forget to take his cook'.[35] The chronicler of Metz also tells us that the duke of Suffolk wore out a dozen horses as he galloped the 40 leagues to Paris without stopping.[36]

It is easy to understand Richard's eagerness. Despite the warming of Anglo-French relations in the last months of Louis' reign, Thérouanne, Tournai and most of Picardy were still in English hands. Therefore, if Francis was determined to fight a second war with the Holy League for Milan, he needed to prevent Henry from renewing his attacks on northern France. As ever, the best way to neutralise any threat from Henry was to cause trouble in England and Scotland so Richard found himself in another anti-Tudor triumvirate with the new French king and the old duke of Albany.

As mentioned earlier, Louis had planned a joint Scots–Yorkist attack on Tudor England, and though this plan had been made redundant by his sudden truce with Henry, Francis saw immense possibilities in its revival. Moreover, the situation in Scotland had changed so radically in the months following the late king's disastrous marriage that Albany already had one hand on the Scottish crown.

Once Margaret Tudor, regent for the infant James V, had alienated most of her support by marrying the unpopular Archibald Douglas, earl of Angus, Albany had been offered the regency in her stead. At first he was reluctant to accept, but Francis wanted a pro-French ruler in Edinburgh and Albany was keen to prove he was a loyal Frenchman. Accompanied by the same fleet of ships the late James IV had lent to the late Louis XII, Albany landed in Scotland on 26 May 1515 and besieged Margaret in Stirling Castle.

Meanwhile, Francis's plans to recapture Milan continued apace and he began to muster a new army in Lyon, the traditional starting point for all French operations in Italy. As befitting his new importance to the French cause, Richard rode with Francis to Lyon and here he was reunited with Fleuranges.[37] Interestingly the Young Adventurer was not just Richard's old comrade-in-arms, he was also his neighbour because he too owned a house in Metz.

Fleuranges' mansion was called Joyous Garde after Sir Lancelot's legendary castle, but owning property in Metz gave him his own quarrel with the Habsburgs.

Though Vigneulles does not go into detail, he tells us that in 1498 Maximilian had seized the Young Adventurer's lordship of Fleuranges and given it to a pro-imperial alderman of Metz named John de Vy. Naturally, Fleuranges had refused to surrender his title and the subsequent feud with de Vy had become so violent all de la Marcks and their retainers had been banned from entering the city under any circumstance. Furthermore, all Messines were forbidden to serve in any military force in which Fleuranges held command.[38]

This law, which had been passed in 1512, meant Richard's friendship with Fleuranges threatened to jeopardise his refugee status, but if his new alliance with Francis and Albany went well he would not be returning to Metz. Unfortunately, Richard's delight at being reunited with Fleuranges was tempered by the arrival in Lyon of the duke of Guelders, but he would not have to share a billet with the man who had betrayed his brother for long.

Within days of his arrival, Guelders was made captain-general of all the German mercenaries in French service,[39] which was the same position Richard had held during the sieges of Pamplona and Thérouanne, yet the White Rose had not been demoted. Despite his evident talents as an infantry commander, Richard was now far too important to be risked on the front line, so instead of accompanying Francis on his quest to reconquer Milan he was ordered to return north, to do what he could to disrupt the English occupation of Picardy.

This proved to be a shrewd move by Francis. Even though the battle of Bosworth had been lost almost thirty years earlier, the Yorkist tree was still able to bear fruit.

18

WILL THE KING HAVE THE SAID ENTERPRISE UNDERTAKEN?

On 16 April 1515, Lord Mountjoy, the English governor of Tournai, wrote to Henry VIII asking for his permission to punish the ringleader of a Yorkist-inspired mutiny. According to Mountjoy, a Welshman named Davy ap Powell had persuaded a significant section of Tournai's garrison to desert to Richard de la Pole, who was rumoured – quite rightly – to be commanding a large French force in Picardy.

In truth, the root of the soldiers' discontent was lack of pay rather than a burning desire for a Yorkist restoration. Nevertheless, the threat to Tournai was real and Mountjoy told Henry that the mutiny had begun with an attempt to lynch the city's English marshal, Sir Sampson Norton.

Despite being named as one of those present at the conspiratorial dinner infiltrated by John Flamank ten years earlier, Norton had returned to royal favour and in 1512 Henry VIII had paid the bluff old soldier's ransom after he had been captured during a raid on Arras. Perhaps unwisely, Henry had put Norton in charge of military discipline in Tournai and this appointment had almost cost him his life; poor Sir Sampson was within seconds of being hanged from one of the city's gates when troops loyal to Mountjoy rescued him. The mutineers' leader, Powell, was not so fortunate; he ended his days at the end of a rope.

Once the mutiny had been quelled, Mountjoy told both the king and Tournai's council that so many of the garrison had been ready to defect to the White Rose it would be impossible to punish them all. He therefore proposed dismissing all but 100 of his most trusted men and increasing their pay to a level that would guarantee their loyalty. The councillors tried to block this added strain on their city's finances by claiming that work on a new citadel, which Henry had ordered to be built, had emptied Tournai's treasury but Mountjoy appealed directly to the king's chaplain, Thomas Wolsey, whose star was on the rise.[1]

As a reward for tending to the king's spiritual needs throughout the Thérouanne campaign, Wolsey had been made bishop of Tournai despite the protestations of the city's French incumbent. Moreover, Wolsey was on the point of being made a cardinal and replacing William Warham, archbishop of Canterbury, as Henry's lord chancellor. The supremely ambitious butcher's son from Ipswich was, therefore, a very useful ally to have at court and Mountjoy's prediction that 'all things will be in hazard'[2] if the garrison's pay was not increased was confirmed by Wolsey's own spies.

'The people of Tournai complain that they are treated like dogs and will revenge themselves by some trick if not well watched,' Wolsey was informed at the end of April 1515.[3] The anonymous author of this report also remarked that Richard's new ally, the duke of Albany, was preparing to negotiate a sham peace treaty that would lull the English into a false sense of security. Incidentally, Wolsey's informant also noted that Richard's French pension was allowing him to live in luxury and he asked that all future correspondence should be sent to him via Paris, rather than Calais, because the English enclave was full of Yorkist spies.[4]

With Albany threatening Carlisle and Berwick, and Richard stirring up rebellion in Tournai and Calais, Henry desperately needed to strengthen his alliances with the other members of the Pope's Holy League, but the king of Aragon let it be known that he would not renew any Anglo-Spanish treaty until the Yorkist threat had been eliminated.

In June 1515, Sir Edward Poynings, who was one of Henry's envoys to the court of Prince Charles, Maximilian's grandson and heir, reported a conversation with his Spanish counterpart. In this typically euphemistic diplomatic exchange, the Spaniard asked if any Englishman still dared to call himself the White Rose, to which Poynings replied 'that there was one whom the Frenchmen called so'. On hearing this, the Spaniard told Poynings 'that it were better for them to do that should be done in time rather than to tarry too long'.[5]

Despite the obfuscating language, the Spaniard's message was clear: Ferdinand would not risk being involved in another bungled English campaign because Henry could not commit all his forces to the war against France until Richard de la Pole was dead. Poynings certainly understood what was being said and his letter to Henry reveals that the most extreme solution to the Yorkist problem – the assassination of Richard de la Pole – had been under discussion for some time.

'Will the king have the said enterprise undertaken, for which frequent suit has been made to me, and, if so, how am I to demean himself towards the parties?' he asked Henry,[6] but Poynings' willingness to commit murder should come as no surprise because he thoroughly detested all Yorkists and the de la Poles in particular.

Having been raised by his Lancastrian mother, Elizabeth Paston, whose family had a longstanding feud with the de la Poles, Poynings had joined Buckingham's plot to depose Richard III. Following the disastrous failure of that rebellion Poynings had thrown in his lot with the Tudor exiles in Brittany and his gamble had been rewarded after Bosworth with both a seat on the Privy Council and membership of the Order of the Garter. In the 1490s, Poynings was sent to Ireland to impose Tudor authority on the strongly Yorkist Irish and he personally led the forces that had defeated Perkin Warbeck at the siege of Waterford.

Besides Irish Yorkists, Poynings had fought anti-Habsburg rebels in the Low Countries not once but twice. In 1491 he had helped Maximilian crush a rising led by Lord Ravenstein and twenty years later he had commanded the aforementioned company of English archers sent to fight for the Emperor during the second Guelders' rebellion.[7] Despite failing to turn the tide in Maximilian's favour, Poynings diplomatic career had continued to prosper and within weeks of reporting his cryptic conversation with the Spaniard he had been ordered to arrange the assassination of the White Rose.

Unfortunately for Poynings, the man he hired to kill Richard suddenly disappeared and command of the operation was handed to Charles Somerset, Lord Herbert, who was now the earl of Worcester.[8] Somerset had received his earldom as a reward for his part in the Thérouanne campaign and after the capture of Tournai he had supervised the repair of that city's defences. It was Worcester who had made sure that the huge round tower at the centre of Henry's new citadel – which still stands – was completed, and his presence in Flanders meant he was perfectly placed to find an alternative to Poynings' missing agent.

'Another gentleman has offered to take the matter in hand and to deliver him [Richard] to me in this town or to make an end of the matter,' Worcester confidently told Wolsey in a letter dated 14 August 1515.[9]

The earl also informed Wolsey that the duke of Lorraine may be channelling funds from the French king to the Yorkists, and his spies were busily attempting to discover if this was true. In the meantime, Worcester sent two of his best men into enemy territory to contact the assassin and finalise the contract. Those chosen for this delicate mission were an Englishman named Sir John Russell and a Burgundian we know only as Captain Thibianville.

Although he was only thirty-one years old, Russell was already a trusted member of the Tudor court. Ten years earlier he had been among the 300 torchbearers who had escorted the shipwrecked king and queen of Castile to Windsor, and as a reward for his exemplary conduct during Philip and Joanna's unscheduled stay in England he had been made a gentleman of Henry VII's privy chamber. When Henry VIII came to the throne, Russell continued in high favour and he too was part of the new king's entourage at Thérouanne.

Russell's exploits as a diplomat and spy would eventually earn him the earldom of Bedford, but while his glittering career is well documented almost nothing is known about his colleague. Judging by his name, Thibianville was born in Thionville, a Burgundian town located 20 miles to the north of Metz and it is likely he was one of the imperial *landsknechts* Maximilian had sent to reinforce Henry's attack on Thérouanne. This would explain how he had ended up in the English garrison occupying Tournai, but he had fallen foul of Mountjoy's purge of suspected Yorkist mutineers.

In a letter to Henry dated 9 September 1515,[10] Worcester named Thibianville as one of the three Flemish captains who ought to be replaced by more trustworthy English officers, but his familiarity with the Moselle valley meant he was retained to act as a guide and interpreter. Thanks to his local knowledge, Thibianville was chosen to accompany Russell on his mission to contact the assassin and their nefarious meeting was to take place in a small town near Nancy called Saint-Nicolas-de-Port. Meanwhile, in Italy, a momentous battle had taken place that added considerable urgency to Russell's task.

After mustering his army at Lyon, Francis had crossed the Alps at the end of August 1515 and by constructing a new road through the mountains he managed to outflank the Papal-Swiss armies defending Milan. Realising they had been thoroughly outmanoeuvred, the Swiss sued for peace but soon changed their minds. Despite signing a treaty, the *reisläufers* treacherously attacked the French camp at Marignano on 13 September 1515 – yet the result was a personal triumph for Francis.

At first, the sheer ferocity of the Swiss attack threatened to overwhelm the duke of Guelders' *landsknechts*, including the 6,000 men of the Black Band once commanded by Richard, but Francis recovered the initiative by personally leading his *gendarmes* in twenty-five heroic charges.[11] Such an onslaught would have driven lesser armies from the field but the Swiss had not become the best infantry in Europe by shirking a fight, and at dusk they renewed their attack.

In the end, it was the superiority of French firepower that was decisive. Lacking cannon and handguns, the Swiss were ruthlessly shot to pieces as they tried to storm the French redoubts and when darkness finally put an end to the slaughter the bloodied survivors slipped away. With no other army in the field, the Holy League was forced to abandon Milan, whereupon Francis took possession of the city. Later he had a medal struck with the motto 'I have vanquished those whom only Caesar vanquished'.

The French victory at Marignano was as complete as the Swiss victory at Novara two years earlier, but as far as Henry VIII was concerned it meant the French king was now free to make good his promise to put Richard de la Pole on England's throne. Such fears meant the White Rose had to die sooner rather than later, so Russell and Thibianville left Tournai at the end of October 1515.

The spies' destination of Saint-Nicolas-de-Port had been chosen because the town's magnificent basilica housed the bones of the eponymous saint. These important relics attracted devotees from all over western Christendom, so the presence of strangers would not attract attention. Accordingly, Russell and Thibianville decided to disguise themselves as humble pilgrims and they had to be particularly careful because the town's feudal lord was the pro-French duke of Lorraine, Antoine the Good.[12]

Although Lorraine was supposed to be an imperial fief, Antoine and his younger brother Claude, comte de Guise had been educated in France, where they had formed lifelong friendships with the seigneur de la Fleuranges, heir to the neighbouring duchy of Bouillon, and the future King Francis. As a consequence, Antoine and Claude had fought for France at Marignano and had greatly distinguished themselves. According to Bayard's biographer, Antoine had rescued the Good Knight from certain death while Claude's selfless courage had prevented the men under his command from being routed by the Swiss.[13]

With stories such as these being widely circulated, Russell and Thibianville would have been in no doubt that they would be hanged as enemy spies if they were caught – and their worst fears were almost realised in a town just north of Nancy.

It was a three-day journey from Tournai to the shrine of St Nicholas, and one of the taverns where the spies hoped to spend the night was in Pont-à-Mousson.[14] However, as the two men sat down to a well-earned supper, three burly constables burst into the room. For a heart-stopping moment Russell and Thibianville thought their true identities had been discovered, but instead of being dragged off to a dungeon the watchmen's captain politely invited both pilgrims to dine with the town's governor, who was also the grand commander of the Hospital Brothers of St Anthony.

An invitation to dine with a senior monk was a rare honour for pilgrims, and the English spies should not have been unduly concerned, but the grand commander's godson was none other than Antoine, duke of Lorraine. Having swum in the murky waters of continental politics for some time, Russell must have known that this close kinship to the pro-French House of Lorraine meant his host was also pro-Yorkist, and he was right.

Once the table-talk had moved on from the French king's spectacular defeat of the Swiss at Marignano, Russell and Thibianville listened in silent terror while the grand commander proudly declared that he had a great deal of sympathy for the 'prince of England' who had been exiled to Metz. Clearly, the pompous prelate thought that Russell and Thibianville were on a secret mission *for* Richard de la Pole, not to arrange his murder.

Wisely, the Tudor spies held their tongues as the grand commander boasted that he had recently helped Richard extricate himself from a terrible business deal he had made with a German count whereby the latter would collect the Englishman's pensions from the kings of France and Hungary, as well as a new annuity he was due to receive from the duke of Lorraine. For reasons that are not entirely clear, Richard had agreed to this proposal but when he discovered that the greedy German was taking more than half the money in commission he had complained to the grand commander. Happily for Yorkist finances, the grand commander had persuaded his godson, Antoine the Good, to have the extortionate agreement cancelled and the German was deported.

After listening intently to what the grand commander had to say, Russell asked why the French king and the duke of Lorraine were so keen to support the White Rose. The grand commander had replied, with a knowing wink, that Francis was happy to support Richard so that 'he might have friends in case England should make some enterprise in France'.[15]

By a strange twist of fate, Russell had found himself breaking bread with an important ally of the very man he was trying to kill, but the grand commander never guessed that his English guests were working for the Tudors. The next day, the two well-fed and well-rested spies were sent on their way with the grand commander's promise to say prayers for the House of York ringing in their ears.

Shortly afterwards, Russell and Thibianville met the assassin. Their detailed account of the assassin's demands, together with a covering letter from the earl of Worcester, was forwarded to Wolsey on 16 November 1515. Incredibly, the original draft of the contract has survived more or less intact.

Memorandum from Captain Thibianville and Captain Russell regarding their discussion with Perceval de Matte, a gentleman from the County Burgundy, concerning how, and under what circumstances, he will undertake the business that we have spoken about and devised.

1. Should the enterprise be discovered, de Matte will be given permission to reside permanently in the English enclave of Calais and granted a pension for life of 200 crowns on which to live.
2. De Matte must be allowed to recruit four companions who will each be paid 50 gold crowns per year (if the enterprise fails) and the same rights of asylum as himself. He also wants to be put in touch with the 'English spy' who has already infiltrated in Richard de la Pole's household and who is well trusted in Metz.
3. If the enterprise succeeds, de Matte is to be paid 400 gold crowns per year for himself and for the aforementioned gentlemen.
4. De Matte also requires 3,000 gold crowns for his expenses, though this will be reduced if a lesser sum is required. Finally, so as not to violate his honour, he requires to be declared a servant of the king and freed from his oath to the lords of Metz.[16]

Having listed his demands, de Matte went on to explain how he intended to 'make the hit' and his plan was chilling in its simplicity.

The assassin had noted that Richard frequently went outside the city to hunt hares or exercise his horses but he did so attended by two or three noble friends and as many as eight servants. De Matte therefore proposed hiring a similar number of men he knew to be trustworthy to lie in wait for their target. De Matte's confederates would travel on foot, because their escape route would lead them through 'tough country' unsuitable for horses, but the ambush could not take place until the ground was hard:

> It will be impossible to complete the enterprise unless it is a beautiful winter's day because the said Richard does not go into the fields unless it is the right time for them to be frozen. Because of this, I do not see myself making haste and I will take care so as to accomplish the thing as desired.[17]

Talk of any delay must have made Russell nervous, but de Matte insisted that the greatest care had to be taken because the Messines would be so outraged by the murder they would search high and low for the perpetrators. That said, the assassin assured his paymasters that he would bribe the captain of the city guard to lead the hue and cry along a false trail. Finally, de Matte gave his solemn oath that if he was not able to run Richard through himself the men in his pay would be more than capable of finishing the job.[18]

Having struck their ignoble bargain, Russell exchanged seals with de Matte – so the Burgundian could recognise future couriers – and promised to give him the king's reply by the end of the month. With that, the assassin returned to Burgundy to await the official go-ahead. Worcester's covering letter ends by insisting that de Matte was the only man skilled enough to complete the mission. However, when no word came from Westminster, Worcester had to write to Wolsey to remind him that the deadline for accepting de Matte's offer was fast approaching.

'It is urgent to know the king's pleasure with regard to it, having promised the gentleman who was to take the enterprise an answer within a month, which expires on Wednesday next,' he wrote in a letter dated 9 December 1515,[19] and Worcester had good reason for insisting that the king made a decision as soon as possible.

In the same letter, Worcester admitted that the threat of a Yorkist insurrection in Tournai was still extremely high because several ringleaders of the previous mutiny had managed to cheat the gallows. According to Worcester, four of those who had escaped were John Cowley, John Lacy, Gilbert Tomson and John Pakeman, who had fled to Saint-Nicolas-de-Port shortly before Russell had arrived in the town to meet Perceval de Matte.[20]

Even if Worcester was unaware of this curious coincidence, there could be no doubt that the Yorkist dagger poised to strike at England was as sharp as ever, which makes Henry's reluctance to give de Matte the green light something of mystery. Perhaps Wolsey and Henry believed that the grand commander in Pont-à-Mousson had deliberately revealed his Yorkist affiliations to Russell in order to make his Tudor employers aware that their entire operation had been compromised.

Considering Wolsey had only just been made a cardinal and Henry desperately wanted to be regarded as a chivalrous, god-fearing prince, it is hardly surprising that they hesitated. Even if they overcame their personal scruples, the damage to both their reputations would be catastrophic if it became public knowledge that they had ordered Richard's assassination. Though several once-powerful noblemen like Edmund de la Pole had been executed on Henry's order, they had been sentenced to death by due process of law, and it should not be forgotten that England's second Tudor king had spared the lives of several Yorkists, such as the marquess of Dorset and William de la Pole, who was still incarcerated in the Tower.

Yet this debate on ethics soon became academic. Whether or not the grand commander in Pont-à-Mousson had succeeded in shaming the king of England into abandoning his plot, the deadline set by Worcester's assassin passed and de Matte disappeared into the shadows whence he had come. Though nothing more was heard of this 'Gentleman of Burgundy', the threat posed by Richard remained, and the information provided by Thomas Spinelli became increasingly important.

We have already met this Florentine financier during the affair of the cockeyed priest who had planned to blow up the English powder magazine at Guînes, but after the de Matte debacle Spinelli abandoned his banking career to become a full-time English spy. Entries in the King's Book of Payments note that between 1509 and 1517 Spinelli was paid an annual salary of £100, plus a £50 bonus, which was a good wage for the time. Equally, Dr Cuthbert Tunstall, one of the official English envoys to the Low Countries and a future bishop of Durham, observed that Spinelli now conducted no private business of his own.[21]

Despite his handsome salary, Spinelli often complained that he had to borrow money because he was kept short of cash by his English paymasters, and poverty was not his only grievance. In several letters to Wolsey, Spinelli bemoaned the fact that his position was constantly being undermined by his jealous colleagues because he had no official standing in the Tudor diplomatic hierarchy. No doubt Spinelli hoped that Henry's sudden need for a larger ambassadorial presence in the Low Countries would advance his career more rapidly, but throughout his time monitoring Richard's activities he remained in the background.[22]

After the death of Philip, king of Castile and archduke of Burgundy in 1506, his sister Margaret of Austria had ruled the former Burgundian territories as regent for her young nephew Charles. However, as the imperial heir was nearing his majority, Charles's court in Ghent had begun to rival that of Margaret in Mechelen. With two competing centres of power in the Low Countries, Henry VIII had to be represented in both, so he appointed Sir Edward Poynings, Dr William Knight and the waspish Dr Tunstall as his ambassadors to Prince Charles.

The prime purpose of this enlarged embassy was to renegotiate the treaties that would renew the Holy League, but for the next two years these men would also labour to frustrate Richard's plots. To this end they ordered Spinelli to increase his surveillance of the Yorkist court-in-exile, and the Florentine banker-turned-spymaster quickly recruited two musicians who were ideally suited to the task.

One was a trombone player, Hans Nagel, and the other was a singer, Petrus Alamire, and the itinerant nature of their professions meant they could travel widely without attracting suspicion. Even more importantly, both men had been employed previously by the Habsburgs, and Nagel already had strong ties to the Tudor court. But in the looking-glass world of espionage, not everything was as it seemed.

19

HE KNOWS ALL THAT GOES ON IN ENGLAND

Unusually for someone of humble origins, we know something about Hans Nagel's early life. He was born in Leipzig around 1470, and his father and brother were also musicians. In 1496 he found a position at the Tudor court, and in 1501 he was listed among the sackbut players who had accompanied an English diplomatic mission to Brussels. In 1503, Nagel and five others performed at Queen Elizabeth's funeral dressed in the new red livery specifically purchased for the occasion, and he continued to be listed among Henry VII's 'lowde mynstrels' until the summer of 1504, when he moved to the Burgundian court.[1]

Two years later, when Philip, archduke of Burgundy and self-styled king of Castile, sailed to Spain to seize his wife's throne, Nagel had been one of the court musicians who had entertained the royal party during the voyage. He had survived the terrible storm that had wrecked the Burgundian armada and travelled to Windsor as part of Philip's entourage. Nagel was also listed among the musicians who were with Philip when he finally reached Spain at the end of April 1506, but he returned to the Low Countries following the king of Castile's sudden death.[2]

It is highly likely that Nagel was recruited as a spy during his first or second stay in England. If so, he would have been on the Tudor payroll for at least a decade by the time Richard was exiled from France and he probably succeeded in infiltrating the Yorkist court-in-exile shortly after the White Rose arrived in Metz.

Consequently, 'the English spy' in Richard's household mentioned by de Matte during his negotiations with Russell may have been Nagel.[3]

Exactly when Nagel met Alamire is not known but the singer was a familiar face in both Habsburg and Tudor circles thanks to his beautifully illuminated music books. These exquisite volumes were eagerly purchased by the imperial family, yet Alamire was not his real name, nor was he a native of Burgundy.

Born in Nuremberg around 1470 to a family of merchants named Imhoff, young Petrus changed his name to the more Dutch-sounding van den Hove when he moved to the Brabant city of 's-Hertogenbosch to become a professional singer. One of his first engagements was with the Illustrious Brotherhood of Our Blessed Lady, a Flemish religious society founded to sing the praises of the Madonna, and another famous member was the painter Hieronymus Bosch.[4]

Whether Bosch had any influence on Alamire's career as an illustrator is a matter of conjecture, but by 1500 the young singer had found regular work performing for the archduke of Burgundy and copying music for the churches of Antwerp. He signed these works with a cipher based on notes in the Italian system of musical notation, A + la-mi-re.[5]

Besides changing his name, Alamire bought a house around this time and married a Flemish girl, Katlijne van der Meeren, but Philip's sudden departure for Spain brought harder times. The Alamires' new house had to be sold in February 1506, and a few weeks later Petrus had to appear before the bailiffs in his wife's hometown of Herentals. Perhaps it was this financial pressure that persuaded Alamire to sell information to Spinelli, but he continued to spy for the English when his fortunes improved. In 1508, Alamire joined the choir of the Imperial Grande Chapelle; he was also appointed scribe and keeper of the books in the private chapel of the Emperor's grandson Prince Charles.[6]

There is no record of Alamire's activities during the early years of Henry VIII's reign, but by the spring of 1515 he had accepted a commission from the Tudor court. A letter he wrote to Henry in May of that year contains his bill for a piece of music for five voices, six small partbooks, thirteen crumhorns and a pedal-operated manicordium to be installed in the king's palace at

Greenwich. Alamire also asked 'for the compensation which has not yet been forthcoming', but what is of greater intertest to us is his report of a new Scots–Yorkist plot.[7]

According to the singer-spy, the duke of Albany was trying to hire a fleet of Danish ships to transport Richard de la Pole's army of French mercenaries across the Channel. Alamire stated that he had learned of this scheme from 'one out of Denmark' and that Nagel had uncovered more evidence of this planned invasion from an Anglo-Flemish customs official. This man, who was called Afere Rason, had fled to Flanders after Wolsey had confiscated goods worth £14,000 from him and he had complained of his treatment to Claus Baaker, a Flemish merchant in Richard's entourage whom Nagel had befriended.

The sudden appearance of Rason in Baaker's household suggested that the fugitive customs officer had been planning to divert the revenues he had collected to the Yorkists, and £14,000 was enough to keep an army in the field for several months. Although Alamire added that Nagel and Baaker had left Richard's court, at least for the time being, he ended his letter by warning Henry that 'the White Rose knows all that goes on in England'.[8]

The plan revealed by Alamire is certainly not without precedent; as far back as 1503, Edmund de la Pole had conspired with the Emperor to conquer England using German *landsknechts* ferried across the North Sea in Danish ships. What was new was the attempt to discredit Wolsey by hinting that the cardinal had sold the goods he had sequestered from Rason and pocketed the proceeds. A little bit of peculation would not have been out of character for the notoriously venal Wolsey, who was also accused of lending the king's money to 'strangers' for his own advantage,[9] but by this time Nagel and Alamire's handler was none other than Thomas Spinelli, and he was beginning to suspect that the musicians were not to be trusted.

At the beginning of October 1515, Spinelli informed Wolsey that the musicians had refused to deliver a package of letters to Richard, which had been entrusted to Nagel, because the countryside around Metz was infested with robbers. To be fair, they did have a point – all the roads of central Europe were indeed plagued by unemployed mercenaries who had turned to banditry after the battle of Marignano made them redundant – but Nagel and Alamire's excuse did not impress Spinelli. What mattered to him was that Richard might suspect the two musicians were working for the Tudors if these vital letters were not delivered.[10]

In the end, the letters were delivered by a more courageous messenger but Spinelli was given further cause for concern by Nagel's increasingly strange behaviour. In the same encoded report for October 1515, Spinelli recounts how Nagel had accepted Sir Edward Guildford's invitation to come to England and perform for the king but only on the condition that he received the king's pardon 'for his dealings with de la Pole'.[11]

This request suggests that Nagel feared Guildford had no idea he was working for the Tudors and was trying to bait a trap. Nevertheless, Nagel's request for a pardon set alarm bells ringing for Spinelli and Dr Tunstall agreed that the trombonist's behaviour was highly suspicious. Their concerns evidently carried some weight because Nagel's Christmas concert was postponed until Easter 1516.

In the meantime, the whole matter was bought to the attention of Dr William Knight, the senior Tudor ambassador to the court of Prince Charles, by none other than Petrus Alamire. No doubt Alamire, who was still employed by the imperial chapel, was trying to calm any fears their paymasters may have had about Nagel, but his efforts did not convince Dr Knight.

In a letter dated 4 February 1516, Knight told Wolsey that inviting Nagel was a terrible idea because he wanted to go to England to 'work treason'. He also insisted that Nagel's request for a pardon was a delaying tactic so he could seek permission for the trip from his true master: Richard de la Pole. As proof of this double-dealing, Knight quoted from a letter the trombonist had written to Alamire in which he had asked the singer to go with him to Metz and assure Richard that his forthcoming trip to England 'would be profitable'.[12]

Of course, Nagel had previously claimed that the roads to Metz were too dangerous for travel, so as far as Knight, Spinelli and Tunstall were concerned the trombonist had been trapped by his own lies. Nonetheless, Knight thought that Nagel could still be useful, provided he did not know he was under suspicion. He therefore advised Wolsey that Nagel's pardon should be granted but his concert should be postponed again, until after Easter, because music was prohibited during Lent.[13]

'And by doing so we may know all de la Pole's enterprises,' the ingenious Knight had told Wolsey,[14] but Nagel was no fool. Realising that a trap was being carefully prepared for him after all, he wisely stayed at home but remained on the Tudor payroll as Knight had suggested. By contrast, Alamire emerged from the affair with his reputation intact.

'Alamire is in so great trust with them all, and so discreet that by his means we shall know the particular ground,' Spinelli had told Wolsey in a letter dated 6 January 1516, adding that he had paid the singer 40 gold crowns to find out what was in the letters Nagel had refused to deliver.[15]

'He hath promised unto us three that at his return, within twenty days at furthest, we shall know all we might had purveyed by some way the letters to be taken,' Spinelli wrote confidently. He can only mean that by playing their hand carefully more could be learned about the suspected invasion of England by the Scots and a Franco-Yorkist army.

As mentioned previously, Alamire had revealed the outline of this plot to Henry back in May 1515, and he had added more details of the scheme in a letter he sent to Spinelli in December of the same year. In this embellished account, Alamire revealed that the negotiations had started badly when Richard accused the herald sent by the duke of Albany of being a Tudor spy. However, after exhaustive enquiries had proved the man to be genuine, Richard gave him a velvet doublet and six gold pieces by way of an apology.[16]

In the light of the Nagel affair it is hardly surprising that Richard had been suspicious, but after this hiccup the preparations for the joint invasion began to gather speed. Richard even took several pro-Yorkist Flemish noblemen into his confidence, and among those who agreed to help were Lord Fiennes, to whom Edmund had written during his imprisonment in Namur, the chancellor of Brabant, and Philip of Cleves, Lord Ravenstein, who had crossed swords with Sir Edward Poynings in 1492.[17]

The Lord of Ravenstein's connections to the White Rose were deep; he was a cousin of the de la Marcks, which meant he was distantly related to Richard de la Pole as well as the seigneur de la Fleuranges, and he had grown up at the court of the Yorkist matriarch, Margaret of Burgundy. Like many Flemish noblemen, his loyalties were fluid and though he had fought for Maximilian during the Flemish revolt of 1482–92 he had joined the French-backed rebels when the Emperor had refused to honour a truce he had brokered.

After being forced to surrender his stronghold of Sluys by Poynings, Ravenstein had fled to France and been made viceroy of French-occupied Genoa for his loyal service during the Italian Wars. The sudden cessation of hostilities in 1514 allowed Ravenstein to return home, but he was not allowed to occupy any position of trust at the imperial court and was denied entry into the prestigious Order of the Golden Fleece.[18]

As far as the king of England was concerned, if Richard was communicating with a pro-Yorkist, pro-French rebel, it could only mean that Continental support for the Yorkists was more widespread than Henry's spymasters had feared. To find out more, Spinelli ordered Alamire to push deeper into Richard's inner circle and the singer obediently befriended Claus Baaker, Nagel's old contact, and Jan van Riet, whose brother Derek had been Richard's steward ever since his trip to Hungary in 1504.[19]

The younger van Riet told Alamire that the Paris–Edinburgh–Metz axis was growing stronger every day and support for the White Rose in England was steadily increasing. He also promised Alamire that he would persuade his brother to write a letter of recommendation so the singer could obtain 'a confidential post' with the White Rose, and the two men agreed to communicate using a codebook disguised as a psalter.

Not for the first time would two brothers find themselves on opposite sides, and it seems that Jan had decided to betray the Yorkists because Richard had failed to repay some money he had borrowed from the van Riets' sister, but more of that later. In the meantime, Jan's claims were verified by another of Alamire's contacts who was 'engaged in the Scotch business' and Spinelli was so pleased with his spy he wrote to Wolsey with a recommendation that the singer should receive another huge bonus of £30 or £40.[20]

More evidence of an imminent invasion was soon forthcoming, this time from Dr Knight, who reported that the imperial foundries in Mechelen were busy casting several large pieces of artillery for

Lord Ravenstein. Knight believed these guns were destined for Scotland because the former rebel had been spotted going into a Mechelen church with the duke of Albany. Knight also claimed that 4,000 *landsknecht* mercenaries had been withdrawn from French garrisons and sent to Bishop Erhard de la Mark in Liege, which could only mean they would be placed under Richard's command.[21]

Though Knight conceded that these mercenaries may be used to reinforce the French-backed rebels in Guelders, he personally believed they would either be sent to Scotland for the invasion of England or brought to bear on Tournai, and his opinions were echoed by Spinelli. In two letters written at the beginning of February 1516, Spinelli informed Wolsey that that the French king had ordered the Guelders rebels to accept a four-month truce and a constant stream of Guelderian troops was now passing through Maastricht.

Though Spinelli noted that these mercenaries were travelling in small groups to prevent the spread of disease, he had little doubt that this force, once assembled, would attack Tournai 'because its recovery is of great consequence to the French'.[22] In the light of these developments, both Knight and Spinelli wrote to the city's governor, Lord Mountjoy, warning him of the danger. For his part, he remained unconvinced.

'I do not believe the reports of troops assembling against Tournay,' he wrote in his February report,[23] but Mountjoy was ignoring the evidence of his own torturers who had been busily mutilating one of the ringleaders of the previous year's pro-Yorkist mutiny.

The unfortunate victim was John Pakeman, who had left his sanctuary in the abbey of Saint-Nicolas-de-Port after receiving assurances that he would be given the chance to clear his name. The promise of an amnesty was a trick, and the moment Pakeman set foot in Tournai he was arrested and 'put to the question'. In his agony, the pain-wracked prisoner revealed that Richard and Fleuranges were now in command of the 'Black Band of Almains' and he gave the names of four East Anglian merchants who were secretly working for the White Rose.[24]

Before he died, Pakeman told his tormentors that the epicentre of this spy ring was the Ship Inn, a tavern in Antwerp's fish market, whose proprietor had a daughter who had 'fallen in with a servant of Blanche-rose'.[25] The girl's lover was probably one of the van Riet brothers, and Pakeman also revealed that the English end of this Yorkist pipeline was run by a man named William of the Stable, who was known to Derek van Riet.[26]

Having been wrung dry of information, the mangled mutineer was hanged, drawn and quartered in May 1516, but Mountjoy knew that a man under torture will confess to anything and he did not believe a word Pakeman said.[27] Moreover, Tournai's governor loathed his job so much he was quite happy to abandon the city to the French.

'I would gladly be discharged of my office, for I wish to go to England at Easter,' he told Wolsey,[28] but he did recruit spies, both inside the city and in Antwerp, to find out the truth. Whatever Mountjoy may have thought, there could be no denying that the king of France, the duke of Albany and Richard de la Pole were up to *something*, and Wolsey became convinced that the Caesar in this triumvirate was the White Rose.

At one level Wolsey's logic cannot be faulted. If Richard was removed from the equation Albany and his French allies would lose the figurehead they needed for a Yorkist uprising in England; on the other hand, the French and Scots rarely needed an excuse to attack the English. Nevertheless, Wolsey remained convinced that assassinating Richard de la Pole was crucial to maintaining Tudor rule on both sides of the Channel. Unfortunately for Wolsey, the two new assassins hired by his spymasters were men of singular ineptitude.

The first of these contract killers, Captain Simond Francoise, was recruited by Sir Edward Poynings, whose track record in finding such men was not good; the fact that another man had to be found after him proves he fared no better than de Matte.[29]

The third assassin to receive the king's warrant to murder Richard de la Pole was called Robert Latimer, but he was arrested while travelling through the Low Countries, and letters from Henry to Lord IJsselstein, commander of the imperial forces fighting the Guelders rebels, were found hidden in his cloak. Though England and the Empire were allies, Henry had overstepped the mark by writing in secret to an imperial general and it took two days of frantic negotiations by Spinelli and Knight to secure Latimer's release.[30]

Undaunted, the assassin declared he was happy to continue with his mission, so Knight ordered him 'to burn certain instructions that he carried ... lest the voyage should be discovered' and sent him off in search of his target.[31] Though accounts of Latimer's fate differ, they all agree that the hapless assassin did not get far. According to Spinelli, Latimer gave himself up shortly after crossing the border into Champagne, but French accounts maintain that he was arrested near Mons after English coins were found in his possession.[32]

In either case, Latimer was detained in the castle of Hayn, where he was questioned by the duke of Vendôme. It is a measure of Richard's importance that his assassin was interrogated by a French prince of the blood royal.[33]

For all his bravado, Latimer was not a man of strong will and he bought his freedom by making a full confession, yet he did not return to England after cheating the gallows.[34] Instead he made his way to Metz and, having convinced Richard that he was a loyal Yorkist, was given a position as a servant.[35] Why Latimer did not simply disappear is something of mystery. Perhaps he feared his Tudor handlers would make him suffer for his failure, or he may have been determined to finish his mission; in either case, we shall hear more of Robert Latimer later.

After these abortive attempts to have Richard killed, the only good news for Wolsey came from Tournai, where it appeared that Mountjoy had been right all along. On 18 April 1516, Sir Richard Jerningham, captain of Tournai's guard, informed the cardinal that the 3,000 men of the Black Band, who had been preparing to attack the English-held city, had been diverted to northern Germany to fight in the Frisian war. Yet this did not mean that the threat of a Yorkist invasion of England had passed.[36]

For some years the rebels against Habsburg rule in Friesland, who had given George the Bearded so much trouble, had made common cause with both the French and the duke of Guelders. As a consequence of this *ad hoc* alliance, Wolsey needed to know if Richard was planning to use Frisian ports to embark his invasion force.

He was also concerned about the loyalties of two imperial commanders in the area. One was Lord Nassau, who had led the imperial forces at the Day of the Spurs, and the other was John, duke of Cleves, who was known as the Baby Maker because he had sired sixty-three illegitimate children *before* his marriage. Incidentally, one of John's granddaughters, Anne, would become Henry VIII's fourth wife, but at this point the significance of the House of Cleves to the Tudors was the fact that they were related to the de la Marcks. This made the Baby Maker a close cousin of Fleuranges and Ravenstein, so it made perfect sense for Wolsey to try and find out if he intended to join the anti-Habsburg party as his kinsmen had done.

Though both Tudor spies were swiftly captured, they managed to escape to Tournai where they reported the departure of the Black Band for Friesland.[37] This news must have set alarm bells ringing in Westminster because, less than two years before, Richard had marched these same mercenaries to St Malo where a French fleet should have been waiting to transport them across the Channel. Only a sudden peace with France had saved Henry from the Yorkists on that occasion, and Spinelli was now insisting that the White Rose was back in French favour.[38]

As ever, separating fact from rumour and misinformation was extremely difficult, but in April 1516 Spinelli wrote directly to Henry claiming that a Devon merchant named Thomas Trysho, who traded between Exeter and Hamburg, had raised 6,000 guilders for the Yorkists and this money had been smuggled to Richard by a Flemish knight called Nicolas van der Hu. Although this information was almost a year old, Spinelli believed it gave weight to the idea that a Franco-Yorkist army would sail from the north German coast and land in Scotland.[39]

To emphasise his point, Spinelli claimed that Richard had recently been summoned to Paris for a secret meeting with the French king. This would have been worrying except that Spinelli admitted his sources were Hans Nagel and Petrus Alamire, who had been paid 50 guilders for this intelligence.[40] It may be recalled that Nagel, who was now known to be a Yorkist double agent, had been kept on the Tudor payroll in the hope he would inadvertently divulge more of Richard's secrets, but as the weeks went by Alamire had also come under suspicion.

'I enclose a letter from Alamire, who went to Metz with Hans Nagel, not knowing of his understanding with me ... I think that Alamire now favours De la Pole, and must not be trusted too much,' Spinelli confessed in a letter to Henry dated 24 April 1516. That same day, Spinelli also wrote to Wolsey, informing the cardinal that he had told the king of his new-found suspicions and asking for further guidance.[41]

To his credit, Spinelli seems to have quickly developed second thoughts about throwing his once-trusted agent to the wolves because in another letter to Wolsey, dated 20 May 1516, he declared that he was 'loath to put any man's life in danger on a mere report'.[42] Spinelli also promised to send Alamire to England to answer his accusers in person, but just at that point the elusive singer disappeared.

20

WHILE I HAVE ONE CROWN TO EXPEND

By the end of May 1516, both jewels in Spinelli's espionage crown were looking somewhat tarnished, which meant his own position was also in serious jeopardy. Spinelli therefore went in person to Alamire's house in Mechelen to find out what was going on. Much to his relief, he found the singer had returned home.[1]

To explain his absence, Alamire told Spinelli that he had travelled to Antwerp to meet Jan van Riet, his contact at Richard's court, who had important news about the long-rumoured Scots–Yorkist invasion. Unfortunately van Riet had been delayed, so the meeting had not taken place, but to set his paymaster's mind at rest Alamire declared he was happy to go to England 'for further instructions'.[2]

The singer duly crossed the Channel on 19 June 1516. When Spinelli wrote to Wolsey advising him that Alamire was on his way, he warned the cardinal that their meeting must be kept secret 'because of his acquaintance with the king's minstrels and Hans Nagel'.[3] Despite this miasma of suspicion, Alamire convinced Wolsey that he was not a double agent and he was sent back to Metz with orders to find out all he could about the French-backed Scots–Yorkist plot. This Alamire did, but Spinelli's apparent success in keeping the singer loyal merely papered over some very serious cracks in the Tudor intelligence services.

Besides the unmasking of Nagel, the arrest of Robert Latimer was a strong indication that there was a French or Yorkist spy operating at the very heart of the king's household and he, or she, had access to the most sensitive Tudor secrets. Finding this mole would not be easy, and the task became immeasurably more difficult when Wolsey learned that another spy on the Tudor payroll was a double agent – and this man was also named Spinelli.

Confusingly, Anthony Spinelli from Genoa had no connection to Thomas Spinelli from Florence, even though both men ran continental intelligence networks for the English king. In fact, Anthony Spinelli was a veteran agent who had spied for the Yorkist kings Edward IV and Richard III before working for the Tudors.

The Genoese spy's troubles had begun in 1513 when he had been arrested and imprisoned by the French. Three years later, in the spring of 1516, Wolsey received an anonymous letter claiming that this Spinelli, like Latimer, had secured his release by agreeing to turn his coat and the traitor was now being paid 400 francs a year to be a 'marvellous great enemy to the king's grace.'[4]

These accusations threw a shadow over Anthony Spinelli's namesake, and as soon as Wolsey learned of the Genoese spy's treachery he took steps to isolate his Florentine counterpart. Shortly after Alamire's disappearance, on 4 June 1516, Thomas Spinelli wrote to Wolsey to complain that he was being excluded from the inner circle of English diplomats in the Low Countries, but the cardinal had more pressing concerns than the Florentine's hurt feelings.[5]

Interestingly, the report about Anthony Spinelli confirmed Thomas Spinelli's claims that Richard had recently travelled to France, and its unnamed author described his curious audience with Francis in some detail:

> Immediately after that the French King was returned from Italy unto Lyon, he sent for Ric. de la Pool, then being in the city of Metz in Lorraine; and as they were both riding upon the said Richard's mule, the king behind the said Richard, the king said these words to unto him. 'I know that the king of England is my utter enemy, intending to destroy and deprive me from my state in Italy, sending his right great sums of money to the Emperor, and retaining the Swisses in his aid for that intent; wherefore glad I would be to serve him with like favours.'[6]

Even if this improbable mule ride is a metaphor, Francis's desire to depose the Tudors is well documented. As far as restoring the House of York was concerned, however, there was a problem. While the overburdened mule plodded its way through the Lyonnaise countryside, Francis explained to Richard that although he was sending men and money to help the duke of Albany hold on to power in Scotland he could not begin the conquest of England until he had consolidated his own hold on Milan. This was not what Richard had expected to hear, yet Francis assured him that the invasion of England had not been cancelled, only postponed:

> ... And because I know your title to be good to the crown of England, I shall but shortly endeavour me to make some peace with the said emperor to stablish my matters there; and, that done, I shall assist you both with men and money for obtaining of your said right, and shall not forsake you in that behalf while I have one crown to expend.[7]

In the meantime, Francis suggested that England's throne might be won by means other than a full-scale invasion and proposed smuggling four hired killers into England to assassinate Henry VIII. For a mere 4,000 francs, which Richard would have to pay, these men would 'by crafty and cautelous means' set fire to the palace where Henry was spending Christmas and burn the Tudor tyrant to death.

Having survived three assassination attempts sponsored by Henry, Richard probably felt he could endorse this early form of the Gunpowder Plot with a clear conscience, especially after Francis had told him about the implications of Robert Latimer's arrest. In particular, Francis warned his Yorkist ally that Latimer's defection might be another trick and that Richard should be aware that there were Tudor spies already operating in his household.

In a mirror image of Richard's problems, Wolsey's informant told the cardinal that there was a Yorkist mole in the Tudor court. Although he did not know the man's name, he had found out that the spy was a marquis who was also Richard's cousin.[8]

As England had only one peer with that title, the traitor had to be Thomas Grey, marquess of Dorset, who was indeed related to Richard, albeit distantly and only by marriage. Adding weight to this accusation were the aforementioned rumours that Dorset had sabotaged the Bayonne expedition to help his Yorkist kinsman, so it can hardly be a coincidence that he was removed from the privy council at this time. Although the much-mistrusted marquis kept his head, it would be four years before he was restored to royal favour.

The realisation that Tudor England was beset by enemies both foreign and domestic must have given Wolsey much food for thought. Yet just as it seemed Yorkist fortunes were on the rise, Thomas Spinelli managed to place another spy inside Richard's inner circle, and this man confirmed that the French were in no position to mount a Yorkist invasion.

The new Tudor agent was a Luxembourger named Jacques de Eesebeke, and besides being the 'bailie' of a small village near Metz he was employed as a messenger in the imperial postal service. Spinelli had recruited him in the spring of 1516 and sent him to Bresse, in Savoy, 'to obtain news of Richard de la Poola',[9] but thanks to the suspicions surrounding Nagel, Alamire, Latimer and Anthony Spinelli, Eesebeke had to be vetted by Dr Tunstall before he was entrusted with an important mission. Fortunately for Thomas Spinelli's battered reputation, Tunstall found Eesebeke to be 'a discreet man'[10] and he was paid 60 gold florins to make 'two journeys into Metz in the matter of Blanche Rose'.[11]

Disguising himself as an itinerant wine merchant, the spy rented lodgings in the city close to Richard's own, and by a remarkable stroke of good fortune a courier carrying packet of letters from the French king turned up at Eesebeke's door by mistake. Though the error was quickly discovered, and Richard sent his secretary to recover the missing mail, Eesebeke learned the letters' secrets by drinking his fellow postman under the table.

As the wine flowed, the French courier confirmed that Francis could not help Richard conquer England while he was preoccupied with Milan. Despite this, Eesebeke's guest also insisted that Francis had not lost interest in the Yorkist cause and he planned to help the White Rose recover his birthright 'at the first good season of the next year'.[12] Though Richard had been depressed by the postponement, and he was seen in church 'with a very poor visage',[13] he had plenty of French gold with which to drown his sorrows.

After making enquiries with Richard's staff, one of whom was a fellow Luxembourger, Eesebeke learned that the French king had given his English ally 3,000 crowns so he could maintain a lifestyle befitting an exiled prince. This money allowed Richard to keep around twenty servants and hold daily banquets to entertain the leading citizens of Metz, though Eesebeke thought that his charm offensive had not been entirely successful.[14]

It should not be forgotten that there were many in Metz who feared that the presence of a pro-French English rebel would upset their delicate relationship with the Emperor, and they persuaded the city council to warn Richard that his secret dealings with Francis must stop or he would be expelled from the city. The White Rose was also told that he had to move into a house belonging to Fleuranges, who still had his own enemies in Metz, because his current landlord, Claude Baudoiche, wanted his troublesome English tenant gone.[15]

All this was reported to Spinelli, who duly informed Wolsey, and Eesebeke's claims that the Franco-Yorkist invasion plan had stalled were corroborated by another wealthy Florentine financier named Leonardo Friscobaldi.

For some weeks, Wolsey had been dealing with an embezzlement scandal involving Friscobaldi, from whom Henry had borrowed 60,000 guilders. This money was supposed to help Maximilian avenge the imperial defeat at Marignano, but, while Henry's gold had saved Brescia and Verona from the French, Friscobaldi had been accused of handling the affair badly.[16] The intricacies of these financial dealings need not concern us here; what is important to us is Friscobaldi's connection to Richard de la Pole.

In a long letter explaining his actions to Henry, Friscobaldi mentioned that a man who owed 200 florins to his father had found a position in Metz as Richard's steward. Realising the debtor's value as a spy, the banker had plied the man with drink and learned that Richard had recently spent ten weeks with the French king, yet the Italian does not depict the White Rose as Francis's equal, riding the same mule. Instead, he portrays Richard as a desperate supplicant who is running out of options:

> So upon a day it fortuned that the steward's master [Richard] was with the French King, and the Queen and the King's mother,

> and made his lamentation unto them, weeping, saying that he was utterly cast away, and wist not what to do, and that he had no help of nobody. The French King said to him with good comfort, be we not here all three cousins? Think you that we will see you cast away? Nay, nay: but I shall bring you to your right, and help you as much as shall be in our power to do.[17]

The banker goes on to say that Francis had accused Henry of being a foul usurper who had dealt so traitorously with his French neighbours that he deserved to be deposed. Francis had also declared that he would not rest until the Tudor despot was in his grave, so Richard should hold himself 'in readiness whensoever he should call him'.[18]

With the benefit of five hundred years of hindsight, we can see that Francis was promising Richard everything and delivering nothing, in much the same way Maximilian had done with Edmund a decade earlier. At the time, though, Friscobaldi could not be sure what he was being told. He therefore decided to investigate further, and his additional enquiries revealed that Richard kept only four servants, not the seventeen or eighteen reported by Eesebeke.

The banker's description of Richard as a desperate exile contrasts sharply with the postman's depiction of the White Rose as a dignified king-in-waiting. Nevertheless, the fundamental message from both sources was the same: Richard de la Pole was no longer a serious threat, at least for the time being. Furthermore, although Wolsey did not know it, Friscobaldi had initially reported his findings to Maximilian *before* he had written to Henry, but the Emperor had no more use for the White Rose either.

Somewhat callously, Maximilian had remarked that he did not care if Richard was hanged, 'for he belongs to the French king',[19] which was a complete reversal of the enthusiastic support he had given the Yorkists fifteen years earlier. Faced with Maximilian's ambivalence, Friscobaldi had toyed with the idea of having Richard kidnapped and sent to England in the hope this would restore his good relations with Henry, but he was told that it would be easier to have the White Rose killed because it would be impossible to capture him alive.

In truth, either plan would have been difficult to execute because in the early summer of 1516 Richard suddenly left Metz.

Contemporary accounts of his movements become confused at this point. On 23 July a Venetian diplomat, Sebastian Giustinian, told the Signory that Richard was back with the French king, but in August Thomas Spinelli told Wolsey that the White Rose was still in Metz and had not been in France 'as some had thought'. Similarly, Hans Nagel thought that Richard had moved to a castle just outside the city whereas Alamire claimed that he had spent the summer with him in Germany.[20]

In Alamire's version of events, the pro-imperial party in Metz had made life so difficult for Richard he had moved to Cochem, another imperial Free City a hundred miles to the north, but the negotiations with Francis had been continued by Nicholas de Hu and the van Riet brothers. These supposedly trusted envoys did their work well, and at the beginning of autumn they delivered a letter from the French king telling Richard that the preparations for an invasion of England were complete and he should bring his men to France with all speed.

According to Alamire, everyone at the French court had supposed that the king's 'great army' was destined for Italy but these rumours had been deliberately manufactured to disguise its real objective, which was England. The singer also told Wolsey that he and Jan van Riet had accompanied Richard to the international trade fair in Frankfurt in order to buy arms.

'Now is the time coming that White Rose, duke of Suffolk, has so long looked for,' Jan had confided to Alamire, and as evidence for his claim he showed the singer a letter from Richard promising to repay 100 gold crowns he had borrowed from the brothers' sister as soon as he had recovered his throne.[21]

Like the good spy he professed to be, Alamire had boasted in his report to Spinelli that he had tried to find out if Jan's claims had any substance by surreptitiously interrogating the van Riets' sister, and the girl had said she had seen five letters insisting that Richard would find 'many friends should he return to England'. Unfortunately, she could not identify the authors of these letters because their names were kept in a separate document.[22]

On the face of the things, Alamire's intelligence contradicted the previous claims from Eesebeke, Friscobaldi and the anonymous reporter of Richard's mule ride, all of whom had stressed that Francis would not contemplate an invasion of England until he had come to terms with the Emperor over Milan. However, that condition had been fulfilled in August 1516, when Francis signed the Treaty of Noyon with Maximilian's grandson Prince Charles.

Following the untimely death of his father, Philip, archduke of Burgundy, Charles had been groomed to succeed his ageing grandfathers, Maximilian of Habsburg and Ferdinand of Aragon, as Holy Roman Emperor and king of Spain respectively. The first part of this enormous inheritance was delivered in January 1516 when Ferdinand shuffled off this mortal coil, yet the king of Aragon's death had plunged Maximilian into the depths of despair. Though he was only fifty-seven, Charles's paternal grandfather had taken to travelling everywhere with his own coffin and had given his grandson a greater role in imperial affairs.[23]

At least the increasingly morbid Maximilian could comfort himself with the thought that his dream of creating a Habsburg superpower was almost a reality, because the moment Ferdinand had been laid to rest Charles had succeeded to all the territories his maternal grandfather had controlled. Besides the kingdoms of Aragon and Upper Navarre, Charles's Iberian inheritance included Castile, which he ruled on behalf of his mentally incapacitated mother, as well as the Aragonese possessions in Sicily and southern Italy. Unfortunately for Charles, he was also bequeathed Ferdinand's Italian problems.

The short-term solution was the Treaty of Noyon, by which Charles recognised Milan as French while Francis withdrew his claim to Naples in return. Yet this diplomatic victory for his patron put Richard in a quandary.

On the one hand the treaty was good news because it fulfilled Francis's requirement to be secure in Milan before attacking England, but on the other, the sudden end to the war had worrying similarities with the events of 1514. On that occasion, Louis and Henry's Treaty of London had ended Richard's plans to invade southern England from Brittany; now the Treaty of Noyon had rendered his invasion of northern England from Scotland unnecessary.

The White Rose was still in Frankfurt when he learned about the treaty, and he discussed its ramifications with Alamire while they strolled around the garden of their inn. Among other things, the two men had talked about the fates of Lambert Simnel, John de la Pole, Perkin Warbeck and the duke of Clarence, after which Alamire had suggested that Richard could avoid their fate simply by making peace with Henry.

'Alamire, you tell me strange things,' Richard had replied, but after thinking for a moment he had asked the singer if he thought that the king of England would indeed grant him a pardon. Alamire answered that Henry was 'most clement', but Richard pointed out that England's second Tudor king had shown his older brothers no mercy.

No one could deny that Henry had signed Edmund's death warrant or that William de la Pole was still locked up in the Tower by his order, but Alamire insisted that both brothers would have received pardons if they had only asked for them. Considering that the de la Poles had been specifically excluded from Henry's amnesty of 1509, this was patently untrue. Richard understandably feared that any attempt to merely contact Henry would backfire.

'If I were to write to his majesty and he were to send the letter to the king of France, I should lose the friendship of France,' he mused, whereupon Alamire advised him to take his case to the Emperor, 'who is a great friend of England'.[24]

Even though both men were unaware of Maximilian's most recent comment to Friscobaldi, about not caring if the last of the Yorkists went to the gallows, this was terrible advice. Richard could hardly forget how Edmund's blind faith in the Emperor had led his brother to the scaffold. Moreover, Richard was not the only Yorkist who was worried by the recent Franco-Imperial rapprochement.

We know little of Sir George Neville's movements after Edmund's execution but by 1516 he was with Richard in Metz. However, shortly before the Treaty of Noyon was signed, he had travelled secretly to France to ask for asylum. When this was refused, he had tried to secure a pardon from Henry. Unsurprisingly, England's king had refused to grant Neville his mercy for a third time, so the veteran rebel had returned to Metz with his tail between his legs.[25]

If Richard had discovered his chief lieutenant's attempted defection only recently it would go a long way to explain his sudden misgivings and that he had told Alamire he would consider making peace with Henry as the singer had suggested. However, the arrival of a messenger bringing 'good tidings'[26] changed everything, and when the two men resumed their talk the following day Richard has recovered his resolve. He made Alamire swear to say nothing of their previous conversation to anyone, and from this point on events appeared to move rapidly in Richard's favour.

On 23 November 1516, Spinelli informed Wolsey that all the exiled Yorkists, including Neville, had been given permission to enter France. This could only mean that something was afoot,[27] yet these rumours had to be treated with a great deal of caution because Spinelli's source was Hans Nagel.

As mentioned earlier, Spinelli now knew Nagel was a double agent and everything the trombonist said could have been part of a carefully planned campaign of misinformation. Equally, Spinelli must have considered the possibility that Alamire's report of Richard's doubts was part of this same smokescreen. If he did, he soon overcame his concerns because he ordered Alamire to find out if the invasion was a reality by intercepting Neville's letters and questioning the schout of Mechelen, who was one of Richard's closest Flemish supporters.[28]

This imperial official should not be confused with Paul Zachtlevent, who was schout of Amsterdam, but he too had no love for the Tudors because his brother had been one of the foreign mercenaries captured and hanged by Henry VII. During which Yorkist rebellion this man met his miserable fate is not recorded, but the result was that Mechelen's schout was happy to help the Yorkists and he regularly supplied Richard's couriers with horses.[29] The obedient Alamire set to work with alacrity, and he quickly confirmed that the invasion was a reality.

At the beginning of December, the singer reported to Spinelli that he had learned from Neville's letters that Francis had ordered the duke of Guelders to turn his four-month truce into a permanent peace with the Habsburgs. While this could have been a condition of the Treaty of Noyon, which contained the usual clauses forbidding the signatories from financing each other's rebels, Alamire also discovered that Francis had arranged for Richard to take command of 4,000 men who had been fighting for Guelders, and this army would be sent to Scotland. Finally, the singer ends his report with the unequivocal claim that 'the Devil was never so anxious to destroy souls as Francis is to destroy the king of England'.[30]

Interestingly, more reliable sources than Alamire and Nagel were insisting that the French king was still plotting a Yorkist restoration. One such source was Wolsey's own protégé, Richard Pace. As Henry's secretary of state, Pace was privy to many secrets, and in October 1516 he informed his patron that the Bastard of Savoy had asked Francis to send Richard across the Channel with 12,000 men.[31] Likewise, Dr Tunstall had told Wolsey that two men of the Tournai garrison had attempted 'to make an enterprise' on the city and that the French king had offered to put Richard de la Pole 'in possession of England'.[32]

Even though Tunstall had declared that this information wasn't worth the 'two angelotts' he had paid for it,[33] the notion that a Yorkist invasion was imminent gained further credence when Francis persuaded Maximilian to sign the Treaty of Brussels. This treaty, which was signed on 4 December 1516, ratified the peace terms already agreed with the Emperor's grandson at Noyon, and three weeks later Spinelli received news that a French-backed Scots–Yorkist invasion of Northumberland would definitely take place during the coming spring.[34]

Once again, this source was neither Nagel nor Alamire. Instead it came from a French noble with a hunched back and a red beard, the latest addition to Spinelli's stable of spies. This man claimed he had fought for France at the battle of Ravenna and was now on his way to Guelders disguised as a Franciscan hermit. His motives for betraying Francis's secrets are not recorded, but he informed Spinelli that the French king was assembling a fleet in Normandy and Brittany, and that these ships would transport an army of Germans under Richard's command to Scotland in March 1517. At the same time, Francis intended to send an army against Tournai, 'where the French had many friends'.[35]

Other pieces of the jigsaw now fell into place. Dr Knight's spies spotted chests of gold being transported through Antwerp, and he had little doubt that this money, rumoured to be in excess of 20,000 guilders, was destined for the Yorkist war chest. Likewise, Spinelli received reports that Richard had met with Fleuranges, who was still commanding the Black Band of mercenaries in French pay. Soon after this, Richard was seen leaving Metz in the company of a mysterious stranger.[36]

21

THIS LORD HAD A MARVELLOUS HORSE

On Christmas night 1516, a rider wearing a heavy disguise arrived in Metz and knocked on the door to the house where Richard de la Pole had taken up residence. Shortly afterwards, the White Rose and his furtive visitor left the city and made their way to Paris for an audience with the French king.[1] According to the chronicler of Metz, Phillipe de Vigneulles, Richard took with him only a few servants, and his mysterious companion was none other than the duke of Guelders.

To outside observers, the fact that the rebel dukes of Suffolk and Guelders had set aside their differences could only mean that they had both been given a command in a French army destined for England. However, if Spinelli, Wolsey or any of their spies thought this was the final proof that Francis had given the invasion the green light, they were very much mistaken.

In the end, the flood of intelligence provided by Nagel, Alamire, Eesebeke, Friscobaldi and a variety of anonymous sources proved to be woefully wide of the mark; the two rebel dukes were actually hurrying to Paris to try and breathe new life into their moribund causes. Just as Richard had feared, the treaties of Noyon and Brussels meant Francis had no more use for foreign rebels in England or the Low Countries, and he even seemed content to leave Thérouanne and Tournai in Henry's hands. As a result, Richard returned to Metz empty handed and facing a very uncertain future.

'During this time, the duke of Suffolk, who was called the White Rose, king of England, was still in Metz and he and his people made their residence in the Rue de la Grande Maison, beyond the church the Holy Spirit, in a house which belonged to Lord Jehan de Vy,' [2] wrote Vigneulles, but Metz was no longer a city at ease with itself.

The three-way tension between the wealthy oligarchs who governed the city, the shopkeepers who paid the taxes and the feudal lords who controlled the surrounding countryside was exacerbated by the incessant Valois–Habsburg wars. Consequently, there were frequent brawls between pro-French and pro-Imperial mobs.[3] No one appreciated the perils of life in Metz more than the chronicler. Back in 1490, Vigneulles and his father had been kidnapped by mercenaries in the pay of the previous duke of Lorraine, Rene, and their relatives had taken more than a year to raise their ransom.[4]

Fast-forward twenty-five years to the spring of 1516, and an alliance of border nobles, led by the notorious German robber-baron Franz von Sickingen and our old friend the seigneur de la Fleuranges, had declared war on the current duke of Lorraine, Antoine the Good.[5] The reason for this war need not concern us here, except to say that it placed Richard in an impossible position because he had close ties to the leading combatants.

On the Lorraine side, Richard was grateful to Antoine for rescuing him from the clutches of the German count who had tried to cheat him of his pension, but he could hardly take up arms against Fleuranges, who was his kinsman and comrade from the Navarrese War. Wisely, Richard chose not to take sides in this bitter feud and Vigneulles tells us that he spent his time 'hunting daily with the other lords or playing games and skits' instead.[6]

If Vigneulles is to be believed, Richard had decided to abandon his quest to restore the House of York, and if this was so we should not be too hard on him. The new world order created by the treaties of Noyon and Brussels meant there was nothing he could do but wait patiently for the political merry-go-round to turn a complete circle. In the meantime, there were plenty of distractions to keep him amused.[7]

Besides the regular tournaments held in the Place-en-Chambre or the Champ à Seille, there were mystery plays performed in front of the city's cathedral and sumptuous society weddings, such as the nuptials of Perette Baudoiche, who was related to Richard's former landlord Claude Baudoiche. Yet Richard's chief passion was horseracing, which had been brought to Metz by those Messines who had fought for France in Italy.[8]

'This Lord [Richard] had a marvellous horse, which he held in the highest esteem, and several times he boasted that it had no equal in Metz or anywhere near about,' remarked Vigneulles.[9] Naturally, such boasting piqued the interest of other a gentlemen of the turf, and Richard was soon challenged to a race by Lord Dex, a former chief alderman.

The contest was to be a steeplechase from the city's Abbey of St Clement to the village of l'Orme-à-Augny 5 miles away, and to make matters more interesting the two men wagered 80 gold crowns each on the result. As this was an affair of honour, Richard and Dex decided to ride their own horses rather than employing jockeys, but the city ordinance forbidding noblemen from participating in such lowbrow pursuits meant their race would have to be run in secret.[10]

At dawn on the great day, the two riders rose early, disguised themselves in the simple garb of peasants and led their mounts to the start line. The sentries had been bribed to open the city's south-western gate a little before the usual hour, and despite the need for secrecy there were plenty of spectators. Among the throng was Vigneulles, who tells us that both horses had been carefully trained for the event, with Dex's horse being fed on a special diet of white wine must instead of hay. The chronicler of Metz also noted that while both men rode without saddles, Dex had shod his horse with specially made lightweight steel horseshoes.[11]

At the appointed hour, the signal was given and Vigneulles says that the two horses set off at such a furious gallop it seemed as if their hooves would 'split the earth'. By the time the riders reached the Leper House at Montigny, Dex had a substantial lead and Richard was forced to use his spurs to so vigorously that blood spurted from the sides of his poor beast. Such brutal treatment achieved nothing, and Dex's slightly sozzled steed crossed the finish line first.

The White Rose had been soundly beaten, but he took his defeat well and paid his bet with good humour. He even challenged Dex to another race, but any rematch would have to wait because

Richard was suddenly summoned to Lyon.[12] This time, he did not have to slip out of Metz in disguise and he was even given an escort of several 'young gentlemen'.

As ever, Vigneulles was among the cheering crowd who watched Richard's departure, but he does not tell us why there was such rejoicing.[13] Perhaps the pro-imperial Messines were simply glad to see the back of their unwanted English guest, or maybe the Francophile party hoped that Francis would broker a peace in the feud between Fleuranges and Antoine the Good. Whatever the reason, Richard arrived in Lyon safely, despite having to travel through a storm that washed away thirty villages,[14] but his hope that an audience with Francis meant a revival of French interest in his cause was premature.

Instead of continuing to plan the much-postponed invasion, Francis ordered Richard to make a pilgrimage to the House of the Annunciation at Loreto, on Italy's Adriatic coast. According to legend, angels had miraculously carried the house where the Archangel Gabriel had told Mary she would be the mother of Jesus to Loreto in 1294, and the city had been attracting the devout ever since. However, as Loreto was under Venetian control, Richard was led to believe that his journey was cover for a spying mission.

In fact, Francis wanted to extend the peace created by the treaties of Noyon and Brussels to England, which meant convincing Henry VIII that his throne and conquests in Picardy were not under threat from Yorkists. Sending the White Rose as far away from northern France as possible would be a good way to achieve this, but Francis's ingenious plan was stillborn.

To enter Venetian territory, Richard needed a passport from the Signory's ambassador in French-occupied Milan, Gian Giacomo Caroldo, but this was refused. In a dispatch dated 12 July 1517, Caroldo explained that he had not allowed the English rebel to cross the Most Serene Republic's border because he feared Henry would retaliate by impounding goods belonging to Venetian merchants in London.[15]

Another Venetian, the diarist Marino Sanuto, tells us that the Signory had approved of Caroldo's decision,[16] yet Richard's Italian pilgrimage would have done nothing to alter Henry's belief that his throne and his nascent empire in France were under threat. The growing legion of Tudor spies on the Continent continued to insist that the White Rose was plotting Henry's downfall with the French and Danish kings, as well as the Scottish duke of Albany, but at this point Alamire overplayed his hand.

In August 1517, the singer sent what would prove to be his final report to Wolsey. He begins by complaining of his harsh treatment. In particular, Alamire was aggrieved at having received no acknowledgment of the five books of music, eight cornets and many lute strings which he had recently sent to Henry; yet he also begs the cardinal not to be displeased by his previous letter, presumably demanding payment, which had been written 'in anger'.[17]

More importantly, Alamire's final report contained several pieces of potentially useful intelligence, including some startling news about the Danish king, Christian II. According to the singer, Richard's personal secretary had shown him letters proving that Christian and the White Rose 'had bound themselves to each other by oaths',[18] but Denmark should have been in the Tudor–Habsburg camp by virtue of Christian's marriage to Maximilian's granddaughter Isabella.

Nevertheless, Alamire insisted that Christian had offered Richard 20,000 men, as well as 'Scots in great number',[19] and because the king of Danes was also related the late king of Scots, James IV, his claims did have a ring of truth. Unfortunately for Alamire, Wolsey no longer believed a word the singer said.

What the cardinal knew, but Alamire did not, was that the duke of Albany had weakened his position as Scotland's regent by imprisoning the popular earl of Lennox. Furthermore, Wolsey had been told by Lord Dacre, the Tudor eyes and ears in the Anglo-Scottish Borders, that Lennox's supporters were on the point of taking up arms and Albany had scuttled back to France in an attempt to raise an army to crush the rebellion.[20]

Although Wolsey could not have known that any troops sent to Scotland would not be led by Richard de la Pole, the fact that Albany had his hands full proved to him that Alamire had either exaggerated the possibility of a Scots–Yorkist–Danish invasion simply to extort more money from his Tudor paymasters or he was a double agent deliberately passing on false information to confound the Yorkists' enemies. Yet the final nails in the coffin of Alamire and Nagel's spying careers were provided by a man named

Thomas Stanley, who had, until recently, served Richard as his gentleman porter.

The name Stanley had a great deal of significance in Tudor circles. The family's support after Henry VII's landing in Wales had been crucial, and Sir William Stanley had led the charge at Bosworth that had ended in the death of Richard III. However, Sir William had been implicated in the Warbeck rebellion and he had been sent to the block in 1495. The Thomas Stanley mentioned in Alamire's report of August 1517 was Sir William's illegitimate son, and he had been imprisoned for fourteen years after his father's execution. Though Thomas had been released in 1509, under the terms of Henry VIII's general pardon, he had been banished and eventually he had joined the other exiled Yorkists on the Continent.[21]

After four years in Richard's household, Stanley had tired of the impoverished life of an exile. Because he believed Nagel and Alamire were working for the Tudors, he arranged to meet the trombonist at the singer's house in the misguided belief they could arrange a full pardon.[22] While waiting for Nagel to arrive, Stanley had told Alamire that the inept assassin Robert Latimer had been arrested yet again, this time by imperial authorities, and charged with carrying letters to Richard.

Other revelations, supposedly from Stanley and which were relayed to Wolsey by Alamire, included the existence of a Yorkist spy based 40 miles from London. This man had been ordered to find out if a list of nobles who had promised to join Richard was genuine, but no further details were forthcoming. In the end, Nagel failed to keep his appointment and Alamire's final report ends with the singer explaining that he could not write in greater detail because the postman was about to leave.[23]

Undeterred by his failure to secure a pardon through Nagel or Alamire, Stanley tried a different approach and a few weeks after his abortive meeting he turned up in Bruges looking for Dr Tunstall. Having admitted that he was Richard's ex-porter, Stanley told Tunstall that he wished to defect because had not seen a penny of the 20 crowns a year he had been promised, and the Tudor envoy to Prince Charles gleefully told Henry the full story in a letter dated 17 September 1517.[24]

According to Stanley's confession, his troubles had begun after he had confronted Neville and threatened to hand in his notice unless he was paid. Much to Stanley's annoyance Neville had dismissed his complaint, saying that Richard never paid any of his servants in case they took his money and ran off, but this was not the end of the matter. Two days later, the aggrieved steward had been rudely awoken by Richard himself and his erstwhile master had been incandescent with rage, as Tunstall explained:

> Pole came into the room with his servants and said, 'Thou false traitor! thou hast been long a spy in my company; thou shalt, before thou depart, show who sent thee hither.' And with that, they all laid hands on him, and took a small cord with pricks, and bound his great toes together, and strained the cord as hard as they could, bidding him confess.
>
> They strained the cord so hard that it brake [*sic*]; but as they were preparing another, he [Stanley] spied the door open, and ran to a monastery of friars, demanding asylum. Pole, being afraid of the slander, sent to him Deryke Rede [Derek van Riet] his chief steward, begging him to return, and after Easter next his wages should be paid, to which he agreed. Pole, when he paid his servants their wages, and gave them liveries of grey and blue, paid Stanley 20 sous, and bid him be gone.[25]

Having been kicked out Metz, Stanley had spent some months in Holland as a servant to the count of Nassau, but he had been treated equally badly by the Dutchman. This was the last straw for Stanley, and he had given himself up to Tunstall in the hope of obtaining a pardon. As a veteran rebel, Stanley knew that a ticket home could only be bought with information so he happily told Tunstall everything he knew about the Yorkist court-in-exile.

Firstly, Stanley insisted that anything Robert Latimer may have said to Tunstall in the past was a lie, which confirmed that his defection to the Yorkists had been genuine. Secondly, he claimed that Richard was still receiving his French pension of 4,000 crowns a year. Thirdly, he maintained that the only Englishman of consequence still with Richard was his chaplain, 'who could only get his wages one crown at a time'. Finally, Stanley insisted that Nagel and Alamire were Richard's spies.[26]

Clearly, Alamire had told Richard about Stanley's previous attempt to defect, which had led to his torture, escape and summary dismissal, but the singer had made a tactical error. Alamire's betrayal of Stanley to Richard proved beyond any doubt that he and Nagel had been serving two masters, and this reflected extremely badly on Spinelli. The disgraced spymaster was quickly packed off to Spain to report on Charles of Habsburg's first visit to his new realm,[27] but the men he had employed were more fortunate.

Once their cover had been blown, Nagel and Alamire wisely retired from the espionage business, yet they prospered after they put away their cloaks and daggers. Alamire's music books remained highly prized and he later accepted an invitation from the Danish king to instruct him in 'the art of mining'. Considering Denmark's lack of mineral resources, this was probably a euphemism for more spying.[28]

Always a favourite of the Hapsburgs, Alamire spent his last years in Mechelen, at the court of Margaret of Austria, and he died there, peacefully, in 1536. Likewise, Nagel continued his career as a trombonist, firstly in Mechelen and afterwards in Antwerp. Nagel was listed in the city accounts for 1530 as being one of the five musicians employed at public expense, and he died the following year. However, none of this was of any interest to Cardinal Wolsey.[29]

Despite the unmasking of Nagel and Alamire, the rumours of a French-and-Danish-backed Scots–Yorkist invasion persisted and Wolsey needed to know how much of what he had been told by the musicians was genuine and how much was pure fabrication. Indeed, Wolsey had been puzzling this conundrum since the beginning of 1517 when he asked the earl of Worcester and Sir Richard Jerningham to find better sources of intelligence.

'You are to send a discreet person, being a Burgonyon [Burgundian], unto Meyse [Metz] in Lorayn [Lorraine] to understand and bring perfect report of Richard de la Pole, where he is and what he doeth,' Wolsey commanded Jerningham,[30] who had been recently promoted from treasurer to deputy governor of Tournai.

This letter was sent on 29 January 1517, long before Stanley confirmed the musicians' treachery, and on St Valentine's Day Jerningham proudly informed Wolsey that he had found a man in the Metz city guard who was prepared to spy on the Yorkists.

He also told the cardinal that he had done everything he could to prepare Tournai for a siege.[31]

Soon afterwards, the earl of Worcester reported that a minor Yorkist called Sir Richard Ponder had offered to defect. In a letter to Wolsey dated 24 March 1517, Worcester described Ponder as the son of a Grantham merchant who wanted to go home after spending ten years in the French army. Though Ponder had admitted he had been one of Richard's mercenaries, he claimed that he was no traitor because he had refused to fight against his fellow Englishmen in Picardy and had been imprisoned by the French as a result.

As evidence of his good faith, the tearful Ponder had revealed that the French were secretly stockpiling arms for an attack on Tournai. This cache included 20,000 pikes, 10,000 suits of armour, 8,000 halberds, 6,000 light handguns, 1,500 heavy handguns and 22 cannon. The loose-tongued knight also revealed that Richard de la Pole had met the French king twice in the last two months, and these meeting had always been held at night. Ponder even insisted that the French had at least two spies in England, one of whom was a Scot masquerading as an Englishman and the other a Parisian merchant.[32]

At the end of his interview with Worcester, Ponder claimed that he had been forced to flee Metz after Richard had become suspicious of him. He had presumably hoped to avoid the painful pedicure inflicted on Stanley, and Ponder's claims that Francis was about to declare war on England gained credence when Wolsey received similar news from a French spy.

'He [the king of France] has made a marvellous and awful plan which, if you don't remedy, you will not fare well,' declared the unnamed author of a report dated 1 August 1517,[33] and he goes on to explain that this plan involved a rebellion in Tournai, whose citizens were ready to drive out the hated English, as well as a Scottish invasion of northern England.

The hyperbole-prone informant went on to claim that the French were sending thirty pieces of artillery to Albany and 'there was no considerable town in France where they are not making cannon'.[34] He also insisted that every shipwright in Normandy was now working on the invasion fleet that would transport 10,000 *landsknechts* under Richard's command to Scotland. Finally, the spy warned that Henry must launch a pre-emptive strike before Albany could return to Edinburgh or he would have lost the war before it had begun.[35]

This spy clearly knew his business, because Albany and Francis had renewed the Auld Alliance on 26 August 1517 and other sources were reporting that Richard was indeed recruiting an army.[36] Shortly before Christmas 1517, Vigneulles noted that the White Rose had been visited by a good-looking German captain who boasted curly blonde hair and a powerful physique. This captain commanded 2,000 battle-hardened veterans of the wars in Italy, and his purse was full of French gold. Vigneulles also tells us that Richard gave his entire household the week off so he could talk to the German in secret.[37]

Of course, Wolsey and Henry did not have access to Vigneulles' chronicle, but they did discuss the matter with IJsselstein, the imperial commander who had led the Habsburg armies against the Guelders and Friesland rebels. IJsselstein was certain that Francis had recently abandoned his policy of *détente* with Henry and was again helping the Yorkists cause trouble. Likewise, Richard Pace reported that the Bastard of Savoy, grand seneschal of Provence, was openly boasting that Francis was planning to use Richard 'to create great dissension' in England to stop Henry from bribing the Swiss to make war on the French.[38]

On top of all this, Sir Richard Jerningham added his voice to those warning Wolsey and Henry that the French were still intent on restoring the House of York. In May 1518, Tournai's deputy governor reported that he had recruited a spy at the French court, named Henry Crossene, who had learned that the invasion plan now included the Danish duke of Holstein. Noting that Richard was already on his way to Copenhagen, Jerningham explained:

> De la Pole is to take ship in Denmark with the duke of Ulske [Holstein], the king of Denmark's uncle, and a certain number of lance-knights to land in England; Albany is to sail from Brittany to Scotland, there to make business against the king; Monsieur de Bourbon [constable of France] and the duke of Vendome are to besiege Tournai. All this is to be done within two or three months.[39]

As proof of Crossene's claims, Jerningham enclosed a letter from a Dutch shipmaster to Richard's chaplain, which had been stolen by his new agent in Metz. Coincidentally, this sailor was called Polle and he had served Perkin Warbeck as well as the de la Poles.[40]

The last voice in this chorus of warnings was from our old friend Thomas Spinelli, who was still following the imperial heir as he toured his Spanish kingdoms. In a letter to Henry dated 2 April 1518, Spinelli revealed that Richard had spent Christmas with Francis, who had given him 'money and promises'.[41] When combined with the reports from Tunstall, Worcester and Pace, Spinelli's latest despatch had to be taken seriously and Wolsey countered by declaring that unless the French king stopped plotting the overthrow of the Tudors, England would not join the Pope's new anti-Ottoman league.

In the aftermath of the Noyon and Brussels peace treaties, Pope Leo X had declared a crusade to drive the Turks out of the Balkans, whereupon Francis, Maximilian and Charles had agreed to make common cause against the Sultan. The odd man out was Henry VIII, who followed his father's example by refusing to sign the necessary treaties until Francis had withdrawn his support for the Yorkists. It was Wolsey who conveyed this decision to the Venetian ambassador, Sebastian Giustinian, and the Signory was duly informed of the English position in a letter dated 29 March 1518.

'He [Wolsey] said that King Henry suspected France of an intention to invade England, as they harboured Richard de la Pole, favoured the duke of Albany and encouraged disturbance in Scotland ... so it was impossible to organise a crusade unless the king of France would give up his ambitious designs,' wrote Giustinian.[42] It is a measure of how much the pious Henry feared Richard that he was prepared to veto an entire a crusade simply to force Francis to abandon the White Rose.

Of course, the rumours of a Scots–Yorkist invasion, combined with an attack on Tournai, could have been deliberately planted by Francis in an attempt to force Henry to renounce his own 'ambitious designs' on the French crown; after the failure of Richard's Italian trip, he certainly needed a new way to bring England's king to heel. Such Machiavellian intrigue was well within Francis's capabilities, and if this was his intention he found an unlikely ally in Cardinal Wolsey.

22

A SIDEWAYS GLANCE

For years the Tudor intelligence services had been crying wolf over French attempts to make Richard king of England, but all the while Wolsey had his eye on a far greater prize: a comprehensive peace treaty that would end the Italian Wars and see Henry secure on his throne. That said, Wolsey's motives were not entirely altruistic.

In spite of the cardinal's loyalty to Henry, which required him to support his sovereign's military campaigns in France, Wolsey dreamed of making himself Pope. With that in mind, bringing peace to war-torn Christendom by uniting its bellicose monarchs against the Turks would make for a great audition. To this end, Wolsey had surreptitiously hijacked the Pope's plan for a crusade and in the autumn of 1518 his grand design became a reality.

On 2 October, the kings of England, France and Spain, the Holy Roman Emperor and the Pope, together with the rulers of twenty smaller nations, signed the Treaty of London, which guaranteed both a five-year truce in Europe and Henry's commitment to Pope Leo X's crusade. Subsidiary treaties, signed two days later, made provision for the peaceable return of Tournai – but not Calais – to France and for the betrothal of Henry's two-year-old daughter, Mary, to Francis's equally young son.[1]

So wide-ranging was the Treaty of London that it became known as the Universal Peace, and among the twenty smaller nations who ratified its terms were three of Richard's most important allies: Scotland, Denmark and Guelders. As was customary, the Treaty of London contained clauses forbidding its signatories from supporting each other's rebels, so, yet again, Richard had been left stranded by the receding tide of international affairs.[2]

Nevertheless, Richard's usefulness to Francis as a sword of Damocles suspended over Henry's head remained, and five weeks after the Treaty of London had been signed the Venetian ambassador, Giustinian, told the Signory that Francis 'favoured the White Rose more than ever' and had even increased the Englishman's pension.[3] The inference here is that although Richard had been sent back into exile in Metz, he and Francis were still secretly plotting the Tudors' downfall.

The increase in Richard's pension certainly suggests that Francis wished to keep the White Rose on his payroll but, on the other hand, the money could have been a bribe to ensure the English rebel toed the line. In either case, Richard was now a rich man and he gained another ally when Jean de Lorraine was enthroned as bishop of Metz.

The new bishop was a younger brother of Richard's old friend Antoine the Good, and he had been appointed to this politically strategic bishopric when he was just seven years old. Despite his tender years, Jean had also been elected bishop of Toul, and when he achieved his majority in April 1518 Francis persuaded the Pope to make him a cardinal as well as the fully fledged bishop of two sees. Such preferment of his supporters was part of Francis's concerted campaign to increase French influence in Metz, so it can hardly be a coincidence that one of Jean's first acts after becoming the city's cardinal-bishop was to present Richard de la Pole with a new home

The house in question was called Haute Pierre and it had once been part of the Abbey of St Symphorien. The old monastery had been burned to ground in 1444 during an unsuccessful siege of the city by Jean's great-grandfather Rene I, duke of Lorraine, and though work on a second abbey had begun in 1481, Haute Pierre was still a ruin when the Cathedral Chapter offered Richard a lifetime lease on the property.[4]

The dilapidated state of the building explains why Richard was charged a peppercorn rent of 10 sun-crowns a year. Considering he had lost 80 sun-crowns on a single horse race this was a trifling sum, but he was required to rebuild Haute Pierre at his own expense. Monsieur F. des Roberts, a nineteenth-century historian and a native of Metz, estimated that Richard spent 2,000 gold florins making his new home the finest private building in the city, and all other construction had to stop because he had engaged every stonemason for miles around.[5] Yet no palace, however grand, is compensation for the loss of a kingdom.

As his new home neared completion, Richard must have wondered if his exile was becoming permanent. Any such fears were groundless. This was an age when the world could be turned upside down by the death of a king, and the passing of Maximilian, king of the Germans, king of the Romans and Holy Roman Emperor, would have a profound effect on Richard's future.

The second of the twelve Habsburg emperors breathed his last on 12 January 1519, and it is a measure of Richard's standing that he was given a prominent role in the memorial service for Metz's feudal overlord. The mass for the repose of Maximilian's soul was held in the city's cathedral on 25 February 1519 and, as ever, Philippe Vigneulles was there.

> And after the torch bearers and candle bearers, came all the members of the three collegiate churches, two by two, after which came all the lords, all dressed in black and in mourning; the duke of Suffolk, whom we call the Blanche Rose, went first, accompanied by the Master Alderman; then came all the other lords in good order, two by two and always the most honourable first.[6]

We can only wonder what Richard was thinking as he led this sombre procession into Metz's cathedral; after all, he had little cause to mourn the man whose scheming had sent his brother to the scaffold and pushed him to the edge of despair. However, this was not to be the only civic occasion of enormous political significance in which Richard played a leading role.

In May 1519, the burghers of Metz held a lavish reception for the French war hero Claude of Lorraine, comte de Guise. Claude was not only a brother of Antoine, duke of Lorraine, and Jean, bishop of Metz, he was also a nephew of the duke of Guelders. As mentioned earlier, Guise had led his uncle's *landsknechts* to victory over the Swiss at Marignano and his name was now mentioned in the same breath as Roland and Bayard.

During the battle's bitter hand-to-hand fighting, Guise had received so many wounds he had been left for dead but survived. He attributed this miracle to his donation of a candle, worth 80 francs, to the Abbey of St Barbara.[7] This monastery, dedicated to the patron saint of artillerymen, was a short ride to the east of Metz and its sumptuous church had been recently rebuilt by Richard's former landlord Claude Baudoiche.

Though Richard had not fought in the battle, his closeness to the French king, and the rise of the French party in Metz, meant he was chosen to lead the official welcoming committee when Guise came to the city to give thanks to St Barbara. Naturally, the hero of Marignano's arrival was recorded in meticulous detail by Vigneulles.

'And then, on this said day of his coming, several of us lords of Metz with all the soldiers and handgunners, and with several citizens went to Joiey,[8] and among the lords was the duke of Suffolk, called Blanche Rose, and he and his people accompanied the Lord of Guise, who went on foot and thus brought him to Metz holding him by the hand,' he wrote.[9] Vigneulles also noted that ordinary people thronged the streets to catch a glimpse of the famous knight and pardons were granted to twenty exiles in honour of his visit.

After being presented with two fine horses, each worth 100 florins, Guise was lodged in the Abbey of St Vincent, where he was entertained with several days of feasting. Eventually, the pious knight was allowed to complete his pilgrimage and Vigneulles tells us that he presented St Barbera with another, larger wax candle, 'which weighed as much as himself in his armour', and a wooden statue 'made in his own likeness and grandeur'.[10]

Such conceit notwithstanding, the timing of Guise's pilgrimage can hardly have been a coincidence. Francis's triumph at Marignano had forced the late Emperor to surrender Milan to the French, and the man who had delivered this victory arrived in one of the wealthiest cities in the Holy Roman Empire on the eve of the election to choose Maximilian 's successor.

By long tradition, a Holy Roman Emperor was chosen by the seven prince-electors of the Empire and, in theory, any Christian monarch could submit their name for consideration. For the election of June 1519, the kings of Spain, France and England put themselves forward, and though the front runner was Maximilian's grandson Charles, king of Spain, his candidature prompted Francis and Henry to stand. In a letter to the banker Jacob Fugger, Francis revealed his motivation:

> You understand, the reason which moves me to gain the Empire is to prevent the said Charles, the King Catholic, from doing so. If he were to succeed, seeing the extent of his kingdom and lordships, this could do me immeasurable harm: he would always be mistrustful and suspicious and doubtless throw me out of Italy.[11]

The rank outsider in the election was the king of England, who had submitted his name against the advice of his own council. As far back as February 1517, Tunstall had urged Henry not to stand because England would be reduced to the status of an imperial province if he won.[12] Typically, the hot-headed Henry had disagreed on the grounds that bringing the full might of the Empire into his war against France was a chance too good to miss.

To thwart the ambitions of their rivals, the three candidates needed to persuade four of the seven prince-electors to vote for them at the imperial diet, which was to be held in Frankfurt. On paper, things began to look promising for Henry because the Germans feared Francis as much as he feared Charles. In the words of Thomas Spinelli, who was desperately trying to rebuild his reputation, 'the Almayns love not the French and the electors and princes fear the greatness of Francis lest he should bring them into more subjection'.[13]

To counter this blatant Francophobia, Francis let it be known that he was prepared to offer each elector a bribe of up to 500,000 ducats,[14] which was almost twice the amount Charles was prepared to spend, and he tried to seize the moral high ground by playing the crusade card. 'If I am elected, three years after the election, I swear I will be in Constantinople, or dead!' he declared.[15] But Charles was not going down without a fight.

All over the Empire, Charles's supporters printed pamphlets and preached sermons that stressed either the German-ness of Charles's Habsburg ancestry or the oppressive nature of French taxation, which regularly levied three tithes in a single year instead of one.

Francis responded by claiming Charles's Teutonic blood had been polluted by spending too much time in Spain, but because the French and Germans were descended from the same ancient tribe, the Sicambri, their customs and traditions were alike.[16]

Unfortunately for Francis, his spurious claims to German ancestry were mercilessly mocked by Frankfurt's balladeers, and Richard Pace, Henry's representative at the proceedings, informed Wolsey that 'all the late emperor's friends are on the king of Castile's side'.[17] Yet Pace was wrong. The utterly venal electors were split 50/50: three for Francis, three for Charles and none for Henry.

With the electoral college in deadlock, the casting vote rested with Louis II, the thirteen-year-old king of Bohemia and Hungary. This was worrying news for the French party because Louis was married to Charles's younger sister Mary of Austria, while Louis's sister Anne of Bohemia was married to Charles's brother Ferdinand of Germany. To complete the Habsburg hold over Louis, the young king's tutor and co-regent was George the Pious, a cousin of Brandenburg's elector.

Though Francis had tried to bribe George, the French envoy had been arrested in Linz and his chest of gold confiscated.[18] Charles was therefore certain Louis would vote for him, but he had reckoned without Richard de la Pole. The White Rose was not only related to the young king's late mother, Anne of Foix-Candale, but had met Louis and George during his years of exile at the Hungarian court. Consequently, Francis sent Richard to Prague with orders to do whatever was necessary to secure Louis' vote.[19]

Back in Frankfurt, an increasingly frustrated Charles had hired Franz von Sickingen to surround the city with *landsknechts* in a brazen display of brute force. This is the same mercenary captain employed by Fleuranges during his feud with the duke of Lorraine, and it did not matter to him that he had already been bribed by the French to stay out of things. The shameless von Sickingen marched 50,000 men to Frankfurt on the pretext of ensuring the electors' safety, and Pace told Wolsey that the imperial count of Nassau was boasting that no Frenchman would enter Germany 'but upon the points of spears and swords'.[20]

Meanwhile, Richard had arrived in Prague too late. Louis' proxies had already left to cast the young king's vote for Charles, and Maximilian's grandson was elected king of the Romans on 28 June 1519. Technically, Charles would only become Emperor when he received his crown from the Pope, a detail which his grandfather had overlooked for most of his reign. Nevertheless, Charles V, as he was now styled, was the *de facto* ruler of a vast empire that stretched from Portugal to Poland and from Naples to the New World.

To make matters worse for Francis, Charles's aunt Catherine of Aragon was married to Henry VIII, meaning France was now surrounded by Habsburg territories and allies. Consequently, the need to detach England from the Habsburg camp became of paramount importance. This time, however, Francis did not immediately turn to Richard. Instead, he continued to pursue the *détente* with England that had produced the Universal Peace of 1518.

This policy would culminate in 1520 in the celebrated conference known to history as the Field of Cloth of Gold. In the meantime, Richard must have been horrified to learn that Francis and Henry had been brought closer together by the election of Charles as Emperor. Whether it was in the freezing snows of Navarre, the cloying mud of Picardy or the glittering palaces of Bohemia, Richard had done everything his French allies had asked of him yet he seemed to be further from his goal than ever.

With his dreams of restoring the House of York yet again in tatters, Richard returned to his adopted city sometime in the late summer of 1519 and immediately found solace in the arms of a beautiful woman. Unfortunately for the man who would be England's king, she was a commoner and already married to a goldsmith. Nevertheless, the two embarked on a torrid affair and Vigneulles recorded all the juicy details with the prurient glee of a modern tabloid journalist.

> In the course of time, everyone, great and small, began to gossip about the behaviour of a woman from Josnes, who was then residing in Metz in the street of Fornerue. She was named Sebille, she was wife to Nicholas the goldsmith, and daughter to Gendin the butcher. The cause of this rumour was that the Lord Blanche-Rose, duke of Suffolk, had been going around town saying that Sebille was one of the fairest women

> who did not belong to the city because she was tall, elegant, proud and pure like the snow.[21]

Besides Richard's casually offensive comments about his fellow Messines, Vigneulles tells us about his scheme to seduce Sebille, which bore a remarkable resemblance to the Biblical tale of David and Bathsheba. In the Old Testament story, King David sent Bathsheba's warrior husband, Uriah the Hittite, on a dangerous mission in the hope he would be killed. In Richard's case, he ordered so many gold and silver dishes from Sebille's husband that the man had to go Paris to buy fresh supplies of the precious metals.[22]

While the goldsmith was away, Richard seduced Sebille, who seems to have been a willing partner in the affair as their first trysts took place in the home of her neighbour, a tailor called Mangenat de Noeroy. According to Vigneulles, the tailor began to worry about his own reputation so he persuaded the lovers to meet in the bathhouse which Sebille's husband had recently built in the nearby village of Jouy-aux-Arches. Vigneulles also tells us that Mangenat paid a local cobbler, Jehan Paillat, to help the adulterers 'take their baths and make good cheer',[23] but meeting outside the city did not keep their illicit encounters secret:

> After a while, the duke seemed to think that everyone was gossiping about him, and he declared that he would beat or kill any such person he met. Things got so bad the aforementioned Mangenat fell into despair and because of this great hatred he and his wife were completely estranged from their male and female neighbours.[24]

By this time the goldsmith had returned from Paris and the slanging-matches between his neighbours had become so frequent the authorities had been forced to intervene. Sebille, her husband and the unfortunate Mangenat were dragged before Metz's magistrates to explain themselves, but Richard was absent from these proceedings.

Incredibly, Sebille managed to convince the magistrates that it was she who had been wronged and she was allowed to keep all her possessions, including her dresses, a casket of jewels and a chest of her husband's money.[25] All of these items would have been forfeit had she been convicted of adultery, but the ruling only made things worse. After a furious row with her husband, who was understandably upset by his wife's behaviour, Sybille grabbed her jewel case and fled with her maid to Richard's palace of Haute Pierre.

For several days nothing was heard of the goldsmith's errant wife save that her maid's mother was accused of stealing from Sebille's husband because some of his belongings were found in the old woman's house. Although this property was returned, Sebille remained with Richard, but when her whereabouts became known the cuckolded husband petitioned the authorities to force her to return. Vigneulles also noted that the goldsmith now went in fear of his life and never left his house unarmed. The following passage justifies his attitude:

> On the Friday after the sixteenth day of the month, the duke was passing through Fornerue with his men, and he saw the said Nicholas, the goldsmith, leaning against a shop with his neighbours. The two said nothing but, as it was said by those who were there, the duke thought that the said Nicholas threw him a sideways glance and had threatened him by making this rude gesture.
>
> The duke, seeing this, replied: 'Now what's that you said? by and by, did you want me?' Then, it is said, he cried out to his people who were standing with him, and, it is said, having drawn his dagger, he made for the said goldsmith but the goldsmith saw the blow coming and sought sanctuary in the house of his neighbour. And then the White Rose, seeing that he had failed in his coup, threw the said dagger with all his strength after his enemy. Why, it was a great scandal that set all the city gossiping![26]

The following Saturday, the aggrieved husband went to the city's cathedral with a sword in his hand and a halberd strapped to his back. Apparently, he had been told that Richard was on his way to the church so he recruited a mob to ambush and kill his wife's lover. Yet Richard had his own spies in the city and they warned him of the danger. Wisely, Richard returned to Haute Pierre but the authorities had had enough. At first they tried to persuade

Sebille to return to her husband voluntarily, but when she refused she was arrested.

> Accordingly, the said Sebille and her maid were placed in the care of a sergeant and locked up in a room in the palace of the War Council. She was here for several days and nights but she was brought good things to eat and drink, paid for by the city, from a nearby tavern called the House of the Angel.[27]

At this point the matter seemed to resolve itself because the despairing goldsmith suddenly moved to Thionville, but although he applied for citizenship in that town he had not admitted defeat. In fact, the goldsmith had left Metz to recruit another gang of toughs to settle his score with Richard. Once again, his plans were scuppered as his wife's lover was warned of the danger. He too left the city and stayed at the castle of Ennery, which belonged to Nicholas de Hu, a long-time de la Pole supporter, but Sebile's irate husband soon picked up his rival's trail. Matters came to head in the deer park surrounding de Hu's castle, and what happened next bore a startling similarity to de Matte's plan to murder the White Rose.

'On the Sabbath after being at the castle for a few days, Richard was ambushed on his way to the recreation fields. In fact, if he had been recognised, he would have been killed or taken prisoner by the Germans whom the said goldsmith had assembled,' Vigneulles wrote.[28] Realising he had only escaped the assassin's knife by pure luck, Richard moved himself and most of his household to Toul, which was still under the control of Metz's bishop, Jean of Lorraine.

If Vigneulles is to be believed, Richard was utterly miserable without Sebille, who was still locked up in the War Council's palace, and she too longed to be with her English Prince Charming. Fortunately, the youthful bishop of Metz and Toul was another of Richard's supporters and he used his influence to secure Sebille's freedom. However, the magistrates could not condone adultery so they would only release Sebille into the custody of her relatives in the hope they would persuade her to return to her husband.

At first the goldsmith's wayward wife went to live with her brother, a sock-maker called François Godin, and then with her cousin, a chandler named Mariette, but both failed to make Sebille see sense. In desperation the magistrates sent Sebille to live with her grandmother and this seemed to do the trick. After a few days, Sebille declared she intended to 'seek St Trotin's pardon', which was a euphemism for abandoning a debauched life.[29]

This sudden desire for respectability convinced the old lady to let her granddaughter leave her house and run errands, but Richard's servants were waiting. With their help, Sebille disguised herself as a grape picker and slipped out of Metz, after which the joyous lovers were reunited in Toul. But the story does not end happily for any of those involved.

Despite the departure of his wife and his rival from Metz, the goldsmith refused to return to the city where he had been humiliated and spent the rest of his days in Thionville. Sebille's maid, the tailor Mangenat and the cobbler Paillat were also banished from Metz, and the lovers' time together was brief. While Sebille's ultimate fate is not certain, it is likely she died giving birth to Richard's only known child, a daughter named Marguerite.[30]

There is evidence to suggest that Marguerite de la Pole became a ward of Marguerite d'Angoulême, who was the French king's sister and a future queen of Navarre, but we will return to the story of the two Marguerites later. In the meantime, suffice to say it is highly probable that Richard asked his royal friend and patron to find a suitable position for his illegitimate daughter because Francis suddenly had need of the White Rose.

While Richard had been romancing Sebille, the kings of England and France had been wooing each other but their rapprochement proved to be as fleeting as the canvas castles erected for the Field of Cloth of Gold. For all its ostentatious pavilions, lavish entertainments and sumptuous feasting, this high-profile conference was an utter failure. The two monarchs could find no common ground and Henry was humiliated when he was beaten by Francis in an impromptu wrestling match.

Having achieved absolutely nothing, this hugely expensive summit broke up on 24 June 1520 and an atmosphere of mutual suspicion quickly settled on both sides of the Channel. Though Henry had surrendered Tournai, he refused to abandon his claims to the French throne and he still held Calais. Throughout the summer of 1520, fears of a pre-emptive invasion by Francis increased and Henry's old foes were at the centre of these rumours.

'There be coming into Scotland, four great men and they be in Dunbar; the one is named the duke of Albany, and the other Richard de la Pole, the third is the duke of Albany's brother, the fourth is Sir Mowncery Mowe,' wrote Richard Pace, who had returned from Frankfurt and resumed his career as Henry VIII's secretary of state.[31] This letter, which is dated 6 August 1520, was addressed to Wolsey and the 'Sir Mowncery Mowe' Pace mentions has to be Anne de Montmorency, who was one of Francis's most trusted courtiers.

The presence of this soldier, diplomat and royal favourite in the list of four great men heading for Scotland would have been more significant if Pace had not thought this news was false because its sources were a drunken cellarman from Thornton Abbey in Lincolnshire and a known fraudster who 'who had been masquerading as the king's messenger'. Nevertheless, Sir Christopher Dacre, who was the brother of Henry's Warden of the Scottish Marches, was sufficiently alarmed to move his cattle away from the border.[32]

Though this invasion also never materialised, and Sir Christopher's cattle continued to graze peacefully in their Cumbrian pastures, it wasn't long before Richard and Albany were again being discussed in the chancelleries of Europe. On 18 October 1520, the new Venetian ambassador to England, Antonio Surian, declared that the dukes of Albany and Suffolk had held more secret talks with the French king.[33]

Though Surian added that Francis's ambassador to England, the aforementioned Montmorency, had tried to quash such rumours, few could deny that the Universal Peace of 1518 was now dead in the water – and, as ever, the most serious bone of contention was Milan.

'My cousin Francis and I are in perfect accord: he wants Milan, and so do I,' Charles is supposed to have said,[34] and even if this pithy witticism is apocryphal, there can be no doubt that the new Emperor was determined to drive the French out of what he regarded as Habsburg territory. Yet the fight for Milan would not begin in Italy.

The next phase of the Italian Wars started with skirmishes in the Ardennes, where Francis was secretly encouraging the de la Marcks to make good their claims to the duchy of Luxembourg, followed by a renewal of the war in Navarre.

23

A VALIANT MAN WORTHY TO BE A GREAT CAPTAIN

Despite the best efforts of Richard de la Pole, the seigneur de la Fleuranges and the Chevalier Bayard, Upper Navarre had remained in Spanish hands ever since Ferdinand's conquest of 1512. So, when the Navarrese king and queen died in 1516 and 1517 respectively, their son Henri d'Albret inherited only Lower Navarre on the French side of the Pyrenees. This partial disinheriting of the pro-French Henri provided Francis with the excuse he needed to strike a blow at the recently elected Emperor, and so a Franco-Navarrese army marched on Pamplona in April 1521.[1]

The French invasion of Navarre was preceded by two diversionary attacks, the first of which was an assault on Fuentarrabia, the Spanish border town where the marquess of Dorset's army had languished during the long, hot summer of 1512. It was led by the candle-lighting comte de Guise, with Guillaume Gouffier, seigneur de Bonnivet and admiral of France, acting as second in command. The second of Francis's feints was an attempt to conquer Luxembourg by the duke of Bouillon, who was Fleuranges' father and another of Richard de la Pole's distant kinsmen.

At first Francis's armies triumphed; in the south, Guise and Bonnivet captured Fuentarrabia, the Castilian garrison in Pamplona surrendered and Luxembourg was overrun, but these victories were soon reversed. An imperial army under the veteran count of Nassau drove de Bouillon out of the Ardennes and besieged a number of French border towns including Tournai, which had been handed back to France in 1519. The Spanish-Habsburg armies in the Pyrenees also rallied and crushed the Franco-Navarrese forces at the battle of Noáin.[2]

After just six weeks of fighting, the French campaigns of 1521 began to mirror the equally disastrous campaigns of 1512, and the defeats in Luxembourg and Navarre were followed by a far more serious reverse in Italy. Almost before Francis knew what was happening, an imperial army under the Italian *condottiero* Prospero Colonna had forced the French to abandon all they had won after Marignano, including Milan, which was seized at the end of November in a surprise night attack.[3]

Emboldened by these successes, Charles was eager to recover the Burgundian territories ceded to the French by his grandfather Maximilian in 1493 under the Treaty of Senlis, and his erstwhile ally Henry VIII was equally keen to reconquer Normandy, Gascony and Anjou. This re-convergence of Tudor and Habsburg ambitions produced the Treaty of Bruges, signed in secret on 28 November 1521 by Cardinal Wolsey for Henry and Margaret of Austria for Charles, whereby both parties agreed to commit 10,000 cavalry and 30,000 infantry to another war against France.

Meanwhile, an increasingly nervous Francis planned to counter the latest Anglo-Imperial threat by reviving his plan for the duke of Albany and Richard de la Pole to invade England from Scotland, though after so many false starts Henry could no longer be caught off guard. Throughout the brief cold war that had followed the Universal Peace, the Tudor spymasters had continued their search for secret Yorkists. Significantly, in April 1521, the king's lieutenant in the duchy of Lancaster, Baron Monteagle, had arrested two men who had been spreading Yorkist sedition in Manchester.

Interestingly, Monteagle was a Stanley and, by virtue of his father's marriage to the widowed Margaret Beaufort, Henry VII's stepbrother. Unlike Thomas Stanley, his illegitimate cousin who became Richard's gentleman porter, Monteagle was a Tudor loyalist and popular tradition credited him with striking down James IV, king of Scotland, at the battle of Flodden.

The plot uncovered by Monteagle had been hatched at the beginning of Lent 1521 and its ringleaders were John Gough, who also used the alias John Strydley, and an unnamed Yorkshire parson who was living 'in sin' with a young woman. According to Monteagle's informant, the amorous cleric had been telling anyone who would listen that he was an accomplished Yorkist spy who had been able to travel freely across Europe by disguising himself as a pilgrim.[4]

The report Monteagle sent to the king also documented the secret meetings Gough had held in and around Manchester, at which he declared that he had met the White Rose in person and found him to be 'a valiant man worthy to be a great captain'. Gough had also maintained that the French king had given Richard 900 ducats to recruit more Englishmen, but these claims had been treated with scorn by his audience, who had insisted that Francis would not support English rebels while he and Henry were at peace.[5]

One of the sceptical Mancunians had told the authorities about meeting Gough in a house owned by Thomas Langton, and here the Yorkist spy had bragged about being hired by Richard's agents in London to kill two prominent Tudor supporters. As soon as Monteagle received this information he had both plotters arrested, whereupon Gough had tried to save his skin by insisting that he had tried to blackmail his Yorkist paymasters by threatening to reveal the names of their intended victims to Wolsey unless he was paid 20 nobles.[6]

Even if Gough and the parson were no more than delusional extortionists, Monteagle's report must have caused Henry some concern. Any Yorkist activity in England's north-west hinted that an invasion would come from Ireland or south-west Scotland and few could forget that Richard's brother John had landed his Irish-Yorkist army in northern Lancashire. However, the exploits of two incompetent blackmailers pale into insignificance when compared with Henry's sudden betrayal by his own sister.

Having painted herself into a political corner by marrying the universally detested earl of Angus, Margaret's only hope of escape was to use Albany's influence with the Pope, to whom he was related by marriage, to obtain a divorce. She therefore offered to drop her opposition to Albany's regency in return for his help, and her rival had accepted this *quid pro quo* with alacrity. Soon after Albany's return to Edinburgh, in November 1521, the unsuspecting Angus had been arrested, charged with high treason and bundled aboard a ship bound for France.

With Angus out of the way, it was rumoured that Albany was planning to wed Margaret himself,[7] and though such a union was unlikely, the two competing regents had made a platonic alliance that greatly increased the chances of an attack on England. To add to Henry's woes, Thomas Spinelli was reporting increased Yorkist activity on the Continent.

Somehow, Spinelli's career had survived the embarrassment of employing not one but two double agents and by the beginning of 1522 he was back in Brussels monitoring Richard's movements. In February, Spinelli informed Wolsey that the White Rose 'with his accustomed train' had met the duke of Lorraine's treasurer, which pointed to Francis still using Antoine the Good to channel funds to the Yorkists.[8]

All of a sudden things looked black for Henry, but on 27 April 1522 the French suffered another crushing defeat in Italy at the battle of Bicocca. As ever, the bone of contention was Milan, which the French had lost the previous autumn, but as the new campaign season opened, a strong force of Swiss, Venetians and French sent to retake the city was annihilated by an imperial army led by Prospero Colonna.[9]

With Francis's troops retreating on all fronts, the triumphant Charles saw an opportunity to deliver the *coup de grâce* and he made a state visit to England to strengthen the agreements made at Bruges in 1521. Under the terms of a new treaty, which was signed at Windsor on 16 June 1522, a Tudor army, bolstered by 10,000 imperial *landsknechts*, would invade Normandy in support of a Habsburg attack on Flanders while Charles would marry Henry's daughter Mary to seal the alliance.

Charles and Henry privately intended to partition all of France between them, but in public their justification for the invasion was Francis's continuing support for Henri d'Albret in Navarre, the duke of Bouillon in Luxembourg, the duke of Albany in Scotland and Richard de la Pole. Indeed, Henry's declaration of war, which was made on 29 May 1522, specifically accuses Francis of breaking his oath by entertaining the king of England's 'rebellious subject'[10] and his accusations were well founded, even though Albany had warned Francis that the Scots were totally unprepared for war.

In a letter sent ten days *before* Bicocca, Albany told Francis that the Scots were still reeling from their defeat at Flodden, fought almost a decade earlier. However, Albany went on to say that an attack on Berwick or Carlisle could be made if his Scottish troops were stiffened with French and Danish mercenaries led by Richard de la Pole. He also advised that any troops sent to Scotland should be transported in ships supplied by the Hanseatic League.

Elsewhere in his letter, Albany stated that England could be conquered with nothing more than 'a strong force of Swiss, a band of brave adventurers, some light cavalry and a small battery of well-equipped artillery',[11] and he urged Francis to send the White Rose to the Danish king, Christian II, to negotiate a suitable alliance. Unfortunately for Richard, Christian's marriage to Charles V's sister made it impossible for him to treat openly with his brother-in-law's enemies. In any case, there was another obstacle to Albany's plan.

In 1518, a rebellion had broken out in Sweden, then under Danish control. The rebels were being financed by the Hanseatic League, so Francis, Albany and Richard could not use Hansa ships for an invasion of England backed by the Danes. However, Christian's uncle Frederick, duke of Holstein offered a solution to both these problems.[12]

As far as Albany was concerned the Hanseatic League's support remained vital, so he suggested that Frederick should act as a neutral intermediary, but Francis thought he could sidestep the issues entirely with the duke's help. Thanks to Christian's mismanagement of the Swedish rebellion, Frederick was on the point of deposing his nephew anyway so Francis offered him French support for his rebellion in return for help putting Richard on England's throne.[13] Naturally, the Holstein–Yorkist alliance would be secured by the marriage of Frederick's daughter Dorothea to Richard.

This was not the first time that the duke had been connected to a Yorkist invasion. Four years earlier, Sir Richard Jerningham had warned Wolsey that Holstein's ports could be used to embark an invading army and now a Yorkist king and a Danish queen were not the only cards Henry's enemies had to play. The reshuffling of the generational deck had brought a new player to the table in the form of James FitzGerald, 10th earl of Desmond.

The FitzGeralds had been fighting a bitter feud with the Butler earls of Ormond for most of the fifteenth century, and these rival clans had taken opposing sides during the Wars of the Roses. The FitzGerald earls of Kildare and Desmond had supported Edward IV, Richard III, Lambert Simnel and Perkin Warbeck, while the Ormonds had backed Henry VI, Henry VII and Henry VIII. As mentioned earlier, an Ormond heir had been the subject of a Yorkist kidnap plot during Edmund's time as White Rose, and Desmond hatred for the Tudors still burned fiercely when James succeeded to his father's earldom in 1520.[14]

At first, James had dreamed of driving the Tudors and their Ormond allies out of Ireland altogether and to do so he had sought help from the House of York's traditional allies, the Habsburgs, but this was a dead end. Although Charles had been alarmed by the warming of Anglo-French relations following the Universal Peace, and had taken Desmond's offer to raise an anti-Tudor rebellion in Ireland seriously, once the treaties of Bruges and Windsor brought Henry back into the imperial fold the Emperor had no more need of Irish rebels.

Fortunately for Irish Yorkism, the dramatic cooling of Anglo-French relations after the failed talks at the Field of Cloth of Gold made Desmond's offer extremely attractive to Francis and he sent two ambassadors to negotiate an alliance. It can hardly be a coincidence that one of these envoys was closely related to Richard's cousin Anne of Foix-Candale,[15] and throughout this period the White Rose continued to fight for France.

A letter dated 8 April 1522, and signed 'Le duc de Suffolk, Rychart', requested a certain captain of Lengey to grant safe conduct to Richard's troops.[16] Lengey is probably Longwy, at the intersection of the modern French, Belgian and Luxembourg borders, and it seems likely that Richard's men were on their way to reinforce Fleuranges, who was guarding this part of the Ardennes.[17]

A month after this letter was sent, the Tudors and Habsburgs declared war. When the region's French commander-in-chief, the duke of Vendôme, learned that imperial troops were preparing to attack his stronghold of Guise, he and Francis devised a plan to lure their enemies into a trap. The bait was a bogus offer from a supposedly disgruntled sentry to open a postern gate, and the imperial commander, Philippe de Croÿ, swallowed it eagerly.

The imperials advanced towards the town of Guise little knowing that Francis, who had decided to lead the operation in person, was lying in wait. However, the planned ambush failed because the hot-headed French king gave the order to attack too early and the two arms of his pincer, which were led by Richard and Fleuranges, were not in position when the charge was sounded. As a result, de Croÿ and his army easily escaped.[18]

Although the town had been saved, de Croÿ's retreat could hardly be called a French victory and the Anglo-Imperial threat continued to grow. All the while, Francis looked to Scotland to distract Henry while his army recovered from the catastrophe of Bicocca but he had to make it clear to Albany that the Scots could expect no military help until the Irish and Holstein alliances were in place.

'[His Majesty] is very grieved he is not able to assist [the Scots] more effectually, for he considers that money sent to Scotland is as profitable as if spent at home, for the prosperity of the one is the defence of the other,' he wrote in a letter to Francois de Charron, the French ambassador in Edinburgh.[19] This letter is dated 13 August 1522, but while the negotiations with the earl of Desmond and the duke of Holstein dragged on there was plenty that Francis could do to assist Albany without resorting to force of arms.

As long as Henry and Wolsey *believed* there was a threat to England's north they would be forced to divert men and resources away from any war on the Continent, so Francis's spies worked hard to convince their English foes that a French invasion fleet, carrying 25,000 men with Richard de la Pole at their head, was about to cross the North Sea. Their lurid reports also repeated the rumours that Albany was planning to murder James V, marry his grieving mother and appoint himself king of Scotland before marching on London.[20]

Further corroboration of the gathering storm came from a Hansa merchant named Pierrepoint, who was another double agent. Born in the Hanseatic town of Deventer on the River Ijssel, Pierrepoint had been a resident of the London Steelyard for several years but in March 1522 he had been recruited by the captain of Boulogne to spy for the French.

On the orders of his new master, the merchant had travelled to Lyon to give the French admiral, Bonnivet, a firsthand report of the Tudor fleet's preparedness for war. After meeting Bonnivet, who spent some time quizzing the merchant about the English warships, Pierrepoint went to Calais and confessed everything to the city's treasurer, Sir William Sandys. The grateful Sandys sent Pierrepoint to Wolsey but the spy had foolishly let it be known that the French believed the cardinal had manufactured the war for his own profit and the furious Wolsey claimed to be too busy to see him.[21]

Eventually Pierrepoint was debriefed by Sir Thomas Boleyn who sent him back to France to spy out French defences and his departure, at the end of May 1522, coincided with Henry's declaration of war. During his second trip to France, the now double agent was asked by the great bailiff of Caen if he knew lord Stafford, whose father, the duke of Buckingham, had been executed the previous year for 'having listened to prophecies of the king's death'.

Presumably, the bailiff thought that Buckingham's aggrieved son would be keen to avenge his father by joining a Yorkist rebellion and he assured Pierrepoint that 50,000 strong-hearted Englishmen would flock to Richard's banner the moment he landed.[22] Interestingly, Pierrepoint was also asked if he would go to Scotland as part of Richard's entourage, and though he declined to do so, saying he was not the right man for the job, he was introduced to the White Rose when both men found themselves back in Lyon.

During their meeting, Richard declared that he had been born in a town 'where he hath made good cheer', which was perhaps a reference to the support he had garnered in the traditionally Yorkist city of London. Yet when Richard was asked how soon he would return to England, he had become vague and would only say that he had travelled to Lyon at the behest of the French king.

Fortunately for Pierrepoint, the duke of Vendôme was more candid and he told the spy that the king of France 'intended to set Richard de la Pole forward with a great number of men, and, with the help of Denmark, land him in England in those parts where the duke of Buckingham had lands, where they would burn and destroy man, woman and child'.[23]

If Pierrepoint or his Tudor paymasters had been able to read Francis's letter to Charron they would have realised that such bellicose talk was just the latest effort in the French king's long campaign of misinformation. Whether Pierrepoint was the knowing or unknowing conduit for this potpourri of half-truths is unclear, but in any case the immediate effect of his revelation was to force Henry to postpone his invasion of Normandy, at least until the threat from Albany and Richard had receded.

Despite repeatedly promising the Emperor that he would fulfil his obligations under the treaties of Bruges and Windsor, Henry's military operations during the summer of 1522 were limited to blockading the French Channel ports and raiding southern Scotland. These operations were an attempt to stop Francis and Richard from assembling a fleet and Albany from recruiting an army, but they did little to mollify Charles, even though his ambassadors to England confirmed that Henry had his hands full.[24]

The burning of the Scottish Borders was led by George Talbot, 4th earl of Shrewsbury, while Brittany suffered under Henry's admiral Thomas Howard, 2nd earl of Surrey,[25] and his vice-admiral Sir William Fitzwilliam. Incidentally, one of the ships under the latter's command was the ill-fated *Mary Rose*,[26] and while her bronze cannon pounded the Breton coast, Wolsey tried to isolate France diplomatically by demanding an end to the Franco-Venetian alliance.

On 21 August 1522, Wolsey's envoy to the Most Serene Republic, Richard Pace, presented the Doge, Antonio Grimani, with a list of eight Anglo-Imperial grievances and topping this list was French support for Richard de la Pole. Pace also pointed out that Francis had invaded Upper Navarre without a formal declaration of war and had used the de la Marcks to fight a proxy war in Luxembourg. Having read out his list not once but twice, Pace insisted that Venetian honour required it to withdraw from such a shameful alliance, but the pro-French Doge rejected the English arguments out of hand.

The elderly Doge's refusal to be intimidated must have come as a welcome relief for Francis, and in Scotland Henry seemed to be doing his best to provoke the invasion he feared. At the beginning of the summer, Henry had ordered all Scotsmen to leave England and wear an identifying white cross of St Andrew on their journey home. He then sent another English fleet into the Firth of Forth to put the coastal towns of Fife and Lothian to the torch while the earl of Shrewsbury pillaged the abbey town of Kelso.[27]

No doubt Henry wanted to terrorise the Scots into abandoning Albany, but burning peaceful farms and fishing villages had precisely the opposite effect. To stop Henry from destroying more of southern Scotland, the Scots put aside their misgivings about fighting the English and Albany was able to raise a huge army of 80,000 volunteers. Yet instead of employing these men defensively, the regent marched on Carlisle even though there was no sign of the promised support from Richard de la Pole, the earl of Desmond or the duke of Holstein.

Without professional soldiers stiffening Scottish resolve, Albany's invasion was doomed. It did not matter that the poorly defended English city could have been captured with ease; as the Scots crossed the marshes at the head of the Solway Firth, they lost their nerve and declared that they would not fight a war that was solely in the interests of France.[28] This was exactly what Albany had feared, and his attempts to shame his men into action only made matters worse.

'You know, or at least you should know, that I have ever set my whole mind and put my body in peril for Scotland, whence I take my name, blood and honour,' he thundered. 'It was an obvious token of this and my good will also when I left in France all delight, cheer, kindness and the delectable friendship of noble men, forsaking distinctions of honour, wealth and prosperity, which I abounded in France, and came to Scotland to set you all at one when each of you was sticking his rapier in his neighbour's belly and you were eating each other up with envy.'[29] His insults were in vain. The Scots marched home and Albany took their recalcitrance as a personal insult.

After negotiating a month-long truce with Lord Dacre, Albany returned to France in high dudgeon but he intended to use the lull in the fighting to put together an army of more reliable foreign mercenaries. Typically, Albany's plan soon became the worst-kept secret in Christendom. Sir Robert Wingfield, England's latest ambassador to the imperial court, was one who realised that the Scottish retreat from Carlise had not ended the Yorkist threat, as evidenced in a letter to Wolsey dated 9 December 1522:

> So as to prevent His [Majesty's] invasion of France next summer. Francis is determined to send Richard de la Pole into

> Scotland, and is intriguing with the earl [*sic*] of Holstein, by assent of the king of Denmark, who dares not openly assist the French against the Emperor. He has sent the earl the order of France, and a sum of money to give assistance to Scotland; all which negotiations pass through Metz in Lorraine.[30]

Wingfield's claims of an imminent invasion were confirmed by the capture of two more Yorkist spies. The first was Aleyn Dawse, a watchman employed by the sheriff of Norfolk, who had hoped to improve his lot by finding a better job. After his arrest, and some less-than-gentle persuasion by his former employer, Dawse confessed that he had been on night duty when two men had approached him with the offer of a position in the household of a nobleman that paid 10*d* a day instead of the 6*d* he earned as a watchman.[31]

Once Dawse had sworn an oath of secrecy he was told by his recruiters, who were named Nicholas Fyske and John Asome, that his new master was to be Richard de la Pole. They assured him that there was no need to be afraid because 'there were 100 more retained in the same manner'. Dawse was also offered a bounty of 6*s* 8*d*, which for some reason he refused, but he agreed to be ready to leave England at an hour's notice.[32]

A few weeks later, the imperial authorities in Flanders caught another Yorkist spy on the road from Cambrai to Valenciennes. Simon of Monmouth, a Welshman, had been travelling with another person who had no rebel connections. The innocent wayfarer had been released but Simon was kept 'in prison and in pain'.[33]

As the rack slowly dislocated his limbs, the Welshman confessed that he had spent several days in Richard's company, after which he had been given 3 gold crowns to go England to discover the extent of Yorkist support and what preparations Henry was making for another invasion of France. Finally, the battered and broken prisoner admitted that Albany was planning to 'raise a great power this summer in France, to land in Scotland and recruit four captains who were to meet in Lorraine'.[34]

The Welshman's confession was sent to Wolsey on 12 January 1523 and it was accompanied by more despatches from Wingfield in which he detailed Richard's plan to recruit an army of

8,000 German and 4,000 Flemish mercenaries to bolster the ranks of hesitant Scots. Two weeks later Wingfield reported that Richard had been forced to enlist Germans and Flemings because the French were such poor fighters,[35] and these claims were corroborated by Richard Pace, who was still in Venice, and a churchman called Peter Vannes who was Cardinal Wolsey's eyes and ears in the Vatican.

On 3 January, Pace reported that Albany had requested 10,000 foot and 500 horse, to be led by Richard, and 'the king of France had liked the enterprise'.[36] Richard's presence in Paris was confirmed by Vannes in a letter dated 29 January, and he tells us that Francis had given Albany 30,000 crowns to fund his return to Scotland.[37]

By 12 March 1523, the Venetian ambassador to France, Giovanni Badoer, was telling the Doge that 'the king of France is making great preparations against the king of England by sea and land'.[38] He also confirmed that the invading army would be commanded by the White Rose and René of Savoy, the French king's half-uncle. However, another of Wolsey's agents produced a surprise: Francis's plans now included the earl of Desmond.

24

MARCH THROUGH THE LAND OF THE ENEMIES IN ORDER TO TRAMPLE IT

In January 1523, an unnamed agent informed Wolsey that 'Albany and Blanche-Rose will be ready to make a descent into Ireland [where] there is an Irish Lord who, by means of a French merchant, has arranged to supply the army with victuals at any spot they please'.[1] For once, the information was good.

Though the secret treaty between the king of France and James FitzGerald would not be signed until 20 June 1523, French envoys had made frequent trips to the castle of Askeaton, which was the main Desmond stronghold in the west of Ireland. As a result, the earl had agreed to provide Richard with 400 horse and 10,000 foot 'with the view of driving Henry VIII entirely out of Ireland and restoring the duke of Suffolk'.[2]

This report finally made it clear to Henry and Wolsey that the previous year's rumours of an invasion were fast becoming a reality, and their response was to appoint the earl of Surrey as lieutenant-general of the north in place of the ageing earl of Shrewsbury. Surrey had spent the previous summer burning Breton fishing villages, and his mission in southern Scotland was the same: put everything to the fire and sword to deter an attack by Albany. Surrey would later boast that he had turned a swathe of the Scottish Borders 12 miles wide into a desert,[3] but Henry could never be sure the north was secure as long as his own sister was making common cause with his enemies.

Fortunately for England's king, Albany's return to France after the debacle at Carlisle had left his sister Margaret dangerously isolated in Edinburgh. The time was now right for Henry to drive a wedge between the two regents. He therefore ordered his Border captains, Surrey and Dacre, to warn Margaret of the dire consequences that would befall her if she continued her alliance with the Tudors' enemies, and Surrey duly wrote to Margaret on 3 August 1523:

> I hear that the Frenchmen in Scotland report that Albany is coming with a great power, and that Richard de la Pole will land in England, but you may be sure this will not come to pass, for the French king would not dare to do it. These are but feigned words to beguile the noblemen of Scotland and that those who believe in Albany's coming will be deceived. The time is coming for doing more damage to Scotland than ever, by destroying their corn, and this will be done without fail, unless the Scottish lords act differently towards the king of England and not to take part with one who favours de la Pole.[4]

A day later, Dacre penned two similar letters to Margaret in which he urged her to abandon the 'false and contrived ways of Albany and Richard de la Pole' for the sake of her son. He did not mince his words; elsewhere in his letters, Dacre called Richard 'one of the vilest *caitiffs* [cowards] of the world'.[5]

These threats had the desired effect on Margaret, and at the end of August 1523 she wrote to Dacre begging him to send an army to rescue herself and her son, but Henry failed to make the most of this opportunity to score a major political victory in the north.[6] Such a failure may appear shortsighted, but developments in France had made Henry feel more secure than ever, and for this he had his navy to thank.

In Surrey's absence, command of the Channel fleet had been given to Sir William Fitzwilliam, and he had continued raiding French ports to prevent Francis, Albany and Richard from gathering a fleet. After several months of terrorising the Breton and Norman coasts, Fitzwilliam was able to inform Henry that his enemies 'would not pass that year into Scotland'[7] and his blockade produced an important, if unexpected, dividend when Charles, duke of Bourbon and grand constable of France, defected to the Anglo-Imperial cause.

Fighting for Milan and filling rebel coffers with gold while Fitzwilliam was slowly strangling revenues from French trade had drained the Francis's treasury. Yet the duchy of Bourbon was a rich vein of wealth that had never been properly mined by French kings. In truth, the verdant lands of central France had originally belonged to the duchess of Bourbon, Suzanne, but she had died in 1521 and bequeathed her vast estates to her husband.

Besides coveting Bourbon's wealth, Francis could not forget that the widowed duke had a claim to the French throne and his newly acquired riches would give him the men and money to mount a rebellion. Moreover, Francis was acutely aware that he had only become king through a series of dynastic accidents and so, like Henry in England, he lived in constant fear of being deposed. Though Bourbon had never shown any signs of disloyalty, Francis became increasingly wary of his constable. Yet rather than consign his rival to a dungeon or the scaffold, he tried to send him to the altar.

To funnel the Bourbon revenues into her son's war chest, Francis's widowed mother, Louise of Savoy, offered to marry the widowed duke but this was not a match made in heaven. Louise was not only fourteen years older than her prospective groom, she was well past her childbearing years and the childless Bourbon desperately needed an heir. Louise's suit was therefore rejected, but insulting the king's mother was a serious blunder. The jilted Louise suddenly remembered she had her own claim to the Bourbon legacy, so she contested the late duchess's will in court.[8]

Suspiciously, the judges ordered the transfer of Suzanne's estates to Louise *before* the case was heard and this blatant abuse of royal power was the last straw for the duke. The fear that Bourbon would mount a challenge for the French throne now became a self-fulfilling prophecy; just as Henry VII had provoked Edmund de la Pole by downgrading his title and confiscating his ancestral lands, so Francis pushed Bourbon into rebellion by doing the same. To complete the coincidence, Bourbon also turned to the Holy Roman Empire for help, but on this occasion the Habsburg Emperor, the Tudor king and the rebel duke were all on the same side.[9]

In July 1523, Charles's envoy met the disenfranchised duke at Montbrison and agreed to supply 10,000 imperial *landsknechts* for his rebellion. These troops would invade France from Alsace, link up with the English marching through Normandy and with them seize Paris.[10] Although this plan was agreed in the absence of Henry's envoy, Dr Knight, who had failed to arrive in time for the conference, Bourbon reached a similar agreement with his deputy, Sir John Russell, three weeks later.

This was the same Sir John Russell who had plotted with Perceval de Matte to kill Richard de la Pole back in 1515, but this time he had disguised himself as a merchant rather than a pilgrim while travelling to Bourbon's castle of La Gayette. Though the rebel duke refused to acknowledge Henry's claim to be the rightful ruler of France, he did agree to help him recover the French lands and titles once held by English kings. This was good enough, and Henry began planning his attack on Normandy as soon as Russell returned to England. However, by this time Francis had learned of the constable's treachery.[11]

According to the Italian chronicler Francesco Guicciardini, two Norman lords who planned to join the English as soon as Henry crossed the Somme inadvertently revealed Bourbon's plot while seeking absolution for their sins from the bishop of Lisieux. Ignoring the sanctity of confession, His Grace had passed this information to the high seneschal of Normandy and he had told Francis. At first the wily duke had managed to mollify his king by feigning illness, but before long he had fled to the Empire.[12]

The constable's sudden betrayal threw the French court into panic. Fleuranges was ordered to take 5,000 men to Guise to prevent an Anglo-imperial army from joining up with Bourbon's rebels, while the duke of Vendôme was sent to Thérouanne with 3,000 Frenchmen and Richard de la Pole, with 4,000 Germans, was ordered to join him. The French chronicler Martin du Bellay tells us that Richard was to use Thérouanne as a base for a mobile force that would 'march through the land of the enemies, in order to trample it',[13] but at the last minute the White Rose and his men were diverted to Lyon.

'The duke of Suffolk, with the *landsknechts* under his command and 2,000 or 3,000 Picardy foot and with a party of gendarmes found themselves at Lyon at the start of August 1523,' added Bellay,[14] but why was Richard sent south when his Tudor nemesis was poised to strike in the north? Incredibly, considering Francis's military, financial and political setbacks, the French king was determined to press ahead with his war to retake Milan and he used his legion of spies to spread rumours that the invasion of England had been called off. To add weight to this lie, Albany was recalled from Brittany where he had been waiting to take ship for Scotland, and Richard was summoned to Lyon.[15]

By these deceptions Francis hoped to lull Henry into a false sense of security, and his plan worked beautifully. On 25 August 1523 the new Venetian Doge, Andrea Gritti, wrote to his ambassador in Rome warning him that the French intended to focus on Italy 'now that the expedition against England, which was to have been effected through the White Rose, has been suspended and renounced'.[16] He, and everyone else, had been fooled.

As far as Henry was concerned, Fitzwilliam's blockade had been a complete success.[17] He ordered his Channel fleet back to port for the winter, but all the while Albany and Richard had been secretly assembling an armada of seventy-two ships and an army of 3,000 men in Brest.[18]

The choice of this Breton port is significant because it indicates that either Richard's negotiations with the duke of Holstein had come to nothing or he and Albany had decided to approach from the west now the Irish earl of Desmond had joined their alliance. Whatever the truth of the matter, the fact that they were able to gather such a sizeable force without Fitzwilliam noticing is testament to the success of Francis's *ruse de guerre*.

We can only imagine Richard's feelings of utter elation as he watched his men embark. At last he was being given the chance to avenge his uncle, his brothers and all the other Yorkists who had died brutal deaths for their cause. Even the capricious Channel weather-gods seemed to smile on his endeavour as the same stiff breeze that blew the Franco-Yorkist cogs and carracks towards western Scotland kept the Tudor ships bottled up in Portsmouth. That said, such a large fleet could not remain hidden in the narrow confines of the Irish Sea for long, and reports of the impending danger soon reached Henry.

Understandably, England's king was furious at being deceived and Wolsey had to write several frantic letters to Fitzwilliam urging him to intercept the Franco-Yorkist fleet. In reply, the unflappable vice admiral had pointed out that he could not make ships sail without a favourable wind and 'if my lord admiral can, I would be right glad to learn in that behalf'.[19]

With Fitzwilliam unable to leave the Solent, Richard and Albany's armada made swift progress and landed at Kirkcudbright, on the Scottish side of the Solway Firth, on 21 September 1523. English chronicler Edward Hall tells us that 'the traytour delapole' was with the French fleet, but he was writing twenty years after these events. At the time, the earl of Surrey's spies insisted that Albany and Richard had divided their forces while still at sea, after which the regent had headed for the Clyde, rather than the Solway, and the White Rose had taken thirty ships to make a separate landing in England.[20]

For the next fortnight, Surrey received conflicting reports about the respective whereabouts of Albany and Richard. According to Dacre, five more French ships had dropped anchor off Kirkcudbright a few days after the main force but Lord Ogle, another veteran border captain, insisted that eighty-seven French transports had arrived at Dumbarton, near Glasgow. According to Ogle, these ships had landed 4,000 pikemen, 500 men-at-arms, 1,000 arquebusiers, 500 light horsemen, and 100 fully armoured horsemen, as well as an arsenal that included 900 handguns and 16 large cannon.[21]

To add to the confusion, Ogle's reports were confirmed by Queen Margaret, who was now desperate to leave Scotland, and other informants told Surrey that Albany had convened councils of war in both Glasgow and Edinburgh. At these councils, said Surrey's spies, Albany had boldly declared that the English border fortresses would fall as soon as they were attacked; once the road south was open, he claimed, the victorious Scots would be joined by Richard de la Pole for a triumphant entry into England.[22]

When all these contradictory pieces of intelligence are pieced together, it seems that the landing in Kirkcudbright was a feint designed to convince Surrey that an attack on Carlisle was imminent whereas Albany actually planned to cross the border further east and had journeyed to Glasgow and Edinburgh to rally the Scottish feudal host. Meanwhile Richard's ships had probably sailed to Ireland, where the earl of Desmond was eagerly awaiting his arrival, which is exactly what his brother had done during the Simnel Rebellion.

Wherever Richard was, Surrey soon realised that a full-scale Scottish invasion was inevitable, so he wrote to Wolsey to inform him that 'either Albany doth marvellously dissemble, or Richard de la Pole has 6,000 or 7,000 men ready to invade England'.[23] But at this crucial juncture Wolsey played down the threat. His typically sycophantic reply to Surrey assured the earl that there was absolutely no danger of a Yorkist rebellion in England because Henry VIII was beloved by all his subjects.

'For assured may ye be, as ye well know there cannot be more integrity, perfect and sure fidelity in lords and subjects to their prince than, thanked be God! the King's highness hath in this realm,' he wrote,[24] but Surrey was far from convinced and he increased his cross-border raids to deny Albany's men the supplies they would need.[25]

As before, the English terror tactics were counterproductive. The burning of towns and villages, such as Jedburgh and Old Jedward, persuaded many Border Scots to support another invasion of England. Nevertheless, Albany was determined to avoid the previous year's mistakes so he ignored the English strongholds of Carlisle, Alnwick and Berwick. Instead, he marched his army over the windswept Lauder Hills to Wark-on-Tweed where there was a ford across the river marking Scotland's eastern boundary with England.

This ford was guarded by a castle, which Hall described as 'little', but George Buchannan, the Scottish chronicler and theologian who actually took part in the 1523 invasion, tells us that Wark was very strongly fortified with a high octagonal keep, surrounded by a double wall enclosing an outer and an inner bailey.[26]

The strategic value of Wark had long been recognised but while the cannons for a new artillery bastion had arrived, the gunners had not and the castle's captain, Sir William Lyle, commanded fewer than 100 men. Albany's force was thirty times greater, and the Scottish train of artillery was the largest ever seen in the Borders, yet Surrey was confident that Wark could withstand a siege. In a letter dated 27 September 1523, he even told Wolsey that he hoped Albany would attack Wark because it was by far the strongest fortress on the Tweed. His wish was soon granted.[27]

The Franco-Scottish army, with Albany at its head and Buchannan in its ranks, reached Wark at the end of October and the regent immediately ordered his cavalry to seal off the approaches to the castle while his artillery battered its ramparts. In no time at all, a breach had been made in the outer bailey's wall and Albany sounded the charge. Shouting their bloodcurdling battle cries, a thousand Frenchmen and five hundred Scots forded the river, stormed the breach and quickly overwhelmed the first line of English defences.[28]

In desperation, Wark's defenders set light to the outer bailey's storehouses and the intense flames forced the attackers back across the Tweed. Under cover of the smoke from the burning barns, Lyle's men retreated to the castle's keep. The Scots believed the keep to be impregnable, so Albany ordered his guns to blast the garrison into submission.[29] After two days of relentless bombardment, during which more than half of Wark's surviving defenders were blown to pieces, Albany ordered a second assault. When Lyle saw his enemy was again fording the river, he urged his men to face death like heroes.

'Sirs, for our honour and manhood, let us go forth and fight with the proud Scots and stately Frenchmen, for more shall our honour be to die in battle then to be murdered with guns,' he cried, and his men shouted their huzzahs as they made a suicidal counter-charge from the castle's battered donjon.

'Then they issued out boldly and shot courageously … and with shooting and fighting they drove their enemies clean out of the place and slew of them, and chiefly of the Frenchmen, 300,' wrote Hall.[30] And unlike in the case of the doomed Spartans at Thermopylae or Texians at the Alamo, help was on its way.

The earl of Surrey had been warned of Albany's attack by Isabella Hoppringle, the pro-English abbess of Coldstream, who was a personal friend of Margaret Tudor. Surrey marched his army to relieve Wark with all speed, and as soon as the English host appeared on the horizon Albany's men fled into the Lauder Hills. Buchannan tells us that only a sudden snowstorm prevented a repeat of the disaster at Flodden. 'The same storm caused the English to disband their army, and return home without effecting anything,' he wrote.[31]

Curiously, neither Buchannan nor Hall make any mention of Richard de la Pole in their accounts of the siege. Though rumours of the White Rose's presence in the Borders persisted,[32] it is most likely that Richard was in Ireland, embarking the earl of Desmond's kerns and gallowglasses, and we can only imagine his utter dismay when he heard the news of his allies' rout at Wark.

On paper, the plan to invade England from Scotland and Ireland had been a good one because the Yorkists had always had strong support among England's Celtic neighbours. Unfortunately for Richard, the Scots formed by far the most important link in this chain and we can hardly blame Desmond for abandoning the enterprise after Albany's defeat. Worse still for Richard, Bourbon's successful escape and arrival in imperial territory allowed Charles and Henry to begin their attacks on France in earnest.

As per the strategy agreed at Montbrison and La Gayette, Bourbon and the 10,000 *landsknechts* he had been given by Charles invaded France from the east. Meanwhile, as he was required to do under the treaties of Waltham and Windsor, the Emperor sent more *landsknechts* to reinforce the Tudor army being assembled in Calais. These men were led by Lord IJsselstein, but overall command of the Anglo-imperial army had been given to the new duke of Suffolk, Charles Brandon.

Though French sources always refer to Richard as duke of Suffolk, the degrading of Edmund and the attainder of all the de la Pole brothers not in holy orders meant he had never officially held this title. Equally, it can hardly be a coincidence that Henry VIII revived the Suffolk dukedom to reward his favourite, Charles Brandon, who had distinguished himself during the 1513 Thérouanne campaign. Though Brandon had soon blotted his copybook by eloping with the king's younger sister, Mary Tudor, he had returned to royal favour by the time Henry launched his latest campaign in Picardy.

The day before Albany landed in Kirkcudbright, the Tudor dragon slumbering in Calais at last stirred. Though Brandon was a capable soldier, the writing was on the wall even before he left the English enclave. IJsselstein had brought with him barely half of the promised imperial reinforcements, and the 10,000 *landsknechts* who were supposed to be advancing on Paris from Alsace with the duke of Bourbon at their head had been routed by the redoubtable comte de Guise as they tried to cross the River Meuse.[33]

Though Bourbon had failed to turn up for his own rebellion, Brandon still had a sizeable army and most of Picardy's defenders were now on the wrong side of the Alps because Francis had continued with his invasion of Italy despite the threat to his rear. Just as Doge Gritti had predicted, Francis had diverted men and money from the conquest of England to the conquest of Italy and Martin du Bellay insisted that Richard de la Pole had been brought back from Scotland to join the fight for Milan.

'Towards the commencement of September in the year 1523, our army composed of 1,400 to 1,500 men-at-arms, close to 5,000 Swiss, 6,000 French infantry, under de Lorges, and an equal number of *landsknechts* under the orders of the duke of Suffolk, marched towards Milan for the purpose of giving battle to the enemy,' he wrote.[34]

If Bellay is correct, Francis had weakened the army he had sent to Scotland either to strengthen his Italian expedition or to deal with Brandon's attack on Paris; this would explain why Richard and Albany had divided their fleet somewhere in the Irish Sea. It was certainly possible for a fast ship to catch up with the cumbersome transports to send an urgent message, but Richard failed to return in time to stop Brandon.

In the end, the French capital was saved not by Richard's mercenaries but by the atrocious weather and the venality of Brandon's imperial allies. After several weeks without pay, the delivery of which had been delayed by torrential rains turning the roads of northern France into quagmires, IJsselstein's *landsknechts* had simply packed up their pikes and halberds and gone home. The departure of these mercenaries had a catastrophic effect on the English troops, and a sudden sharp frost finally broke their spirit. Cries of 'Home, home!' began to echo around the English camp, and, faced with the prospect of widespread mutiny, Brandon turned his men around. The exhausted, frostbitten remnants of Henry's mighty army limped into Calais shortly before Christmas 1523.[35]

More by good luck than good management, Paris had held, but Francis failed to capitalise on Brandon's failure. Instead of driving the demoralised English out of Calais, he continued with his quest to reconquer Milan, yet he did not lead this campaign in person. Unsure of Bourbon's movements, Francis remained in Lyon to deal with any uprising in the rebel duke's duchy. Command of the Milanese expedition was given to Bonnivet.

We have already met France's admiral during the Pierrepoint affair and the successful French attack on Fuentarrabia in 1521 but while this had been Bonnivet's only military experience, his progress was rapid because Charles had made the same mistake as Francis. Valuable resources intended to strengthen the Habsburg army in Italy had been diverted to Brandon and Bourbon, leaving the outnumbered imperials no choice but to withdraw into Milan, yet Bonnivet chose to besiege the weakened city instead of ordering a full-scale assault.[36]

In many respects this was a sound military decision, but the contemporary Italian chronicler Francesco Guicciardini insisted that 'the evil genius of the French, darkening as usual their intellects, would not permit them the profit of so fine an opportunity'.[37] Leaving Guicciardini's chauvinism aside, Bonnivet faced the same problems in Italy as Brandon had in France, and the worsening weather forced him to retreat into winter quarters at Abbiategrasso.

Just as Paris had remained French, so Milan stayed in imperial hands. By the end of 1523 there existed a situation, perhaps unique in military history, whereby all sides had lost. Albany's Scots had failed in Northumberland, Brandon's English had failed in Picardy, Bourbon's rebels had failed in Alsace, and Bonnivet's French had failed in Lombardy, yet none of these defeats ended the war. As far as the protagonists were concerned, all the campaigns would begin again in the new year.

25

ALL I HAVE IN THIS WORLD IS OWING TO YOU

The ignominious collapse of the latest Franco-Scottish plan to restore the House of York would have broken lesser men, but not Richard de la Pole. Instead of retiring to Metz to spend the rest of his days racing horses and chasing other men's wives, the White Rose returned to France, where he was made most welcome by the French king.

The failure of Brandon's invasion notwithstanding, Francis desperately needed his Yorkist terrier to keep snapping at Henry's heels, so Richard was deeply involved in the French king's plans for the 1524 campaigns. First the Danish connection was revived; it may be recalled that Frederick, duke of Holstein, had been plotting to overthrow his royal nephew, Christian II, because he had failed to crush the Swedish rebellion. In the summer of 1523, Frederick had marched on Copenhagen and ousted Christian, who found refuge with his brother-in-law Charles V. Soon afterwards, the Emperor had written to Henry VIII, his aunt's husband, asking for England's help in restoring Christian to the Danish throne.[1]

In August 1523, Charles and Henry had sent a joint embassy to Frederick with a warning that he must reinstate his nephew within a fortnight or face the consequences.[2] Naturally, Tudor–Habsburg support for Christian made a Valois–Yorkist alliance an attractive proposition for Frederick, so he recommenced his negotiations with Richard.

On 13 April 1524, the stalwart Dr Knight, who was still representing Tudor interests in the Low Countries, reported that Fredrick's envoy, Dr Brent, had arrived in Antwerp and had been seen in the company of Derek van Riet, Richard's long-serving steward. Knight asked Wolsey if he should have these men arrested by the imperial authorities or merely keep them under surveillance.[3] Wolsey's reply has not survived, but Richard's covert dealings with Copenhagen were not the only spying missions being undertaken by Yorkists.

In the same letter to Wolsey, Knight asked the cardinal to reward an imperial sentry who had arrested a Franco-Yorkist agent as he crossed the Flemish border near Valenciennes. This man was a servant of the same duke of Aarschot who had almost been trapped by Richard's ambush during the attack on Guise in 1522, but the Yorkist camp was also riddled with spies, moles and defectors.

Typical of this murky world of ever-shifting loyalties was the somewhat farcical attempt by Sir William Sandys, treasurer of Calais, to persuade one of Richard's German mercenaries to change sides. According to Sandys' report of the affair, which is dated 5 September 1524, he had been approached by a shady character named Henry Crookshanke who had offered to broker the German's defection. Though Sandys suspected Crookshanke of being a double agent, he sent one of his sergeants to investigate.

The two men had met in the border town of St Omer, at a seedy tavern called The Boot, and Crookeshanke had told the sergeant that he had the disgruntled German hidden in a nearby safehouse because he lacked the money to bring him to Calais. The sergeant left St Omer to fetch the required cash, and a few days later Sandys sent an archer named Robert Elvish, who was also master of the posts at Calais, together with an armed guard back to The Boot with the money.[4]

Interestingly, Elvish was acquainted with another spy, the aforementioned Deventer merchant called Pierrepoint, whom he had helped with legal advice during a dispute with the captain of Boulogne.[5] This experience would stand Elvish in good stead because the slippery Cookshanke suddenly insisted that he would not surrender the Yorkist defector until he had spoken to Wolsey in person.

To the undoubted surprise of Elvish, Crookshanke claimed he was fed up with other people taking the credit for his work and this rather feeble explanation was accepted. A few days later Crookshanke went Rouen, where he claimed he had a ship waiting to take him to England, but his story began to unravel when a report reached his Tudor handlers that contrary winds had forced this ship to put into Dunkirk. Once again, Elvish was sent to find out what was going on, but when he arrived at Dunkirk there was no sign of either the ship or Crookshanke. In vain, Elvish searched for the missing spy, and after three days it became painfully clear that his bird had flown.[6]

The most likely explanation for Crookshanke's sudden disappearance is that he and his defector, if such a man had ever existed, were nothing more than swindlers, but it is also possible that this was an attempt to infiltrate another Yorkist mole into the Tudor spy network. Why it failed, and what happened to Crookeshanke, is something of a mystery but Richard was adept at using double agents, such as Hans Nagel and Petrus Alamire, and a closer examination of Crookshanke's conversations with Elvish suggests that he was deliberately inflating the Yorkist position in order to mislead his Tudor enemies.

To begin with, Crookshanke told Elvish that there was a steady stream of Yorkists making for Metz by way of Winchelsea and Rye. He also claimed he had met two of these volunteers at Rouen, but no other source mentions Normandy as the preferred entry point for Yorkist refugees. Likewise, although Crookeshanke confirmed that Frederick, the usurping king of Denmark, was now firmly in the Franco-Yorkist camp, his claim that another French invasion was imminent was too outlandish to be true.

'Before the league between the king [of Denmark] and the French king, Richard de la Pole came from over the mountains to the French court ... and the French king clapped him on the shoulder, saying, my lord of Suffolk, I will set you into England with 40,000 men within few days,' Crookeshanke told his prospective employers.[7]

While the existence of the Franco-Danish negotiations were corroborated by Dr Knight's spies, the idea that Francis could spare 40,000 men to invade England was pure fantasy. That said, Crookshanke's claims about the duke of Albany had some substance.

According to Crookshanke, Albany had returned to France after the failed siege of Wark and had recruited a new army of

4,000 foot and 800 horse. These men were now billeted near the Franco-Flemish border, and he also told Sandys that French privateers were seizing Flemish fishing boats to transport these men to Scotland.[8] Curiously, Crookshanke insisted that the French claimed to be acting in the name of the Danish king when they hijacked the unlucky fishermen's boats, but while these claims also have to be treated with caution, there is little doubt that Albany, like Richard, had not given up his fight.

Though the defeat at Wark had alienated almost all of Albany's supporters in Scotland, he had refused to resign the regency and, instead, had returned to France in the hope of raising a new army to bolster his flagging regime. Albany arrived in Paris in January 1524, but his absence allowed his enemies to declare that the twelve-year-old James V had achieved his majority and would henceforth rule as king. This meant the regency was now unnecessary, and could be dissolved, but Albany and Francis had other ideas.

The duke of Albany's chief stronghold in Scotland was the castle of Dunbar, on the North Sea coast so, if he was plotting to recover the Scottish regency with French and Danish help, it made sense to base any invasion force close to the eastern end of the English Channel. Furthermore, Henry was told by his imperial allies that they had captured fourteen carts full of military hardware and they believed these supplies were destined for Francis's fortresses surrounding the Calais Pale, such as Thérouanne and Tournai.[9]

Though the fiasco of Brandon's campaign meant another English invasion of Picardy was unlikely, at least for the moment, Francis could never be sure that northern France was safe so long as Calais remained in Tudor hands. As ever, a pre-emptive strike on the Pale was a necessary precursor to any French operation in Italy, but in the spring of 1524 Francis's army was not as strong as his enemies believed. The sudden recapture of Fuentarrabia by the Spanish in February 1524[10] imperilled the French south-west, and Bonnivet was rapidly losing ground in Italy to the duke of Bourbon, of all people.

The new year had brought a complete change of command in the imperial armies in Italy, with the duke of Lannoy, who ruled Naples and southern Italy as the Emperor's viceroy, replacing Prospero Colonna, who had died in December 1523. Shortly after receiving his marshal's baton, Lannoy was ordered to drive the French back over the Alps, depose Francis and replace him with Bourbon.

The dismal failure of Bourbon's first tilt at the French throne notwithstanding, the rebel duke had managed to convince both the Habsburg Emperor and the Tudor king of England that the French people still yearned for him to save them from Valois tyranny. Fortunately for Bourbon, his ambitions matched those of Charles so he was given permission to lead an imperial army into Provence, but this could not be done until Bonnivet's French, then overwintering in Abbiategrasso, had been defeated.

The imperial army in Milan, which had survived Bonnivet's siege of the previous autumn, was reinforced by a large force of Lannoy's Spaniards and Neapolitans at the end of December 1523. All was now ready for a counterattack but Lannoy decided to do nothing until the spring, when he would be further strengthened by 6,000 German *landsknechts* and 7,000 Venetians under the duke of Urbino.[11] The addition of the Venetians was an especially bitter blow for the French because it completed the Most Serene Republic's abandonment of their former allies.

Though Francis tried to counter the build-up of imperial forces in Lombardy by recruiting yet more Swiss mercenaries, these troops soon deserted. Bonnivet was now seriously outnumbered, and he was forced to abandon the Milan campaign. To his credit, the admiral supervised the French rearguard during their retreat over the Alps in person but his army was caught and massacred by the imperials at what became known as the battle of the Sesia River. Among those slaughtered was the Chevalier Bayard, Richard's old comrade from the Navarrese War, and Bonnivet himself was seriously wounded.[12]

'The French have been so seriously weakened by their attacks on towns and castles, and the plague and famine from which they have several times suffered, that out of 1,500 *gendarmes* only 350 have returned to France,' wrote Charles in a gleeful letter he sent to his ambassador in England, Louis de Praet, on 21 May 1524.[13]

The Emperor certainly had every reason to be pleased with this victory. Not only had Lannoy succeeded in driving the French out of Italy, the destruction of Bonnivet's forces had opened the road to Marseille for Bourbon. But while Charles was still keen to give the renegade duke his wholehearted support, Wolsey had warned Henry not to risk another embarrassing defeat by invading Picardy on the rebel duke's behalf.[14]

On the face of things, the cardinal's advice was sound. Brandon's abortive march on Paris had shown that Bourbon lacked the popular support he claimed, and the Tudor army had yet to recover from the debacle. However, Wolsey's motives may have been more self-serving. According to a letter written by the dean of Windsor, the cardinal was keeping England out the wars in France and Italy in order to curry favour with the recently elected Pope Clement VII, who was trying to broker another Universal Peace. In return, Wolsey hoped to be appointed both bishop of Durham and papal legate to England.[15]

Whatever Wolsey's motives for blocking another English attack on France, Henry did agree to continue paying for the imperial troops spearheading Bourbon's rebellion, even though the English garrisons guarding the Calais Pale were ordered not to respond to any French provocation.[16] This command did not impress Sir William Fitzwilliam, the fire-breathing English admiral, who had been moved from the Tudor navy's Channel fleet to the captaincy of Guînes at the start of the year.

It is not clear whether Sir William's transfer to Guînes was a promotion for having organised the successful blockade of France's northern ports in 1522, or a demotion for having failed to intercept Albany and Richard's Franco-Scottish armada in 1523. In either case, as soon as he arrived in Guînes, Sir William had written to Wolsey describing the feebleness of his imperial allies as well as their French enemies.

'Though the Burgundians and French were within gunshot of each other they did not venture to fight,' he snorted in a typically candid letter he sent to Wolsey on 10 May 1524.[17] Fitzwilliam also boasted that the pusillanimous French could be thrashed by a few resolute Englishmen, and at this point in his report he dropped a bombshell: the White Rose had bloomed again in Picardy.

'By all that I hear, the French are not more than 18,000 strong and, except a few Almains led by Richard de la Pole, are no soldiers. Considering that this wretched traitor is in the field, haste over some men to give courage to the Flemings, who are men enough if their hearts were good,' he wrote.[18] Fitzwilliam also claimed that the gluttonous French were running short of food and urged Wolsey to let him make the most of this opportunity.

'They consume the victuals as fast as they come ... I wish the king [of England] had some more men on this side the sea. If we were but 15,000 English, besides these I have here ... we should make them a good breakfast!' he thundered.[19]

It seems that Sir William had forgotten the events of the previous autumn, when Brandon's army had demanded to go home when they were just 50 miles from an undefended Paris. Nevertheless, in a second report he sent to Wolsey a few days later, the new captain of Guînes admitted that Henry's own men were not entirely reliable and several members of the Calais garrison had tried to join the Yorkist cause.[20]

These deserters, one of whom was called Thompson, had been arrested by an imperial patrol as they tried to cross the border into France but when Sir William wrote to the imperial governor of Flanders, Lord Fiennes, asking for them to be returned for interrogation and execution, he denied all knowledge of the incident. All Fiennes would say was that one of his archers had seen a group of English Yorkists entering the border town of St Omer; perhaps they too had a secret appointment with Henry Crookeshanke at The Boot.[21]

One explanation for Fiennes' refusal to hand over his Yorkist prisoners is that he was hoping to keep any ransom for himself. Alternatively, if this was the same Lord Fiennes whom Edmund de la Pole had asked for help during his imprisonment in Hattem and Namur, it is possible that he had set the deserters free so they could join Richard's men. That said, Fiennes had no qualms about handing over two confidential letters from Richard that his patrols had seized from a captured courier.[22]

Although these letters, which are written in French and dated 8 May 1524, contain nothing of earth-shattering significance, they do offer a fascinating insight into Richard's state of mind during this period. The first is addressed to Francis's mother, Louise of Savoy, who had been appointed regent while her son hurried south to defend Provence, and it graphically illustrates Richard's deep debt to his French patrons:

> To the French Queen Mother: I believe that Vendôme and Brienne have informed you about the King's affairs here. I am

> sorry our enemies have not awaited us, for I and my band have the best desire to live and die in the King's service. All I have in this world is owing to you.[23]

The second letter, which is addressed to the king is more prosaic. 'I beg you to hasten the pay of the *landsknechts*, because they have not a dernier,' he wrote. This lack of military resources confirms that Francis was now so preoccupied with Bourbon's rebellion that Richard's role in Picardy had to be purely defensive.[24] If the White Rose could weaken the Calais garrisons by attracting a steady stream of deserters so much the better; indeed, his propaganda value to the French is dramatically illustrated by a curious meeting that took place in the middle of May 1524.

A few days after intercepting Richard's letters, Sir William Fitzwilliam sent a spy to the French camp at Hesdin, 40 miles to the south of Guînes, under the pretext of delivering his own letters to his French counterparts, the duke of Vendôme and the seigneur de Pont-Rémy. Typically, this meeting had produced nothing except empty threats, such as Pont-Rémy claiming that Francis was marching to Guînes at the head of a huge army and would begin a siege of the castle within the next four days. This was an obvious lie, but the offer of a huge bribe if Sir William surrendered Guînes was genuine.

'Trumpet, say this, tell your master [if] he will join us with the said 10,000 men, and beat these coward Flemings who run away, I shall give him a good part of the booty,' said Pont-Rémy.[25] In reply, the herald had said that the English would do no such thing, because they were looking forward to a good fight, yet Sir William needed hard facts, not idle boasts.

On 15 May, a second English emissary arrived at Hesdin. This man was no lowly herald but an important member of Calais' ruling council. Although Sir William refers to the man simply as 'Calais' in his report, he was probably the city's treasurer, William Sandys,[26] and his time with Vendôme had ended with a jaw-dropping surprise.

As before, nothing of importance was agreed and Vendôme had closed the fruitless meeting by asking if there was anything more to be said. This had prompted Sandys to say no, except that Sir William was sorry the French had not kept their promise to come to see him at Guînes because he had gone to a great deal trouble preparing a suitable welcome. Despite this taunt, it was Vendôme who had the last laugh. With a wry smile, the Frenchman gestured to a servant who opened a curtain at one end of the tent, and in walked Richard de la Pole.

'Here is your king!' Vendôme had cried in triumph.

'He is not my king!' Sandys had spluttered, and Sir William's report to Wolsey adds that the Tudor envoy had been so insulted at being confronted by the last of the Yorkist bogeymen that there had been an almighty row.

'Calais will explain to you himself how they bandied words,' wrote Sir William, yet even after Sandys had stormed out of Vendome's tent this was not the end of the matter.[27] While making his preparations to leave, the Englishman was taken to one side by Pont-Rémy, who whispered that he wanted to end the fighting.

'There is no man living who desireth peace more than I, for I am a Picard born myself, and my country is destroyed by the war,' he said. In reply, Sandys had told him that peace could be made easily if Francis agreed to Henry and Charles's demands, whereupon Pont-Rémy had suggested that Sir William should write to Henry with the details of any truce because he 'knew how to manage it'.[28] With that Sandys returned to Calais, but as he left he noticed that the French were preparing their own departure from Hesdin.

Was Pont-Rémy's peace proposal genuine, and if it was, had he been acting with the knowledge of the French king? If Francis was offering an olive branch in the north to better defend the south then he was pushing at an open door, for Wolsey was also in favour of peace. However, before Pont-Remy's offer reached the cardinal, news arrived of Bonnivet's disastrous defeat at the River Sesia and Wolsey had to rethink his policy of keeping England out of any war in support of Bourbon.

Put simply, all that mattered to Wolsey was securing the papal tiara for himself and the crown of France for Henry, but the destruction of Francis's army in Italy meant Bourbon held the key to both these doors. Consequently, Wolsey had to *appear* to reverse his previous policy of vetoing another English attack on Picardy, and he persuaded Henry to accept a treaty with Charles that reaffirmed Tudor support for the French rebel.

'The duke of Bourbon with a sufficient army shall invade France with all possible speed, so as not to give the enemy time to recover strength [and] the emperor will send with Bourbon the troops he was bound to keep in the duchy of Milan. Each prince will provide 100,000 gold crowns for the payment of the remainder of the army, the contribution to commence as soon as Bourbon is in French territory,' read the first two clauses of the treaty which Henry signed on 25 May 1524.[29]

In spite of this, Wolsey had no intention of diluting Henry's claims to the French throne and he instructed Richard Pace, who had accompanied Bourbon to his camp near Turin in order to supervise the payment of the promised subsidy,[30] to withhold the money until the renegade duke had publicly declared that the French crown rightfully belonged to the House of Tudor. Moreover, Pace was ordered to withdraw the English offer entirely if Bourbon flatly refused to acknowledge Henry as his king.[31]

The cardinal's letter went on to inform Pace that although Henry's treaties with Charles required the English to invade northern France in support of Bourbon, he was reluctant to do so unless the rebel's victory was certain.

'The [English] army is in readiness, if, on the duke of Bourbon's advance into France, any revolution should arise which would require the presence of the king [of England]. You are to encourage the duke to enter France, though the king is not minded to assist until he sees his advantage,' he wrote, though it sounds like it was Wolsey who was reluctant to risk another Brandon-style military embarrassment rather than Henry.[32]

How much Richard's presence in Picardy affected Wolsey's thinking is debateable, but it cannot be denied that the Yorkist and Bourbon problems were inextricably linked. On the one hand, Wolsey dared not weaken England by sending men and money to Bourbon if Francis, Richard and Albany were about to attack Calais or Northumberland. On the other, funding Bourbon had its merits; after all, the White Rose would lose his only ally if Francis was deposed.

Of course, Bourbon knew none of this and he was utterly appalled when Pace presented Wolsey's demand that he meekly hand to Henry the crown he believed to be his. Yet Pace was a skilled diplomat and he managed to convince the rebel duke that his cause was doomed without English gold to pay his imperial army. Almost certainly against his better judgement, Bourbon took the oath recognising Henry as king of France on 25 June 1524.

'I promise unto you, upon my faith, that I, the duke of Bourbon, will, by the help of my friends, put the crown of France upon the king [of England], our common master's head.'[33] With that, Bourbon sold his birthright for a mess of English potage.

As an example of Machiavelli's new style of unscrupulous statecraft Wolsey's double-dealing cannot be bettered. Pace even persuaded Bourbon to attack without any sign of Sir John Russell, who was supposed to deliver the first £20,000 of Henry's promised £100,000 war chest. Russell did not catch up with Bourbon until late August, and his excuse was that he had been forced to take long detours to avoid the 'diverse ambushes' that had been set for him.[34]

No doubt the rebel duke had no intention of keeping any promise he made to the upstart Tudors when he crossed the River Var, which marked the Italian–French border, on 1 July 1524, especially as the imperial victory at the Sesia two months earlier meant he was more than strong enough to overwhelm the feeble French forces opposing him.[35]

On 7 August 1524, Bourbon entered Aix, the Provençal capital, and two days later he had himself proclaimed comte de Provence by the region's parliament.[36] Incredibly, the conquest of south-east France had taken less than six weeks and cost the lives of only ninety-three imperials.[37] However, this was the apogee of Bourbon's campaign. As the summer of 1524 turned to autumn, his fortunes rapidly declined.

26

AT LEAST THREE HUNDRED MEN DIED IN THAT PLACE

Under the treaties signed by Charles and Henry, the duke of Bourbon was supposed to receive support from a Spanish army making an attack from the south-west while the English invaded France from the north, but both these operations failed to materialise. Despite ruling an enormous empire, Charles V did not have enough resources to wage a full-scale war in the Pyrenees as well as the Alps, but at least he had given Bourbon the means to conquer Provence. By contrast, Wolsey repeatedly ignored the rebel duke's appeals for the English to open a second front in Picardy.[1]

'It is very necessary that the king of England should invade France with a large army, for it is not easy to conquer the kingdom [of France] without it being attacked in several places,' Bourbon pleaded in two identical letters he sent to Henry and Wolsey on 25 June 1524.[2] Furthermore, despite his promise to enter the war once Bourbon had secured a bridgehead, Wolsey paid no heed to his own envoy, Richard Pace, who claimed that the French crown would fall into Henry's lap.

'Bourbon says hourly that France is now the king's, if he will take it [and] if we had the money we would be able to go where we pleased, and fight the whole of France. You [Wolsey] must consider this, for the king was never so likely to recover his rights in France as now,' Pace insisted in a letter he sent to the cardinal on 16 July, but it was all to no avail.[3]

Even when Russell reached Aix with the promised gold, which he did on 26 August 1524, Wolsey remained convinced that the French rebels had no chance of success. Another letter from Bourbon begging Wolsey 'to hasten the English expedition' was met with complete indifference, and the descendant of Henry V was not allowed out to play.[4] To add to Bourbon's worsening plight, his Hispano-Italian co-commander, Marshal Pescara, would not march his men to Paris until Marseille had been captured.

Initially, Bourbon had wanted to invade France via Lyon, which was closer to his ancestral domains where he presumed his support was strongest, but the campaign's first objective was changed to Provence so the imperial army could be resupplied by sea once winter snows had closed the Alpine passes.[5] The key to this strategy was the capture of Marseille's large harbour, but the city remained resolutely loyal to Francis.

As Bourbon's army approached, the citizens of Marseille slammed shut their gates and the imperials were forced to dig in for a siege. To counter the invaders' trenches and gun pits, the defenders strengthened their ancient walls while assassins infiltrated the imperial camp and cut the throats of sleeping sentries. These fearsome volunteers stripped naked and covered themselves in olive oil before going into action, a somewhat bizarre tactic but one that would give them the edge in any hand-to-hand combat.[6]

In spite of these surreal countermeasures, Bourbon remained confident that Marseille could be opened 'like an oyster' but his first assault on the city was beaten back with heavy losses.[7] Moreover, the failure of Bourbon's allies to make their promised diversionary attacks meant Francis was free to concentrate all his forces on the relief of the city. Crucially, Wolsey's decision to do nothing in the north allowed the 6,000 mercenaries defending Picardy to join Francis's army, and their captain was Richard de la Pole.

'The king [of France] likewise, seeing the army of his enemy before Marseille ... sent to Switzerland to raise 14,000 men and 6,000 *landsknechts*, 3,000 under the charge of François, monsieur de Lorraine, and 3,000 under the charge of the duke of Suffolk, the Rose-Blanche, whom I have mentioned several times in these memoires,' wrote Martin du Bellay.[8]

The monsieur de Lorraine spoken of here is François, comte de Lambesc, who was the youngest of two brothers of the duke of

Lorraine who fought in the campaign. The other was Louis, comte de Vaudémont, and theirs were not the only familiar faces Richard met on the road south. Also answering Francis's call to arms were Fleuranges, who had recruited the aforementioned Swiss,[9] and the duke of Albany.

Despite the best efforts of the French king, Albany had been removed from power in May 1524 when an Act dissolving the regency and declaring the twelve-year-old King James V to be an adult was passed by the Scottish parliament. However, Albany was still Scotland's heir presumptive, as well as a powerful French landowner, so his support was vital for Francis during the Bourbon crisis. Therefore, as a reward for his faithful service, he was offered a senior position in the loyalist army being assembled at Caderousse, near Avignon.[10]

Naturally, Francis's march to Marseille did not go unnoticed by Bourbon who now agreed that Provence could not be held over the winter unless the city's port was in his hands. He therefore ordered another assault but Marseille's defenders had built a massive earthwork behind the city's outer wall and buried barrels of gunpowder in the open spaces between the two ramparts. Although Bourbon's men braved the defenders' withering gunfire, nothing would induce them to cross this rudimentary minefield and they fell back in disarray.[11] Though Bourbon continued the siege, his last throw of the dice had failed and it soon became clear that his position even in Provence was untenable.

'The Lord of Bourbon, feeling the power of the king himself approaching, ordered his retreat and to do this he sent his large artillery to Genoa by sea and had the smaller guns taken to pieces so they could be carried on the backs of mules over roads where it was impossible to drive a cart,' wrote Bellay,[12] but Honoré de Valbelle, a resident of Marseille who watched Bourbon's withdrawal, tells us that the imperials were so afraid of being surrounded that they buried their cannon to speed their escape.[13]

Buried or not, the French king had wasted so much time hanging rebel sympathisers on his journey south he found nothing but empty gun-pits and abandoned trenches when he finally reached Marseille. Perhaps if Francis had been more merciful he might have trapped Bourbon in his own siegeworks. Even so, although the rebel duke had slipped through his fingers, Bourbon's defeat had reopened the door to Milan.[14]

The king of France was not a man to waste such an opportunity, but he had to act before the imperials could regroup. Francis therefore divided his army into three columns, the first of which would follow Bourbon as he retreated along the slower, but easier, coastal road to Genoa. The second would try and overtake the fleeing imperials by marching straight through the Alps and the third, led by Francis himself, would swing north, to Briançon on the Savoy border. Here Francis would rendezvous with a large contingent of Italians being recruited by the pro-French Michel-Antoine de Vasto, marquis de Saluzzo.[15]

Coincidentally, Richard was related to Saluzzo, whose mother, Margaret de Foix-Candale, was the aunt of Anne de Foix-Candale, late queen of Hungary.[16] Their shared ancestor was Michael de la Pole, 2nd earl of Suffolk, but whether Richard met his distant cousin at Briançon is not known. Nevertheless, Bellay insists that both men were with Francis when the third French column entered the Po Valley on 17 October 1524.[17]

Francis crossed the Alps with almost 40,000 men, but incessant rain slowed their advance to a crawl. Such sluggish progress allowed Bourbon and the imperials to reach the safety of Pavia, 20 miles to the south of Milan, but they had to abandon all their baggage to stay ahead of the French. Consequently, Bourbon's bedraggled army arrived in Lombardy's ancient capital footsore, starving and unarmed.[18]

The survivors of the Marseille campaign were greeted by the despairing Charles de Lannoy, the imperial commander-in-chief, who had been forced to move his own army to Pavia from Milan after plague had struck the larger city. Having to abandon the central objective of the war was bad enough, but the sight of Bourbon's ragged men limping across the bridge over the Ticino must have sent Lannoy into a panic. Although 700 imperials were still garrisoned inside Milan's impregnable castle, the plague-ravaged Milanese had been unable to repair the city's outer fortifications or stockpile enough food to withstand a siege.[19]

One of the wealthiest cities in northern Italy had therefore been left practically undefended, and in desperation Lannoy tried to reinforce the beleaguered imperial garrison by ordering Bourbon to march his men to Milan. What the exhausted soldiery thought of this is not recorded, but Lannoy's plan was thwarted by the Milanese themselves. In order to spare their city the customary three-day sack, they surrendered to Saluzzo's advance guard and Bourbon was again forced to retreat.[20]

The sudden fall of Milan, combined with a further deterioration in the weather, meant Lannoy had to rethink his whole plan for the defence of northern Italy. To begin with, he moved two-thirds of his army to winter quarters in Lodi, 30 miles to the east of Milan, but he left 9,000 veteran *landsknechts* in Pavia to guard the city's strategic bridge over the Ticino. These men were commanded by the highly capable Spaniard Antonio de Leyva.

If Francis wanted keep hold of Milan, he would have to destroy the imperial armies in Lodi and Pavia before they could be reinforced by fresh troops recruited in Germany and Naples. This would be no easy task. Even with their overwhelming numerical superiority, the French were not strong enough to besiege two cities at once, so Francis held a council of war to decide whether his principal objective should be Lannoy in Lodi, or de Leyva in Pavia.[21]

Those who favoured attacking Lannoy included the veteran commanders Louis de Trémoille and Jacques de la Palice, who argued that Lodi would fall more easily because its defences were weak and its defenders disorganised.[22] Those who urged Francis to attack Pavia included the duke d'Alençon, who was the king's brother-in-law, and Admiral Bonnivet, who had failed to recapture Milan in 1523.[23] Typically, Francis chose to follow the advice of his relatives and favourites rather than that of his seasoned generals.

There was a persistent rumour that Bonnivet was so keen to capture Pavia because the Lady Clarice, his mistress from his previous campaign, was still living there.[24] Indeed, her daring escape from the besieged city is depicted in the fifth of the seven tapestries woven in 1530 to commemorate the subsequent battle, but most modern historians dismiss this story as a romantic fiction.[25] No doubt Guicciardini was closer to the truth when he said that Francis was simply wise enough not to turn his back on 9,000 heavily armed imperials.[26]

Whatever Francis's motives, once his mind was made up nothing would change it. After leaving Trémoille with 4,000 men to occupy Milan, he led the rest of his army across the fertile plain created by the mighty River Po and marched on Pavia. The French host arrived before the city's walls on 28 October 1524, and with them was Richard de la Pole.[27]

We know from Bellay that Richard and François de Lorraine had been placed in command of the elite Black Band of mercenaries, and Fleuranges tells us that these renegade *landsknechts* were part of the French vanguard billeted in the Abbey of San Lanfranco, a mile to the west of Pavia.[28] Interestingly, the abbey's monks venerated St Thomas Becket, the English archbishop whose life – and murder on the orders of a royal despot – closely mirrored that of their monastery's founder, Bishop Lanfranco.

As generations of de la Poles had also suffered at the hands of ruthless kings, perhaps Richard was shown the abbey's famous fresco depicting Becket's death and invited to pray for God to grant him justice. Equally, Richard's nineteen-year-old co-commander, François de Lorraine, must have asked God for the chance to emulate his older brother's heroics at Marignano, especially as the site of the celebrated French victory was only 15 miles from Pavia. If so, the hot-headed youth would soon have his prayers answered.

While the Milanese had been busy trying to placate the advancing French, de Leyva had been strengthening Pavia's defences. Despite being crippled by gout, which forced him to supervise the works from a litter, he and his men managed to build a number of earth-and-timber blockhouses at strategic points around the city's walls. These strongpoints persuaded the French commanders that Pavia could only be taken by siege.

Initially, Francis based his headquarters with Richard's vanguard in San Lanfranco's abbey, and they were soon joined by the French rearguard, led by the duke d'Alençon, a force of specialist assault troops led by the master of the king's household, and the French artillery. On the other side of the city, the Swiss mercenaries under Fleuranges, Palice and the duke of Albany took up positions between an outlying watchtower called the Torre de Gallo and a group of five ancient abbeys clustered around the road to Lodi.[29]

Besides preventing Lannoy from reinforcing Pavia from the east, the Swiss were ordered to guard the French baggage park, which had been established at the Castel Mirabello. This palatial hunting lodge was located a mile to the north of Pavia, in the centre of a vast walled deer park created for Milan's Visconti dukes. Meanwhile, the duke of Montmorency was given the task of sealing off the southern approaches to the city by capturing the new blockhouse that guarded the bridge over the Ticino.

To Montmorency's fury, this redoubt had been built on an islet formed by the confluence of the Ticino and its tributary, the Gravalone. It could therefore be resupplied indefinitely by boats from Pavia, and a direct assault was out of the question because the ground between the two rivers was an impassable marsh. Only cannon could dislodge the Spanish mercenaries defending the blockhouse, but the heavy French guns could not be brought to Montmorency because the Ticino bridge was in imperial hands. Until French engineers built an alternative, all Montmorency could do was set up camp in the hamlet of Sant'Antonio and wait. Unfortunately for him, Francis was becoming impatient.[30]

The foul winter weather was taking a steady toll on the French army, so Francis decided to ignore his generals' advice and risk assaulting the city from San Lanfranco, where his heavy guns were already emplaced. A bombardment to batter a hole in Pavia's western wall began at first light on 1 November, but it took more than a week to make a breach wide enough for an attack.

At dawn on 9 November, the French trumpets sounded the charge. The imperial defenders were ready, and the attack was easily repulsed. Among those killed was the sixteen-year-old Claude, duke of Longueville, whose late father had been captured at the Day of the Spurs. Shot through the shoulder, the boy had cried, 'I'm dead!' and expired.[31]

Undeterred by the slaughter of young Longueville and countless others, Francis decided on a much bigger assault that involved simultaneous attacks from all directions and he sent as much artillery as he could spare to the camps at Mirabello, the Five Abbeys and San Antonio. By now a pontoon bridge across the Ticino had been completed, but only four culverins reached Montmorency before this crossing was swept away in a flood.

Despite the lack of heavy artillery, Montmorency was able to pound the Gravalone blockhouse into submission and no doubt the Spanish defenders expected they would be either ransomed or released, provided they took an oath to return home. This was certainly the normal practice in mercenary armies, but

Montmorency had been humiliated by the Spaniards' stubborn resistance and he ordered their instant execution.

'Having seized the tower, he hanged those he found inside, for having been so outrageous as to try and defend such a chicken coop from the whole French army,' wrote Bellay.[32]

These men may have been enemies but they deserved better. They had fought bravely, and the sight of their dangling corpses so outraged de Leyva he wrote to Montmorency warning him that would be hanged from the same gallows if he ever fell into imperial hands. Francis was also shocked by Montmorency's blatant disregard for the rules of war and sent de Leyva a grovelling apology.[33] In spite of this, the incident was neither forgiven nor forgotten, and the fight for Pavia became characterised by an almost modern lack of chivalry.

Once the Gravalone blockhouse had been subdued, and the rest of the French guns had been dragged overland to the camps at Mirabello and the Five Abbeys, the ring of French steel around Pavia was complete. At last Francis could prepare for a mass assault, and his artillerymen restarted their barrage. At dawn each day, the French cannons roared into life and jagged gaps began to appear in the ramparts on opposite sides of the city.

As soon as Pavia's walls began to crumble, de Leyva ordered his men to dig ditches in front of the breaches and pile the excavated earth into embankments to shelter his handgunners. These men were armed with heavy hackbuts, which took their name from the iron hook under the barrel that could be used to brace the weapon against a wall or earthwork. Thanks to its large calibre, a hackbut could fire anything that could be rammed down its muzzle, so de Leyva's men began smashing up Pavia's churches because sharp-edged marble was more lethal than smooth pebbles.[34]

By 21 November, Francis was ready to storm both breaches and the attacks would be coordinated by trumpet signals from the recently captured Gravalone blockhouse. In the east the honour of leading the assault fell to Fleuranges and Albany, but in the west the attack would be led by the king himself, with the comte de Lambesc and Richard de la Pole acting as his lieutenants.

'And the *landsknechts* were led by Monsieur François and the duke of Suffort, who called himself the Blanche Rose, and count de Wolf and afterwards came the king with all his *gendarmerie*,' wrote Fleuranges, who adds that the French knights had to fight on foot because horses were of no use when storming city walls.[35]

Despite being reduced to the status of lowly infantry, the nobly born *gendarmes* insisted on wearing their magnificent suits of armour. The morning sun glinting off the highly polished metal must have dazzled the defenders, but it also made them excellent targets, and steel plate was no barrier to a few ounces of lead fired at close range from a well-aimed arquebus.

Furthermore, the imperials had learned valuable lessons at the siege of Marseille and de Leyva had created similar minefields by burying kegs of gunpowder in the bottom of the ditches that had been dug in front of the breaches. He also ordered *petereaux* to be placed at each end of the trenches, and these large-calibre mortars, like the smaller hackbuts, could be filled with anything that would shred frail human flesh.[36]

Little knowing what awaited them, Francis's *gendarmes* and Richard's *landsknechts* charged towards the western breach, but the French bombardment had done little damage to de Leyva's blockhouses. Safe inside these strongpoints, the imperials were able to unleash a blizzard of lead shot and the combined firepower of their arquebuses and hackbuts had the same effect as First World War machine guns. Scores of Frenchmen were scythed down before they reached the imperial trenches, and this was only the beginning of the slaughter. When the surviving attackers tried to scramble across the muddy ditches, the imperials fired their *petereaux* and exploded their mines.

'This gave the defenders wonderful pleasure because they killed many people. At least 300 or 400 men died in that place, killed immediately without being wounded, and among those butchered was the standard bearer of the king's Scottish Guard,' wrote Fleuranges.[37] He also tells us that the French king was 'enjoying fighting as a simple captain', but while Francis was having a fine time dispatching low-born imperial sword-fodder, no one was directing the battle.

Without their king to lead them, the French attackers soon degenerated into a confused, disordered rabble, and all the while the imperial handgunners continued to pour a murderous storm of fire onto their hapless enemies. Eventually, even the battle-crazed

Francis realised that the breach was too strong to be taken and ordered a retreat.[38]

The assault on the western breach had achieved nothing, and the attack in the east had fared no better. The first wave of Swiss had been repulsed with equally heavy casualties and these fleeing 'lost children', as Fleuranges called them, ran into Albany's second wave. The gallant Fleuranges had tried to lead his troops around the confused mass of men but it was futile. The commander in the east, Lord Palice, had no choice but to call off his attack and the battered Swiss had limped back to their billets in the Five Abbeys.[39]

Another attempt to take Pavia by storm had ended in bloody failure, and Francis had to admit that his only option was to try starve the city into submission. Sieges in winter were no easy task, however. Already, the French army had been seriously weakened by disease and desertion, and the atrocious conditions in their camp only made matters worse. It was therefore understandable that most of Francis's captains advised him to go home and renew the campaign in the spring, but Bonnivet was strongly in favour of continuing the siege.

According to Fleuranges, who was present during these councils of war, Bonnivet was not only an inveterate gambler 'who always liked to play quits or double',[40] he was worried that he would be blamed if the war achieved nothing. Bonnivet certainly had a point, because it had been he who had persuaded Francis to attack Pavia in the first place, and Fleuranges believed that the king continued to side with his boyhood friend because he too feared for his reputation.

'The kings of France had never failed to take a city, so long as they supervised the siege in person,' he explained in his memoirs.[41]

To be fair to both Francis and Bonnivet, their spies were reporting that Pavia's defenders were running short of food and ammunition, but again Fleuranges tells a different story. According to the self-styled Young Adventurer, de Leyva had stockpiled enough corn, wine and parmesan cheese to last at least two years, and he had even solved the problem of paying his mercenaries.[42]

When the captain of the imperial *landsknechts*, the German-born Count Sorne, threatened to open Pavia's gates to the French unless his men received their wages, de Leyva had melted down the city churches' plate and minted his own coins. These ducats were stamped with the slogan 'Pavia under Caesar will triumph', and when there were no more churches left to loot the mercenary captain had suddenly and conveniently died.[43]

Some said that the bibulous count had simply drunk himself to death, which was not unusual for a *landsknecht*, but others swore that Sorne had been poisoned on de Leyva's orders. Whatever the truth of the matter, Sorne's death and the timely arrival of 3,000 ducats, smuggled into the city inside a wine barrel, were enough to quash any mutiny.[44].

Meanwhile, Francis thought he had found a way to end imperial resistance in Lombardy by opening a second front. This time, the diversionary attack would not be made on Navarre, Northumberland or the Ardennes. Instead, Francis would attack the 'soft underbelly' of the Habsburg empire by reasserting French rights to the crown of Naples.[45]

27

NOT A DOZEN LANCES BUT A THOUSAND

The most recent struggle for control of southern Italy between the kings of France and Spain had ended in 1503 when the Spanish had trounced the French at the battle of Garigliano. Following this victory, Ferdinand of Aragon had become king of Naples, Sicily and Sardinia, which he had ruled until his death in 1516. All his Spanish and Italian territories should have then passed to his daughter Joanna, but her supposed insanity meant that her son Charles had succeeded to his grandfather's Hispano-Italian empire.

Three years later, Charles's election as Holy Roman Emperor had added the German and Roman crowns to his already bulging jewel house and this, together with the renewals of the imperial alliances with England in 1521 and 1522, had completed the Habsburg encirclement of France. The goal of the entire Pavia campaign had been to break this stranglehold, but, with the fighting in Lombardy at a stalemate, Francis would need the help of the new Pope to wriggle free.

Like his predecessors, Francis became convinced that conquering Naples was the only way to guarantee French independence but the papal territories in central Italy blocked all roads from Milan to the south. To complicate matters further, Clement VII, who had ascended the throne of St Peter in November 1523, had been the imperial candidate in the election to succeed Adrian VI. However, the 219th pontiff was also a Medici and the imperial viceroy,

Lannoy, had angered him by refusing to put down a rebellion that had driven his family from Florence.

Following Lannoy's failure to restore the Medici, Clement sent his envoy to Francis's camp at Pavia with an offer to endorse his claims to Naples and allow the French army free passage across papal territory in return for help recovering Florence. Naturally Francis had accepted this offer, but Clement was playing a double game and sent a secret message to Lannoy claiming that he had been forced to agree to French demands.[1]

As Richard took no part in the Neapolitan campaign, there is no need to examine its progress in detail. What is important to our story is that Francis sent a third of his army south under the command of the duke of Albany, whose sister-in-law Madeleine de La Tour d'Auvergne had married into the Medici clan.[2] The former regent of Scotland left Pavia shortly before Christmas 1524, and he took with him 4,500 foot and 500 horse.[3]

No doubt Richard was among the many French captains who wondered why their army at Pavia was being denuded of valuable troops at this crucial point in the siege, but Francis did take steps to plug the gaps in his ranks caused by Albany's departure. Besides recruiting more mercenaries in the Swiss canton of Grison, Francis managed to persuade the celebrated *condottiero* Ludovico di Medici to swap sides.

Confusingly, Ludovico is better known by his *nom de guerre*, Giovanni of the Black Bands, but his men should not be mistaken for the Black Band led by Richard de la Pole. Giovanni had earned his soubriquet in 1521 by placing black stripes on his coat of arms to mourn the death of Pope Leo X, his cousin and previous employer,[4] whereas Richard's men derived their name from their practice of blackening their armour with soot to prevent rust.[5] Nevertheless, both groups were considered elite units and Giovanni's defection was a considerable propaganda coup for the French.

In his second volume of memoirs, Fleuranges tells us that Ludovico/Giovanni had joined the French because the Emperor had failed to keep 'certain promises', but this was only half the story. As his name suggests, Ludovico di Medici was Pope Clement's nephew and it is highly likely he was ordered to turn his coat by his uncle. Whatever the truth, Francis made a very public show of paying the Italians their first month's wages.[6]

Meanwhile, Lannoy was trying to revitalise his own army, which had been seriously weakened by Bourbon's failure in Provence, and the man he hoped would put some backbone into his men was the fire-breathing Georg von Frundsberg. Though this ageing warlord, who had created the original *landsknecht* companies for Maximilian, was supposed to be retired, Lannoy sent Bourbon to persuade him to buckle on his sword once more.

The renegade duke proved to be a better diplomat than a general, and the man known as the 'Father of Landsknechts' agreed to reinforce the imperial army with 15,000 veteran mercenaries. These men were every bit as tough as their grizzled field captain, and the worst blizzards in living memory could not stop them from crossing the Alps in record time. Frundsberg's Germans reached Lannoy's camp at Lodi on 10 January 1525.

The news that the Empire's most famous mercenary captain had beaten his ploughshare back into a sword gave Francis serious cause for concern, especially as Albany had failed to reach Naples. In a repeat of what had happened to him in Edinburgh, the ex-Scottish regent had become trapped in an inescapable labyrinth of Florentine politics.

With his Neapolitan plan in tatters and his own army now outnumbered, Francis was in no doubt that Lannoy would try and relieve Pavia as soon as the weather improved. But as the French cannons lit up the dawn of each day with a new barrage, he had a flash of inspiration: he would end the siege with a jousting match. This was not as far-fetched as it may sound. Thanks to the expense of hiring mercenaries, the ancient custom of using champions to decide the outcome of battles had survived into the late Middle Ages and the man whom Francis chose to issue his formal call-to-arms was Richard de la Pole.

Venetian chronicler Marino Sanuto recorded the event in his diary:

> On 31 December, the duke of Suffolk, in the name of the French king, and accompanied by a single drummer, ventured forth to deliver a letter of challenge to Antonio, that is the Signor da Leyva [the Pavia garrison's commander]. If one of us could best one of them in the breaking of a dozen lances, for the sake of gentility and the love of a lady, then the king [of France] would surrender the field.[7]

With the destiny of kingdoms hanging in the balance at Pavia, Francis must have thought that the royal blood flowing through Richard's veins made him the only person of sufficiently high rank to deliver such an important message. Unfortunately for the French, de Leyva did not share Francis's ideals of chivalry.

'On the first day of January, 1525, one of our drummers, conveyed the aforementioned Signor Antonio's reply to the aforementioned duke of Suffolk. [He said] that, little by little, our army would come closer and when they took the field against the French king they would break not a dozen lances but a thousand,' writes Sanuto.[8] He then goes on to describe another surprise that the imperial herald had in store for Richard.

To emphasise de Leyva's point, the herald showed the White Rose a cart loaded with bags of money and remarked that his master could pay any number of mercenaries for as long as they were needed.[9] Clearly, de Leyva was pulling the same stunt that Francis had employed with his special pay parade for Giovanni's Black Bands, but these claims were more than mere bravado. Thanks to messages smuggled into the city, de Leyva knew that Lannoy and Frundsberg's relief force was already on the march.

The revitalised imperial army, which now numbered around 24,000, left Lodi on 24 January 1525 and the French outposts at San Angelo and Ladirago were easily brushed aside. An attempt by Bonnivet to stop Lannoy in his tracks was defeated at Belgioioso and the imperial host reached the eastern outskirts of Pavia on 3 February.[10]

Within hours of their arrival, Frundsberg's men began constructing a complex series of earthworks and gun emplacements to counter the French siegeworks while Lannoy established his headquarters in a large villa known as the Casa del Levrieri. This 'House of the Greyhounds' took its name from the nearby kennels where the Visconti and Sforza dukes kept their hunting dogs, but Lannoy was after bigger game than hares.

From this vantage point, the imperial viceroy could observe the French positions in the eastern sector of the battlefield, and Francis responded by moving his own headquarters to a more central position. The spot he chose was the Castel Mirabello in the centre of the vast, diamond-shaped deer park, which occupied more than 5,000 acres of woods and heathland to the north of Pavia.[11]

The French baggage train, with its attendant throng of pedlars and prostitutes, had been encamped at Mirabello since the beginning of the siege and the Visconti's sumptuous hunting lodge offered more comfortable lodgings than a tent.

Despite resembling a domed Byzantine chapel, Mirabello boasted luxurious sleeping quarters and a lavish feasting hall. Even more importantly, it was surrounded by a moat, high walls and a drawbridge designed to create a place of refuge for Pavia's feudal overlords during periods of civic unrest. In addition to Mirabello's defences, the park itself was protected by a solid wall 15 feet high, with gateways that were heavily fortified.[12]

These advantages were not lost on Francis, but shortly after moving his headquarters to Mirabello he decided that the hunting lodge was too close to the front lines so he moved to a third camp located near the park's north-western gate, called the Porta Repentina. Besides being more than a mile away from Mirabello, and well out of range of imperial guns, there was plenty of dry, open grassland where the French knights could pitch their tents and graze their horses. As an added bonus, the mews where the Visconti dukes kept their hawks was nearby and the hunting-mad Francis had brought his own birds with him.[13] However, the Florentine Guicciardini was appalled by the French king's growing lack of interest in the siege:

> The whole care of managing the army lay on the Admiral, the king wasting the greatest part of his time either in idleness or in vain pleasures, without finding spare hours for business or serious thoughts, holding in contempt all other commanders, consulting only with the Admiral, and hearkening also to Anne de Montmorency ... great favourites, but of little experience in military affairs.[14]

Nevertheless, the move was completed by 20 February and the king's new camp at the Porta Repentina became the epicentre of French operations. Besides Francis and his noble gendarmes, the other troops billeted here included the *landsknechts* led by Richard and Lambesc.[15]

It is a measure of Richard's continuing favour with Francis that he and the French king were always billeted together at Pavia, but weakening the forces guarding the city's western approaches almost proved fatal for the Pope's nephew. Having been left in San Lanfranco to defend the first French camp, Giovanni and his men suffered repeated raids and during one imperial sortie the *condottiero* had been shot in the foot. Fleuranges tells us that the badly wounded Giovanni had to be taken to Piacenza for treatment, and Guicciardini adds gleefully that these successful raids persuaded many of Francis's newly hired foreign mercenaries to desert.[16]

The first to go were Giovanni's Italians, who were understandably aggrieved at having to bear the brunt of the fighting in the San Lanfranco sector; the crippling of their captain had been the last straw.[17] Refusing all incentives to stay, Giovanni's men joined their captain in Piacenza and their withdrawal was followed by the departure of the Grisons Swiss.

Pleading the necessity of defending their homes from imperial raids, the 6,000 Grisonaise left Pavia three days after Giovanni's men, which meant the French had lost around a third of their strength in just seventy-two hours.[18] If Francis did not stem this haemorrhaging of manpower, the imperials would win the war without firing a shot. Luckily for him, Lannoy had problems of his own.

In spite of de Leyva's boast that his treasury was full, he had only enough gold to keep his mercenaries at their posts until the end of February.[19] To compound de Leyva's predicament, Lannoy's men were also threatening to mutiny unless they too were paid and there was no sign of the 200,000 ducats that had been promised by Charles and Henry.[20] This was because the increasingly impatient Emperor believed Lannoy was not making sufficient use of Frundsberg's reinforcements, and he had told his viceroy that not another florin would be sent until the stalemate had been broken.

With the situation rapidly approaching critical, Lannoy had to do something to keep his Emperor happy and his army in the field, so he decided to attack the French baggage train at Mirabello. Apart from being a soft target, the loot seized in a successful raid would solve all his financial problems, at least in the short term, but there might have been more to Lannoy's thinking than simple burglary.

Some modern historians have maintained that Lannoy was labouring under the delusion that Francis was still lodged at Mirabello and planned a lightning raid to snatch the sleeping French king from his bed. This, in theory, would end the war at a stroke, but French writers of the time like Fleuranges and Bellay maintained that Lannoy only wanted to create a diversion so that de Leyva's garrison could break out of the besieged city.[21]

Regardless of Lannoy's intentions, if things went well for the imperials, either Francis would be captured and his army forced to abandon the whole of Italy, or de Leyva would escape from Pavia. Even if the French prevented the garrison's breakout, Lannoy could retreat to Lodi, claim he had done his best to end the siege and offer to renew the campaign in the spring, when the Spanish treasure ships arrived from the New World.[22]

Once Lannoy had decided to attack the French camps, the only serious obstacle he had to overcome was the high wall surrounding the deer park. Fortunately for the imperials, Francis had believed the north of the park was too far away from the front lines to be worth defending, and one section in particular was screened from the few French sentries stationed at the Porta Pescarina by a dense wood. Even so, the Spanish engineers would have to break down this hidden section of the wall by hand, and under cover of darkness, to avoid raising the alarm.

Once a breach had been made, Lannoy planned to send a crack force of 3,000 Neapolitan arquebusiers to seize the French baggage park at Mirabello. Meanwhile, the rest of the imperial army would attack the main French camp at the Porta Repentina. Having stirred up a hornet's nest in the park, de Leyva could take advantage of the confusion to lead Pavia's garrison to safety.

The Italo-Spanish marquis de Vasto was chosen to lead the attack on Mirabello while the remainder of the imperial troops would be commanded by Frundsberg, Pescara, Bourbon, and Lannoy himself. As the march north would take place at night, Lannoy instructed his men to wear white shirts over their armour, so they could tell friend from foe, and to cover his army's departure he ordered the imperial artillery to bombard the French positions at the Five Abbeys. Last but not least, Lannoy set the time and date for the attack at dawn on 24 February 1525, which was the Emperor's birthday.[23]

At dusk on 23 February, the Spanish engineers collected their mattocks and mauls and scurried away to break down the wall while the rest of the imperials assembled at their various muster points. Yet it took longer than expected to organise de Vasto's Neapolitans, Pescara and Lannoy's Spaniards and Frundsberg and Bourbon's Germans into their proper divisions, meaning the imperial batteries could not begin their covering bombardment until much later than planned.[24]

The roar of the imperial guns must have deafened Lannoy's troops when they eventually shuffled out of their camp at the Casa de Levrieri, but the sheer volume of men, combined with the lack of a moon, made their progress through the frosty landscape painfully slow. By now the imperial battleplan was more than six hours behind schedule, yet the Spanish pioneers were still struggling to demolish the deer park wall when their comrades arrived.

'About midnight, the Spaniards began to empty their camp and to make, as I told you, a great noise and began to break the wall of the park, which was of well-seated bricks, in three places,' wrote Fleuranges, who still commanded 4,000 Swiss in French pay.[25] These men had not returned home after the departure of their countrymen from Grison, and being stationed at the Porta Levrieri meant they were the targets of the imperial bombardment. However, instead of disguising the imperial march, the thunderous cannon fire had alerted Fleuranges to the danger.

The Young Adventurer quickly marshalled his men into their battle formations, and he was not the only French captain to realise that an attack was underway. Despite Lannoy's orders to maintain strict silence, a French cavalry patrol inside the park heard the imperial artillerymen on the other side of the wall whipping their horses.[26]

At first the patrol's captain, Charles Tiercelin, seigneur de la Roche-du-Maine, thought that Lannoy was abandoning Pavia altogether, but when it became clear that the imperials were trying to outflank the French positions he sent an urgent messenger to his sleeping king. Nevertheless, even as Fleuranges and Tiercelin were trying to organise the park's defenders, a sizeable section of the wall collapsed.

Adam Reissner, Frundsberg's secretary, biographer and a veteran of Pavia, described the moment:

> As the day dawned, the wall fell ... Alphonsus Margrave von Guasta [de Vasto] was first into the park with three imperial flag-companies, which included the most skilful Spanish. In all, he had five thousand men and the Margrave of Pescara spoke to him; Dear brother, you should now make sure that you capture the House of Mirabello, and that nothing stops you. Do not fear the enemy, whom we have beaten before, but if you are too weak, God will turn against you and so, in truth, you should die so that we may win.[27]

The Neapolitan raiders were now on a collision course with both Fleuranges' infantry and Tiercelin's cavalry, but the entire battlefield suddenly disappeared under a thick blanket of pre-dawn fog. In the gloom, Fleuranges and Tiercelin missed de Vasto and instead blundered into Georg von Frundsberg's much stronger force.[28]

After de Vasto's advance guard had rushed into the park, the Spanish engineers had broken down more sections of the wall and these extra breaches allowed the rest of the imperial army to enter in two columns. The first of these, under Lannoy, Bourbon and Pescara, marched west to protect de Vasto's right while the second, led by Frundsberg and his lieutenant, Marx Sittich von Ems, headed east to cover de Vasto's left.[29]

Besides his 8,000 *landsknechts*, Frundsberg's column had a squadron of Spanish light horsemen, called *jinetes*, and a battery of sixteen field guns but it was impossible to maintain a proper formation while scrambling through the narrow gaps in the wall. Consequently, Frundsberg sent his *jinetes* and artillery into the park first with orders to protect his infantry from attack while they formed their pike squares.[30]

Despite the mist obscuring their enemy's manoeuvres, Fleuranges' Swiss knew the sound of artillery being dragged into position when they heard it so they followed their usual practice of trying to rush the enemy guns before they could fire. At Marignano and Bicocca this suicidal tactic had ended in bloody defeat, but at Pavia the Swiss charge was hidden by the fog. Before the imperial gunners knew what was happening, they were being slaughtered by the wraith-like *reisläufers* while Tiercelin's cavalry scattered the Spanish horsemen.[31]

This skirmish lasted no more than a few minutes but the units annihilated by Fleuranges were only the vanguard of Frundsberg's column and the imperial squares, nicknamed *igels* or hedgehogs, were rapidly growing their spines. Before Fleuranges could retreat, both of Frundsberg's *igels*, bristling with pikes, arquebuses and halberds, emerged from the gloom and battle was joined.

Whilst Frundsberg and Fleuranges slugged it out near the Porta Pescarina, de Vasto's Neapolitans reached the French baggage park at Mirabello, and Pescara's order to let nothing stand in their way was obeyed to the letter. After a lethal volley of gunfire had dispatched the sleepy sentries, de Vasto's men fell upon the unarmed camp-followers like hounds on a wounded deer. The pedlars and sutlers were systematically plundered, the *kampfrau* raped and anyone who resisted was butchered in an orgy of brutal violence.[32]

At this point, the 9,000 imperials garrisoning Pavia were supposed to break out of the city and link up with de Vasto's men but the heavy winter rain had flooded a broad swathe of land between the hunting lodge and Pavia's northern gate. Faced with an impassable morass, de Leyva had to lead his men towards the drier ground at the Five Abbeys but this detour brought them into contact with the 3,000 Swiss led by the duke of Montmorency.[33]

'Here, there was great slaughter,' wrote Fleuranges, and it is hardly surprising that the fighting at the Five Abbeys was particularly vicious.[34] Pavia's garrison had a score to settle with the man who had hanged their comrades defending the Gravalone blockhouse, and a number of luckless civilians who had fled the massacre at Mirabello were caught in the crossfire.[35] Fleuranges claimed that his own tent was plundered by de Leyva himself.

But in the midst of all this, where was Richard de la Pole?

When the battle of Pavia began, the last Yorkist and his Black Band were sleeping peacefully in the royal camp near the Porta Repentina. Besides the mounted knights of the *gendarmerie*, Richard shared this billet with several companies of French foot soldiers under the seigneur d'Amboise and another contingent of Swiss who had remained loyal to their French paymasters.[36] All of these men tumbled out of their tents the moment the alarm was raised by Tiercelin's messenger, but even in good weather it could take up to twenty minutes to encase a knight in his steel carapace;

at Pavia, the squires' fingers were so numb with cold that the buckling on of breastplates and vambraces took much longer.

While Francis waited for his army's shell to harden, he ordered Bonnivet to take fifty light horsemen and find out what was happening in the east of the park. It was still dark when the admiral galloped off into the mist, but the sound of gunshots led him straight to Fleuranges' fight with Frundsberg's gunners. Bonnivet helped Tiercelin drive off the Spanish *jinetes*, who were supposed to protect the imperial artillery, and the ease of this victory convinced him that the imperial attack was nothing more than a raid.[37]

In typical fashion, Bonnivet had totally misread the situation, and when he returned to the Porta Repentina he compounded his error by insisting that there was no need for undue haste. Equally typically, Francis believed his favourite and prepared for battle thinking he was facing only a small part of Lannoy's army. That said, Francis was no fool and he realised that the imperials would have to cross the broad heath between the French tents at the Porta Repentina and the wood at the Porta Pescarina if they wanted to attack his camp.

The open heath was perfect ground for cavalry so Francis drew up the 3,600 men of his *gendarmerie* in four ranks; if any imperials dared to challenge the French horsemen, these fully armoured knights would trample them into the mud.[38]

As he eyed the serried ranks of his paladins, Francis must have felt supremely confident. Mounted noblemen, sheathed in iron, had dominated European battlefields for a thousand years and a French *gendarme* was the supreme expression of feudal military might. Dressed in plumed helmets, expensive plate armour and long surcoats decorated with the wearer's ancient badges of rank, a *gendarme* was an awe-inspiring sight, and the most magnificent of them all was the king himself.

A painting completed soon after the battle shows Francis wearing gilded armour beneath a scarlet surcoat emblazoned with the white cross that had been adopted as the identifying mark of French armies during the latter stages of the Hundred Years War. By contrast, the French king's horse was caparisoned in royal blue, decorated with gold fleur-de-lys.[39]

Besides his magnificent *gendarmerie*, two factors added to the strength of Francis's position. Firstly his flanks were well protected; to his left the park wall was still standing, while to his right an artillery redoubt covered the road between the Porta Repentina and the Castel Mirabello. Secondly, Francis was still in contact with his supporting infantry, led by the White Rose. Fleuranges tells us that 'the duke of Suffort', the comte de Lambesc and Count Wolf commanded 4,000 men of the Black Band as well as 3,000 Swiss 'from the Upper Cantons', and Bellay adds that these men were drawn up in two squares.[40]

The pike squares of the sixteenth century performed the same function as tanks on a modern battlefield, so Francis had no doubt he could repel the imperial column that was slowly groping its way towards the Porta Repentina. Nonetheless, the French king should have heeded the Biblical proverb that 'pride goeth before destruction and an haughty spirit before a fall'.

28

IT WAS A BLOODY BATTLE

The first imperial troops to emerge from the wood on the far side of the heath belonged to Pescara's brigade, but massed infantry advancing over open ground presented a perfect target for the French guns protecting Francis's right flank. At such short range they could not miss, and Bellay described how the imperial foot soldiers were blown to pieces:

> The Lord Jacques Galliot, grandmaster of the artillery of France, had sited his guns in a place so advantageous for us ... that suddenly the cannonballs were punching great holes in their ranks, so that all that could be seen were arms and heads flying through the air.[1]

In the face of this vicious onslaught, Pescara's Spaniards hastily retreated into the safety of trees, but help was on its way. Throughout the barrage, Lannoy's cavalry had been skirting around the northern edge of the wood and they found themselves facing their French counterparts when they too reached the heath.[2]

It was now dawn, and as soon as the bellicose French king spotted Lannoy's horsemen he thanked God for giving him the chance to win another glorious victory. Leading his *gendarmes* in a magnificent, battle-winning charge would be the greatest joust of his career, so he ordered his knights to lower their lances and spur their steeds. On the far side of the heath, Lannoy watched this avalanche of Gallic steel gather momentum and knew there was no escape. Even though his men were outnumbered, and wore much less armour than the French, they would have to fight.

'There is no hope except God, follow me and do as I do!' the imperial viceroy cried, ordering his trumpeters to sound the charge.[3]

Yard by yard, horses on both sides picked up speed until their trot became a canter, then a gallop, but the impetus was with the heavily armoured French. They smashed into their lightly armed enemies like a wrecking ball. Hundreds of Spaniards were skewered on lances or cloven in two by broadswords, and those who survived being unhorsed were trampled to death by the mighty French warhorses.

Among the few who managed to escape the carnage was the imperial viceroy, and he followed his fleeing men into the same wood where Pescara's embattled infantry had also sought shelter. Much to the Spaniards' relief, the wood's labyrinth of trees prevented the much larger French horses from following.

Cursing his luck, Francis reined in his men at the edge of the wood, but the impenetrable undergrowth should have been the least of his worries. What Francis had failed to realise was that chasing Lannoy had taken his knights too far to the east, so the French guns protecting his flank had to cease bombarding Pescara's men for fear of killing their own king. Worse still, the French *gendarmes* were now separated from Richard's supporting *landsknechts* by a considerable distance, as Adam Reissner explained:

> The first brigade of [French] armoured knights, charged towards the imperial knights, and attacked them on the right side with great impetuousness, and all of a sudden they left the Swiss and the Black Brigade of the Germans behind, and the French artillery had to hold their fire, because the gunners had to take care not to hit their countrymen.[4]

Whether Reissner was present in this part of the battlefield is not known, and while his explanation that the French remained at the edge of the trees because they were hoping to capture Bourbon is plausible, the rebel duke was actually on the other side of the wood. According to Bellay, Bourbon was busy forming the last of the imperials to enter the park into pike squares, and though he agreed that Francis's charge had forced the French gunners to cease firing he thought that the king had not pressed home his advantage because he thought that the entire imperial army was in full retreat.[5]

'Now I really am the duke of Milan!' Francis is supposed to have cried,[6] but he had spoken too soon. Lannoy's cavalry had indeed been scattered and Pescara's infantry were pinned down in the west, but in the eastern sector of the battlefield Frundsberg's counterattack had cut Fleuranges' Swiss to ribbons.

After being bested by Frundsberg's much larger force, Fleuranges had made a fighting retreat towards his camp at the Porta Levrieri but during this vicious melee he had been knocked unconscious by a blow from a halberd. As soon as his men saw their captain fall, they lost their will to fight. Throwing away their weapons, Fleuranges' Swiss ran for their lives. They were shown no mercy; hundreds were shot in the back by Frundsberg's arquebusiers.[7] When the Young Adventurer recovered his wits, he found himself a prisoner.

Though Frundsberg's victory over Fleuranges had been total, the battle was far from won and the beleaguered Pescara was still sending urgent messages to all the imperial captains pleading for help. Having grasped the situation quickly, the Father of Landsknechts hastened to the marquis's rescue and on the way he was joined by both Bourbon, whose pike square was now ready for battle, and de Vasto, whose raiders had failed to link up with de Leyva.[8]

The race to the wood proved to be the pivotal moment of the battle. If Francis had retreated and allowed his artillery to finish off Lannoy and Pescara's men hiding in the woods, Richard's Black Band could have blocked Frundsberg's advancing pike squares with ease. As it was, Francis failed to realise that his charge had not only left his *gendarmes* dangerously exposed and blocked his gunners' field of fire but had split his army into several different groups, none of which could support the other.

In the east, Fleuranges and Tiercelin were now prisoners. The few survivors of their shattered brigades were fleeing towards a new pontoon bridge which had been built by the French to replace the one swept away. Likewise, the Pavia garrison had overwhelmed Montmorency's positions at the Five Abbeys and the butcher of the Gravalone blockhouse had also been captured. In spite of de Leyva's threats, Montmorency was held for ransom instead of being hanged as a war criminal, and those of his men able to run joined Fleuranges' Swiss in their headlong flight to the pontoon bridge.[9]

As events would prove, Montmorency had been extremely lucky. Francis still had no idea that his army to the east of Pavia had collapsed. Now the only French units still capable of fighting were in the west, and these consisted of the duke d'Alençon's rearguard, billeted in the abbey of San Lanfranco, and Richard's Black Band, who had been stationed at the Porta Repentina. Unfortunately for Francis, d'Alençon's Gascons were too far from the heath to be of any use, which meant the only man who could rescue the French king from disaster was the putative king of England.

Whether Richard appreciated the irony of this situation is not known, but most sources agree that the White Rose marched his men towards Francis as soon as he spotted the danger. However, the Black Band was still crossing the heath when Frundsberg's 15,000 *landsknechts* arrived to block their advance. A battle royal between these two bitter rivals was now inevitable. Reissner takes up the story:

> The German *landsknechts* on the French side, called the Black Brigade, approached the imperial foot soldiers with a great desire to punish them. They wanted to serve their king [Francis], who had paid them a lot of money in wages, with honour and live honestly, but the imperial *landsknechts* and those of Frundsberg were equally eager to fight the Black Brigade. This was because, despite being Germans and subjects of the Emperor, they served the French king, who was the state enemy of the Emperor, and they fought against their brother Germans, who were of their blood.[10]

However, a *landsknecht* ritual had to be observed before the butchery could begin.

The king of France was not the only person at Pavia who believed that a battle could be decided by single combat, and as soon as Frundsberg's men were within earshot one of Richard's captains dashed out of the Black Band's ranks and challenged Frundsberg to a duel. The man was a German from Augsburg by the name of Langenmantel.[11]

Unfortunately, Langenmantel's challenge made even less of an impression on Frundsberg than Richard's similar offer had done on de Leyva. After declaring that he did not bandy words with traitors, the Father of *Landsknechts* treacherously ordered his men to attack before Langenmantel could return to the safety of his own lines. Frundsberg's men needed no second bidding. They surged forward and Langenmantel was the first to be hacked to pieces.

'The hated Augsburger was struck down with many weapons, and a land-knight held up his severed hand, still wearing the arm-bracers and the fingers with the gold rings, as a sign of victory,' noted Reissner.[12] Moments later, the two enemy pike squares were locked together in the bitter hand-to-hand fighting that contemporaries called 'bad war'.[13]

A fight between pike squares was a brutal, bloody trial of strength, with those in the front ranks slashing at their foes with their long halberds or short 'cat-skinner' swords while the pikemen behind pushed for all they were worth. When the ground became slippery with blood and entrails, men kicked off their shoes to get better purchase in the gore-soaked slime. Bellay gives us the French version of Richard's epic battle with Frundsberg:

> Our *landsknechts*, who could not number more than four or five thousand and over whom François Monsieur de Lorraine, brother of the duke of Lorraine, and the duke of Suffolk, called Rose-Blanche were in charge, walked with their heads bowed, straight to the large imperial battalion, which came to attack the king; but being few in number (as I have said) they were surrounded by two large German pike squares and defeated, despite fighting bravely.[14]

According to Reissner's account, Richard's young co-commander was one of those killed in the first charge,[15] and he too described how the Black Band was encircled.

'In this attack, Georg von Frundsberg and Marx Sittich von Ems crushed the enemy with another cunning battle-plan. While von Frundsberg pecked out the eyes of his foes, von Ems took his brigade to one side, and another wing of the army swung around the other, so the enemy were trapped in the middle,' he wrote.[16]

Somewhere in this tangled knot of blood-crazed berserkers was the White Rose, who was now fighting for his life as well as for the future of the Yorkist cause, but it was hopeless. As Richard tried to hack his way out of the imperial net, he was mortally wounded.

'Reichart, a nobly born prince of Suffolchiae of the royal house from England called the White Roses, who had land and power in Britannia, and who was the leader of the Black Brigade because of his skill in war, perished here,' wrote Reissner.[17]

It was all over in a heartbeat. The de la Poles' forty-year struggle to restore the House of York came to an end in the blood-soaked mud of Pavia. When the fog of war had lifted, a pile of mangled corpses, all wearing smoke-blackened armour, marked the spot where the Last Yorkist and his men had met their heroic fate.

'They killed them all, so that almost none of the black-clad foot soldiers escaped,' crowed Reissner.[18] With the annihilation of Richard and his men, any hope that Francis may have had of snatching victory from the jaws of defeat also perished. Put simply, as soon as Pescara's arquebusiers realised that Francis had cut himself off from all forms of rescue, they ran out of the woods and began picking off his attendant *gendarmes*.[19]

'Whilst von Frundsberg and von Ems routed and drove off the enemy foot soldiers, the king's horsemen were torn apart and killed by the imperial musketeers and cavalry ... It was a bloody battle, and the French had to fall, because the Spaniards quickly surrounded them and shot lead bullets at them from all sides, mortally wounding them,' says Reissner.[20]

With no room to manoeuvre, Francis's *gendarmes* were easy targets, and their expensive armour offered no protection from cheap handguns fired at close range. The imperial arquebusiers simply blasted the French horsemen out of their saddles, and any noble knight who was merely wounded was swiftly despatched the moment he crashed to the ground. One of those who died in this way was Jacques de la Palice, Lord Chabannes. After his horse was killed with a pike, the ageing warrior, having first tried to defend himself, was shot the moment he surrendered.[21]

At least Richard's old commander from Navarre and Picardy had died with a sword in his hand; that other elderly veteran of the Italian Wars, the sixty-four-year-old Louis de la Trémoille, suffered a truly ignominious end. He too was unhorsed, and as he lay helpless in the mud a Spanish handgunner shoved the muzzle of his weapon under the skirts of the Frenchman's armour and pulled the trigger. A flash of light, a loud bang and Trémoille's remains had to be scraped out of his metal skin 'like a lobster from its shell'.[22]

Other members of the French nobility who were killed at the edge of the wood included René of Savoy, the Great Bastard, who was pinned under his dying mount and suffocated. When his corpse was recovered, it was described as being blue, like that of a drowned man, while his eyes and tongue bulged from his head as if he had been hanged. Equally unlucky was Galeazzo di San-Severino, master of the king's horse, who was accidentally beheaded by a backswing from a friend's sword, but the most important Frenchman to die in this massacre was Bonnivet.

'He who had advised the king about this battle and had persuaded him to remain in this camp did not want to suffer the disgrace for the defeat, so he opened his helmet, charged into the midst of the enemy and allowed himself to be stabbed to death,' wrote Reissner.[23]

Although the admiral of France had been hopelessly at sea during both his Italian campaigns, he had at least breathed his last fighting for his king as a chivalrous knight should. Nevertheless, with Bonnivet dead and the rest of the *gendarmerie* being hewn or blown to pieces, Francis soon found himself alone and surrounded by hordes of hostile Spaniards.

'What is happening?' Francis cried as he slashed at his tormentors with all the desperation of a baited bear.[24] He could not keep his enemies at bay forever, and when he was wounded in the leg he had no choice but to surrender.[25] In the space of an hour, the French king had been transformed from conqueror to captive. All the while, the last remnants of his army were crumbling away like sandcastles in the tide.

When Alençon heard that Francis was a prisoner, he withdrew his rearguard from San Lanfranco to the safety of Milan. With the benefit of hindsight, his decision is entirely justifiable; the battle was clearly lost after Francise surrendered. Nevertheless, Alençon was severely criticised for having done nothing to rescue his king. To compound his disgrace, he was also accused of destroying the pontoon bridge over the Ticino to prevent any imperial pursuit, though it is far more likely that someone else ordered its demolition.

Whatever the truth, breaking down the bridge trapped the survivors of Fleuranges and Montmorency's companies on the wrong side of the river, condemning them to slaughter.[26]

The retreat of Alençon completed the imperials' resounding victory. The king of France had been captured, his army shattered and the French nobility decimated. Indeed, Francis's defeat at Pavia would prove to be every bit as disastrous for the French as the catastrophe of Agincourt a century earlier, and though Henry VIII had not won the French crown, as he had intended, the destruction of the House of York was still great cause for celebration. Realising this, the English ambassadors across Europe were quick to inform both the king and Cardinal Wolsey of the Tudors' final triumph over the de la Poles.

'Sure-word has come that the French king is taken, and [with him] an infinite number of his lords; among them the king of Navarre, and La Rosa Blancha, Edmund de la Pole's brother ... make up the trinity of kings taken in the field,' wrote Bishop John Clerk, the Tudor envoy in Rome, in a letter he sent to Wolsey just three days after the battle.[27] The sometime bishop of Bath and Wells also remarked that the duke of Albany had been left stranded in central Italy by the French defeat.

Also quick off the mark was Sir John Russell, who was still serving as the Tudor liaison officer to the duke of Bourbon. In a letter he sent to Henry on 11 March 1525, Russell told his king that the man he had been ordered to assassinate back in 1515 was at last in his grave.

'The lance-knights fought very well against their own nation, but few escaped and Richard de la Poole, their captain, was slain,' he wrote. The following day, Russell's superior, Richard Pace, informed Wolsey that the Tudors' most implacable enemy had been killed at Pavia, and he adds that the beleaguered Albany was intending to 'steal away by sea into Provence', but Henry had already heard the news.[28]

According to Robert Maquereau, a contemporary Burgundian chronicler, it was almost midnight on 9 March when an imperial messenger, who had fought at Pavia, arrived in London with the official account of Charles's victory. Though Henry had been sleeping, he hurriedly donned a nightgown and read the letter handed to him with tears in his eyes. When he had finished, the king of England fell to his knees and thanked his All-Knowing Creator for his good fortune.

'My friend, you are like St Gabriel, who announced the coming of Jesus Christ,' Henry said to the messenger as he rose to his feet. He then asked what had become of Richard de la Pole.

'The White Rose is dead in battle, I saw him with the others,' the messenger declared proudly.

'Then may God have mercy on his soul, all the enemies of England have passed away!' Henry cried joyfully, and the Burgundian chronicler adds that the bearer of these glad tidings was very generously rewarded, 'as much for the death of the White Rose as for the victory'.[29]

While much of Maquereau's account may be fanciful, the king's delight was genuine. The English chronicler Edward Hall tells us that the moment Henry heard of Richard's demise he sent heralds to proclaim the glad tidings across London; beacons were lit and free wine was distributed to allow the poor to toast their king's health. At the other end of the social scale, Henry celebrated his triumph over the Houses of York and Valois with a great feast served 'in a goodly tent' erected on Tower Hill to which the ambassadors of Rome, Flanders and Venice were invited. These festivities were followed by a magnificent service of thanksgiving held in St Paul's Cathedral.[30]

A few weeks later, Dr Richard Sampson, the English ambassador to the imperial court, presented Wolsey with a book, written in Spanish, recounting the imperial victory.[31] A letter from Charles V to Louis de Praet, his ambassador to Henry, shows the full measure of the de la Poles' significance in Tudor–Habsburg relations. In this missive, which is dated 26 March 1525, the Emperor ordered de Praet to make special mention of 'the defeat of the White Rose and the danger Albany faced' when he gave Henry the final list of casualties.[32]

Outside the rarified atmosphere of official diplomatic circles, one of Wolsey's Continental catspaws was equally delighted to hear of the death of the White Rose. This man, a Fleming called John Hédin, saw an opportunity to make a quick florin by volunteering to wind up Richard's affairs, even though he had bequeathed almost nothing to his descendants.

'I have learned from friends at Metz that he who was called Blanche Rose, and died in battle beyond the mountains, has left some goods in that town, of no great amount. Though it will not be easy, I will endeavour, by the king's authority, to obtain them for such persons as Your Eminence may designate. [I also] request the gift of them for myself,' he wrote in a letter to Wolsey dated 27 March 1525.[33]

No doubt Hédin was underplaying the value of Richard's estate in the hope of deterring more powerful vultures, and he was not the only man trying to profit from the butchery at Pavia. As was customary, the victorious imperial troops stripped everything of value from the dead noblemen before selling their bodies to the deceased's servants, whose duty it was to bring home whatever was left of their late masters. This practice led to a grisly meat market with the naked, putrefying cadavers laid out in Pavia's churches and the vendors calling out the prices they would accept.[34]

The contemporary French historian Jean Bouchet remarked that the shredded corpse of La Trémoille could only be identified by the length of the big toenail on its right foot, which the noble lord had grown especially long for precisely this purpose.[35] He also tells us that after Trémoille's mangled remains were claimed, they were embalmed with myrrh and aloes before being shipped to his grieving relatives. Alas, there would be no such homecoming for Richard de la Pole.

The body of an attainted English pretender killed in the service of France could never be returned to England, yet Richard's corpse was not thrown into the pits hastily dug for the common soldiery. Rather, his remains were claimed by no less a person than the duke of Bourbon, who insisted on arranging a proper funeral and officiating as chief mourner. Perhaps Bourbon took on this role by way of apology; after all, both he and Richard had fought for France in Navarre, and they had only ended up on opposite sides at Pavia because of their respective kings' shameless ambition.

Whatever Bourbon's motives, he certainly ensured Richard spent eternity in good company. On his orders, the White Rose was laid to rest in Pavia's Augustinian cathedral, now San Pietro in Ciel d'Oro,[36] where he shares eternity with the early Christian theologian St Augustine of Hippo, the late Roman philosopher Boethius and the great Lombard king Liutprand.

Yet this is not the end of the de la Pole story.

Epilogue

THE FIRST AND LAST YORKISTS

Almost seventy years after Richard's death, an Elizabethan travel writer named Fynes Moryson made a pilgrimage to Pavia to see the tomb of Saint Augustine and was surprised to find a memorial to Richard de la Pole in the same church. Though Moryson included only part of Richard's lengthy epitaph in his memoir, the full text can be found in the writings of the eighteenth-century poet, traveller and co-founder of *The Spectator* magazine, Joseph Addison:

> The French King Francis the first, being taken by Caesar's army near Pavia, the fourteenth [*sic*] of February in the year 1525, among other lords these were slain: Francis duke [*sic*] of Lorraine, Richard de la Pole, Englishman and duke of Suffolk, banished by his tyrant King Henry VIII. Their bodies lay buried, without honour fifty-seven years in this Convent. At length, Charles Parker of Morley, a near kinsman of the duke of Suffolk, who had been banished from England by Queen Elizabeth for the Catholic Faith, and who was supported in Milan by the bounty of the Catholic King Philip, invincible Monarch of Spain, erected this monument, the best his slender means could afford, to his most dear kinsman and these most illustrious Princes, recommending a better and more honourable one to the Lorrainers. Passer-by pray for the repose of their souls.[1]

So who was Charles Parker?

The *Dictionary of National Biography* states that Parker had indeed fled England to escape the Elizabethan persecution of Catholics, and he had been created titular bishop of Man while in exile. At the end of his ecclesiastical career Parker had retired to Pavia, where he had discovered Richard's tomb, and in 1611 his request to be buried next to his kinsman had been granted.[2] No doubt the similar tribulations he and Richard had suffered at the hands of the Tudors persuaded Bishop Parker to mark and share the last resting place of the White Rose, yet the two men were not as closely connected as the elderly cleric believed.

Their relationship was through the marriage of Richard's sister Elizabeth de la Pole to Charles's maternal great-great-uncle Henry Lovel, Lord Morley.[3] After Lovel had been killed at the siege of Dixmude in 1491, his Morley titles had passed to his sister Alice, who had married into the staunchly Yorkist Parker family. Alice was Bishop Charles's great-grandmother and her husband, Sir William Parker, had been Richard III's standard bearer at Bosworth. Evidently, Bishop Parker was fiercely proud of his White Rose ancestry because he provided Pavia's Augustinians with another monument to commemorate Lionel of Antwerp bearing the following legend:

> Lionel duke of Clarence, son of Edward III, king of England, who married Violanta, daughter of Galeazzo, who had the duke of Milan for his brother, who died at Alba in the Year of Salvation 1368. [This memorial is dedicated] with great honour [because] the tomb was taken away afterwards, by a decree of the Council of Trent. [Erected] in the Year of Salvation 1590 [by] Charles Parker of Morley, an Englishman who is of the same Clarence stock, who was exiled for thirty years for remaining true to the faith of the Catholic Church.[4]

Even though the actual ancestor of the House of York was Edmund of Langley, the fifth surviving son of Edward III, a stronger Yorkist claim to the throne originated with Lionel of Antwerp, Edward's second surviving son; but here is not the place to examine the tangled stems that produced the Wars of the Roses. As far as Bishop Parker was concerned, both the first and last Yorkists had died at Pavia.

This strange coincidence came about because the five-month wedding feast that had followed Lionel's second marriage, to the only daughter of Galeazzo Visconti, lord of Pavia, had proved too much for the English prince's constitution. The gluttonous groom had breathed his last on 7 October 1368 and his body had been buried in Pavia's Augustinian cathedral, which had become the customary resting place for notables who had died in the city. However, as Parker's memorial states, Lionel's remains were repatriated some years later by a special order of the Council of Trent.[5]

After Lionel's body had been returned to England, it was reinterred in the Augustinian priory at Clare, in Suffolk, which had been founded by the family of his first wife. The principal mausoleum of the de la Poles is also in Suffolk, in the village of Wingfield's parish church of St Andrew, but Richard's body was destined to remain in Italy – and his bones were not allowed to rest in peace.

During the French Revolutionary Wars, anti-clerical hysteria forced the Augustinian monks to leave Pavia, and their abandoned cathedral soon fell into disrepair. Though the church was reconsecrated in 1896, and the tombs of St Augustine, Boethius and Liutprand restored, Bishop Parker's memorials to Richard and Lionel were destroyed by Napoleon's soldiers when they turned the vacant building into an arsenal. Ironically, the palace of Haute Pierre, which had been Richard's home during his exile in Metz, suffered a similar fate around the same time, but at the hands of a French king rather than French revolutionaries.

Under the terms of the 1648 Treaty of Westphalia, which had ended the Thirty Years War, Metz became a fully French city. In the following century, Haute Pierre was purchased by Louis XVI to use as a mansion for the city's governor. The old medieval palace, which had been renovated by Richard at his own considerable expense, was demolished in 1777 and replaced with the elegant Neoclassical structure we see today.

Incidentally, one of the last residents of the old palace was the marquis de Lafayette, hero of both the American and French revolutions, and it was at Haute Pierre, in 1775, that he decided to join George Washington's Continental Army. During the Napoleonic Wars the building became Metz's chief courtroom, and it is still the city's Palais de Justice. Moreover, its modern address is 3, rue Haute Pierre.

The fate of Richard's tomb and palace notwithstanding, his memory was preserved in less tangible ways. Philippe de Vigneulles thought Richard's death was of sufficient importance to record it in his journal, though he mistakenly reported that the White Rose had been drowned in the River Po while trying to escape the bloody aftermath of Pavia.[6] Likewise, the canons of Metz's cathedral honoured the last Yorkist by holding an annual requiem mass for Richard until the French Revolutionaries who took over Metz put an end to such practices. Although his mass is no longer said, the original dedication has survived:

> In April of the year 1525, in the conflict at Pavia, the city where Francis, king of the Gauls, was captured by the army of the Roman emperor and led captive to Spain, there died the illustrious Richard duke of Suffolk, who having obtained our house called la Haute-Pierre, which had been previously leased to him for life by us, very sumptuously restored it, wherefore we now decree that our church should celebrate the anniversary [of his death] every year, in perpetuity, for the safety of his soul.[7]

Sadly, all these monuments and masses cannot hide the fact that Richard's quest for England's throne had ended in failure, and his death at Pavia marked the Tudors' final victory over the House of York. As neither Richard nor his siblings left legitimate male heirs, there were no more de la Poles to challenge Henry VIII or his descendants, but the Suffolk branch of the White Rose did not disappear entirely.

Against all odds, Richard was survived by his illegitimate daughter, Marguerite, who became a lady-in-waiting to the king of France's sister, also called Marguerite. As Marguerite de la Pole left a will dated 1599, it is safe to assume that she died sometime after that date, and there can be little doubt that Richard was her father because her marriage contract says so.[8] However, while Marguerite de la Pole's paternity can be established with some certainty, the identity of her mother remains a matter of debate.

A seventeenth-century French monk and chronicler, Anselme de Sainte-Marie, thought that Richard's daughter was the product of his brief affair with a woman called Marie of Sicily. Unfortunately for future genealogists, the only source he gives is 'a proof supplied by a canon of St Jean de Lyon',[9] and Anselme's work is woefully prone to errors. For example, he confuses Marguerite de la Pole with Margaret Kerdeston, who was her great-great-aunt.

On the other hand, Richard's love affair with Sebille is well documented so it is far more likely that Marguerite's mother was the adulterous wife of Metz's goldsmith. Furthermore, because Sebille had died young and Richard had been extremely close to the French king, it is equally probable that their daughter became a ward of Francis's sister, Marguerite d'Angoulême.

The plot thickens when we realise that Queen Marguerite's first husband was the same duke of Alençon who had done little to prevent Francis's defeat. As he was one of the few French noblemen who had escaped from Pavia intact, Alençon had shouldered most of the blame for his brother-in-law's capture and he had been unable to bear the disgrace. He had died shortly after his return to France, and the following year his thirty-four-year-old widow had married the twenty-three-year-old king of Navarre.

Though the dashing Henri d'Albret had also been taken prisoner at Pavia, his daring escape from an imperial castle had done much to restore his reputation. Such heroics had certainly won Marguerite d'Angoulême's heart, yet she became the more accomplished monarch. Her patronage of the arts, political skills and talents as an author have earned her the title of First Modern Woman, but it was her custom of fostering the impoverished daughters of noblemen that concerns us here.

The high-born girls taken under Marguerite d'Angoulême's wing included Mademoiselle d'Estouteville, Isabeau de Rohan and Charlotte de Laval.[10] As Richard had been killed in the service of France, it makes perfect sense for the French king's sister to take care of his daughter, and Marguerite de la Pole's presence at the court of Marguerite of Angoulême is proved by her marriage contract.

In this document, Marguerite de la Pole is described as a 'lady of honour to the queen of Navarre' as well as 'daughter of Richard de la Pole, son of the last duke of Suffolk'; it also tells us that the bride took her wedding vows on 21 May 1539 in the presence of the queen and her kinsman the marquis of Saluzzo.[11] As we have seen, both Saluzzo and Richard had fought at Pavia, and they shared a common ancestor in Michael de la Pole, 2nd earl of Suffolk, but with whom did Richard's daughter tie the knot?

Once again the answer can be found in Marguerite's marriage contract, which states that the bridegroom was Sibeud de Tivoley, seigneur de Brénieu, a 'squire of honour to the French queen, Eleanor of Austria', who was Charles V's sister. Eleanor's marriage to Francis, which had taken place in 1530, was part of the peace agreement that had freed the French king from Habsburg captivity after Pavia.

Following their wedding, Francis and Eleanor had taken up residence in the royal palace of Fontainebleau, where Henri and Marguerite of Angoulême were also living, so the marriage of her lady-in-waiting to a gentleman in the service of her new sister-in-law may have been intended to build bridges between the two queens' households. The fact that Eleanor, queen of France, was godmother to the third of Sibeud and Marguerite's eight children, who was named Éléonore in her honour, certainly adds weight to this theory.[12]

In time, Éléonore de Brénieu-Suffolk became a lady of honour at the Navarrese court, like her mother, but owing to the Spanish occupation of Pamplona, which her grandfather had fought so hard to prevent, Navarre's monarchs ruled only their territories on the French side of the Pyrenees. As a result, the White Rose's granddaughter spent much of her life at the Chateau de Nerac, ancient seat of the Lords d'Albret and *de facto* Navarrese capital.

The importance of this city increased in 1555 when Jeanne d'Albret, the only surviving child of Queen Marguerite and King Henri, succeeded to Navarre's throne and converted her entire realm to Calvinism. During the French Wars of Religion, Nerac became a haven for Huguenot refugees and Éléonore de Brénieu-Suffolk grew up to be a committed Protestant.

In July 1564, Éléonore married the governor of Nerac's castle, Jean de Secondat, seigneur de Roques. She was nineteen while he was nearly fifty, and his chief claim to fame is that he was related to the famous Calvinist theologian Joseph Justus Scaliger. It is a measure of Monsieur and Madame de Roques' standing in both Navarrese and Calvinist circles that Scaliger advised another prominent Huguenot, Pierre Pithou, to entrust his secret messages to Éléonore.[13]

Despite his age Jean fathered five sons with Éléonore, but four of them were killed fighting for the Protestant cause. Jason, Jaques, Henry and Paul died at the battles of d'Ivry, de Nuits, Middleburg and Ostend respectively, but the youngest son, Pierre, became a royal counsellor and lieutenant-general of Guyenne under Jeanne d'Albret's son, and France's only Protestant king, Henri IV. Pierre's nephew Jacob was badly wounded during same siege of Ostend that had killed his father, Paul, but he survived to have children, who had children.[14]

The Enlightenment philosopher Charles-Louis Secondat, baron de Montesquieu, who created the Separation of Powers principle that underpins the American Constitution, is Jacob's great-grandson,[15] but space precludes listing all those who can trace their pedigree back to Richard de la Pole. All that needs to be said is that Marguerite de la Pole-Suffolk and Sibeud de Brénieu had seven more children beside Éléonore.

The full list of Richard's grandchildren includes Jean, seigneur de Brénieu; Pierre, canon of St Denis; Claude, canon of d'Evry; Catherine, who married Gilbert de Colomb; Marguerite, who married Claude d'Orgeoise; Louise, who married Jean de Montchenu; and Sebastienne, who married Andre Berenger de Guas.[16] So, although two of his immediate descendants entered Holy Orders, the rest married and had children of their own. As a result, Richard de la Pole could have descendants living somewhere in the world today.

As modern genealogists have discovered the 11x-great-grandchildren of Richard's aunt Anne of York, duchess of Exeter, living in Canada, it is certainly possible that his daughter's line has also survived, which leads us to this intriguing thought: if the House of Windsor should ever become extinct, perhaps one of Marguerite de la Pole's descendants will step out of the shadows and pick up the White Rose reluctantly dropped by her father five centuries ago.

NOTES

Introduction: The Origin of the de la Poles

1. Kingsford, *Dictionary of National Biography* (1885-1900), Vol. 46, p. 48
2. Fryde, *William de la Pole, Merchant and King's Banker* (Hambleton Press, 1988), p. 15
3. Napier, *Historical Notices of the Parishes of Ewelme and Swyncombe* (1858), pp. 271–285
4. Napier, p. 315
5. Historical Manuscripts Commission, Third Report (1872), p. 279
6. Jackanapes was medieval slang for a pet monkey.
7. Napier, p. 75
8. *Hall's Chronicle*, p. 219

1 No Slight Distinction

1. Seward, *The Last White Rose*, p. 137
2. Hall, p. 495
3. Namely Roland de Vielleville, Henry's illegitimate son 'by a Breton lady', and Matthew Baker – Penn, p. 47
4. Hall, p. 495
5. The future James IV – Napier, pp. 142 & 158
6. *Rolls of Parliament*, Vol. 6, p. 398a
7. The Sarum Missal, containing the words and music for the Catholic mass, which is inscribed with Humphrey's name and was presented to the college chapel by him in 1498, still survives. Lower Library Aa.1.38 (G.A.S. 86)

8. Upcher, *History of Hingham, Norfolk, and its church of St. Andrew* (1921), p. 34
9. Napier, p. 162
10. Napier, p. 165
11. Leland, *Collectanea*, Vol. 4 (1770), pp. 238, 229, 230, 243, 245 & 255
12. Napier, p. 158
13. Hall, p. 445
14. *Chronicle of Calais*, p. 22
15. Hall, p. 446
16. Ellis, *Original Letters of Richard III & Henry VII*, p. 118
17. Leland, *Collectanea*, Vol. 4, p. 238
18. Hall, p. 464-6
19. *Chronicle of Calais*, p. 22
20. Bacon, *The History of the Reign of King Henry VII* (Folio Society), p. 127
21. Bentley, *Excerpta Historica*, p. 88
22. *Rolls of Parliament*, Vol. 6, p. 475
23. Gairdner, *L&P HVII*, Vol. 1, Appendix A, p. 392
24. Blatchly & Haward, 'Sir Robert Lord Curson Soldier Courtier & Spy', *Proceedings of the Suffolk Institute of Archaeology and History*, Vol. XLI (Part 3) (2007), p. 343
25. Bindoff (ed.), *The History of Parliament: the House of Commons 1509-1558, A-Z Member Biographies* (1982)
26. Davey, *The Pageant of London*, Vol. 1 (Methuen, 1906), p. 310
27. There is some debate as to which of the boys was the younger; Napier believes Richard was the fifth son of the 2nd duke of Suffolk and William the sixth, but most of the evidence suggests Richard was the youngest of the de la Pole brothers.
28. Gairdner, *L&P HVII*, Vol. 1, Appendix A, pp. 394–5
29. Ibid., p. 395
30. ibid., p. 396
31. ibid., pp. 396–8
32. ibid., p. 400
33. Gairdner, *L&P HVII*, Vol. 1, Appendix A, pp. 400–401
34. Cockayne, *Complete Peerage*, Vol. II, p. 76
35. Gairdner, *L&P HVII*, Vol. 1, Appendix A, p. 401
36. 29 September 1495 – Bentley, *Excerpta Historica*, p. 105

2 *Departed out of This Realm*

1. Leland, *Itinerary* (Bell, 1907), parts I–III, p. 113
2. 14 October 1495 – *Rolls of Parliament*, Vol. 6, pp. 474–7
3. Napier, pp. 166 & 170
4. Leland, *Collectanea*, Vol. 4, pp. 229–230
5. *Rolls of Parliament*, Vol. 6, p. 458
6. Beltz, *Memorials of the Order of the Garter* (Pickering, 1841), clxix
7. Archbold, *DNB* (1885-1900), Vol. 57, p. 288
8. Cockayne, *Complete Peerage*, Vol. VII p. 307
9. Vergil, *Anglica Historia* (Hay ed.), Book XXIV, p. 83
10. ibid., p. 87
11. Arthurson, *The Perkin Warbeck Conspiracy*, p. 144
12. Vergil, *Anglica Historia*, Book XXIV, p. 89
13. An Gof means 'the smith' in Cornish and he is also known as Michael Joseph.
14. Hall, p. 477
15. Bacon, p. 174
16. Hall, pp. 479-80
17. Shaw, *Knights of England*, p. 29
18. Hall, p. 479
19. *Select Cases in the Council of Henry VII* (Selden Society), pp. xxix-xxx
20. Hall, p. 483
21. ibid., p. 485
22. ibid., p. 486
23. Napier, p. 168
24. Gairdner, *The Paston Letters*, Vol. VI, Letter 1065, p. 160
25. Napier, p. 172
26. Gairdner, *The Paston Letters*, Vol. VI, Letter 1065, p. 160
27. Bacon, *The Reign of Henry VII* (CUP, 1885, Lumby ed.), p. 186
28. Sewell, *Memoirs of Sir James Tyrell* (1878), pp. 128, 137
29. ibid., pp. 137–8
30. Confusingly Sir James's son was also called Thomas but he was not knighted until 1513 – Sewell, p. 161
31. Bentley, *Excerpta Historica*, p. 123
32. Gairdner, *L&P HVII*, Vol. 1, pp. 132–3
33. *Fabyan's Chronicle*, p. 686
34. Hall, p. 490
35. Bergenroth, *CSP Spain*, p. 206
36. Bentley *Excerpta Historica* p. 120-122

37. Bergenroth, *CSP Spain*, p. 206
38. Hall, p. 491
39. ibid., p. 490
40. Penn, p. 38 & Cunningham, p. 96
41. Molinet, *Chroniques*, Vol. 47 (1828 ed.), p. 118
42. ibid., p. 119
43. Penn, p. 74

3 The Goodliest Plumes

1. Hall, p. 491
2. Cunningham, p. 189
3. Ryssangles is now the Suffolk village of Rishangles – Napier, p. 172, fn4
4. Gairdner, *DNB* (1885–1900), Vol. 46, p. 22
5. Miguel was the son of Joanna and Catherine's older sister, Isabella of Aragon, who had married the king of Portugal in 1498 but had died in childbirth the following year.
6. Hall, p. 491
7. *Chronicle of Calais*, p. 3; see also Molinet, p. 130 & Gairdner, *L&P HVII*, Vol. II, p. 87
8. ibid., pp. 50-51
9. Hall, p. 492
10. *Chronicle of Calais*, p. 50
11. Gairdner, *Henry VII*, p. 176
12. Hall, p. 851
13. *Chronicle of Calais*, p. 50
14. Molinet, *Chroniques*, *Vol. V* (1828 ed.), p. 130
15. Bergenroth, *CSPS*, Vol. 1, pp. 277–278, p. 231-3
16. Vergil, p. 125
17. Blatchly and Haward, p. 335
18. ibid., p. 335
19. ibid.
20. Principally James Gairdner, the nineteenth-century curator of the state papers relating to this period and the author of *Henry VII* (pp. 186–7) and Wilhelm Busch, German author of *England Under the Tudors* (pp. 364–5)
21. In Latin: A MOY NE TIENT and PARLESQUI VOULDRAS – Blatchly and Haward, p. 335
22. Gairdner, *L&P HVII*, Vol. I, XVIII, p. 134

23. Busch, Vol. 1, p. 365
24. Maximilian had tried once before to bring Spain into the Habsburg sphere of influence by marrying his daughter, Margaret of Austria, to Ferdinand and Isabella's son, John. Unfortunately John had died in 1497 and though Margaret was pregnant by her husband at the time of his death, the child was stillborn.
25. Gairdner, *Henry VII*, p. 136-156
26. Vergil, Book XXIV [XXVI], p. 123 & Hall, p. 495
27. Gairdner, *L&P HVII*, Vol. 1, XXIV, p. 226
28. Vergil, Book LXXIV, p. 125
29. Ellis, pp. 34–6
30. Gairdner, *L&P HVII*, Vol. 1, XXIV, p. 226
31. ibid., p. 227

4 *My Most Dear and Well-beloved Cousin*

1. Stowe, *Annals of England*, p. 807
2. Cockayne, *Complete Peerage*, Vol. 12, p. 253 fn (g)
3. Anon. (trans. Sneyd), *A Relation of the Island of England about the year 1500*, p. 27
4. Gairdner, *L&P HVII*, Vol. 1, LV, p. 312
5. ibid., XVIII, p. 143
6. ibid., XVIII, p. 134
7. ibid., p. 143
8. ibid., p. 144
9. Count Enzenberg, *Schloss Tratzberg* (1958), pp. 41–44
10. Gairdner, *L&P HVII*, Vol. 1, Letter XVIII, p. 135
11. ibid., p. 135
12. ibid., XVIII, p. 135
13. ibid
14. ibid., XVIII, pp. 144–5
15. ibid., XVIII, p. 136
16. 7–22 August 1485
17. Gairdner, *L&P HVII*, Vol. 1, XVIII, p. 137
18. Osprey, MAA58, *The Landsknechts*, p. 3
19. Gairdner, *L&P HVII*, Vol. 1, Letter XVIII, pp. 136–7
20. ibid., pp. 152–3
21. Somerset was a paternal second cousin to the king's mother, Margaret Beaufort.

22. Warham had already negotiated several treaties with the Habsburgs and was a future archbishop of Canterbury.
23. Gairdner, *L&P HVII*, Vol. 1, Letter XVIII, p. 153
24. ibid., XIX, pp. 154–5
25. A gold coin, first issued by Edward IV, worth 6*s* 8*d* – Gairdner, *L&P HVII*, Vol. 1, Letter XIX, pp. 160–1
26. ibid., XIX, pp. 157–8
27. ibid., XX, p. 168
28. ibid., XXI, p. 149
29. ibid., XVIII, p. 147
30. ibid., XX, p. 169
31. ibid., XX, pp. 175–6
32. ibid.
33. ibid., XX, p. 177
34. ibid., XVIII, p. 137
35. ibid., XVIII, pp. 137–8
36. ibid., XVIII, p. 138
37. ibid
38. ibid., XVIII, pp. 138–9
39. i.e. 27 February 1502 – *Chronicle of the Grey Friars of London*, p. 27
40. Speed, *Historie of Great Britain*, p. 992 and Fabyan, p. 688

5 *I Thought at This Hour to Be Very near England*

1. Napier, p. 175
2. *The Victoria County History Volume II: Hampshire*, pp. 143–144
3. Napier, p. 175
4. Penn, p. 81
5. Gairdner, *L&P HVII*, Vol. 1, p. 181
6. Sewell, *Memoire of Sir James Tyrell*, Vol. 5, p. 171
7. Gairdner, *L&P HVII*, Vol. 1, p. 181
8. Fabyan, p. 687, see also Gairdner, *L&P HVII*, Vol. 1, p. 139
9. Sewell, p. 161 [fn] & p. 177–8
10. *Grafton's Chronicle* (1809 ed.), Vol. II, p. 118
11. ibid., p. 118
12. Vergil, Book XXIV (XXVI), p. 127
13. More, *History of King Richard III* (CUP, 1883 ed.), p. 83
14. Leland, *Collectana*, Vol. 4, pp. 258–9
15. Buck's *Richard the Third* (1647 ed.), Book V, p. 142
16. Vergil, p. 125

17. Hall, p. 496
18. Speed, p. 991
19. Sewell, p. 177
20. Gairdner, *L&P HVII*, Vol. 1, p. 180
21. Arthurson, pp. 75, 82 & 167
22. 1 March 1502 – Gairdner, *L&P HVII*, Vol. 1, p. 180
23. Fabyan, p. 687
24. ibid., see also *The Chronicle of the Grey Friars of London*, p. 28
25. Sewell, p. 176
26. Fabyan, p. 687
27. ibid., XXI, p. 180
28. Hall, p. 496
29. Gairdner, *L&P HVII*, Vol. 1, XXI, pp. 183–4
30. ibid., XXI, p. 178
31. ibid., p. 182
32. ibid., XVIII, p. 139
33. ibid., pp. 139–40
34. ibid., p. 140
35. ibid., pp. 140–41
36. ibid., p. 141
37. ibid., p. 150
38. ibid., pp. 141-2
39. ibid., p. 142
40. ibid.

6 *Burn That Book and a Vengeance Take the First Writer*

1. Gairdner, *L&P HVII*, Vol. 1, XIX, p. 156
2. ibid., Preface, p. xliv
3. *Calendar of Patent Rolls*, 1495–1509, p. 272
4. Gairdner, *L&P HVII*, Vol. 1, p. 139
5. Leadam, *Transactions of the RHS*, Vol. 16 (1902), p. 141
6. Rolls of Parliament for the reign of Henry VII (Rot. Parl.), Vol. 6, p. 504, b
7. Leadam, p. 142
8. Gairdner, *L&P HVII*, Vol. 1, XXIII, p. 224
9. Leadam, pp. 142–3
10. Gairdner, *L&P HVII*, Vol. 1, XXI, p. 178
11. Fabyan, p. 688
12. Napier, p. 174

13. Cunningham, pp. 189–90
14. Fabyan, p. 688
15. Penn, p. 123
16. Fabyan, p. 688
17. Bindoff, 'Flamank, John', *The History of Parliament Online: The House of Commons, 1509-1558, Members Biographies*
18. *Cal. Pat. Rolls Henry VIII*, vol. ii, 365
19. Gairdner, *L&P HVII*, Vol. 1, XXVL, p. 231
20. ibid., pp. 232–3
21. ibid., p. 233
22. ibid., p. 235
23. Gairdner, *L&P HVII*, Vol. 1, p. 236
24. ibid., p. 236
25. ibid., p. 237
26. ibid., XXVL, p. 237
27. ibid.
28. ibid., p. 238
29. ibid., p. 239
30. ibid., p. 240
31. Penn, p. 232

7 *Provided They Make Declaration of All They Know*

1. Hasted, *The History and Topographical Survey of the County of Kent, Volume* 2, p. 393. Incidentally, Stone Castle had once belonged to the Killingworth family and it is located not far from seat of another of Henry's 'new men', Sir Thomas Boleyn, at Hever. The daughters of these two parvenus, Anne Boleyn and Bridget Wiltshire, were close friends until they quarrelled over the latter's choice of third husband. Tragically, it was Bridget's indiscreet letter that helped send Anne to the scaffold but all that lay in the future.
2. *Calendar of Close Rolls*, Henry VII, Vol. II, 1500-1509 (1963 ed.), No. 161, p. 57
3. Gairdner, *L&P HVII*, Vol. 1, XXIII, p. 222
4. ibid., pp. 222–3
5. ibid., pp. 224–5
6. ibid., pp. 220–1
7. ibid., p. 225
8. ibid., pp. 226–7
9. ibid., p. 227

10. ibid.
11. ibid., pp. 227–8
12. ibid., p. 228
13. ibid.
14. ibid., p. 229
15. Hasted, *The History and Topological Survey of the County of Kent*, Vol. 7, pp. 94–5
16. Hall, p. 394
17. Leadam, p. 139
18. ibid., p. 140
19. ibid., p. 152
20. ibid., pp. 153–4
21. ibid., pp. 154–5
22. ibid., pp. 155–6
23. ibid., p. 157
24. ibid., pp. 147 & 157–8
25. ibid., p. 158
26. ibid.

8 We and King Henry of England, of the Red Rose, Have Made a Contract

1. Gairdner, *L&P HVII*, Vol. 1, XXI, pp. 186–7
2. ibid., p. 187
3. ibid., pp. 187–8
4. *The Statutes of the Most Noble Order of the Garter* (1814 ed.), p. 35
5. Gairdner, *L&P HVII*, Vol. 1, XXII, p. 205
6. ibid., XXI, p. 189
7. Gairdner, *L&P HVII*, Vol. 1, XXVII, pp. 196–9
8. ibid., p. 204
9. ibid., p. 205
10. ibid.
11. ibid., p. 206
12. ibid., p. 207
13. ibid., pp. 210–11
14. ibid., p. 212
15. ibid., pp. 212–219
16. 3 July 1503 – Gairdner, *L&P HVII*, Vol. 1, XXV, pp. 229–230
17. Ellis, L, pp. 126–7
18. Oostkerke in modern Belgium.

19. Not to be confused with the aforementioned Bastard of Oyskerk.
20. Gairdner, *L&P HVII*, Vol. 1, XXXIX, p. 272
21. Ellis, XLVIII, p. 123 & XLIX, p. 124
22. ibid., LV, p. 134
23. Gairdner, *L&P HVII*, Vol. 1, XXXVI, p. 264
24. ibid., pp. 264–5
25. Ellis, XLIX p. 124 & L, p. 127
26. Gairdner, *L&P HVII*, Vol. 1, XXV, p. 207
27. Cockayne, *Complete Peerage*, Vol. IV, p. 340
28. E. C. Lodge, *The Barony of Castelnau, in the Médoc, during the Middle Ages* (1907), p. 93 & C. M. Hansen, 'Suffolk's Niece: The Identity of Margaret, the wife of Jean de Foix, earl of Kendal, Captal de Buch, K.G.', *Genealogists' Magazine*, Vol. 22, no. 10 (1988), pp. 373–77
29. J. Strachey (ed.), *Rotuli Parliamentorum* (1767–1775), Vol. 5, XXVIII, Hen VI, 31, p. 179
30. John's descendants continued to use their Gallicised English title until 1714.
31. Brown, *CSP Venice*, Vol. 1, 805, p. 287 & Engel, *The Realm of St Stephen*, p. 360
32. Arthurson, pp. 70–71 *et al.*
33. Busch, *England under the Tudors*, Vol. 1, p. 181
34. Probably Derek van Riet.
35. Ellis, L, pp. 125–6
36. ibid., p. 126
37. ibid.

9 *And After All Things Were Known*

1. *Rolls of Parliament*, Vol. 6, p. 545
2. *ibid.*
3. Hall, p. 496
4. Blatchly & Haward, p. 335
5. Curson's rehabilitation was continued by Henry VIII who gave Sir Robert his third pardon on 8 May 1509, barely two weeks after his accession – Blatchly & Haward, p. 335
6. Hall, p. 496
7. *Chronicle of the Grey Friars of London*, p. 27; see also Speed, p. 992 & Fabyan, p. 688
8. Vergil, XXIV [XXVI], p. 125
9. Busch, p. 179

10. ibid., p. 181
11. Bergenroth, *CSP Spain*, Vol. I, 401 p. 335
12. ibid., p. 335
13. Gairdner, *L&P HVII*, Vol. 1, XXX, p. 253
14. Bergenroth, *CSP Spain*, Vol. I, 402, p. 337
15. ibid., pp. 335–6
16. Gairdner, *L&P HVII*, Vol. 1, XXX p. 253
17. Ellis, LIX, p. 142
18. Gairdner, *L&P HVII*, Vol. I, Preface, pp. xlvii–xlviii
19. Hannay, *Letters of James IV*, Vol. 45, Letter 14, p. 10
20. Gairdner, *L&P HVII*, Vol. I, Preface, p. xlix
21. ibid., l
22. ibid., XXXII, p. 257
23. ibid., XXX, pp. 254–5
24. ibid., XXXII, p. 257
25. ibid., XXXI, p. 255
26. ibid., XXXII, p. 257
27. ibid., p. 256
28. ibid.
29. ibid., p. 258
30. ibid., XXXVI, p. 265
31. ibid., p. 263
32. ibid., p. 264

10 To Keep the Bit in the Mouth of the King of England

1. Brown, *CSP Venice*, Vol. 1, 847 & 848, pp. 302–3
2. ibid., 849, p. 303
3. ibid., pp. 303–4
4. ibid., 846, p. 302
5. ibid., 844, p. 301
6. Bergenroth, *CSP Spain*, 432, p. 354
7. Gairdner, *L&P HVII*, Vol. 1, XXXII, pp. 260–1
8. Prescott, pp. 363–4
9. Brown, *CSP Venice*, Vol. 1, 851, p. 305
10. Bergenroth, *CSP Spain*, 432, pp. 354 & 357
11. Gairdner, *L&P HVII*, Vol. 1, XXXIII, p. 258
12. ibid., XXXV, p. 261
13. ibid., pp. 262–3
14. Brown, *CSP Venice*, Vol. 1, 851, p. 304

15. ibid., 853, p. 305
16. ibid., 845, p. 302
17. ibid., 853, p. 305
18. Gairdner, *L&P HVII*, Vol. 2, XXIV, p. 133
19. ibid., p. 142
20. ibid.
21. Ellis, LIII, p. 131
22. ibid., pp. 131–2
23. Ellis, LIV, pp. 132–3
24. ibid., pp. 132–4
25. Gairdner, *L&P HVII*, Vol. I, XXXVIII, pp. 266–7
26. ibid., p. 269
27. Brown, *CSP Venice*, Vol. 1, 858, pp. 307–9
28. ibid., p. 308

11 Here at the King's Command

1. Ellis, LVIII, p. 140
2. Gairdner, *L&P HVII*, Vol. I, XXXIX, pp. 271–2
3. ibid., XL, p. 273
4. ibid., p. 273
5. ibid., pp. 274–5
6. Gairdner, *L&P HVII*, Vol. I, XLI, p. 276
7. ibid., pp. 276–7
8. ibid., XLII, pp. 277–8
9. Brown, *CSP Venice*, 861, p. 309
10. Hall, p. 496
11. Vergil, Book XXVI, para 44
12. Peter the Martyr Letters (Elzevir of Amsterdam ed., 1670), Epistle 282, p. 161
13. Brown, *CSP Venice*, Vol. 1, 861, pp. 309–10
14. Brown, *CSP Venice*, Vol. 1, 860, p. 308
15. ibid., pp. 308–9
16. ibid.
17. Brown, *CSP Venice*, Vol. 1, 863, p. 310
18. ibid., 863 & 864, pp. 310–11
19. ibid., p. 311
20. ibid., p. 311
21. ibid., 865, p. 312
22. ibid., p. 312

23. ibid., pp. 312–13
24. ibid., 864, p. 311
25. ibid., p. 312
26. ibid.
27. Gairdner, *Memorials of Henry VII, A Narrative of the Reception of Philip, King of Castile*, p. 302; see also Hall, p. 500 & Vergil, p. 135
28. Hall, p. 500 & Vergil, p. 135

12 Till He Might Possess His Prey

1. Hall, pp. 500-1 & Vergil, p. 137
2. Gairdner, *Memorials of Henry VII*, p. 283
3. ibid., p. 292
4. Vergil, p. 137; Hall, p. 501; see also Bacon, *The Reign of Henry VII* (1885), p. 205
5. Gairdner, *Memorials of Henry VII*, pp. 294 & 297
6. ibid., p. 302
7. Vergil, p. 137; Hall, p. 501 & Bacon, p. 204
8. Brown, *CSP Venice*, Vol. 1, 870, p. 316
9. Gairdner, *L&P HVII*, Vol. 1, XLIII, pp. 278–9
10. Gairdner, *L&P HVII*, Vol. 1, XLIV, p. 280
11. ibid., p. 281
12. ibid., p. 282
13. ibid., pp. 282–3
14. Tomlinson, *A History of the Minories*, pp. 68–9
15. Gairdner, *L&P HVII*, Vol. 1, XLIV, p. 284
16. Bergenroth, *CSP Spain*, Vol. 1, 452, pp. 380–1
17. ibid., 453, p. 381
18. ibid., 455, p. 384
19. Gairdner, *Memorials of Henry VII*, p. 301
20. Hall, p. 501
21. Brown, *CSP Venice*, Vol. 1, 869, p. 315
22. Stowe, *A Survey of London* (Thomas ed., 1842), p. 26
23. Hall, p. 501
24. Ellis, LVIII, p. 140–1
25. Brown, *CSP Venice*, Vol. 1, 869, p. 315
26. ibid., p. 315
27. ibid., pp. 314–5
28. *Chronicle of Calais*, p. 5–6
29. ibid., p. 66

30. Brown, *CSP Venice*, Vol. 1, 867, p. 313
31. *Chronicle of Calais*, p. 66
32. Vergil, p. 139
33. ibid.; Fabyan, p. 689 & Hall, p. 502
34. Vergil, p. 139–41; Hall, p. 502
35. Selden Society, *Select Cases in the Council of Henry VII*, pp. xxix–xxx
36. ibid.
37. ibid.
38. ibid.
39. Vergil, p. 141
40. Fabyan, p. 689

13 To Caesar's Greatest Displeasure

1. Later, Erhard changed sides and become a staunch supporter of the Habsburg Emperor Charles V.
2. He was later released and resumed his place at court.
3. Maximilian continued to style himself 'King of the Romans and of Hungary' even after Pressburg.
4. Brown, *CSP Venice*, Vol. 1, Table 7, p. cxliii
5. ibid., 822 p. 293
6. *Sanuto Diaries*, Vol. VI, 1506–7, p. 438; see also Brown, *CSP Venice*, Vol. 1, 889, p. 325
7. Brewer, *L&P HVIII*, Vol. II, pt 1, 1163, p. 307
8. Gairdner, *L&P HVII*, Vol. 1, LIV p. 310
9. ibid., pp. 310 & 313–4
10. ibid., p. 315
11. ibid., p. 316
12. ibid.
13. ibid., p. 313
14. ibid., p. 317
15. ibid., pp. 316–8
16. ibid., p. 318
17. ibid.
18. ibid., p. 319
19. ibid., p. 320
20. ibid., LVII, p. 321
21. ibid., LVIII, pp. 322–3
22. *Chronicle of Calais*, p. 66
23. Du Bellay, *Mémoires de Martin et Guillaume du Bellay*, Vol. I, p. 7

24. Herodotus, *The Histories*, II, c. 121
25. Brewer, *L&P HVIII*, Vol. I (Part 1), 11, pp. 7–8
26. ibid., p. 8
27. Gairdner, *L&P Richard III & Henry VII* [1863 ed.], Vol. II, p. 378
28. Gairdner, *L&P HVII*, Vol. 1, XXXII, p. 256
29. Brewer, *L&P HVIII*, Vol. I, 594, p. 84
30. Spelled *bogye* in original MS. Cox, Noel, 'Tudor Sumptuary Laws and Academical Dress', *Transactions of the Burgon Society*, Vol. 6, p. 29 fn 112
31. Brewer, *L&P HVIII* (1867 ed.), Vol. 1, pp. lxxiv & (1920 ed.) 886, p. 465
32. Le Glay, *Correspondence of Maximilian & Margaret*, Vol. 1, Letter 269, pp. 355–6 quoted in Brewer, *L&P HVIII* (1920 ed.), Vol. I, 646, p. 362

14 *An Exalted Individual*

1. Baumgartner, *Louis XII*, pp. 191–2
2. Eleanor was the eldest daughter of Philip and Joanna; she is therefore known as both Eleanor of Austria and Eleanor of Castile.
3. Brown, *CSP Venice*, Vol. 1, 915 & 916, p. 332
4. In Basque, Pasaia.
5. Hall, p. 528
6. The Treaty of Blois.
7. Prescott, *The Reign of Ferdinand & Isabella*, pp. 476–7 fn 12
8. Vergil, Book XXV [XXVII], p. 179
9. In Basque, Hondarribia; in French, Fontarrabie.
10. Hall, p. 528
11. Vergil, pp. 181–3
12. Bergenroth, *CSP Spain*, Vol. 2, 68, p. 67
13. Brown, *CSP Venice*, Vol. 2, 172, p. 65
14. Hall, pp. 528–9
15. Bergenroth, *CSP Spain*, Vol. 2, 68, p. 65
16. Hall, pp. 530–31
17. ibid., p. 529
18. Bergenroth, *CSP Spain*, Vol. 2, 68 pp. 65–6
19. Vergil, pp. 179–81
20. Gairdner, *L&P HVII*, Vol. 1, Preface, p. lvii, see also Ellis, LIX, p. 141
21. Fleuranges, *Mémoires*, Vol. 1, Prologue, pp. 2–7
22. ibid., pp. 71–2
23. ibid., pp. 100–1

24. ibid., pp. 104–7
25. Boissonnade, *Histoire de la réunion de la Navarre à la Castile*, p. 376
26. Fleuranges, *Mémoires*, Vol. 1, pp. 105–6
27. Bellay, Book 1, pp. 1–2, para C
28. Fleuranges, *Mémoires*, Vol. 1, pp. 106–7
29. ibid., p. 108
30. du Bellay, pp. 1-2, para B

15 I Pray You Give Me This Day Something

1. Fleuranges, *Mémoires*, Vol. 1, p. 109
2. Garibay, *Compendio*, Vol. 3, Bk 29, ch. 26
3. Mailles, *The Right Joyous and Pleasant History of the Chevalier Bayard*, Vol. 2, p. 132
4. ibid., p. 133
5. ibid., pp. 134–5
6. ibid., p. 136
7. ibid.
8. ibid., p. 137–8
9. Fleuranges, *Mémoires*, Vol. 1, p. 109
10. Brewer (1920 ed.), Vol. 1, 1509 [3584] p. 695
11. Fleuranges, *Mémoires*, Vol. 1, p. 109
12. ibid.
13. ibid., p. 110 & fn1
14. Mailles, p. 139
15. ibid., pp. 138–9
16. Brewer (1920 ed.), Vol. 1, Part 1, 1509 [3584], p. 695
17. Kastrexana, *A Guide to the War in Navarre in 12 Scenes*, p. 54
18. Mailles, p. 140
19. ibid., p. 141
20. Brewer (1920 ed.), *L&P HVIII*, Vol. 1, Part 1, 1155 (3138), p. 546
21. The treaty was signed 22 May 1512 – Brewer (1920 ed.), *L&P HVIII*, Vol. 1, Part 1 (1206), 3218 p. 559
22. Not to be confused with the Dr Thomas West who had been ambassador to Venice and an envoy to the Hungarian court in 1502 – Brown, *CSP Venice*, Vol. 1, Table 7, p. cxliii
23. Brewer (1920 ed.), *L&P HVIII*, Vol. 1, Part 1, 1315 [3347], p. 604
24. ibid., 1297 [3320], p. 593
25. ibid., 1302 [3326], p. 599
26. ibid., 1206 [3218], p. 559

27. ibid., 1314 [3346], p. 603 & 1340 [3372], p. 623
28. ibid., 1317 [none], p. 609 & 1323 [4388] p. 611
29. Bergenroth, *CSP Spain*, Vol. 2, 68, pp. 68–9
30. ibid., p. 69
31. Brewer (1920 ed.), *L&P HVIII*, Vol. 1, Part 1, 1484 [none], p. 677
32. ibid., 1533 [3602], p. 710 & 1559 [none], p. 716
33. ibid., 1564 [3633], p. 717
34. ibid., 1566 [3651], p. 719
35. Bergenroth, *CSP Spain*, 84, p. 91
36. Bergenroth, *CSP Spain*, Vol. 2, 97, p. 112
37. Brewer (1920 ed.), *L&P HVIII*, Vol. 1, Part 1, 1657 [4038] p. 745; see also Bergenroth, *CSP Spain*, 79, p. 84
38. ibid., Part 2, 2072 [4324], pp. 944–5
39. Vergil, p. 203
40. Fabyan, p. 695
41. *Rolls of Parliament*, vi. 545 et seq.
42. Brown, *CSP Venice*, 248, p. 104
43. Brewer (1920 ed.), Vol. 1, part 2, 2072 [4324], p. 944

16 A Marvellously Pretty Army

1. As Elizabeth/Anne is not mentioned in her mother's will, which was granted probate on 15 May 1515, she may have predeceased her – Cockayne, Vol. VII, p. 307; see also Tomlinson, *A History of the Minories*, pp. 68–9 & p. 73–5
2. Talbot's ancestor, John Talbot, 1st Earl of Shrewsbury, had been known as the English Achilles for his exploits in the Hundred Years War and he had shared command of the English army at the siege of Orleans with the de la Pole brothers' grandfather William, duke of Suffolk.
3. Brewer (1867 ed.), *L&P HVIII*, Vol. 1, 3989, p. 556
4. Dorset was grandson of Edward IV's queen, Elizabeth Woodville, and Essex was the son of her sister Anne.
5. Bergenroth, *CSP Spain*, Vol. 2, 97, p. 112; see also Brewer (1920 ed.), Vol. 1, Part 1, 1750 [3861], p. 799
6. Hall, p. 538
7. Brewer (1920 ed.), *L&P HVIII*, Vol. 1, Part 2, 2391 [4284], pp. 1057–8
8. ibid., p. 1058
9. du Bellay, *Mémoires*, p. 44
10. ibid., p. 3

11. Brown, *CSP Venice*, 268, p. 109
12. Fleuranges, *Mémoires*, Vol. 1, p. 137
13. ibid., p. 138
14. Hall, p. 54; see also Brewer (1920 ed.), *L&P HVIII*, Vol. 1, Part 2, 2391 [4284], p. 1058
15. Cruikshank, *Army Royal*, p. 43
16. ibid., p. 29
17. Brewer (1920 ed.), *L&P HVIII*, Vol. 1, Part 2, 2391 [4284], p. 1058
18. Fleuranges, *Mémoires*, p. 137; see also Mailles, *Mémoires*, p. 2 & Hall, p. 541
19. Brewer (1920 ed.), *L&P HVIII*, Vol. 1, Part 2, 2391 [4284], p. 1058 & Hall pp. 541–3
20. Hall, p. 541
21. ibid.
22. ibid., p. 542
23. Fleuranges, p. 137; see also Mailles, p. 2 & Hall, pp. 541-3
24. Brewer (1920 ed.), *L&P HVIII*, Vol. 1, 2102, p. 954
25. Brown, *CSP Venice*, 269, p. 110
26. Bellay, p. 44
27. M.F. des Roberts, *Un Pensionnaire Des Rois de France a Metz*, p. 241
28. Hall, p. 543
29. Brown, *CSP Venice*, 291, p. 120
30. Hall, p. 543
31. Brown, *CSP Venice*, 259, pp. 107; 266, p. 109 & 279, p. 114
32. Brewer (1920 ed.), *L&P HVIII*, Vol. 1, Part 2, 2259, p. 1013; see also Brown, *CSP Venice*, 328, p. 139
33. Brown, *CSP Venice*, 266, p. 109
34. Brewer (1920 ed.), *L&P HVIII*, Vol. 1, Part 2, 2157, p. 972
35. Hall, p. 545 – F.D. Roosevelt described the Japanese attack on Pearl Harbor as 'a day that will live in infamy'.
36. Brewer (1920 ed.), *L&P HVIII*, Vol. 1, Part 1, 1297 [3320], p. 593; 1302 [3326], p. 599 & 1314, [3346], p. 603

17 The Hungry Man of Pamplona

1. Behrens, 'The Career of Thomas Spinelli', *Transactions of the Royal Historical Society*, Vol. 16 (Fourth Series, 1933), pp. 161–95
2. ibid., p. 167
3. Brewer (1920 ed.), *L&P HVIII*, Vol. 1, Part 2, 2083 [4328], p. 949 & Vol. 1, Part 1, 1265 [4329], p. 580

4. ibid.
5. Brown, *CSP Venice*, 308, p. 126
6. Mailles, Vol. 2, p. 147
7. Hall, p. 549
8. Mailles, Vol. 2, pp. 147-9
9. Oman, *History of the Art of War in the 16th Century*, p. 295
10. Bellay, p. 44
11. Hall, pp. 560–3
12. Bellay, p. 5; see also Mailles, Vol. 2, p. 159
13. *Grafton's Chronicle*, p. 278; see also Cruikshank, p. 127
14. Wolf, *Odd Bits of History*, p. 64
15. Bellay, p. 7, para C
16. Robert, *A Pensioner of the French King in Metz*, p. 242
17. ibid., p. 242
18. i.e. Brighton – Hall, pp. 568–9
19. Robert, p. 240
20. Hall, p. 569
21. Brewer (1920 ed.), *L&P HVIII*, Vol. 1, Part 2, 2974 [5151], p. 1288
22. Hall, p. 569
23. Vigneulles, *Gedenkbuch des Metzer Burgers*, p. 265
24. Bellay, pp. 5–6, paras F-A see also Vigneulles, p. 264–5
25. Robert, p. 243
26. Vigneulles, p. 265
27. Robert, p. 244
28. In the Middle Ages *cleret* or *clairet* was a light-pink rosé, not the full-bodied reds called claret today.
29. Vigneulles, p. 265
30. Robert, p. 245
31. Baudoiche had been knighted at Louis' coronation – Robert, p. 244
32. Robert, p. 245
33. Vigneulles, p. 265; see also Fleuranges, p. 163
34. Bellay, *Mémoires*, p. 8, para C
35. Vigneulles, p. 291
36. ibid., p. 291
37. Fleuranges, p. 172
38. Robert, p. 247
39. Fleuranges, p. 173; see also Bellay, p. 9, para C

18 *Will the King Have the Said Enterprise Undertaken?*

1. Brewer (1864 ed.), *L&P HVIII*, Vol. 2, Part 1, 326, p. 104
2. ibid., 325, p. 104
3. ibid., 399, p. 117
4. ibid., 399, pp. 117–8
5. ibid., 609, p. 167
6. ibid.
7. Hall, p. 523
8. Brewer (1864 ed.), *L&P HVIII*, Vol. 2, Part 1, 742, p. 195
9. ibid., 809, p. 215
10. ibid., 891, p. 244
11. Oman, p. 166
12. Ellis, LXXXIII, p. 212
13. Mailles, p. 184
14. Brewer (1864 ed.), *L&P HVIII*, Vol. 2, Part 1, 1163, p. 307; see also Ellis, LXXXIII, pp. 202–12
15. ibid., 1163, p. 307
16. ibid., pp. 306–7
17. ibid., p. 307
18. ibid.
19. Brewer (1864 ed.), *L&P HVIII*, Vol. 2, Part 2, Appendix 16, p. 1528
20. ibid., Part 1, 1509, p. 420; see also ibid.
21. Behrens, pp. 168–9, fn 3
22. Eventually, Spinelli did become part of the accredited English embassy to the Habsburgs – Brewer (1864 ed.), *L&P HVIII*, Vol. 2, Part 1, 2207

19 *He Knows All That Goes on in England*

1. Bouckaert & Schreurs, *Tielman Susato & the Music of His Time*
2. ibid., p. 105–7
3. Brewer (1864 ed.), *L&P HVIII*, Vol. 2, Part 1, 1163, p. 307
4. Schreurs (contrib.), *The Treasury of Petrus Alamire*, p. 15
5. ibid., p. 16
6. ibid.
7. A manicordium is a type of clavichord – Brewer (1864 ed.), *L&P HVIII*, Vol. 2, Part 1, 541, p. 150
8. ibid.
9. ibid., 1238, p. 325
10. ibid., 981, p. 264
11. ibid.

12. ibid., 1478, p. 411
13. ibid.
14. ibid.
15. ibid., 1388, p. 381
16. ibid., 1299, p. 348
17. ibid.
18. Koenigsberger, *Monarchies, States Generals and Parliaments: The Netherlands in the Fifteenth and Sixteenth Centuries*
19. Brewer (1864 ed.), *L&P HVIII*, Vol. 2, Part 1, 1339, p. 360 & 1980, p. 575
20. ibid., 1339, p. 360
21. ibid., 1478, p. 411
22. ibid., 1479, p. 412 & 1498, pp. 417–8
23. ibid., 1510, p. 420
24. ibid., 1510, p. 420–1
25. ibid.
26. ibid., 1510, p. 421
27. ibid., 1894, p. 547
28. ibid., 1510, p. 421
29. ibid., 1239, p. 325
30. ibid., 1496 & 1497, p. 418
31. ibid., 1497, p. 418
32. ibid., 1913, p. 553 & 1973, p. 573
33. Probably Ville-sur-Haine, on what is now the Franco-Belgian border.
34. Brewer (1864 ed.), *L&P HVIII*, Vol. 2, Part 1, 1581, p. 437 & 1913, p. 553
35. ibid., 2410, p. 752
36. ibid., 1780, p. 505
37. ibid., 1782, p. 505
38. ibid., 1783, p. 505
39. ibid., 1727, p. 485; 541, p. 150; 1478, p. 411; 1496, p. 417; 1498, p. 418; 1553, p. 431; 1665, p. 464
40. ibid., 1727, p. 485 & 1783, p. 505
41. ibid., p. 518
42. ibid., 1913, p. 553

20 *While I Have One Crown to Expend*

1. Brewer (1864 ed.), *L&P HVIII*, Vol. 2, Part 1, 1939, p. 563
2. ibid., 1980, p. 575 & p. 581, 1994

3. ibid., 2081, p. 624
4. ibid., 1973, p. 574
5. ibid., 1994, p. 581
6. ibid., 1973, p. 573
7. ibid.
8. ibid.
9. ibid., 1939, p. 563
10. ibid., 2081, p. 625 see also Ellis Letter LXXXIII p. 205-6
11. ibid., 2072, p. 618
12. ibid., 2081, p. 624
13. ibid.
14. ibid., 2081, pp. 624–5
15. ibid., 2081, p. 624
16. ibid., 2023, p. 597 & 2024, p. 598
17. ibid., 2113, p. 639
18. ibid., p. 639
19. ibid., 2113, p. 639
20. ibid., 2205, p. 672; 2244, p. 690; 2419, pp. 755–6 & Vol. 2, part 2, 2767, p. 889
21. ibid., 2419, pp. 755–6
22. ibid., 2419, p. 756
23. Benecke, *Maximilian I*, p. 10
24. ibid., 2419, p. 756
25. ibid., 2136, p. 645
26. ibid., 2419, p. 756
27. ibid., 2585, p. 804
28. ibid., 2673, p. 841
29. ibid., 2673, p. 842
30. ibid.
31. ibid., 2473, p. 770
32. ibid., 2671, p. 841
33. ibid.
34. ibid., 2767, p. 890
35. ibid.
36. ibid., 2840, p. 913

21 *This Lord Had a Marvellous Horse*

1. Vigneulles, p. 301
2. ibid., p. 306

3. Robert, p. 250
4. Vigneulles, p. 378
5. Fleuranges, p. 231 & Vigneulles, pp. 293–4
6. Vigneulles, p. 306
7. Robert, p. 250
8. Vigneulles, pp. 300 & 306
9. ibid., pp. 306–7
10. ibid., p. 307
11. ibid.
12. ibid., pp. 308 & 311
13. ibid., pp. 310 & 311
14. ibid., p. 310
15. Brown, *CSP Venice*, 927, p. 405
16. ibid.; see also *Sanuto Diaries*, Vol. 24, p. 407
17. Brewer (1864 ed.), *L&P HVIII*, Vol. 2, Part 2, Appendix, RO. 39, p. 1540
18. ibid.
19. ibid.
20. ibid., Part 1, 2273, p. 700
21. ibid., Part 2, 3690, p. 1164
22. ibid., Appendix, RO. 39, p. 1540
23. ibid.
24. ibid., 3690, p. 1164
25. ibid., pp. 1163–4
26. ibid., p. 1164
27. ibid., 4056, pp. 1252–5
28. Bouckaert & Schreurs, p. 113; see also Schreurs (contrib.), *The Treasury of Petrus Alamire*, pp. 19–20
29. Bouckaert & Schreurs, pp. 114–5
30. Brewer (1864 ed.), *L&P HVIII*, Vol. 2, Part 2, 2846, p. 914
31. ibid., 2926, p. 944
32. ibid., 3048, p. 977
33. ibid., 3550, p. 1127
34. ibid.
35. ibid., pp. 1127–8
36. Teulet, *Papiers d'État*, Vol. 1, pp. 39–43
37. Vigneulles, p. 321
38. Brewer (1864 ed.), *L&P HVIII*, Vol. 2, Part 2, 4057, p. 1256 & 4071, p. 1262

39. ibid., 4201, p. 1301–2
40. ibid., 4201, p. 1302
41. ibid., 4056, p. 1254
42. ibid., 4047, p. 1250; see also Brown, *CSP Venice*, Vol. 2, 1019, pp. 437–8

22 *A Sideways Glance*

1. Brewer (1864 ed.), *L&P HVIII*, Vol. 2, Part 2, 4469, 4470, 4471, 4472, 4475, 4476 & 4477, pp. 1372–4
2. ibid., 4469, p. 1372
3. Brown, *CSP Venice*, Vol. 2, 1106, p. 475
4. Vigneulles, p. 358
5. Robert, 259–60
6. Vigneulles, p. 359
7. ibid., p. 361
8. Probably Jouy-aux-Arches, 6 miles to the south-east of Metz.
9. Vigneulles, pp. 361–2
10. ibid.
11. Knecht, *Renaissance Warrior & Patron*, p. 165
12. Brewer (1864 ed.), *L&P HVIII*, Vol. 2, Part 2, 2911, p. 939
13. ibid., 4178, p. 1293
14. Brown, *CSP Venice*, 1165, p. 497
15. Wolf, *Odd Bits of History*, p. 73
16. Barillion, *Journal*, Vol. II, pp. 125–6
17. Brewer (1867 ed.), *L&P HVIII*, Vol. 3, Part 1, 300, p. 104
18. ibid.
19. 'Instructions given by Francis I to the duke of Suffolk', Mss Colbert, vol. 385 (Bibliothèque Nationale de France), p. 11
20. Brewer (1867 ed.), *L&P HVIII*, Vol. 3, Part 1, 326, p. 116
21. Vigneulles, *Gedenkbuch*, p. 365; see also Vigneulles, *Das Journal: Aufzeichnungen eines Metzer Burgers*, pp. 325–8
22. ibid., p. 365
23. ibid., p. 369
24. ibid., p. 365
25. ibid., p. 366
26. ibid., pp. 366–7
27. ibid., pp. 367–8
28. ibid., p. 368
29. ibid.

30. ibid., pp. 368–9
31. Ellis, *Original Letters Illustrative of English History*, Third Series (1847 ed.), CXV, pp. 325–6
32. ibid., CXV, pp. 325–6
33. Brown, *CSP Venice*, Vol. 3, 130, p. 90
34. Blanc, *Letters on England*, Vol. 1, p. 296

23 *A Valiant Man Worthy to Be a Great Captain*

1. One of those wounded during the second siege of Pamplona was Ignatius Loyola, founder of the Jesuits – Oman, p. 173
2. Also known and the battle of Esquiroz – ibid., p. 174
3. ibid., p. 176
4. Brewer (1867 ed.), *L&P HVIII*, Vol. 3, Part 1, 1221, pp. 461–2
5. ibid., p. 462
6. ibid., pp. 461–2
7. Brewer (1867 ed.), *L&P HVIII*, Vol. 3, Part 2, 2292, p. 970
8. ibid., p. 873
9. Oman, pp. 176–85
10. Brewer (1867 ed.), *L&P HVIII*, Vol. 3, Part 2, 2292, p. 970
11. Teulet, *Papiers d'État*, pp. 31–4
12. ibid., pp. 33–34
13. ibid., p. 35
14. Cockayne, *Complete Peerage*, Vol. IV, D-F, pp. 85–6
15. The other was the more prosaically titled Francis de Bergagni.
16. Brewer (1867 ed.), *L&P HVIII*, Vol. 3, Part 2, Appendix, 32, p. 1581
17. Pardoe, *The Court and Reign of Francis the First, King of France*, pp. 466–7
18. ibid., p. 467
19. Brewer (1867 ed.), *L&P HVIII*, Vol. 3, Part 2, 2435, p. 1025
20. Bergenroth, *CSP Spain, Further Supplements to Vol. 1 & 2, Vienna*, British History Online, pp. 141–48
21. Brewer (1867 ed.), *L&P HVIII*, Vol. 3, Part 2, 2446, pp. 1030–33
22. Brewer (1867 ed.), *L&P HVIII*, Vol. 3, Part 2, 2446, p. 1031
23. ibid., 2446, p. 1032
24. Bergenroth, *CSP Spain, Further Supplements*, pp. 141–8
25. Son of the first earl, who had been created 1st duke of Norfolk in 1514.
26. Brewer (1867 ed.), *L&P HVIII*, Vol. 3, Part 2, 2419, p. 1021
27. Stuart, *The Scot Who Was a Frenchman*, p. 133

28. ibid., p. 144
29. ibid., p. 145
30. Brewer (1867 ed.), *L&P HVIII*, Vol. 3, Part 2, 2708, p. 1141
31. ibid., 2737, p. 1152
32. ibid.
33. ibid., 2769, pp. 1164–5
34. ibid., 2769, p. 1165
35. ibid., 2768, p. 1164 & 2798, p. 1176
36. ibid., 2755, p. 1158
37. ibid., 2800, pp. 1177–8
38. Brown, *CSP Venice*, 639, p. 305

24 *March through the Land of the Enemies, in Order to Trample It*

1. Brewer, *L&P HVIII* (1867 ed.), Vol. 3, Part 2, 2799, p. 1177
2. ibid., 3118, pp. 1306–7
3. ibid., 3321, p. 1383
4. ibid., 3222, p. 1340
5. ibid., 3224, p. 1341
6. ibid., 3268, p. 1355
7. Hall, pp. 660–1
8. Knecht, p. 204
9. ibid., p. 205–6
10. Brewer (1867 ed.), *L&P HVIII*, Vol. 3, Part 2, 3194, p. 1330 & 3225, pp. 1341–2
11. ibid., 3225, p. 1342; see also Guicciardini, *History of Italy*, Vol. 8, Bk XV, pp. 131–3
12. Guicciardini, Vol. 8, Bk XV, pp. 57–8; see also Giono, *The Battle of Pavia*, p. 62 and Knecht, p. 207
13. Bellay, Book II, p. 45, para F, p. 46, para C
14. ibid., p. 47, para E
15. Stuart, p. 159
16. Doge Grimani died in May 1523 – Brown, *CSP Venice*, Vol. 3, 742, p. 337
17. Brewer (1867 ed.), *L&P HVIII*, Vol. 3, Part 2, 3237, p. 1345
18. Hall, p. 665
19. Bindoff, 'Fitzwilliam, Sir William', *The History of Parliament 1509-1558, Member Biographies*

20. Brewer (1867 ed.), *L&P HVIII*, Vol. 3, Part 2, 3360, pp. 1396–7 & 3365, p. 1400; see also Hall, p. 665
21. ibid., 3403, p. 1421
22. ibid., 3362, p. 1398; 3381, p. 1413–4 & 3445, p. 1433–4
23. ibid., 3445, pp. 1433–4
24. ibid., 3447, p. 1434
25. ibid., 3360, p. 1397 & 3381, p. 1413–14
26. Buchannan, *History of Scotland* (1827 ed.), Vol. II, p. 287
27. Brewer (1867 ed.), *L&P HVIII*, Vol. 3, Part 2, 3365, pp. 1400–1; 3381, p. 1414
28. Hall, p. 666
29. Buchannan, Vol. II, p. 287
30. Hall, p. 666
31. Buchannan, Vol. II, p. 288
32. Brewer, *L&P HVIII* (1867 ed.), Vol. 3, Part 2, 3456, p. 1437
33. Bellay, Book II, p. 54, para C
34. Bellay (1853 ed.), Vol. 1, pp. 320–1
35. Brewer, *L&P HVIII*, Vol. 3, Part 2, 3601, p. 1498
36. Bellay, Book II, p. 53, para A
37. Guicciardini, *History of Italy*, Vol. 8, p. 62

25 *All I Have in This World Is Owing to You*

1. Brewer (1867 ed.), *L&P HVIII*, Vol. 3, Part 2, 3250 & 3251, p. 1350
2. ibid., 3287, p. 1369
3. Brewer (1870 ed.), *L&P HVIII*, Vol. 4, Part 1, 243, p. 96
4. ibid., 631, p. 279
5. Brewer (1867 ed.), *L&P HVIII*, Vol. 3, Part 2, 2446, p. 1030
6. Brewer (1870 ed.), *L&P HVIII*, Vol. 4, Part 1, 631, pp. 279–80
7. ibid., 631, p. 280
8. ibid.
9. ibid.
10. Guicciardini, *History of Italy*, Vol. 8, Book XV, p. 125
11. ibid., p. 106
12. Bellay (1569 ed.), Book II, p. 59, para A–C
13. Brewer (1870 ed.), *L&P HVIII*, Vol. 4, Pt 1, 351, p. 143
14. Scarisbrick, *Henry VIII*, pp. 131–2
15. Brewer (1870 ed.), *L&P HVIII*, Vol. 4, Part 1, 446, pp. 188–9
16. ibid., 365, p. 148
17. ibid., 324, p. 134

18. ibid., 324, p. 135
19. ibid.
20. ibid., 330, pp. 136–7
21. ibid., 334, p. 138
22. ibid., 324, p. 134
23. ibid., 317, p. 132
24. ibid., 318, p. 132
25. ibid., 325, p. 135
26. Or possibly the city's Lord Deputy, John Bourchier, Baron Berners.
27. ibid., 335, p. 138
28. ibid., 335, pp. 138–9
29. ibid., 365, p. 148
30. Guicciardini, Vol. 8, Book XV, p. 137
31. Brewer (1870 ed.), *L&P HVIII*, Vol. 4, Part 1, 365, p. 148 & 374, p. 158
32. ibid., 374, p. 158
33. ibid., 442, p. 188
34. ibid., 570, p. 249
35. Guicciardini, Vol. 8, Book XV, pp. 134–5
36. Knecht, p. 214
37. Giono, p. 77

26 *At Least Three Hundred Men Died in that Place*

1. Guicciardini, Vol. 8, Book XV, pp. 131–8
2. Brewer (1870 ed.), *L&P HVIII*, Vol. 4, Part 1, 444 & 445, p. 188
3. ibid., 503, pp. 210–11
4. ibid., 510, pp. 213–14; 595, p. 265 & 606, p. 271
5. Guicciardini, Vol. 8, Book XV, p. 133
6. Giono, p. 80
7. ibid., p. 79–81
8. Bellay (1569 ed.), Book II, p. 60, para B & D
9. Fleuranges, Vol. 2, pp. 148–54
10. Bellay (1569 ed.), Book II, p. 60, para D
11. Giono, p. 81
12. Bellay (1569 ed.), Book II, p. 60, para C; see also Guicciardini, Vol. 8, Book XV, p. 140
13. Mignet, *Rivalry of Charles V & Francis I*, pp. 500–510; see also Fleuranges, Vol. 2, p. 149
14. Guicciardini, Vol. 8, Book XV, p. 139

15. Konstam, *Pavia 1525*, p. 30
16. Pattou, 'Seigneurs de Grailly & Captal de Busch', *Racines et Histoire*, p. 12
17. Bellay, Book II, p. 60, para D
18. ibid., para C
19. Guicciardini, Vol. 8, Book XV, pp. 141–2
20. Bellay, Book II p. 61, para B
21. ibid., para C
22. Guicciardini, Vol. 8, Book XV, p. 146
23. Giono, p. 108
24. Roederer (1825 ed.), *Louis XII & François I*, Vol. 2, p. 78
25. The Pavia tapestries, created by Bernard van Orley, are on display in the Museo di Capodimonte, Naples.
26. Guicciardini, Vol. 8, Book XV, p. 11
27. Bellay, Book II, p. 62, para D
28. Fleuranges, *Mémoires*, Vol. 2, p. 177
29. ibid., pp. 177–8
30. ibid., Vol. 2, p. 178; see also Bellay, Book II, p. 61, para E & Guicciardini, Vol. 8, Book XV, p. 151
31. Fleuranges, *Mémoires*, Vol. 2, p. 175, see also Bellay, Book II, p. 61, para F
32. Fleuranges, *Mémoires*, Vol. 2, p. 179, see also Bellay, Book II, p. 61, para E
33. Fleuranges, *Mémoires*, Vol. 2, p. 179
34. Giono, p. 117
35. Fleuranges, *Mémoires*, Vol. 2, pp. 185–6
36. ibid., Vol. 2, p. 183
37. ibid., Vol. 2, p. 186
38. ibid.
39. ibid., pp. 186–7
40. ibid., p. 190
41. ibid., p. 191
42. ibid., p. 190–91
43. ibid., p. 181
44. ibid., fn 1; see also Guicciardini, Vol. 8, Bk XV, p. 181 & Bellay p. 63, para A
45. Guicciardini, Vol. 8, Book XV, p. 158

27 *Not a Dozen Lances but a Thousand*

1. Guicciardini, Vol. 8, Book XV, pp. 153–5
2. Stuart, p. 171
3. Guicciardini, Vol. 8, Book XV, p. 158
4. Guicciardini , Luigi, *The Sack of Rome*, p. 139
5. Miller, *The Landsknechts*, p. 37
6. Fleuranges, *Mémoires*, Vol. 2, pp. 193–4
7. *Sanuto Diaries*, Vol. 37, p. 458, para 276
8. ibid.
9. ibid.
10. Konstam, *Pavia 1525*, p. 46
11. Guicciardini, Vol. 8, Book XV, p. 189; see also Fleuranges, Vol. 2, p. 214
12. Fleuranges, Vol. 2, p. 212, fn 1
13. Konstam, pp. 50 & 55
14. Guicciardini, Book XV, p. 190
15. Konstam, pp. 55 & 62 (map)
16. Fleuranges, Vol. 2, pp. 219–20; see also Guicciardini, Vol. 8, Book XV, pp. 202–3
17. Oman, p. 196
18. ibid., pp. 196–7
19. Konstam, p. 55
20. Guicciardini, Vol. 8, Bk XV, pp. 203–4; see also Brewer, *L&P HVIII*, Vol. 4 Pt1, 1064, p. 465 & 1087, p. 478
21. Fleuranges, Vol. 2, p. 226; see also Bellay, Book II, p. 68 para A
22. Oman, p. 198; see also Giono, p. 144 & Konstam, p. 55
23. Guicciardini, Book XV, p. 204
24. ibid., Vol. 8, Book XV, p. 205
25. Fleuranges, Vol. 2, p. 223
26. ibid., Vol. 2, p. 224
27. Reissner, *Historia Herrn Georgs und Herrn Kaspars von Frundsberg* (1572 ed.), pp. 42b & 43a
28. Fleuranges, *Mémoires*, Vol. 2, p. 225
29. Reissner, p. 43b
30. Konstam, p. 62 (map)
31. Fleuranges, Vol. 2, pp. 224–25
32. Giono, p. 148; see also Konstam, p. 64
33. Giono, p. 148
34. Fleuranges, Vol. 2, p. 231

35. ibid.
36. ibid., p. 229; see also Bellay, Book III, p. 68
37. Giono, p. 147
38. Konstam, p. 62 (map)
39. Anonymous (painting), *The Siege and Battle of Pavia* (Ashmolean Museum, Oxford)
40. Fleuranges, *Mémoires*, Vol. 2, p. 229; see also Bellay, Book III, p. 68

28 It Was a Bloody Battle

1. Bellay, Book III, p. 68 para B
2. Konstam, p. 69
3. Giono, p. 152
4. Reissner, p. 44a
5. Bellay, Book III, p. 68, para C
6. Giono, p. 152
7. Fleuranges, Vol. 2, p. 228
8. Giono, p. 153; see also Konstam, p. 72
9. Fleuranges, Vol. 2, pp. 230, 234, 236
10. Reissner, p. 45a
11. Reissner maintains he was called Hans Langenmantel but other sources insist he was Hans' brother George.
12. Reissner, pp. 45a–45b
13. *Schlechten Krieg* (*Bad War*) is the title of a drawing by Holbein.
14. Bellay, Book III, p. 68, para D
15. Reissner, p. 45b
16. ibid.
17. ibid.
18. ibid.
19. Bellay, Book III, p. 68, para C
20. Reissner, p. 46a
21. ibid.
22. Giono, pp. 154–5
23. Reissner, p. 46b
24. Giono, p. 155
25. Bellay (1908 ed.), p. 356
26. ibid., p. 356, fn 1
27. Brewer (1870 ed.), *L&P HVIII*, Vol. 4, Part 1, 1131, p. 497
28. ibid., 1175, p. 518 & 1178, p. 519
29. Maquereau, *Histoire Generale de l'Europe*, p. 231

30. Hall, p. 693
31. Brewer (1870 ed.), *L&P HVIII*, Vol. 4, Part 1, 1237, p. 543
32. ibid., 1213, p. 530
33. ibid., 1217, p. 532
34. Giono, pp. 163–4
35. Bouchet, *A New Collection of Stories Illustrating the History of France*, Vol. IV, ch. 23, p. 477
36. Banks, *The Dormant and Extinct Baronage of England* (1808 ed.), p. 159; see also Burke, *The Vicissitudes of Families*, p. 128 & Wolff, *Odd Bits of History*, p. 79

Epilogue: The First and Last Yorkists

1. Moryson, *Itinerary*, Vol. 1, pp. 363–4; see also Addison, *Remarks on Several Parts of Italy in the years 1701, 1702 & 1703* (1753 ed.), pp. 24–5
2. Lee, 'Parker, Henry, Charles's father', *DNB* (1885-1900), Vol. 43, p. 239 & Addison, p. 26
3. Banks, *The Dormant and Extinct Baronage of England* (1808), Morley family tree, p. 360; see also Cockayne, *Complete Peerage*, Vol. V, p. 372
4. Gough, *Sepulchral Monuments in Great Britain*, Vol. 1, Part II, p. 216
5. Tout, 'Lionel of Antwerp', *DNB* (1885-1900), Vol. 33, p. 337
6. Robert, pp. 265–6
7. ibid.
8. This elusive document is supposedly kept in the Marriage Records of the Bibliothèque Municipale de Lyon but this author has not been able to see a copy first hand. The quotes are therefore taken from modern secondary sources: Richardson's *Plantagenet Ancestry*, Vol. 2, p. 293 & Reynaud, 'Mises Au Point Sur Les Genealogies Colomb', *Rochette et Coppier*, pp. 14–15
9. Anselme, *Histoire Généalogique et Chronologique de la Maison Royale de France*, Tome 3, p. 383
10. Robinson, *Margaret of Angoulême* (1886 ed.), p. 88
11. Richardson, *Plantagenet Ancestry*, Vol. 2, p. 293
12. Montesquieu, *Revue de L'Agenais*, No. 1 (Janvier–Mars, 1981), p. 8
13. *Unpublished Letters of Joseph Justus Scaliger* (1879 ed.), Letter XLIII, p. 139 & fn 3
14. Montesquieu, Revue de L'Agenais, No. 1, Janvier-Mars, p. 9
15. ibid., p. 11
16. Richardson, *Plantagenet Ancestry*, Vol. 2, p. 293

SELECT BIBLIOGRAPHY

Addison, Joseph, *Remarks on Several Parts of Italy in the years 1701, 1702 & 1703* (London: Tonson & Draper, 1753)

Amin, Nathen, *Henry VII and the Tudor Pretenders* (Stroud: Amberley Publishing, 2020)

Anselme, Père, *Histoire Généalogique et Chronologique de la Maison Royale de France* (Paris: BnF Gallica, 1768)

Arthurson, Ian, *The Perkin Warbeck Conspiracy 1491-1499* (Stroud: Sutton Publishing, 1994)

Bacon, Francis, *The History of the Reign of King Henry VII* (Cambridge: Cambridge University Press, 1885)

Bacon, Francis, *The History of the Reign of King Henry VII* (London: Folio Society, 1971)

Barillion, Jean, *Journal de Jean Barrillon secrétaire du chancelier Duprat, 1515-1521*, Tome 2 (Paris: Bnf Gallica, 1899)

Baumgartner, Frederick, *Louis XII* (New York: St Martin's Press, 1996)

Bayne, Charles, *Select Cases in the Council of Henry VII*, Vol. 75 (London: Selden Society, 1958)

Behrens, Betty, 'The Career of Thomas Spinelli', *Transactions of the Royal Historical Society*, Fourth Series, Vol. 16 (Cambridge: Cambridge University Press, 1933)

Beltz, George, *Memorials of the Order of the Garter* (London: W. Pickering, 1841)

Beneke, Gerhard, *Maximilian I, An Analytical Biography* (London: Routledge & Keegan Paul, 1982)

Bentley, Samuel, *Excerpta Historica* (London: R. Bentley, 1833)

Bergenroth, G. A., *Calendar of Letters, Despatches, and State Papers – Spain*, Vols I & II (London: Longman Green, Longman, & Roberts 1862 & 1866)

Bindoff, S. T., *The History of Parliament 1509-1558, Members' Biographies A-Z* (London: Boydell & Brewer, 1982)

Blanc, Louis, *Letters on England*, Vol. I (London: Sampson, Low, Son & Marston: 1866)

Blatchly, John & Haward, Bill, 'Sir Robert Lord Curson: Soldier, Courtier & Spy', *Proceedings of the Suffolk Institute of Archaeology and History*, Vol. XLI, Part 3 (Ipswich: Suffolk Institute of Archaeology and History, 2007)

Boissonnade, P., *Histoire de la Réunion de la Navarre à la Castile* (Paris: BnF Gallica, 1893)

Bouchet, J., *A New Collection of Stories Illustrating the History of France*, 1st Series, Tome IV (1837)

Bouckaert & Schreurs (contrib.), Polk, Keith (editor), *Tielman Susato & the Music of His Time* (New York: Pendragon Press, 2005)

Brewer, J. S. (editor), *Letters & Papers, Foreign & Domestic of the Reign of Henry VIII* (London: Longman, Green, Longman Roberts & Green, 1864, 1867 1870 & 1920)

Brown, Rawdon, *Calendar of State Papers & Manuscripts – Venice*, Vol. I & II (London: Longman, Green, Longman Roberts & Green, 1864)

Buchannan, George, *The History of Scotland*, Vol. II (Glasgow: Blackie, Fullarton & Co., 1827)

Buck, George, *History of the Life and Reign of Richard the Third* (London: W. Wilson, 1647)

Burke, Bernard, *The Vicissitudes of Families* (London: Longman, Green, Longman, and Roberts, 1863)

Burke, John, *Dictionary of the Peerage and Baronetage*, 6th Edition (London: Henry Colburn, 1839)

Busch, Wilhelm, *England under the Tudors* (New York: Burt Franklin, 1895)

Cockayne, G. A., *Complete Peerage*, Vols I–VIII (London: George Bell & Sons, 1887)

Cornish, Paul, *Henry VIII's Army*, Men-at-Arms Series, 191 (Oxford: Osprey Publishing, 1987)

Cruikshank, C. G., *Army Royal, Henry VIII's Invasion of France 1513* (London: Oxford University Press, 1969)

Cunningham, Sean, *Henry VII* (London: Routledge, 2007)

Davey, Richard, *The Pageant of London*, Vol. 1 (London: Methuen & Co., 1906)

De la Marck, Robert III, *Mémoires de Maréchal de Floranges, dit le Jeune Adventureux*, Tomes I & II (Paris: Goubaux et Lemoisne, 1913)

Demarolle, Pierre, *La Chronique de Philippe de Vigneulles et la mémoire de Metz* (Caen: Éditions Paradigm, 1993)

Dodsworth, William, *An Historical Account of the Episcopal See and Cathedral of Salisbury* (Salisbury: Brodie & Dowding, 1815)

Doubleday, H. Arthur & Page, William (general editors), *The History of Hampshire and the Isle of Wight, The Victoria History of the Counties of England*, Volume II (Westminster: Archibald Constable & Co., 1902)

Du Bellay, *Mémoires de Martin et Guillaume du Bellay* (Paris: l'Huillier, 1569)

Du Bellay, *Mémoires de Martin et Guillaume du Bellay* (Paris: Durand, 1853)

Du Bellay (Bourrilly, V. et Vindry, F. editors), *Mémoires de Martin et Guillaume du Bellay* (Paris: La Société de L'Histoire de France, 1908)

Banks, T. C., *The Dormant and Extinct Baronage of England*, Vol. II (London: J. White, 1808)

Ellis, Henry, *Original Letters Illustrative of English History*, Third Series, Vol. 1 (London: R. Bentley, 1846)

Engel, Pal, *The Realm of St Stephen* (London: I.B. Tauris, 2005)

Enzenberg, Sighard, *Schloß Tratzberg: Ein Beitrag zur Kulturgeschichte Tirols* (Innsbruck: Schlern-Schriften & Wagner University Press, 1958)

Fabyan, Robert, *The New Chronicles of England and France* (London: F. C. Rivington *et al.* 1811)

Fryde, E. B., *William de la Pole, Merchant and King's Banker* (London: Hambleton Press, 1988)

Fynes, Moryson, *The Itinerary of Fynes Moryson Gent.*, Vol. I (Glasgow: J. Maclehose & Sons, 1897)

Gairdner, James, *Letters and Papers Illustrative of the Reigns of Richard III & Henry VII*, Vols I & II (London: Longman, Green, Longman, Roberts 1861 & 1863)

Gairdner, James, *Henry VII* (London: Macmillan & Co., 1909)

Gairdner, James, *Memorials of Henry VII (A Narrative of the Reception of Philip, King of Castile)* (London: Longman, Brown, Green, Longmans and Roberts, 1858)

Gairdner, James (editor), *The Paston Letters*, Vol. VI (London: Chatto & Windus, 1904)

Garibay, Esteban, *Compendio Historial de Las Chronicas y Universal*, Vol. 3 (Barcelona: S. de Cormellas, 1628)

Giono, Jean, *The Battle of Pavia* (London: Peter Owen, 1963)

Gough, Richard, *Sepulchral Monuments in Great Britain*, Vol. 1 Part II (London: J. Nichols, 1796)

Grafton, Richard, *Grafton's Chronicle*, Vol. II (London: J. Johnson *et al.*, 1809)

Gross, Anthony J., 'The Last Yorkist Revealed? Richard de la Pole, Charles Duc de Bourbon and a contentious panel portrait of the 1520s', *The Fifteenth Century, Volume XX: Essays Presented to Rowena E. Archer*, ed. Linda Clark (Woodbridge: The Boydell Press, 2024).

Guicciardini, Luigi, *The Sack of Rome* (London: J H McGregor, 1993)

Guicciardini, Francesco, *The History of Italy*, Vol. VIII (London: John Towers, 1755)

Hall, Edward, *The Union of the Two Noble and Illustrious Families of Lancaster and York (Hall's Chronicle)* (London: J Johnson *et al.*, 1809)

Hannay, James Kerr, & Mackie, R. L., *The Letters of James IV 1505-1513*, Vol. XLV (Edinburgh: Scottish History Society, 1953)

Hardyng, John, *The Chronicle of John Hardyng* (London: F. C. Rivington *et al.*, 1812)

Hasted, Edward, *The History and Topographical Survey of the County of Kent*, Vol. 2 (Canterbury: W. Bristow, 1797)

Herodotus, *The Histories* (London: Penguin, 1972)

HMSO, *Calendar of Patent Rolls Henry VII*, Vols I & II (London: HMSO, 1914)

Kastrexana, Joxerra, *A Guide to the Conquest of Navarre in 12 Scenes* (Andoain: Txertoa, 2012)

Knecht, Robert Jean, *Renaissance Warrior & Patron, The Reign of Francis I* (Cambridge: Cambridge University Press, 1994)

Koenigsberger, H. G., *Monarchies, States Generals and Parliaments: The Netherlands in the Fifteenth and Sixteenth Centuries* (Cambridge: Cambridge University Press, 2001).

Konstam, Angus, *Pavia 1525*, Campaign Series, 44 (Oxford: Osprey Publishing, 1996)

Latham, R. E. (editor), *Calendar of Close Rolls, Henry VII*, Vol. II, 1500-1509 (London: HMSO, 1963)

Le Glay, André Joseph Ghislain (editor), *Correspondence de l'Empereur Maximilian 1er & Marguerite d'Autriche*, Vol. 1 (Paris: de Crapelet, 1839)

Leadam, Isaac Saunders, *Transactions of the Royal Historical Society*, Vol. 16 (London: Royal Historical Society, 1902)

Leland, John, *De Rebus Britannicus Collectanea*, Vol. IV (London: Jo. Richardson, 1770)

Leland, *The Itinerary of John Leland* (London: Bell & Sons, 1907)

Leslie, Stephen (editor), *The Dictionary of National Biography*, Vols 1–63 (London, Smith, Elder & Co., 1885)

Liliencron, Rochus, *Deutsches Leben im Volkslied um 1530* (Berlin: W. Speman, 1884)

Des Roberts, M. F., 'Un Pensionnaire Des Rois de France a Metz', *Société d'Archéologie Lorraine et du Musée Historique Lorraine*, Troisième Série (Nancy: G. Crepin-Leblond, 1878)

Mailles, Jacques, *The Right Joyous and Pleasant History of the Chevalier Bayard*, Vol. II (London: John Murray, 1825)

Maquereau, Robert, *Histoire Generale de l'Europe depuis la Naissance de Charles-Quint, Jusqu'au Cing Juin MDXXVII* (Louvain: L'Imprimerie Academique, 1765)

Mignet, M., *Rivalité de François Iier et de Charles-Quint*, Tome I (Paris: Didier, 1876)

Miller, Douglas, *The Landsknechts*, Men-at-Arms Series, 58 (Oxford: Osprey Publishing, 1976)

Molinet, Jean, *Collection des Chroniques Nationales Françaises*, Tome IV (Paris: Verdiere, 1828)

Montesquieu, Philippe, *Revue de L'Agenais*, 108e année, No. 1, Janvier-Mars (Agen: Société Académique d'Agen, 1981)

More, Thomas, *The History of King Richard III* (Cambridge: Cambridge University Press, 1883)

Napier, Henry Alfred, *Historical Notices of the Parishes of Ewelme and Swyncombe* (Oxford: J Wright, 1858)

Nichols J. G. (editor), *The Chronicle of Calais in the Reigns of Henry VII & Henry VIII* (London: Camden Society, 1846)

Nichols J. G. (editor), *Chronicle of the Grey Friars of London* (London: Camden Society, 1852)

Oman, Charles, *History of the Art of War in the 16th Century* (Uckfield: Naval & Military Press, 2017)

Pardoe, Miss (Julia), *The Court and Reign of Francis the First, King of France*, Vols I & II (London: Richard Bentley, 1849)

Pattou, Etienne, *Seigneurs de Grailly & Captal de Busch* (Online Article: *racineshistoire.free.fr*, 2008)

Penn, Thomas, *The Winter King* (London: Penguin, 2012)

Peter Martyr D'Anghera, *Opus Epistolarum (Letters)* (Amsterdam: Daniel Elzevir, 1670)

Peter Martyr D'Anghera, *De Orbe Novo (Eight Decades)*, Vol. I (New York: Putnam 1912)

Prescott, William H., *History of the Reign of Ferdinand & Isabella*, Vol. II (London: George Routledge & Sons, 1867)

Pugh, T., *Henry VII and the English Nobility* (Manchester: Manchester University Press, 1992)

Reissner, *Historia Herrn Georgs und Herrn Kaspars von Frundsberg* (Leipzig: Voigtländer's Source Books, 1909)

Reynaud, Jerome, *Mises Au Point Sur Les Genealogies Colomb, Rochette et Coppier* (Online Article: jeromereynaud.free.fr, 2008)

Richards, John, *Landsknecht Soldier*, Warrior Series, 49 (Oxford: Osprey Publishing, 2002)

Richardson, Douglas, *Plantagenet Ancestry*, Vols II & IV, Second Edition (Salt Lake City: Richardson, 2011)

Robinson, *Margaret of Angoulême, Queen of Navarre* (London: W. H. Allen & Co., 1886)

Roederer, P. L., *Louis XII et François I*, Tome II (Paris: Bossanges Frères, 1825)
Sanuto, Mario, *The Diaries*, Vols IV, V, VI, XXXVII & XLI (Venice: Nicolo Barozzi, 1880)
Scarisbrick, J. J., *Henry VIII* (London: Eyre & Spottiswoode, 1968)
Schiller, Frederick, *History of the Revolt of the Netherlands* (New York: Harvard Publishing Co., 1895)
Schreurs, Eugeen (contrib.), Kellman, Herbert (editor), *The Treasury of Petrus Alamire* (Ghent: Ludion, 1999)
Seward, Desmond, *The Last White Rose* (London: Constable & Robinson, 2011)
Sewell, W. H., 'Memoirs of Sir James Tyrell', *Proceedings of the Suffolk Institute of Archaeology and History*, Vol. 5 (Yaxley: Sewell, 1878)
Shaw, William A., *The Knights of England*, Vol. II (London: Sherratt & Hughes, 1906)
Sneyd, Charlotte, Augusta (translator), *A Relation of the Island of England about the year 1500* (London: Camden Society, 1847)
Speed, John, *The Historie of Great Britain* (London: George Humble, 1623)
Strachey, J. (editor), *Rotuli Parliamentorum*, Vol. 5 (London: Parliament, 1767)
Stow, John, *Survey of London* (London: Whittaker & Co., 1842)
Stuart, Marie W., *The Scot Who Was a Frenchman* (Edinburgh: William Hodge & Co., 1940)
Teulet, *Papiers d'État Relatifs à l'Histoire d l'Écosse*, Tome 1 (Paris: Plon Frères, 1851)
Thorpe, Markham John, *Calendar of State Papers – Scotland*, Vol. I (London: Longman, Brown, Green, Longmans & Roberts, 1858)
Tomlinson, Edward Murray, *A History of the Minories* (London: Smith Elder & Co., 1907)
Larroque, Philippe, *The Unpublished Letters of Joseph Justus Scaliger* (Agen: J. Michel, 1879)
Upcher, Arthur, *History of Hingham, Norfolk, and Its Church of St Andrew* (East Dereham: A. F. Mason, 1921)
Vergil, Polydore (Hay, Denys, translator) *Anglica Historia* (London: Royal Historical Society, 1950)
Vigneulles, *Das Journal: Aufzeichnungen eines Metzer Burgers* (Saarbrucken: Conte Verag, 2005)
Vigneulles, *Gedenkbuch des Metzer Burgers (Chronicle of Metz)* (Stuttgart: Heinrich Michelant, 1852)
Wolf, Henry, W., *Odd Bits of History* (London: Longmans, Green & Co., 1894)

INDEX